Mixed-Blood
HISTORIES

Mixed-Blood HISTORIES

Race, Law, and Dakota Indians in the Nineteenth-Century Midwest

Jameson R. Sweet

UNIVERSITY OF MINNESOTA PRESS
MINNEAPOLIS • LONDON

The University of Minnesota Press gratefully acknowledges the generous assistance provided for the publication of this book by the Department of American Studies and the School of Arts and Sciences at Rutgers University.

Portions of chapter 1 are adapted from "A Vast Indigenous World: Moving Away from Eurocentric Conceptions of North American History," *William and Mary Quarterly* 81, no. 1 (2024): 93–102, https://doi.org/10.1353/wmq.2024.a918187. Portions of chapter 5 are adapted from "Native Suffrage: Race, Citizenship, and Dakota Indians in the Upper Midwest," *Journal of the Early Republic* 39, no. 1 (2019): 99–110, https://doi.org/10.1353/jer.2019.0008; copyright 2019 Society for Historians of the Early American Republic. Portions of chapter 6 are adapted from "Makhóčhe Khípi: A Dakota Family Story of Race, Land, and Dispossession Before the Dawes Act," in *Allotment Stories: Indigenous Land Relations Under Settler Siege,* ed. Daniel Heath Justice and Jean M. O'Brien (University of Minnesota Press, 2021).

Published by the University of Minnesota Press
111 Third Avenue South, Suite 290
Minneapolis, MN 55401–2520
http://www.upress.umn.edu

ISBN 978-1-5179-2033-3 (hc)
ISBN 978-1-5179-2034-0 (pb)

A Cataloging-in-Publication record for this book is available from the Library of Congress.

Printed in the United States of America on acid-free paper

UMP BMB 2025

Contents

Introduction

Over a four-day Memorial Day weekend in 2007, members of the extended Trudell family met on the Santee Indian Reservation in northeastern Nebraska for a family reunion. Home of the Santee Sioux Tribe, the reservation is primarily composed of members of the Bdewákhaŋthuŋwaŋ (or Mdewakanton in English) tribe of Dakota Indians. The reunion comprised the descendants of Francis Trudell and Ičíyapiwiŋ, who had been married by Dakota custom in Minnesota about 1835. Over one hundred relatives showed up at the Santee Community Center in Niobrara. Over the weekend, getting to know these distant relatives and seeing their faces, I was struck by how diverse the family is. Most of the family members who still lived on the reservation were phenotypically Indian and were fully immersed in Dakota culture. Other family members were phenotypically white, many of whom only had a vague notion of their Dakota heritage and had lived away from the reservation for generations. Most of the family fell on some spectrum in between or bore African American features. This is typical of a Native American extended family in the Midwest. However, it is important to remember that race and culture are disparate concepts; the perceived phenotype of the Trudell family members did not necessarily match up with their ethnic or racial identity or cultural knowledge.

The extended family had been brought together in an unlikely way. A court case, *Wolfchild v. United States,* filed in 2003 and which ultimately failed in 2013, included over seven thousand potential plaintiffs in a case involving the land of Bdewákhaŋthuŋwaŋ Dakota peoples in Minnesota going back to the nineteenth century.[1] Although I chose not to be a plaintiff in the case, some members of the Trudell family did. To qualify as a plaintiff, it was necessary to prove descent from particular Dakota people in the nineteenth century who had been perceived by the United States government to be loyal during the U.S.-Dakota War in 1862. A flurry of genealogical research by these thousands of potential plaintiffs in the early 2000s had the unexpected effect of connecting far-flung relatives, including those unconnected to the lawsuit. For the Trudell family, this culminated with the 2007 family reunion.

During the reunion, I observed my relatives, few of whom I had met before. I noticed that the relatives local to the reservation bore most of the cost and conducted most of the labor for the reunion, nearly all of whom were women. Only a few relatives spoke the Dakota language, most notably Roger Trudell, the tribal chairman; some relatives heard Dakota spoken for the first time at the reunion. The traditional practices observed at the reunion were commonplace for some, while they were one-time novelties for other relatives. During the long weekend, two young male members of the family had performed the haŋbdéčheya ceremony, or "vision quest," in which they had fasted and prayed. Before each meal, we made a spirit plate and a family member led us in prayer. We later visited the graves of our ancestors and relatives in the local reservation cemeteries, leaving offerings of tobacco.

It was not lost on me that we were the descendants of an interracial marriage that had taken place 170 years before our reunion. Observing the diversity of my relatives brought to mind a document I had recently seen, an affidavit from 1855 in which my great-great-great-grandfather was giving evidence to ensure that his mixed-ancestry children would receive lands guaranteed under federal legislation the previous year. "I, Francis Trudell of Dacotah Co[unty] Min[nesota] Ter[ritory] (near Mendota), do solemnly swear that I am a Canadian Frenchman. About twenty years ago I was married by Indian custom to a Sioux woman of the Medawahkanton band. At her baptism she was called Mary. She is now about 36 years of age & I am 48. We live together & have seven children now living. . . .

They are Half Breeds and all live with us."[2] In this document, Trudell delineated his own ethnicity and race from that of his wife and assigned yet a third racial category to his children, as "Half Breeds." This demonstrates how multiple racial and ethnic categories could exist in one family, which must have been confusing for the children who grew up in these mixed families and were categorized as something different from either of their parents. Making sense of the racial diversity of one Indian family in the twenty-first century and the curious racial aspects of this mid-nineteenth-century document, coupled with the legal situations that prompted both events, elicited many of the questions from which this book emerges.

Centuries of intermarriage between Euro-Americans and American Indians in the Midwest have resulted in a significant population of Indigenous people of mixed ancestry, or what contemporaries called "half-breeds" or "mixed-bloods." So as not to legitimize or normalize the Euro-American racial discourse of "blood" forced upon them, I use the term "mixed ancestry." Government officials were mystified as to their status and legal rights. E. A. Hitchcock, an army officer tasked with distributing $100,000 in treaty funds to Ho-Chunk people of mixed ancestry, stated in 1838, "Half-breeds are neither white men nor Indians, as expressed in their name; and the proper treatment of them is neither defined in the regulations, nor, perhaps, established by usage. If it is said they are not Indians, and must therefore be treated as white men, it may more plausibly be said they are not white men, and ought therefore to be treated as Indians."[3] Tribal leaders contributed to the complexity of this history when they insisted on separate provisions of land or money for their mixed-ancestry relatives in treaties. To be clear, despite this confusion, Indians of mixed ancestry were just that—Indians. Some coalesced into the Métis community in the Red River Valley of southern Manitoba and some families merged into the white American community over time, but most maintained connections to their Indigenous nations.

This book analyzes the history of mixed-ancestry Indians in the Midwest, particularly the Očhéthi Šakówiŋ (Seven Council Fires), or the Dakota and Lakota, often called "Sioux," in the nineteenth century. The book explores how the study of law, kinship, and culture at this moment critically shifts understandings of race, nation, and Indian–white relations in the United States. Through treaties, legislation, court cases, and state constitutions, the American legal and racial systems in the Midwest solidified "half-breed" or "mixed-blood" as a separate legal and racial category, which included rights, albeit ambiguous, inconsistent, and often temporary, that other Indians did not have, such as the right to sue and testify in court, buy and sell land, vote, and serve in public office. They also enjoyed entitlements to land and money enumerated for them in treaties between the United States and Indigenous nations. While they received short-term benefits, this period of American racial creation coupled with the foundation of "mixed-blood" as a separate legal category ultimately led to intratribal divisions. In many respects, these legal rights and treaty provisions were predicated on whiteness rather than mixedness. American legal understandings defined "mixed-bloods" as those of mixed white and Indian "blood." Those few mixed-ancestry Dakota and Lakota families with African ancestry were usually, but not always, excluded from enjoying these legal rights and excluded from the status of "mixed-bloods" by the federal government and local governments. By the end of the nineteenth century, the solidification of the "mixed-blood" racial category in American racial perceptions ensured that Indians of mixed ancestry would face much the same racial discrimination as their full-ancestry relatives, while simultaneously Euro-Americans denied their Indigenous identities—although for much of the nineteenth century a less than full blood quantum worked to one's advantage.

The title of this book, *Mixed-Blood Histories,* refers to the consequences of moments when the United States and white Americans initiated laws, policies, and practices that sought to delineate people of mixed ancestry as white, as Indian, or more often as the nebulous and ill-defined category of "half-breed." Such racial and legal contradictions and inconsistencies are baked into settler colonialism and white supremacy to give settlers and white supremacist institutions the flexibility to enact contradictory laws and policies or employ contradictory racial ideas when necessary to bolster white supremacy and settler power. Most often, settlers and American officials worked to portray them as racially, legally, politically, socially, or economically distinct from Indians. In other words, typical "mixed-blood histories" were when Americans tried to socially construct or codify into law Native Americans of mixed ancestry as something else, or, in Hitchcock's words, "neither white men nor Indians." The chapters that follow chronicle some of these histories among the Dakota people in the nineteenth century, yet I argue that, for the most part, people of mixed ancestry were simply Indians. Yes, their experiences, histories, and motivations were distinctive. This distinctiveness is indicative of the diversity of Native American history and the Indigenous experience rather than evidence of their otherness. In these moments, Indians of mixed ancestry adapted to new realities and contended with American colonialism in their own ways, at times making decisions that were at odds with their full-ancestry Indian relatives.

Just as there was no homogeneous Indian or Dakota experience, mixed-ancestry Dakota people were not a monolith. They lived and traveled across a broad geography where they had varied experiences with different Euro-American empires and settler colonial nations and institutions. They faced different legal, political, economic, and cultural realities and encountered manifold and uneven pressures of assimilation and racialization. They also held varying legal rights and citizenship status. Their one common trait was some connection to the Dakota Nation or some inkling of a Dakota identity. Their racial mixedness did not equate to a shared identity or to a guarantee of a similar lived experience.

American officials regularly employed the language of blood quanta by the 1820s and began to meticulously record the blood quanta of Indigenous people of mixed ancestry. Blood quantum is a colonially imposed concept to mathematically measure Indian "blood," typically expressed in fractions. But it was not until the turn of the century that the United States began to define "Indian" and tribal citizenship through blood quantum. By this time, blood quantum became a settler colonial tool of exclusion. For most of the century, though, the U.S. government did not use blood quantum to define Indianness. While the federal government sometimes used blood quantum as an exclusionary tool, it was primarily meant to define people within the new legal category of "half-breed." The primary catalyst for Indians of mixed ancestry as "other" was that American policymakers perceived Indians of mixed ancestry as assimilable and a potential assimilative influence on their full-ancestry relatives and because officials recognized that they had influence on their full-ancestry relatives and hoped to exploit and manipulate that influence.

As Patrick Wolfe argues, "Settler colonialism destroys to replace."[4] This destruction might include genocide, but it also included other elements, such as forced assimilation, the individualization of Indians, and the implementation of blood quantum to eliminate Indigenous people on paper. For Indians of mixed ancestry, this meant that the United States might incorporate them into the nation. Not because they wanted to. Making Indians into individuals meant they could be separated from their Indigenous nations and separated from their inherent land rights. "Non-Indian ancestry compromised their indigeneity" in the eyes of the American legal system, Wolfe asserts.[5] Part of the American settler colonial project of othering mixed-ancestry Indians was to make them no longer Indian and separate them from the land and their sovereign nations. The American challenge to the sovereignty and nationhood of Indigenous people, coupled with white Americans' increasing obsession with "blood," led, over time, to the American perception of Indians as racial minorities rather than as sovereign nations.

The historical focus on Indians of mixed ancestry emerged out of fur trade scholarship in the late 1970s and early 1980s with influential work by Jennifer S. H. Brown, Sylvia Van Kirk, and Jacqueline Peterson.[6] Works of ethnohistory, they centered the role of mixed families in the fur trade. They focused on the upper Great Lakes region and conflated Indians of mixed ancestry with the Métis and replicated the federal government's assertion that mixed-ancestry people were something else—not white and not Indian. Subsequent scholarship retained the ethnohistorical methodological focus, often continued the mischaracterization of mixed-ancestry Indians as Métis, and emphasized their distinctiveness to the point where they divorced mixed-ancestry people from their tribal contexts, reifying settler colonial notions of mixed-ancestry people as "other." Part of the project of this book is to place mixed-ancestry Indian histories back into the tribal and cultural contexts to which they belong.

More recently, Métis scholars argue that Métis identity has been misunderstood as being rooted in racial mixedness and contend that the

Métis are an Indigenous people distinct from Indians with a unique culture and a common identity and a common sense of Indigenous nationhood. I contend that Indians of mixed ancestry are not Métis, nor are they distinct to the point of losing their Indianness. Jace Weaver argues that "too many want to see mixed bloods . . . as somehow diminished in Indianness" and asserts that "to be bicultural is to be *bicultural*—not to be somehow non-Native."[7] The old trope of Métis-as-mixed has been sustained by modern phenomena of claiming Métis identity on the basis of the discovery of an Indian ancestor from long ago, thereby circumventing generations of cultural practice, belonging in a community, kinship connections, and a national identity.[8] There is much to learn from Métis historiography, but the conflation of mixed-ancestry Indians and Métis has resulted in scholars divorcing Indians of mixed ancestry from their tribal contexts and masking their identities as tribal members. Studying Indians of mixed ancestry, then, is simply a way to broaden our understandings

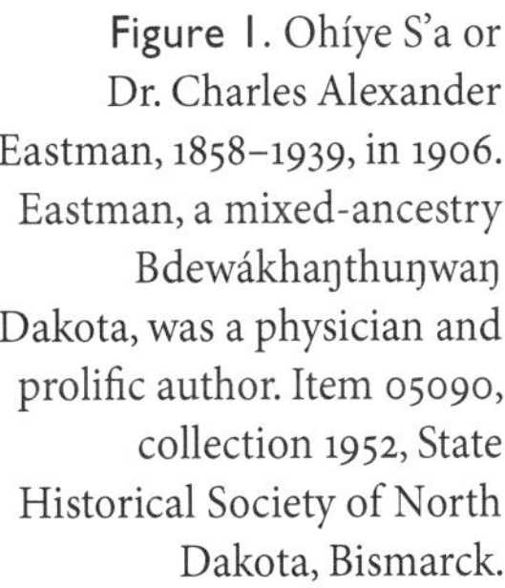

Figure 1. Ohíye S'a or Dr. Charles Alexander Eastman, 1858–1939, in 1906. Eastman, a mixed-ancestry Bdewákhaŋthuŋwaŋ Dakota, was a physician and prolific author. Item 05090, collection 1952, State Historical Society of North Dakota, Bismarck.

of the Indian past, not the past of some nebulous group of in-between or peripheral people.

For their part, most mixed-ancestry Dakota and Lakota people continue to think of themselves as tribal members into the present. Only a handful of mixed-ancestry Dakota and Lakota people born in the nineteenth century left book-length writings. Invariably, these authors upheld the value and importance of Očhéthi Šakówiŋ culture and history and noted the negative effects of Western culture. This was summed up by another mixed-ancestry Dakota observer, James Garvie, born in 1862, who wrote that the Dakota "were corrupted and ruined by the introduction of the low, debasing civilization of the white man."[9] Marie Buisson McLaughlin (1842–1924), a mixed-ancestry Bdewákhaŋthuŋwaŋ Dakota, published a book of traditional Dakota stories in 1916. In the dedication she wrote, "In loving memory of my mother, Mary Graham Buisson, at whose knee most of the stories contained in this little volume were told to me."[10] This reveals the importance of kinship and the role of women as the carriers of culture among the Dakota.[11] Probably most famous among them was Charles Eastman (1858–1939), a Bdewákhaŋthuŋwaŋ Dakota physician and author of eleven books, primarily on Dakota history and culture.[12] His contemporary Susan Bordeaux Bettelyoun (1857–1945), a Sičháŋǧu Lakota, with the aid of a mixed-ancestry Húŋkpapȟa Lakota woman, Josephine McCarthy Waggoner (1872–1943), wrote a book manuscript in the 1930s, a memoir of Bettelyoun and history of the Lakota, posthumously published.[13] Some of Waggoner's additional historical writings were recently edited and published by Emily Levine.[14] Two Iháŋkthuŋwaŋ Dakota women born later in the century—Zitkala-Ša, or Gertrude Simmons Bonnin (1876–1938), an author and activist, and anthropologist Ella Deloria (1889–1971)—left a significant body of work on Dakota history and culture.[15] Zitkala-Ša wrote of her loathing for Euro-Americans because of their ill treatment of Indigenous people, while Deloria dedicated her life to preserving Očhéthi Šakówiŋ history, culture, and language. Sičháŋǧu Lakota historian and nephew of Susan Bordeaux Bettelyoun, William J. Bordeaux (1884–1962) published his book *Conquering the Mighty Sioux* in 1929, in which he referred to white Americans as invaders and feared that his people were becoming too mixed.[16] The attitudes of mixed-ancestry people were diverse. Some were like Emma Robinson Valandry, an Oglála Lakota woman born in the early 1860s who witnessed the Wounded Knee Massacre in 1890 and lived her entire life among the Lakota and spoke Lakota, who was reluctant to adopt a Lakota identity, played up her whiteness, and exhibited internalized anti-Native racism in an interview with Ella Deloria in 1935.[17] Most Dakota and Lakota people of mixed ancestry of this era maintained a close connection to their people and their culture. But they were never a monolith; their attitudes regarding their mixed heritage varied widely.

Scholars often describe the history of mixed-race people in North America as a "hidden history" or describe them as "hiding in plain sight."[18] This was never a hidden history nor were mixed-race people hiding. Interracial marriage and mixed-race Americans had always been visible; Americans debated it in their media and wrote an extensive literature on mixed-race Americans. William J. Scheick reveals how tropes of the

Figure 2. Marie Louise Buisson McLaughlin, 1842–1924. A Bdewákhaŋthuŋwaŋ woman of mixed ancestry, she was an author and instrumental to the career of her husband, James McLaughlin, an Indian agent at Devil's Lake and Standing Rock agencies. Photo taken January 28, 1864. Item 03108, collection 1952, State Historical Society of North Dakota, Bismarck.

"half-blood" pervaded nineteenth-century American literature.[19] Had it been hidden, Americans would not have constantly made laws, which utterly failed, attempting to curtail these relationships or created specific racial language for mixed-race people. Instead, white Americans employed an actively constructed amnesia to forget or remain willfully ignorant of mixed-race Americans. By the turn of the twentieth century, Americans were obsessed with racial mixture, turning to scientific racism and eugenics. "Fears of racial mixture preoccupied policymakers, scholars, lawyers, scientists, and journalists," Lauren L. Basson argues, because they were perceived as threats to white supremacist understandings of the state.[20]

Many scholars have studied the connections and mixed-ancestry offspring of the French and Indigenous peoples in the Great Lakes and Mississippi River Valley.[21] Despite the divergent histories of racialization of African Americans and Native Americans under settler colonialism, they often converged in nineteenth-century conversations about race among white American officials who debated their rights under American law. Several scholars have explored the complexities of Indigeneity and Blackness, but much work remains to be done.[22] Susan Sleeper-Smith argues that "Indian communities successfully incorporated European traders as well as other strangers, and even enemies through intermarriage," which "transformed French fur traders into friends, family, and allies." She centers Indigenous women in these encounters and asserts that these kinship connections turned economic practices "into a socially accountable practice."[23] "Blood" has become a ubiquitous descriptor of Indigenous identity, but J. Kēhaulani Kauanui argues that "blood quantum logic presumes that one's 'blood amount' correlates to one's cultural orientation and identity," which is certainly not the case.[24] In broader American culture, blood quantum came to be the yardstick for measuring Indianness, but according to Theda Perdue, understandings of race and belonging through blood "privileges European cultural norms and male power" and damages the claims to Indigeneity of mixed-ancestry people.[25]

The American obsession with racial mixedness and blood quantum in relation to Indigenous people has shaped how the general American population perceives American Indians: as racial or ethnic minorities.

"Indianness" is a political category, not simply a racial one, and tribal nations are inherently sovereign and have political and legal status in the United States. Indigenous nations predate the United States as "pre-existing sovereigns whose existence is not beholden to the Constitution or to the federal or state governments."[26] Legal scholar David E. Wilkins challenges the idea of the infallibility and perceived legitimacy and unassailability of American legal institutions, asserting that American legal rulings have often "had little to do with logic, reasoning, or legal ideals," especially when it comes to the rights of Indigenous people.[27] The American obsession with race continues to privilege the idea of race-based Indianness and in the process erases tribal sovereignty.[28] Indians, particularly those of mixed ancestry, were also subject to state and territorial law, which helped shape much of federal Indian policy during the nineteenth century.[29]

Because of the conflation of Métis with Indians of mixed ancestry that often appears in the literature, more must be said to differentiate the two. Chris Andersen challenges the idea that the Métis people can be regarded in simple terms of hybridity, or Métis-as-mixed, and he challenges how historians of mixed-ancestry people in the Great Lakes have characterized their subjects as Métis or métis. The Métis-as-mixed trope erases their Indigeneity and erases their sovereignty as an Indigenous nation. Andersen explains that the practice of denominating mixed-ancestry Indians as métis, while meant to differentiate them from the Métis people, has backfired. It simply reinscribes the mischaracterization that Métis identity is grounded in mixedness and ascribes an identity to Indians of mixed ancestry that they did not hold. Such assumptions also uphold erroneous notions of racial purity of members of tribal nations and erases the Indigeneity of Indians of mixed ancestry.[30]

Terminology

The Dakota Nation is composed of seven different divisions, what the Dakota call the "Očhéthi Šakówiŋ" (or the Seven Fireplaces in English, sometimes called the Seven Council Fires). Historically, non-Dakota people referred to all divisions of the Očhéthi Šakówiŋ as "Sioux," abbreviated from the earlier French "*Nadouesioux*," a corruption of an Ojibwe derogatory term. The Očhéthi Šakówiŋ comprise three main mutually intelligible dialect groups with some minor cultural differences, but they are the same people. The farthest west and largest tribe being the Thítȟuŋwaŋ (or Teton in English), more commonly called the Lakota, who speak their own dialect also called Lakota. East of the Thítȟuŋwaŋ are the Iháŋkthuŋwaŋ (Yankton) and Iháŋkthuŋwaŋna (Yanktonai), which I refer to as the "Western Dakota," who speak a distinct dialect that incorporates aspects of the Lakota dialect and the Eastern Dakota dialect. Further east are the Eastern Dakota, made up of four tribes: the Bdewákhaŋthuŋwaŋ (Mdewakanton), Sisíthuŋwaŋ (Sisseton), Waȟpékute (Wahpekute), and Waȟpéthuŋwaŋ (Wahpeton). All seven tribes are divided into subgroups, historically called bands, sub-bands, or villages. The four Eastern Dakota tribes and the Iháŋkthuŋwaŋ are the primary focus of this book. I use the Dakota forms of these names, or simply "Dakota," except when quoting sources or in the proper names of places, such as the Santee Reservation, Sisseton Reservation, or Yankton Reservation.

The racial terminology of this research is a challenge. Historically, nineteenth-century sources refer to mixed-ancestry Indians as "half-breeds" or occasionally "mixed-bloods." According to James A. Clifton, "half-breed" first appeared in print as a racial category in 1773 but did not come into common usage until the nineteenth century.[31] American officials occasionally debated the term "half-breed"; some believed it meant those of literally one-half blood quantum, while most argued that it was an all-encompassing term that had no blood quantum connotation. This confusion led many nineteenth-century documents to refer to both "half-breeds" and "mixed-bloods." Constructing race or belonging on a foundation of blood is a Euro-American concept based in exclusion, not in how Indigenous people perceived themselves. As early as 1705, American colonial institutions imposed the practice of quantifying Indian blood, but it has been especially prevalent since the nineteenth century.[32] This quantification, called blood quantum, has been employed by the U.S. government to exclude Indians from their treaty-guaranteed rights and privileges. Systematic exclusion of mixed-ancestry Indians with a blood quantum deemed too low to be Indian effectively lets the government off the hook for their treaty obligations to Indian nations.

Most scholars use the term "mixed-blood," and this is the term in common usage today in Indian communities. Other scholars use hyphenated terms, but what this work has in common is that it ignores Indigenous people's own concepts for race and racial mixedness. Indigenous languages have concepts for Indians of mixed ancestry. The Dena'ina of Alaska use "niłdulchinen," the Blackfeet say "aanáó'kítapiikoan," the Plains Cree "âpihtawikosisân," the Ute "navayi-tʉ-m-mʉ," and the Sahaptin say "shitkumshawáash." Most language dictionaries simply translate these terms as "half-breed" or "mixed-blood," but they often come from very different concepts of race. For instance, an Ojibwe word for mixed-ancestry Indians is "wissâkodéwinini," which means "half-burned-wood-man." The idea being that mixed-ancestry Indians are like a log that is half in and half out of a fire: the unburned end is white while the burned end is black.

The Dakota people have a racial language that is just as complex, and often just as problematic, as racial language in English. Although the etymology is uncertain, the Dakota term that refers to Euro-American people, "wašíču," is often translated to "fat taker." Among Dakota people today, many see this as an innocuous term, while others perceive it as a racial slur. One of the terms used in the nineteenth century to mean "mixed-ancestry Indians" was "wašíču číŋčapi," meaning literally "offspring of white men." The other most common term of the period, which is still used today, is "iyéska," which means "translator."[33] The term "iyéska" suggests that the Dakota perceived mixed-ancestry Indians as holding a kind of mediator role, while the phrase "wašíču číŋčapi" suggests that the Dakota wanted to push mixed-ancestry Indians away, as being offspring of whites, not the Dakota. Revealing the complexity of racial discourse in the Dakota language, both terms have evolved over time. While both terms still refer to mixed-ancestry Indians, both can have derogatory connotations. Today, "iyéska" is sometimes used as an insult to suggest someone talks or acts like a white person. Scott Richard Lyons complicates these terms further. "Iyéska" and "wašíču číŋčapi" do not contain a connotation of "blood" but rather of kinship and culture. As Lyons asserts, one "doesn't need to possess a certain degree of blood or conform to a particular phenotype to be considered a 'full-blood.' The truly important things are mind-set and action."[34] In this paradigm, one needs to act or think as an Indian to be a "full-blood," while "acting white" makes one a mixed-ancestry Indian.

Further illuminating the complex language of race is a term in the Lakota dialect, "áozi," which means "Indians of mixed-ancestry" but literally translates to "yellow armpit." This term too is problematic. "Áozi" comes from a nineteenth-century Lakota stereotype, the belief that whites sweat more than Indians and therefore that Indians of mixed ancestry would sweat more than their full-ancestry relatives and yellow the armpits of their shirts. Speakers of the Lakota dialect also differentiated between mixed-ancestry Indians and Métis in the nineteenth century. The Lakota used the word "Slót'a" specifically for the Métis people around Turtle Mountain, later coming to mean all Métis people descended from the original Red River core. "Slót'a" means "slippery with grease" or is sometimes translated as "greasy people," referring to Métis people's extensive buffalo hunting. The Dakota also have an ethnic discourse to talk about people from different tribes, nationalities, or ethnicities. The Dakota call their Ojibwe neighbors "Ȟaȟátuŋwaŋ Oyáte," or "the Nation That Dwells at the Falls," or the Omaha "Oyátenuŋpa," "Two Nation." When Germans began their heavy settlement among the Dakota in Minnesota in the 1850s, the Dakota called them "Iyásiča," or "Bad Talkers." Apparently, the Dakota felt that German was an ugly language. They referred to the British as "Šagdáša" or "Šagdášiŋ," which has come to be a synonym for mixed-ancestry Indians on the Spirit Lake Reservation in North Dakota. This just scratches the surface of the racial and ethnic discourse of the Dakota; other tribes have similarly rich discourses and concepts of race, which expresses the strong need for scholars to analyze Indian cultures and languages to understand these distinct discourses.[35]

Each of the eight chapters in this book analyzes a particular mixed-blood history. These were legal moments often representing shifts in federal Indian policy toward mixed-ancestry Indians, and each chapter reveals the evolution of racial thought and discourse among white Americans and the Dakota people. Throughout the book, I interweave the stories of families, particularly branches of my own family's history, to demonstrate how these events affected mixed-ancestry people and their families. In earlier chapters, I focus on the Dorion family, an Iháŋkthuŋwaŋ Dakota and Sičháŋǧu Lakota family. In later chapters, I examine the history of the Trudell family, a Bdewákhaŋthuŋwaŋ Dakota family. Occasionally, a third family, the Iháŋkthuŋwaŋ and Sičháŋǧu Langdeau family, makes an appearance in the narrative. Anne F. Hyde argues that the nineteenth century of the American West to 1860 can best be understood through an analysis of families rather than national or ethnic identities.[36] This is especially apt for the history of mixed-ancestry Dakota people; as different colonial powers claimed suzerainty over Dakota country, as the boundaries of American territories and states advanced and receded, and even after the population of Dakota country became increasingly Euro-American, mixed-ancestry Dakota families remained, enduring all of these changes. I use family history methods in conjunction with an analysis of Indigenous kinship, which coincides with the traditional pursuit of passing on oral history from generation to generation, is in keeping with Dakota values, and is a culturally appropriate academic practice.[37] Indeed, as Raymond J. DeMallie asserts, "because kinship is so much a part of the context of Native American life, the extent to which it permeates all aspects of culture is easily overlooked."[38]

Chapter 1 examines the early history of the rise of the mixed-ancestry Dakota community from the mid-1600s to the early nineteenth century through the fur trade and examines how members of these mixed families became important diplomats and go-betweens. Chapter 2 centers on the 1830 Treaty of Prairie du Chien and how this and other treaties had the unintended consequence of solidifying "half-breed" as a separate legal and racial category. I also analyze the federal Indian policy of the period focused on assimilation of mixed-ancestry Indians and how they quickly took to American legal institutions. Shifting to the 1837 Treaty of Washington, chapter 3 analyzes how mixed racial status and kinship became intertwined with the American capitalist economy in which Americans placed economic value on mixed-race status while Dakota people began to place monetary value on the fulfillment of kinship obligations. Nationhood and a series of unratified treaties in the 1840s are the subject of chapter 4, in which the federal government negotiated directly with the mixed-ancestry Dakota, nearly recognizing them as their own sovereign nation apart from the Dakota Nation. Chapter 5 explores state constitutions and local laws written in the mid-nineteenth century that enfranchised Indians of mixed ancestry, guaranteeing U.S. citizenship for Indians of mixed ancestry and denying it for those of full-ancestry. Indians of mixed ancestry served in political office and, for a time, held political power and influence in the Midwest. Land is the subject of chapter 6. The 1830 Treaty of Prairie du Chien had founded two Indian reservations for the exclusive use of Indians of mixed ancestry, but in the 1850s they sought individual landownership. Indians of mixed ancestry enjoyed rights to land that their full-ancestry relatives did not, but they quickly became inundated with settler colonial dispossession tactics. Chapter 7 reveals how years of colonial divide-and-conquer strategies resulted in animosities and major divisions between those of mixed and full ancestry that were laid bare in the U.S.-Dakota War of 1862. Dakota people of mixed ancestry fought on both sides in the war, but especially on the American side, while the full-ancestry Dakota captured over 160 mixed-ancestry Dakota people and threatened them with death. In the subsequent military tribunals, mixed-ancestry Indians were crucial witnesses that sent dozens of their relatives to the gallows. Finally, chapter 8 explores the complex aftermath of the U.S.-Dakota War and how Dakota people of mixed ancestry gravitated closer to their full-ancestry relatives. As racial categories became more solidified in the United States by the end of the century, they found challenges to claims of both Indianness and whiteness.

CHAPTER 1

The Emergence of the Mixed-Ancestry Dakota Community, 1660–1815

Dakhóta wóyakapi kíŋ dé héčha (this is a Dakota story). Marie, an Iháŋkthuŋwaŋ Dakota woman, was probably born in the 1750s. Her people primarily followed the buffalo on the Missouri and Des Moines Rivers and their various tributaries in what settlers renamed northwestern Iowa, southwestern Minnesota, and eastern South Dakota. They also hunted smaller game, fished, and grew crops in the river valleys, especially corn. Marie would have grown up living in tipis and perhaps earth lodges and would have helped her mother tend the corn, search for wild edibles, and process animal hides. Her parents' names are unknown, but some sources refer to her father as a chief, which means he likely led an Iháŋkthuŋwaŋ thiyóšpaye, a small unit of related families who lived together in a small village and typically traveled and hunted together.[1]

By the time of Marie's marriage in the 1770s through a Dakota ceremony to fur trader Pierre Dorion, the Dakota had been intermittently trading with Europeans for over a century, although mostly the Iháŋkthuŋwaŋ people's eastern relatives, the Bdewákhaŋthuŋwaŋ Dakota. In the aftermath of the Seven Years' War, the Iháŋkthuŋwaŋ welcomed more consistent trade from the British out of Prairie du Chien and Michilimackinac and the Spanish out of Saint Louis, although most of the traders themselves, like Dorion, were French Canadians. The British and Spanish were long in competition with each other over gaining the favor of tribes in the Midwest.[2] Dorion was among this early wave of traders. Born in Quebec

City in 1740, Dorion grew up in New France, a colony of the French Empire in North America, but later worked in the fur trade in the Dakota homeland for the British, Spanish, and, later, the Americans. With his marriage to Marie, Dorion married into the complex Dakota kinship system, which, as a fur trader, gave him distinct advantages such as a customer base that was obligated to trade with him the furs they acquired through hunting and trapping. The marriage also came with kinship obligations for Dorion; his new relatives expected him to supply them with goods, such as tools, cloth, and whiskey. His long relationship with the Dakota came with the trust of his Dakota kin, and he was called on from time to time by colonial officials to facilitate diplomacy with the Dakota, a not uncommon activity for long-term fur traders. This situation also gave Marie a modicum of authority as the linchpin of this reciprocal kinship relationship.

By the end of the War of 1812, after over 150 years of contact between the Dakota people and Euro-Americans, there was a significant population of mixed-ancestry Dakota Indians. This chapter chronicles this contact and the intermarriages between white men and Dakota women that led to the rise of this population. The primary inducement for these interactions was the fur trade. Beyond simply economic relationships, the fur trade was inherently political and was intended by the Dakota and the various Euro-American empires they traded with to further their diplomatic needs, such as military alliances. Diplomacy and trade were indistinguishable for Indians, and Euro-American empires like New France relied on the fur trade "as an instrument of its foreign policy" with Indigenous nations.[3] Historians often portray how Indians became reliant on the fur trade, but Euro-American empires also needed alliances with tribal nations.[4] For the Dakota, trade relations and diplomatic relationships required that the fur traders they encountered become kin—either by informal or formal ceremonial adoption or through marriage. It was these kinship requirements that were the main catalyst for intermarriages and thus the rise of the mixed-ancestry Dakota population.[5] This chapter examines the history of the Dorion family, an Ihángkthuŋwaŋ Dakota fur trade family who honored complex Dakota kinship practices, were deeply enmeshed in the fur trade between the Mississippi and the Pacific, and served as diplomats between the Dakota Oyáte, or Dakota Nation, and the British, Spanish, and American empires.

This history features a complex coalescence of several different elements: Indigenous and colonial powers all vying for regional power, the vast economic importance of the fur trade that brought these powers together, the Indian requirement of kinship ties, and the diplomacy necessary to make this all work. Indigenous men, Indigenous women, and white men each had their own overlapping roles to play. Indian men were leaders of their nations and warriors who could make peace or war, as well as the primary laborers in the fur trade who hunted the fur-bearing animals. Indian women were laborers and the linchpin of the all-important kinship connections that made trade possible. They held influence with their Indigenous relatives, their white husbands, and their mixed-ancestry children. White men in the fur trade were the tie to coveted Euro-American manufactured goods, laborers, and sometimes emissaries of empires. They also largely adopted Indigenous material culture and food and some Indigenous beliefs and practices.[6] All held different roles as laborers in the fur trade and any could potentially act as facilitators of trade, translators, negotiators, or diplomats. Mixed-ancestry Indian men and women grew up in the midst of this world and could take on any of these roles. The history of the Dorion family well illustrates the coalescence of these elements and the role that mixed-ancestry families played in them.

Trade and kinship were always at the heart of diplomacy between Indigenous nations and Euro-American empires as they continually challenged each other for power.[7] "Native Americans interact with one another first and foremost as relatives," Raymond J. DeMallie argues, and kinship pervades every part of Indian life—economic, political, religious, diplomatic, and cultural.[8] Many scholars examine the intersections of these topics, particularly focusing on differing power relations in various regions of North America and how fortunes changed over time.[9] Diplomacy is at the center of other studies, especially among the Iroquois in the seventeenth and eighteenth centuries and how they successfully played the British and French off of each other to their own benefit.[10] Several scholars examine the role of women, families, and kinship in this history, but few illustrate the centrality of Indians of mixed ancestry in the intersections of the fur trade, power dynamics, diplomacy, and kinship.[11] Lesley Wischmann describes fur trader Alexander Culbertson and his Kainai wife Natawista as "an active diplomatic team" on the Great Plains.[12] In looking at Creek diplomacy in the eighteenth-century Southeast, John T. Juricek argues that mixed-ancestry Creek people were crucial in diplomatic relationships between the Creek and the British and were invaluable in keeping the peace between them.[13] Through an analysis of the Dorion family history, we get a view into just how influential and deeply enmeshed a singular mixed-ancestry Indian family could be in the convergence of power dynamics, the fur trade, Indigenous kinship systems, and diplomacy, giving a true measure of the importance of mixed-ancestry Indians in this history.

Kinship and diplomacy were inextricably linked for the Dakota people, as observed in the Dakota language. In diplomatic negotiations, Dakota leaders frequently addressed people as relatives. The U.S. president became known as "Thuŋkášida," a formal term for "grandfather." "Thuŋkášida" became so ingrained as the term for "president" that it formed the basis for other words related to the U.S. government. "Thuŋkášida Othí" became the name for Washington, D.C. The Dakota refer to the U.S. government as "thuŋkášidayapi," and "thuŋkášida" forms the root for terms for the Senate and House of Representatives.[14] The use of relative terms in negotiations was a diplomatic tactic. By referring to the president and the federal government as "grandfather," they were signaling that the president, as a grandfather, had kinship responsibilities to the Dakota people and as a relative had the duty to treat them fairly.

In 1660, the Dakota received a strange visitor, Pierre-Esprit Radisson, a French fur trader and explorer, who wrote of the Dakota, "that the dores of their villages, cottages of their wives and daughters, weare open at any time to receive us, being wee kept them alive by our marchandises." Radisson might have meant or thought that Dakota women were available to French Canadian traders for sexual liaisons because of Dakota dependence on European manufactured goods, and that might be the case, but this also likely meant that Dakota women were available for marriage in order to create kinship connections and facilitate trade and diplomatic relations. The women of the Dakota "were the dearest thing they had in the world," Radisson said of the Dakota men.[15] Another telling aspect of Radisson's narrative is that it suggests that during this first recorded account between the Dakota Nation and Europeans he claims that the Dakota people were already dependent on European manufactured goods, suggesting the possibility of significant earlier contact.

The fur trade was a catalyst for Indian–white interaction, and it was a family business in more ways than one. For the Dakota, the vast majority of Euro-Americans that they came into contact with were connected to the fur trade, and quite often those traders played a diplomatic role between the Dakota and various European powers. Dakota kinship conventions required that in order to trade, fur traders must become kin. This was most commonly achieved through intermarriage—white fur traders regularly married Dakota women, which cemented reciprocal kinship obligations and facilitated trade.[16] Over time, this resulted in a significant population of Dakota people of mixed ancestry, who themselves often entered the fur trade or married fur traders. Although, as Carolyn Podruchny argues, high-ranking fur traders often married to create kinship obligations for trade, whereas lower-ranking voyageurs often married simply for a new life but created reciprocal kinship obligations nonetheless.[17]

In the dedication of his 1933 book *Land of the Spotted Eagle,* Luther Standing Bear summed up the Lakota and Dakota attitude toward women and mothers: "For it is the mothers, not the warriors, who create a people and guide their destiny."[18] Indeed, the Indian women who married white men created the mixed-ancestry Indian population. They gave birth to them, but more importantly, they shaped them and ensured they maintained their identities as Indians and remembered their kinship obligations. For centuries, white, Indian, and mixed-ancestry women also were as much a part of far-flung networks across the continent within and beyond the fur trade.[19] These women were important for transmitting culture and beliefs to the next generation and as significant historical actors beyond simply the mainstays of kinship connections.

Through these marriages, the woman's relatives were obligated to trade with the husband, while the fur trader then had obligations to his wife's relatives.[20] Trading in Dakota country meant being incorporated into a Dakota family, and it also meant creating a nuclear family. Most of the offspring of such marriages grew up in the fur trade. Men, women, and children all worked together in the trade. The fur trade also served as the vehicle for diplomatic relationships between the Dakota and the various colonial powers in North America. From the 1650s to the 1810s, the Dakota held relationships with the French, British, Spanish, and, finally, the Americans.

Ella Deloria, a mixed-ancestry Dakota anthropologist born in 1889, describes the vital part that kinship had long played in Dakota culture: "I can safely say that the ultimate aim of Dakota life, stripped of accessories, was quite simple: One must obey kinship rules; one must be a good relative." The Dakota concept of "being a good relative" was the most important character trait and one that all Dakota strove for.[21] In seeking this goal, "every other consideration was secondary—property, personal ambition, glory, good times, life itself. Without that aim and the constant struggle to attain it, the people would no longer be Dakotas in truth." Kinship was the center of Dakota life; in fact, kinship and the central concept of being a good relative was the very basis of Dakota identity.[22]

Marriages in the fur trade era between white fur traders and Native women were considered by fur traders to be in the "custom of the country," and historians continue to use this phrase to describe such marriages as temporary or inferior to Euro-American marriage practices.[23] But this is incorrect; usually they were marriages conducted through the established ceremonies or practices of the cultures from which the Native women came. They were no less valid than marriages conducted by Christian clergy, even if some traders acted as if they were. Rarely are such marriages preserved in the historical record, while those conducted by Christian clergy often do appear in historical documents.

My earliest known Dorion relative to visit the Mississippi River was Joseph Dorion, born in Quebec City in 1717. In 1749 he married a Native woman in Cahokia, when it was then still part of New France. His wife, Marie Anne Padoka, was a widow of Louis Richard and she was likely from the Arikara Nation, as she was referred to as "Desricaras."[24] Joseph survived Marie's death in 1757, but nothing is known of him after. His much younger first cousin, my ancestor Pierre Dorion, also had a Catholic marriage recorded in Cahokia in 1788. He married an Iháŋkthuŋwaŋ woman called Marie in the parish register. But they had already been married by Dakota ceremony, probably at least a decade earlier as five of their sons were baptized on the same day as their marriage.[25]

Pierre-Esprit Radisson, who wintered with the Dakota in 1659–1660, described an elaborate, multiday kinship ceremony that occurred when he and his men met a delegation from the Dakota Nation, or what he called the "Nation of the beefe" for their reliance on buffalo. In the process of making Radisson and his fellow travelers their kin, the Dakota first stripped them naked and gave them new clothes, made from tanned white buffalo hides, much like their own. The following day, after much gift exchange, the group's interpreter told the Dakota, "We take you for our brethren by taking you into our protection," revealing that they well understood that they were being incorporated as kin to the Dakota and were reciprocating the sentiment.[26] Eight days of feasting followed, when the main body of Dakota arrived to meet the French travelers. More ceremonies and gift giving followed with the Dakota making clear they were willing to die in their new kinship and military alliance with the French. The French responded, "Acknowledging you for our brethren and children, whom we will love henceforth as our owne."[27]

Aquipaguetin, a chief among the Dakota, began a journey down the Mississippi in 1680 to take revenge on the Miami Indians, a party of whom had killed his adult son. Before reaching the Miami, his party ran into a canoe of three Frenchmen led by a Catholic missionary named Louis Hennepin. The Dakota debated what to do with the newcomers. Some thought they should be killed, while others suggested the Dakota take Hennepin back to their villages where they might learn about the French from him. In hopes of placating those Dakota who debated his death, he gave them some of the goods he was carrying—axes, knives, and tobacco. Hennepin believed that those who wanted to kill him only did so because they could not avenge their lost loved ones by killing Miami Indians and saw him as an alternative target. "But those who liked European goods," Hennepin claimed, "were much disposed to preserve us, so as to attract other Frenchmen there and get iron, which is extremely precious in their eyes."[28] At this early date, the Dakota saw the importance of trade, and it became an important factor in how they dealt with Europeans. In this case, it dissuaded them from killing potential enemies that they encountered in enemy territory.

In his account, Hennepin complained of suffering from hunger and felt that he was ill-treated by his Dakota hosts. Another chief, Wazíkhute (Pine Shooter), agreed, scolding those who had "insulted men who brought them iron and merchandise, which they had never had." Chief Wazíkute was showing once again the value the Dakota placed on trade with the French and believed the people should treat their new relatives as such in order to ensure future trade.[29] Hennepin's visit among the Dakota was short; he soon returned southward to join with other Frenchmen in the region. His account demonstrates that in 1680, the Dakota were eager for European goods, especially guns, and that they were willing to ceremonially adopt Europeans that they encountered to make them kin and facilitate trade.

On his trip through the Great Lakes region from 1678 to 1680, Hennepin observed numerous mixed-ancestry children among the nations he visited, although it is unclear whether he met any among the Dakota. He claimed, "If these children are of a French father, you can detect it in the face and eyes. Those of the Indians are entirely black, and they can see further than Europeans, and they have a more piercing eye. If the Indian women were capable of contracting marriage, we might marry as many as we would to our Frenchmen."[30] Despite Hennepin's misguided racial assumptions about Indians, his account is revealing. Not only did he record a significant mixed-ancestry population in the Midwest by 1680, but he also noted their difference only in physical appearance. As he observed these children in Indian villages and does not mention any continued familial connections by the white fathers, it is likely that these early mixed-ancestry generations were not exposed to Euro-American culture to any great degree.

The earliest direct evidence for the birth of mixed-ancestry Dakota children comes from about 1700, but it is quite possible earlier meetings between the Dakota and French Canadians resulted in sexual relationships that produced mixed-ancestry children. Writing sometime in the 1890s, Joseph Buisson wrote about his family tree. He narrated the story of a French ancestor named Penishon who came to Minnesota in 1700, presumably as part of Pierre-Charles Le Sueur's expedition that year. Penishon married a Dakota woman and had a daughter whom Buisson named as Ištázidaŋ, but Penishon and the other Frenchmen were forced to return to New France. Two decades later, Penishon returned and found his daughter married to a chief and with a young son named Čataŋnaye. Buisson claimed that Penishon named his grandson after himself, and Penishon the younger went on to marry and have seven children, one of whom was a chief, also called Penishon, who signed the 1805 Pike Treaty. Buisson claimed that his grandmother Házaȟotawiŋ (Gray Huckleberry Woman) was the granddaughter of the grandson of Penishon. Buisson's family passed on the story of Penishon orally, while explorers and modern historians assume that the Penishon who signed the 1805 treaty was simply a

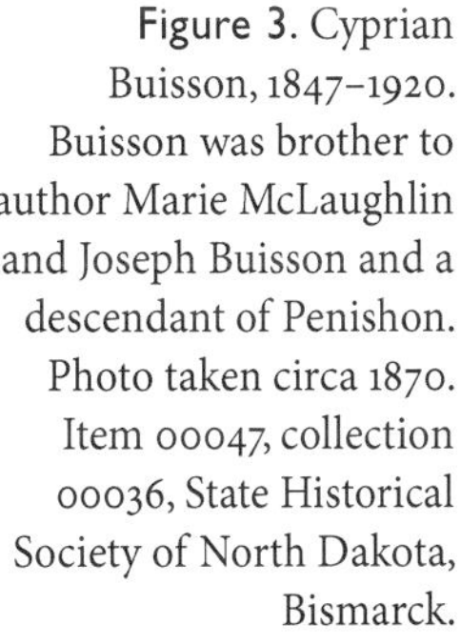

Figure 3. Cyprian Buisson, 1847–1920. Buisson was brother to author Marie McLaughlin and Joseph Buisson and a descendant of Penishon. Photo taken circa 1870. Item 00047, collection 00036, State Historical Society of North Dakota, Bismarck.

Dakota called by a French name or the son of a fur trader named Penishon, when in fact, according to Buisson, the Dakota Penishon family had a long history dating back to 1700 in Minnesota.[31]

We will never know the true extent to which interracial trysts occurred, but considering that fur traders of all ranks and social classes frequently married Indian women, it was probably quite extensive.[32] Many of these early French traders probably intermarried with the Dakota in order to facilitate trade, and as we have seen, the Dakota were interested in doing the same. While early French missionaries were unlikely to engage in sexual relationships with Dakota women, they did occasionally make record of the offspring of Dakota women and French men.

Early missionary and church records attest to interracial marriages and mixed-ancestry families among the Dakota, but they also reveal how the institution of slavery led to mixed-ancestry Native children. Father de la Morinee baptized a three-year-old child in 1747 at Mackinac, Michigan, the son of Charles Chevalier and a "Sioux slave." The same register records the baptisms of other mixed-ancestry Dakota well into the nineteenth century.[33] A mixed-ancestry Odawa fur trader and chief, Charles Langlade, enslaved a Dakota woman who bore him children in the 1740s.[34] Brett Rushforth compares Indigenous and European institutions of enslavement in New France and demonstrates the magnitude of the trade in enslaved Indians. Rushforth found numerous instances of enslaved Dakota people going back to the early 1700s.[35] This enslavement resulted in nonconsensual and perhaps some consensual relationships, many of which produced offspring of mixed ancestry who were not enslaved.

The trade relationships between the Dakota and the French continued for another century. Nicolas Perrot began trading with the Dakota in 1665.[36] As early as 1687, the French began establishing forts in the region, particularly around Lake Pepin, to trade with the Dakota. Le Sueur founded a trading post by 1687 and an additional post in 1695.[37] In 1700, Le Sueur returned to the region, building Fort L'Huillier near the mouth of the Blue Earth River.[38] The French kept up a constant trade with the Dakota in the 1720s and 1730s, and the French supported a trading fort at Lake Pepin most of those years.[39] Trading forts would have included both traders and small garrisons of soldiers, any of whom might have had relationships with Indian women. According to Peter Lawrence Scanlan, in 1735 alone Louis Nolan led at least twenty traders with him to trade among the Dakota, bringing numerous men in contact with Dakota women.[40] By 1737, however, the relationship between the Ojibwe and Dakota deteriorated into warfare, resulting in a strained relationship between the French and the Dakota. The French abandoned their fort but kept up trade on a smaller scale.[41] Fur trader Paul Marin, who married a Sac woman, kept up trade and diplomacy among the Dakota during the 1750s.[42]

When the Spanish took over administration of the Louisiana Territory after the Seven Years' War, their policy differed little from the French. The Spanish never had a settler population sizable enough to Christianize or force labor on Plains Indians as they did in California and other parts of Latin America. Instead, they took nominal charge of the French and some of the Indian residents of the region. The Spanish lieutenant governor of Upper Louisiana in 1777, Francisco Cruzat, in his report on the tribes on the northern plains and Upper Mississippi to Louisiana governor Don Bernardo de Gálvez, spoke of the Dakota: "We have been unable to acquire information concerning the number of warriors of this tribe, for they are very numerous and are settled in distinct districts." Cruzat continued, "They are located on the meadowlands of the Misisipy in the Spanish district, about two hundred and thirty leagues from this village [Saint Louis]. Their occupation is that of the hunt, but no profit results to this district therefrom, for the traders from the English district are gaining entrance . . . one hundred and fifty leagues from the Misisipy, in order to trade with them."[43] As Cruzat explained, the British still dominated the Dakota fur trade despite the Spanish claiming Dakota territory. But the Spanish were trading with the Iháŋkthuŋwaŋ Dakota on the Des Moines and the Iháŋkthuŋwaŋ and Lakota on the Missouri River. The volume of trade increased in the following decades but never rivaled that of the British among the Dakota on the Mississippi and Minnesota Rivers.[44] Dakota country was long coveted by Euro-American empires, who long competed for suzerainty over the area.

It was not until the 1770s that we start to see many mixed-ancestry children growing up using the names of their white fathers. Among the Iháŋkthuŋwaŋ, the Dorions were probably the oldest mixed-ancestry

Figure 4. Zephier Rencontre, born circa 1798. Photo taken in Washington, circa 1867. Rencontre, a mixed-ancestry Iháŋkthuŋwaŋ Dakota, was active in affairs between the U.S. government and the Dakota Nation, serving as an interpreter and treaty signatory as late as 1865. Edward E. Ayer Digital Collection, Newberry Library, Chicago.

family, followed by the Rencontre family in the 1790s. Mixed families were more common among the Bdewákhaŋthuŋwaŋ in the 1700s, starting with the Renville, Auge, Rock, and Lamouche families in the 1770s, the LaChapelle, LaPointe, and Kinzie families in the 1780s, and the Aird, Couder, and Dubois families in the 1790s. The Campbell family arose among the Waȟpéthuŋwaŋ and the Dickson family among the Sisíthuŋwaŋ, both in the 1790s. Most of these early Bdewákhaŋthuŋwaŋ families descend from the Wápahaša or Wabasha family of chiefs, as do a number of later mixed families.

Many of the towns and cities in the Midwest had their start as fur trade crossroads or entrepôts and were populated by a diverse population of Indians and mixed-ancestry people of many tribes, French Canadians, and occasionally enslaved or free African Americans. Most of these towns were predominantly Indian in their early histories, including well-known cities like Detroit, Green Bay, Saint Louis, and Saint Paul. Dozens of lesser-known towns in the region got their start in this way too, including Prairie du Chien, Wisconsin; Wabasha, Minnesota; Council Bluffs, Iowa; Winnipeg, Manitoba; and Vincennes, Indiana. Indians of mixed and full ancestry also frequently visited or resided in settler cities. Towns like these were crucial in the creation of the mixed-ancestry Indian population of the Midwest, serving as sites of trade and diplomacy but also as sites where Euro-American and Indigenous practices converged.[45] White Americans swarmed these towns, making Indigenous people a small minority by the second half of the nineteenth century.[46]

Historians often underestimate the importance of the interior of the continent, especially the Mississippi River Valley and the Great Lakes. Barry Gough asserts that the strategies of colonial powers involved in the Seven Years' War, the Revolutionary War, and the War of 1812 centered on control of the interior.[47] During the Revolutionary War, the Dakota and the Dorion family found themselves embroiled in the war. Pierre Dorion worked as a diplomat for the Spanish government, which was allied with the Americans. In May 1780, a British force of as many as 1,500, primarily Indians, attacked Saint Louis, an important trade hub and diplomatic site.[48] Among them were about two hundred Dakota warriors under chief Wápahaša.[49] While the force failed to take Saint Louis, they killed dozens of Saint Louisans and wounded or captured dozens more. The Dorion family was living there during the Battle of Saint Louis on May 25, when approximately 10 percent of the civilian population was killed, captured, or wounded. The Dorions were one of at least four mixed-ancestry Dakota families living in Saint Louis in the 1770s who were likely residing there at the time of the attack.[50] Six days after the battle, Dorion wrote in French to George Rogers Clark, older brother of William Clark. The elder Clark was commander of the Kentucky militia and highest-ranking American officer in the Northwest. Dorion informed him that he had taken an oath of fealty to the United States and stated his wish to move from Saint Louis, on the Spanish side of the Mississippi, to Cahokia, on the American side.[51]

In the months following the battle, there were rumors (later proved to be unfounded) that eight hundred Dakota warriors and other Indian allies of the British were making ready for a second attack on Saint Louis. The residents of Saint Louis were understandably alarmed at what would have been a sure defeat and a major blow to the Spanish in Louisiana.[52] In response, Spanish officials worked to sway the loyalties of tribes allied with the British and get them on the side of the Spanish. Lieutenant Governor Cruzat tasked Pierre Dorion, with his fur trade experience and kinship connection with the Dakota, to go among them on the Upper Mississippi to get them to change their allegiance to the Spanish. Pierre had been working out of Prairie du Chien among the Dakota on the Mississippi River as a fur trader in 1779 and probably earlier.[53]

Dorion left Saint Louis on January 26, 1781, loaded with goods to give as gifts to the Dakota. He returned to Saint Louis in July of that year with a delegation of Dakota leaders who affirmed to Spanish authorities that Dorion had succeeded in acquiring Dakota loyalty, and they agreed to end their relationship with the British and their traders. The Dakota leaders asked that Dorion be sent among them again with more goods, to which Cruzat agreed. The Spanish government spent over 1,240 pesos on Dorion's successful mission.[54] In his capacity as fur trader, Dorion was also a successful diplomat for the Spanish government, although the influx of needed goods, as well as kinship obligations, may have been a greater influence than Dorion himself.

After the war, Dorion continued to work in the fur trade out of Saint Louis, at first on the Des Moines River and later up the Missouri and James Rivers. In the 1790s he was trading with the Iháŋkthuŋwaŋ Dakota and Ioway on the Des Moines River in present-day Iowa. Jean Baptiste Faribault traded among the Iháŋkthuŋwaŋ Dakota on the Des Moines River from 1799 to 1804 at a post called Redwood. Faribault needed an interpreter and hired a man who "was old, having lived many years among the Yankton Sioux, and was well acquainted with their character and their language." Most accounts refer to this man simply as "Deban," but this was most likely Pierre Dorion, as he is the only man that fits the bill and there is documentation of his presence on the Des Moines at the time. While trading on the Des Moines, "Mr. Faribault narrowly escaped assassination at the hands of a half-breed," who Faribault's biographer, Henry H. Sibley, described as "jealous of the intrusion of a white man into his favored land." This was possibly a member of the Dorion family, too. Faribault soon left to trade on the Minnesota River, where he married a mixed-ancestry Bdewákhaŋthuŋwaŋ woman and had an extensive family.[55]

There is some documentation of the activities of the Dorion family on the Des Moines River at the turn of the nineteenth century. The journal of Francois Cailhol mentioned that Pierre Dorion had caused turmoil among the Sac and Fox and the Dakota with "a thousand lies" in 1798.[56] In 1799, Dorion sent a request to the newly appointed lieutenant governor of Upper Louisiana, Charles de Hault Delassus, asking for a grant of land on the Des Moines. In his appeal, he explained that he had "been in the service of His Catholic Majesty" the King of Spain and that he had proven himself capable to operate among the tribes of the region.[57] There is no evidence that Dorion ever acquired title to land under the Spanish, but one of his relatives, Louis Honoré Tesson, did. Tesson's wife, Susanna Liberge, was a descendant of the Dorion family in Canada; she was the granddaughter of Dorion's first cousin, also named Pierre Dorion, born in 1715. Tesson's landholdings were short-lived, as Dorion was witness to the seizure of Tesson's land by Delassus around 1800.[58]

Their kinship connection aside, Tesson repeatedly snitched on Dorion to Delassus. Just two weeks after Dorion requested his land grant, Tesson complained of the expansion of the illegal British fur trade west of the Mississippi in territory claimed by the Spanish. Tesson alleged that Dorion was working with British merchants out of Michilimackinac to trade their goods to the Dakota.[59] Over the following weeks, Tesson wrote several letters to Delassus, noting Dorion's trade on the Des Moines. On October 10, Tesson now complained that two of Dorion's mixed-ancestry sons were working for a British fur trader, "Mr. Croford," on the Des Moines to trade with the Ioway under a permit given them by their father.[60] Mr. Croford would have been either Lewis or Redford Crawford, brothers who traded with and had families among the Dakota.

Apparently the Dorion family was up to other mischief while on the Des Moines. In the spring of 1800, Jean Baptiste Baupelar accused the elder Dorion of convincing the Dakota to burn Baupelar's lumber and a stand of timber he claimed.[61] A month later, Tesson wrote to Delassus on behalf of several Sac chiefs to let him know that Dorion and his sons had killed a Sac man on the Des Moines.[62] This may be why by 1803 Dorion was trading far from the Des Moines, working for Regis Loisel at his Cedar Island post on the Missouri River north of the Big Bend.

Lakota and Iháŋkthuŋwaŋna Dakota have their own histories that attest to intermarriages with Euro-Americans: winter counts. Winter counts are historical documents kept by some Great Plains tribes that recorded one important event for each year or "winter," by which that year became known. Originally, these were written as pictographs on animal hides, and the reading of these pictographs was carefully passed down to each succeeding generation. Over time, the hides degraded and the winter counts were transferred to new hides or, by the middle of the nineteenth century, to paper. As part of this process, many discontinued the pictographs, and winter count keepers translated them into Lakota or Dakota text. Most extant Očhéthi Šakówiŋ winter counts cover the last third of the eighteenth century to the last third of the nineteenth century, but some extend significantly earlier and later.[63]

The earliest known mention of Euro-Americans comes from the John K. Bear winter count, an Iháŋkthuŋwaŋna document. "Wašíčuŋ thokáȟčiŋ ahí kíŋ," the entry for 1684 states, or "The very first white man they had ever seen came among them." Anthropologist James H. Howard suspects this to be Nicolas Perrot, a trader who built a trading post in 1683 near modern-day Red Wing, Minnesota.[64] The same winter count records several interactions over the following decades. The 1699 entry "Makhá thó Wakpá ed wašíčuŋ kičhí úŋpi" ("They lived with a white man on Blue Earth River") refers to the trading post of Pierre-Charles Le Sueur in south-central Minnesota. The winter count mentions that a white man joined in a Dakota ceremony in 1708. Other entries record indirect interactions, such as the 1687 burning of a cabin that was probably a French fort.[65] Despite these early entries, mentions of interactions with Euro-Americans are uncommon until the turn of the nineteenth century.

Some winter counts mention intermarriages or make reference to people of mixed ancestry. "Dakhóta wíŋyaŋ wáŋ wašíčuŋ hihnáye," the 1785 entry of the John K. Bear winter count states, or "A Dakota woman took a white man for a husband."[66] Another winter count relates the story of a Lakota woman who was killed in 1804–1805 by a man name Ponca. According to the winter count, the woman received a death sentence for being unfaithful to her white husband.[67] The earliest known reference to Indians of mixed ancestry comes in 1768 when multiple winter counts mention a fight: "Iyéska kíčizapi," or "Mixed-bloods fought."[68] The 1825 entry in the Sičháŋǧu Lakota Big Missouri winter count mentions two Lakota boys of mixed ancestry who died after eating the meat of a dead buffalo they found.[69] While mentions of white traders are quite common after 1800, references to intermarriages and mixed-ancestry Indians are rare. Such intermarriages themselves were not rare; most likely winter count keepers saw such events as commonplace and therefore unworthy of mention. Similarly, by the late 1700s mixed-ancestry Indians were no longer a novelty among the Očhéthi Šakówiŋ, nor did winter count keepers often find it necessary to mention the racial mixedness of those mentioned in their work.

As early as 1797–1798, these winter counts mention "Good White Man" and his associate "Little Beaver" who came among them over the next several years to trade. Edward S. Curtis suggests "Good White Man" was Pierre Dorion's employer Regis Loisel and that "Little Beaver" may have been Pierre Dorion Jr., "for intelligent descendants in their conversation with Indians call their mixed-blood ancestor by that name."[70] Some historians speculate that Pierre Dorion Sr. might be the Good White Man mentioned in Lakota winter counts at the turn of the nineteenth century.[71]

Pierre Tabeau gave an account of his visit to the Cedar Island post in late 1803, while Pierre Dorion was there. A band of Lakota was encamped near the fort; they were in the midst of internal political strife, which spilled over onto the traders. Loisel gave several examples of the mistreatment of traders: "Mr. Dorion escapes the tomahawk of a rogue by drawing a pistol; he is threatened with assassination by another and obliged to spend three days without going out; a man named La Rivierre escapes a gun-shot; there is a plan to kill us on leaving a feast; Mr. Dorion is insulted by the young people who often blow out his candle and throw it on the ground." Tabeau continued, "The kettles, the tools, the clothes, the cash-boxes of the engagés are carried off every day; the pipes, the tobacco, always kept in the house by Mr. Dorion for the annoying use of the public, disappears frequently."[72] The incident demonstrates the difficulties that Dorion and other traders faced in carrying out their occupation. Perhaps Dorion was leaving the Cedar Island post when he met Meriwether Lewis and William Clark in 1804.

On June 12, 1804, as Lewis and Clark headed north up the Missouri toward Lakota country, they met two boats traveling south, probably destined for Saint Louis. On one of the boats, they met Pierre Dorion Sr., from whom they purchased three hundred pounds of buffalo grease. Lewis and Clark decided to hire Dorion as an interpreter and to lead a delegation of Dakota Indians to Washington after they were done with his services as interpreter. Members of the Corps of Discovery noted Dorion's usefulness. Dorion was "a verry confidential friend" of the Dakota, Clark wrote in his journal, "he haveing resided with the Nation 20 odd years."[73] Along with his kinship connections and long residence among the Dakota, Sergeant John Ordway commented that Dorion "could Speak Several languages, among the indians for a long distance."[74] He was also able to describe much of the region to Clark, including the Des Moines, Big Sioux, and Minnesota Rivers and the pipestone quarry where Dakota and many other tribes collected their red pipestone to make their pipes.[75] They found Dorion useful for his kinship connections, his knowledge of the land and the people, and his diplomatic abilities.

On August 27, Lewis and Clark sent Dorion and Sergeant John Pryor to invite the Iháŋkthuŋwaŋ chiefs to a council. Two days later they returned with five chiefs, about seventy Iháŋkthuŋwaŋ men and boys, and Dorion's son, probably Pierre Jr., who had been trading among them. Clark gave Pryor and the younger Dorion tobacco, corn, and kettles to give to the Dakota and to inform them that Lewis and Clark would hold the council the next day. Lewis and Clark gave the chiefs medals and clothes and asked that they go to Washington to visit the American president. The elder Dorion translated for the chiefs, giving their assent to travel to Washington, and they expressed interest in diplomacy and trade. The head chief, whom Ordway called "Weucha," said that the British had also given him a medal and clothes, but when he visited the Spanish, they gave him nothing, and he asked that the Americans send more traders.[76] This was probably a subtle hint that now that the Spanish were out of the picture the British might be competition for the Americans as they vied for the loyalty of the Dakota. Lewis and Clark told the council that they were not traders but that they were clearing a path for traders to come after them and that they "would Supply their wants on better terms than ever they had got them before."[77] The other chiefs expressed similar sentiments, that they were poor and hoped the Americans would take pity on them by providing them goods. Pierre Sr. had traveled with Lewis and Clark for two and a half months, but they tasked Dorion with a new job. "We gave Mr. Peter Dorion, a Commission to act with a flag and some Cloathes & Provisions & instructions to bring about a peace" with the various tribes on the Missouri River "and to employ any trader to take Some of the Cheifs of each or as many of those nations as he Could Perticularly the Seuouex" to Washington. The Dorions then left the expedition, rejoining their Dakota kin.[78]

On September 12, 1806, Pierre Dorion met Lewis and Clark on the Missouri River once again. This time Dorion was headed north with a boatful of merchandise to go winter with the Iháŋkthuŋwaŋ Dakota, while the Corps of Discovery was on their return voyage to Saint Louis. In the time between their encounters, Dorion had led a delegation of Iháŋkthuŋwaŋ and Omaha chiefs to Saint Louis, but little came of the trip. Lewis and Clark tasked Dorion yet again with assembling a delegation of chiefs, this time specifically Iháŋkthuŋwaŋ and Lakota chiefs, and bringing them to Saint Louis the next spring.[79] In May 1807, by which time Thomas Jefferson appointed Clark as superintendent of Indian Affairs, Dorion brought the delegation of Oglála, Sičháŋǧu, and Saóne Lakota and Iháŋkthuŋwaŋ Dakota chiefs to speak with Clark. In their speeches, all the chiefs expressed their acute need for traders and a desire for building an alliance with the Americans through trade. A Lakota soldier summed up the main point of the chiefs: "We are in a place where no goods are taken. I hope you will take pity on us and send a Trader." But Clark responded, saying that because the Lakota had been stopping traffic up the Missouri, traders had stopped coming, but he told them if they were friendly to the traders, they would be allowed to return to their country. During the council, several of the chiefs pointed to Dorion and his words that brought them there and after the council they "requested that Mr. Durion might be persuaded to return to give Council to their Bands."[80] This incident demonstrates yet again that Pierre Dorion Sr. was an adept diplomat, interpreter, and trader who was well-respected among his Dakota and Lakota kin. Unfortunately, the Americans were not able to expand the trade to the level that the Lakota people required.

With tribes in the region desperate for trade, the British maintained their foothold in the Upper Mississippi valley and to a lesser degree on the Missouri River. Traders like Pierre Dorion were willing to operate under any colonial flag—Spanish, British, or American—as long as it netted them profits. Just as Dorion tried to walk a line of trading under both the Spanish and British in Spanish Louisiana, after the Louisiana Purchase, Dorion and other traders were suspected by the Americans of working with the British. The fur trade was key to military alliances with Indigenous nations, and the competition between the British and the Americans came to a head during the War of 1812.[81] Frederick Bates complained that some of the employees of the government, like "that old hypocrite Dorion," often bad-mouthed the U.S. government when providing Indians with gifts or payments, which Bates felt was at the very moment that they should be working to cement alliances. He felt that the government should "discharge these faithless people" and only allow U.S. citizens to conduct diplomacy with Indians.[82]

Both the elder and younger Pierre Dorion were involved in a diplomatic mission, leaving Saint Louis in late May 1807 to escort Mandan chief Shahaka, or Big White, to his people in modern-day North Dakota. William Clark tasked Ensign Nathaniel Pryor to lead the escort. Pierre Dorion Sr. happened to be in Saint Louis at the time with a delegation of Iháŋkthuŋwaŋ leaders; a separate escort, under the command of Lieutenant Joseph Kimball, was to accompany Dorion and the Iháŋkthuŋwaŋ back to their territory. Also in Saint Louis at the time, Pierre Dorion Jr. was outfitting a party of ten fur traders to trade among the Iháŋkthuŋwaŋ. Yet another party, Pierre Chouteau and thirty-two traders, were headed up the Missouri to trade with the Mandan. All the parties decided to travel together.[83]

When they reached the Iháŋkthuŋwaŋ country, Lieutenant Kimball and his men, all of the Iháŋkthuŋwaŋ, and Pierre Dorion Jr. and his men all left the expedition, while Pierre Dorion Sr. continued up the Missouri as interpreter. Upon reaching the lower Arikara village on September 9, they discovered that the Arikara were unwilling to let them pass, and the Arikara fired on their boats. Dorion and another man, Rene Jessaume, were let off the boat to speak to the Arikara and traveled by land through the Arikara villages. The Arikara told Dorion that they and their Lakota allies were at war with the Mandan and would not let them pass to give aid to their enemies. Dorion and Jessaume returned to the boats and a battle soon commenced. On the boats, three of Chouteau's men were killed and three more severely wounded. Three of Ensign Pryor's men were also wounded, including the other interpreter, Jessaume, as was the Lakota Chief Tȟatȟáŋka Sápa (Black Buffalo) who led the Lakota warriors. The mission was a failure and Ensign Pryor ordered the retreat back to Saint Louis. Big White and his family were not able to return home until 1809.[84]

Meriwether Lewis, Governor of Louisiana Territory, argued in 1808 that the British were responsible for "all our pending evils on the frontier." Lewis gave instructions to Dorion to keep the British out of the territory. He accused the British of actively working toward turning the Indians west of the Mississippi against the United States. Lewis also asked that Dorion get two of his sons, Baptiste and Louis, who were working for

British traders, to end their employment so that they could be hired by the U.S. government as interpreters. Lewis then sent the three Dorion men and others to try to make peace among the Sac and Fox, the Ioway, and the Dakota in Iowa. The mixed-ancestry Dorion family were ideal interpreters and negotiators, and the U.S. government frequently hired them to work on the nation's behalf.[85]

By 1807, William Clark, now Superintendent of Indian Affairs at Saint Louis, referred to Pierre Dorion as an Indian subagent for the Dakota. Dorion brought a delegation of Dakota leaders to Saint Louis, whom Clark described as "representativs of several of the most Noumerous and Vicious Bands of that nation inhabiting the Missouri." Dorion wanted to bring them on to Washington to meet the president, but Clark felt that such a trip would be too costly. Instead, Clark sent them home loaded with gifts. Clark wrote of the delegation to Secretary of War Henry Dearborn, "Mr. Durion has great influence with the Sieoux haveing resided near thirty years with those people, and can be of great Service to the government in keeping those vicious Tribes at peace."[86] Clark believed that Pierre Dorion was valuable to the U.S. government because of his influence among both the Lakota and Dakota. The Lakota especially were perceived by American officials at this time to be particularly warlike and a danger to American interests. Clark placed his faith in Dorion that he could keep the Očhéthi Šakówiŋ from going to war with the United States.

After Pierre Dorion died at Fort Osage in 1810, a small inventory of his personal belongings was recorded by the Saint Louis County probate court, which gives some insight into his life. Among his belongings were a mix of goods of Euro-American and Native manufacture. Among the Native items were four "Indian pipes," two "Indian medicine bags," two "Indian shott bags," and three pairs of moccasins, two of them well-used. Upon his death at age seventy, he had spent at least half of his life incorporated into Dakota society through his marriage to Marie. The moccasins and bags might have been produced by Marie herself—or, at least, Dorion found use in these Native manufactured items. Beyond Euro-American clothing and a few small items adjudged "being old and of no use," Dorion owned a silver watch, a gun, an old sword, trunks, a brass inkhorn, a large iron spoon, a pair of spectacles, and an old Spanish medal. Such items would not have been out of place among a fur trader's effects. At auction, Dorion's estate sold for $35.371/2, a meager showing for his decades of work in the fur trade, but the itinerant nature of fur trade life was not conducive to amassing a great many possessions.[87] This document and his possessions demonstrate connections to multiple colonial powers who had been competing for power in the region, his kinship connections, and his work as a fur trader.

The next generation of the mixed-ancestry Dorion family were also deeply entrenched in this world. The story of Pierre Dorion Jr.'s career with the short-lived Pacific Fur Company reveals much about the lives of fur traders, Indians of mixed ancestry, and Native women in the fur trade. John Jacob Astor, founder of the American Fur Company, of which the Pacific Fur Company was a subsidiary, was looking to expand trade to the Pacific and to blaze an overland trail to the West Coast. He hired Wilson Price Hunt to put together an expedition across the continent and build a fur trade post at the mouth of the Columbia River. After signing employees at Michilimackinac, Hunt traveled to Saint Louis in early 1811 to engage more hunters and an interpreter who could converse with the Lakota and Dakota, whose territory he planned to traverse. There was only one man who fit the bill in Saint Louis, Pierre Dorion Jr.

Unfortunately for Hunt, there was competition for Dorion's services. Dorion had previously worked for Manuel Lisa and his Missouri Fur Company on the upper Missouri River. During his previous employment with Lisa at Fort Mandan, Dorion had accrued a considerable debt to the company, primarily liquor, although Dorion disputed the debt. Lisa was planning his own expedition to trade on the upper Missouri and hoped to retain Dorion for his skills as interpreter and so that he could work off his debt.[88]

Washington Irving, the well-known author, historian, and later ambassador to Spain, made much of Dorion's alcoholism in his 1836 book *Astoria* and used it to cast aspersions on his character and mixed heritage. "He had proved himself faithful and serviceable while sober," Irving asserted, "but the love of liquor, in which he had been nurtured and brought up, would occasionally break out, and with it the savage side of his character."[89]

Irving explained Dorịon's liquor debt to the Missouri Fur Company, claiming that "he had been seized with a whiskey mania" while at Fort Mandan, and because the company store was the only place to acquire it, he accumulated a large debt. The company charged his account ten dollars for every quart of whiskey he drank. Dorion disputed the debt, "the mere mention of which was sufficient to put him in a passion."[90]

Hunt succeeded in hiring Dorion away from the Missouri Fur Company, which proved beneficial to Dorion and prompted Lisa to take drastic measures. For Dorion, the competition for his services as hunter and interpreter earned him a salary of $300 per year with $200 paid up front. In an unusual move, Dorion's second wife Marie, a full-ancestry Ioway woman, accompanied the expedition at Dorion's request, as did Dorion's two children, Paul (who was actually the son of Pierre Jr. and his first wife, an Iháŋkthuŋwaŋ Dakota woman named Wíhmuŋke Wakháŋ Wíŋ, or Holy Rainbow Woman) and John Baptiste (Pierre Jr.'s son with Marie).

The party left Saint Louis in several boats and was to arrive in Saint Charles the next day at noon, where Lisa had alerted the authorities to arrest Dorion when he arrived. However, two members of Hunt's party, John Bradbury and a man named Nuttall, heard of the plot and were able to catch up with the boat during the night and warn Dorion before they arrived in Saint Charles. To thwart the arrest attempt, the boat landed and the Dorion family, with all their belongings, left on foot to walk around Saint Charles and reboard the boat upriver, on the other side of the town.[91]

For Hunt, this was a worrisome first day of employment for his interpreter, who was off the boat with his family, all his possessions, and $200 of Hunt's money. But there was nothing else to be done; the authorities at Saint Charles would surely take Dorion into custody if he continued on the boat. From Hunt's perspective, since Dorion had already shown unfaithfulness to his previous employer by avoiding the liquor debt, he had little reason to believe that Dorion would reappear. When the expedition arrived in Saint Charles, the local authorities looked in vain for Dorion and held Hunt's party until the following morning.[92]

The next day, however, upon leaving Saint Charles, the expedition quickly caught up to Dorion, but he was alone. Dorion had apparently beaten Marie, and she refused to accompany him, taking the children and their belongings with her. Hunt sent one of his men to look for Marie and the children, and the expedition camped on an island, waiting. Before sunrise the next morning, Marie and the children caught up to the party, saw their fires, and called from the bank. The family was reunited, for now.[93]

The expedition continued, reaching Fort Osage, east of modern-day Kansas City, where they stayed for three days. Near the fur trade post was an Osage village where the Dorion family and other members of the expedition witnessed dances and celebrations by the Osage. Marie wanted to stay among the Osage, possibly to escape her husband's abuse. Dorion forced her to accompany him onto the boat, where he beat Marie again, quite severely, causing a disturbance among the expedition members.[94] If they had been living in a Native village, such domestic abuse probably would have been dealt with by relatives. But among a group of mostly white men, far from government authorities, Marie lacked the protection afforded by Dakota or Ioway kinship and American law.

Lisa eventually completed hiring members for his expedition in Saint Louis and followed the Hunt party, hoping to catch up. Incidentally, Sacagawea, famous for her role as guide to Lewis and Clark, and her fur trader husband, Toussaint Charbonneau, accompanied Lisa. When the two parties finally united on June 2, the Dorion family would have met Sacagawea.[95] At the same time, the reunion of Lisa and Dorion did not go well. For several days, Dorion and Lisa avoided each other, and the two expeditions encamped near each other in separate camps. However, the uneasy peace was not to last.

Lisa finally invited Dorion to his boat and tried to convince him to leave Hunt's employ and rejoin his. When his words failed to convince Dorion, he reminded him of the whiskey debt, which enraged Dorion, who believed he had been cheated. John Bradbury explained that Dorion believed "that he had been charged the most exorbitant prices for articles had at Fort Mandan, and in particular ten dollars per quart for whiskey."[96] Dorion left the boat and returned to Hunt's camp and Lisa soon found an excuse to follow him. This time, harsh words led to violence, with Dorion punching Lisa. Lisa returned to his boat for a knife while Dorion took up a pair of pistols belonging to Hunt, awaiting Lisa's return.

Lisa ventured back into Hunt's camp with his knife. When members of the Hunt party learned that Lisa had tried to steal Dorion away, they were angered, and Hunt challenged Lisa to a duel with pistols. Lisa returned to his boat to collect his own pistols, where he was talked down by members of his expedition who also smoothed things over with the Hunt camp.[97] Violence between fur traders was not uncommon, particularly between those from rival companies.[98]

By mid-July 1811, the expedition reached the Arikara village, and owing to reports of unrest among the Blackfeet further up the Missouri, Hunt decided to leave the boats and head toward the Pacific by foot. They had over eighty horses, loaded with food, goods, ammunition, and traps, but not enough for all the members to ride. Dorion was allotted a horse for the use of him and his family and to carry their belongings. According to Irving, Marie mostly "trudged on foot, like the residue of the party; nor did any of them show more patience and fortitude than this resolute woman in enduring fatigue and hardship." And they were indeed to experience much hardship. At this point the expedition bid adieu to Lisa's party, many of whom, including Lisa, doubted the expedition would make it to the Pacific alive.[99]

As the expedition continued, the party ran the risk of starvation, which was not an uncommon problem in the fur trade.[100] Their supplies dwindled; they lost horses and were compelled by hunger to eat some of them. They occasionally replenished their supplies of food or horses by trading with Indians along the way. At one village, they secured "a supply of fish and dogs from the natives; and two of the men were fortunate enough each to get a horse in exchange for a buffalo robe. One of these men was Pierre Dorion, the half-breed interpreter, to whose suffering family the horse was a most timely acquisition." The horse turned out to be an object of dispute as the expedition continued and the men wanted to eat it. By this time, as their journey became more difficult, they realized that Marie was expecting and quite far along in her pregnancy. The children, aged two and four according to Irving, "she had frequently to carry on her back, in addition to the burthen usually imposed . . . yet she had borne all her hardships without a murmur and throughout this weary and painful journey, had kept pace with the best of the pedestrians." Irving's stereotype of Indian stoicism aside, Marie proved an able member of the expedition. Despite her pregnancy, she walked as much as any member of the expedition, she cooked and dressed skins, and she took care of two young children, among other duties.[101] Irving's description may have been exaggerated, as nineteenth-century observers frequently wrote of Native American women as beasts of burden for Indian men.[102]

Eventually, the members of the expedition began to starve, even after eating the remaining horses. The extreme lack of water in some locales prompted expedition members to drink their own urine.[103] Some of the men were too weak and began slowing down the party. Hunt tried to keep everyone together, but men began to abandon the slower people and moved on ahead. Dorion was one of these. "Pierre owned the only remaining horse; which was now a mere skeleton. Mr. Hunt had suggested, in their present extremity, that it should be killed for food; to which the half-breed flatly refused to assent" and abandoned Hunt on his skeletal steed.[104]

The next day, December 10, 1811, Hunt and the three men still with him caught up to the expedition members who had gone ahead. All Hunt and his men had to eat was a beaver skin. Hunt was resolved to sacrifice Dorion's horse, but Dorion again refused. The men supported Dorion, believing it was best to save the horse as a last resort, and Hunt relented. Later that day, the expedition encountered a small camp of Shoshone and scared them off. The Shoshone left five horses, one of which the men began to immediately butcher and devour.[105]

The expedition continued on foot during the winter, killing their remaining horses when they needed food. On the morning of December 30, Marie went into labor. The expedition continued, while the Dorion family remained in camp and welcomed their new child. The Dorions caught up with the expedition the next day at a Shoshone village, with Marie riding the bony horse, carrying her baby.[106] Tragedy struck. The baby only survived eight days, passing on January 7, 1812. Yet the party continued, with their stock of horses dwindling to Dorion's emaciated steed and another in a similar condition.[107]

They eventually arrived on the Columbia River, where they met another Indian camp. Dorion was saddened when his horse, which had survived so much, was stolen in the night.[108] They made their way to the coast, where they erected Fort Astoria. However, the Pacific Fur Company proved untenable, as they were in heavy competition with the North West Company. The Pacific Fur Company dissolved in 1813, and many of the men either joined the North West Company or acted as independent traders or hunters. Some headed back east.

Upon reaching Astoria, Dorion worked primarily as a hunter for the Pacific Fur Company. Dorion frequently hunted alongside another hunter in the employ of the company, Ignace Shonowane, an Iroquois Indian. Dorion and Shonowane had difficulty finding game that spring, but the company's logbook notes them bringing in their first recorded game, two elk, on May 27, 1812.[109] The families of Dorion and Shonowane often spent time with each other and hunted together. Fort Astoria featured a diverse set of employees. On July 30, 1812, the Dorion family, Shonowane and his family, Thomas McKay, and two Native Hawaiians left the post for an extended hunting trip together on the Columbia River.[110] McKay was the son of one of the cofounders of Fort Astoria, Alexander McKay, who had been killed the previous year, and his mother was a mixed-ancestry Cree woman with Swiss ancestry. From August through October, Dorion, his friend Shonowane, and several others were employed in making canoes out of cedar for the use of the company before going back to hunting with their families in November.[111]

In the winter of 1813–1814, the Dorion family joined John Reed and others, traveling to the interior. They planned to winter on the Snake River, in modern-day Idaho, where they built a house and trapped beaver and traded with any Indians that came along. Upon reaching the Snake River in mid-August, the Reed party constructed a house for the winter and set about trapping beaver. After being harassed by some local Indians, they decided to move and build a new house farther up the river. Marie stayed at the house with Reed and several other of the men while Dorion, Gilles Leclerc, and Jacob Regner were in a trapping camp about two days' journey away. On January 10, an Indian came to the house and informed Reed that a band of "Snake" Indians (a collective name for Bannock, Shoshone, and Northern Paiute Indians) had burned the first house and were heading toward the second house.[112]

Upon hearing this, Marie and her two children set off on a horse to Dorion's camp to warn him and the other trappers. Because of a storm, it took three days for Marie to arrive at the trappers' camp. Approaching the camp, she ran into a badly wounded Leclerc, who informed her that her husband, Pierre Dorion, had been killed, along with the other trappers, by Indians. Marie immediately set off to return to Reed's house with a wounded Gilles Leclerc, who died on the return journey. When she arrived she found "Mr. Reed and the men were all murdered, scalped, and cut to pieces."[113] Her husband and all the men had been murdered; Marie and her children were the only survivors. She was stuck in the mountains in the dead of winter with two young children, no shelter, and in constant fear of attack.

She knew the house had many provisions before the attack; she didn't know what might remain, and she was too afraid to approach the house for fear the attackers might still be nearby. She scouted the house from high ground, and after dark she entered and found "plenty of fish scattered about." She returned the next night to carry off more supplies, and after two days she set off with the supplies on her horse with her two children. She found an inconspicuous place to camp where she killed her horse for food and waited out the winter until she could walk out of the mountains. After waiting fifty-three days for better weather, she began the trek back to Fort Astoria. She traveled fifteen days, exited the mountains, and her and her children were in near-starving condition when she found a Sahaptin village, who treated Marie and the Dorion children kindly.[114]

Days later, Marie and the children traveled down the Columbia River in a canoe accompanied by two canoes of Sahaptin Indians, hoping to meet some fur traders. Gabriel Franchère recorded running into the three canoes. "We heard a child's voice cry out in French" to stop, presumably one of the Dorion children. "We put ashore, and the canoes having joined us, we perceived in one of them the wife and children of a man named Pierre Dorion. . . . This woman informed us, to our no small dismay, of the tragical fate of all those who composed that party."[115] Marie remained on the Pacific coast until her death in 1850. She married two more fur traders and had children with both.[116] Paul and John Baptiste Dorion grew up on the Columbia and later went their separate ways. Paul returned to his people on the Missouri, where he married several Lakota women and had many children. John Baptiste married a Métis woman and moved to Canada, where his family and descendants blended into the Métis community in Manitoba.

Through the story of the Dorion family, we can see the rise of the mixed-ancestry Dakota community, how they were integral parts of the new economic systems introduced through the fur trade, and their role in diplomacy between the Dakota Nation and settler empires. Indians of mixed ancestry were born of the fur trade, but their labor in the trade and their diplomatic skills were crucial to maintaining trade. They also served as important linkages in the broad kinship networks that developed through the intermarriage of Indigenous people and Euro-Americans. At the same time, Indians of mixed ancestry learned to navigate settler colonial societies and operate in both Indigenous and settler colonial worlds.

By the early nineteenth century, a significant mixed-ancestry community had developed among the Dakota and other Indigenous nations. As illustrated by the Dorion family, mixed families were deeply involved in the contests over power between Indigenous nations and settler empires, the fur trade, Indigenous kinship systems, and diplomacy. Pierre Dorion earned the trust of the Dakota Nation. But he and his mixed-ancestry sons sometimes involved themselves in the competition between empires for alliances with Indigenous nations. Family members had worked in the fur trade for the Spanish and Americans but also illegally for the British.[117] In 1815, the Omaha chief Big Elk complained to William Clark that Baptiste Dorion urged his people to rebuff the Americans and develop ties with the British.[118] All of the Dorion men worked in the fur trade for various companies. They were coveted for their skills as laborers, hunters, interpreters, and negotiators. Pierre Dorion Sr. married among the Iháŋkthuŋwaŋ Dakota and gained reciprocal kinship obligations with the extended family of his wife Marie. The children were born with those kinship connections, and at least two of the sons married among the Ioway Nation, gaining additional reciprocal kinship obligations with them. The Dorion family history reveals a complex world of settler empires vying for alliances with the Dakota and other tribal nations, the centrality of the fur trade in economic life, the importance of Indigenous kinship systems, and the necessity of mixed-ancestry Indian families to aid in negotiation and diplomacy between these disparate Indigenous and colonial powers. Indians of mixed ancestry had proven themselves adept and invaluable at navigating this world.

CHAPTER 2

The Creation of "Half-Breed" as a Legal Concept

An 1824 land cession treaty between the United States and the Sac and Fox contained a provision that a tract of land in modern-day Iowa between the Des Moines and Mississippi Rivers was "intended for the use of the half-breeds belonging to the Sock and Fox nations; they holding it, however, by the same title, and in the same manner, that other Indian titles are held."[1] American officials engaged in legal debates over the legal definition of "half-breed" in this and treaties with similar provisions. Numerous treaties mentioned half-breeds as a class of people entitled to land but never provided a definition. Figuring out the rightful claimants to the land resulted in hundreds of competing land claims and many court cases, some of which reached the U.S. Supreme Court.[2] Isaac Galland published a brief pamphlet in which he worked through his thoughts on the legal definition. Galland contemplated many questions as to who counted as a half-breed, the legal rights of mixed-ancestry Indians, and jurisdiction over their land. There was some question among local white people whether the land was intended for "civilized" mixed-ancestry Indians or if those deemed "uncivilized" were also eligible. Galland also expressed anxieties that the term "half-breed" included full-ancestry Indians who had one-half Sac or Fox ancestry, for the treaty made no distinction as to "cast[e], class, birth or blood." Did they need a legal guardian or could they make their own legal decisions concerning their land? When they died, could they pass the land to their heirs, or could they inherit land?

Should rights only extend to those actually living on the land? As the land was within the bounds of a quick succession of territorial governments—Michigan, Wisconsin, then Iowa—did the territory or the federal government have the right to define "half-breed" or hold jurisdiction over the land?[3] With numerous treaties containing the ill-defined legal term "half-breed," such debates continued across the Midwest and in the federal government for decades.

Between 1816 and 1833, there were thirty treaties that set aside land for mixed-ancestry Indians, twenty-five of them in the Midwest. These provisions appeared in treaties because tribal leaders demanded them and because the federal government believed that mixed-ancestry Indians who owned individual lands would assimilate into American culture and would influence their full-ancestry relatives who, by their example, would also assimilate. Mixed-ancestry Indians were not only influential in this way; one observer claimed that they "have often exercised more sway in Indian affairs than chiefs," suggesting their influence went far beyond assimilation.[4] This policy, however, had the unintended consequence of creating a new legal racial category, that of "half-breed," and set in motion the first of several mixed-blood histories among the Dakota and many more among other tribes in the Midwest.

At the same time, during the first half of the nineteenth century, Indigenous people of mixed ancestry gravitated closer to American culture and American institutions. Increasingly, mixed-ancestry Dakota people attended school, executed deeds and powers of attorney, worked for the government as interpreters, and even bought and sold enslaved people. Their involvement in American culture notwithstanding, mixed-ancestry Dakota people in these early decades did not give up their Dakota culture or kinship responsibilities. The first few decades of the nineteenth century were a formative period as Indians of mixed ancestry increasingly engaged with American legal and political institutions while also experiencing a slow calcification of their legal and racial status as mixed-bloods or half-breeds. As they were leaning into becoming American by inserting themselves into these legal institutions, American officials worked to assimilate them while simultaneously and contradictorily trying to solidify a definition of them as something different from both Indians and white Americans.

For centuries, Euro-American officials in North America employed laws to regulate the rights of mixed-race people and place them within a racial social hierarchy.[5] Indeed, race and racial mixedness were frequently at issue in court cases, legislation, and marriage statutes.[6] While terminology for mixed-race people was plentiful, the terms "half-breed" and "mixed-blood," or some variation, came into common use in the Midwest in reference to Indians of mixed ancestry and Métis people in the first half of the nineteenth century. These terms, or wording related to blood quantum, sometimes used interchangeably and sometimes as distinct expressions, appeared in treaties, federal, state, and territorial legislation, and state constitutions. This legal terminology was never clearly defined and was debated for decades. At the same time, Indians of mixed ancestry increasingly sought out opportunities to engage with American legal institutions, sometimes complicating the issue when their names appeared on legal contracts, land deeds, court cases, and other legal documents.

Ideas about assimilation through intermarriage and the creation of a mixed-ancestry population were not new in American politics. In 1804, President Thomas Jefferson wrote of Indians: "You will unite yourselves with us . . . and we shall all be Americans; you will mix with us by marriage, your blood will run in our veins, and will spread with us over this great island."[7] This oft-mentioned quote was not a magnanimous gesture that would lead to a hybrid culture. Jefferson was suggesting a kind of intermarriage where only Indian genetics would be passed on; his claim came with the assumption that Native American cultures would be completely stamped out, leaving people of Indian ancestry but fully of American culture.

Treaties often named individuals who were to receive allotments of land, most commonly eighty acres. Before 1824, treaties rarely explicitly called the individuals therein named "half-breeds," but as the vast majority of those named had Euro-American names, it is likely that the majority of allottees were Indians of mixed ancestry. In a treaty with the Wyandot, Seneca, Delaware, Shawnee, Potawatomi, Odawa, and Ojibwe in 1817, article 8 named numerous individuals who were to receive land. Several "quarter-blood Wyandot Indians," the children of a white man (William McCollock, who was killed in action in the War of 1812), each received 640 acres. The treaty set aside another 640 acres to "Anthony Shane, a half blood Ottawa Indian"; siblings Rachel and Joseph Williams, the children of "the late Isaac Williams, a half-blood Wyandot," received 160 acres each.[8] An 1818 treaty with the Miami named numerous individuals, without any mention of blood quantum, but the treaty refers to a handful of them as "half-blooded." The treaty granted to Rebecca Hackley, "a half-blooded Miami," a section of land "located at the Munsey town, on White river."[9]

After 1824, however, treaty negotiators were more explicit that the lands were intended for mixed-ancestry Indians. For instance, a land session treaty with the Osage in 1825 stated in article 5, "From the above lands ceded and relinquished, the following reservations, for the use of the half-breeds, hereafter named, shall be made." The treaty went on to name forty-six individuals and the locations at which they were to receive 640 acres of land.[10]

By 1826, treaties definitively stated that these lands were for assimilative purposes. A treaty with the Ojibwe that year stated in article 4: "It being deemed important that the half-breeds, scattered through this extensive country, should be stimulated to exertion and improvement by the possession of permanent property and fixed residences." Here, "stimulated to exertion and improvement" implies the Jeffersonian ideal of yeoman farmers and suggests that land would "improve" or assimilate them. The article goes on to explain, "the Chippewa tribe, in consideration of the affection they bear to these persons, and of the interest which they feel in their welfare, grant to each of the persons described in the schedule hereunto annexed, being half-breeds and Chippewas by descent" 640 acres each.[11] This treaty reveals that the federal government wanted these mixed-ancestry allotments for the purpose of assimilation, while it also illustrates tribal leaders' interest in the welfare of their mixed-ancestry relatives.

The typical treaty language for these provisions reveals that tribal leaders wanted these lands set aside for their mixed-ancestry kin. Tribal leaders wanted, and fought for, separate provisions of land for their relatives of mixed ancestry. A treaty with the Wyandot in 1817 allotted lands to eight named members of the tribe "at the special request of the said Indians."[12] Article 10 of an 1832 treaty with the Ho-Chunk used similar language: "At the special request of the Winnebago Nation, the United States agree to grant, by patent, in fee simple, to the following named persons, all of whom are Winnebagoes by blood."[13] This kind of language was common in these treaties and is borne out in the treaty negotiations that tribal leaders in the Midwest thought it was important to put land in the hands of their mixed relatives. The records do not reveal exactly why tribal leaders wanted this; certainly, their mixed-ancestry relatives requested it, and leaders felt it would be a benefit to the mixed-ancestry members of their tribe.

American officials wanted these provisions too, often proclaiming the importance of putting parcels into the hands of individual mixed-ancestry Indians and how it would aid in the assimilation of all Indians. Lewis Cass argued in 1826 for the allotment of land to mixed-ancestry Indians, claiming that "to secure their permanent attachment to our Government is an important object, while the grants they receive, unalienable as they are, would insure their fidelity."[14] The Superintendent of Indian Affairs at Saint Louis, William Clark, went further in 1825, writing, "Each of the treaties contains several reservations of a mile square in favor of half breed Indians & their children. Reserves of this kind have been heretofore made in behalf of such persons, and in my opinion have a good effect in promoting civilization, & as their attachment is created for a fixed residence & an idea of separate property is imparted without which it is vain to think of improving the minds or morals of the Indians, or making any progress in the work of civilization."[15] John Johnson wrote to the commissioner of Indian Affairs in 1826 about the Sac and Fox mixed-ancestry lands, arguing that the government should provide them with agricultural implements and education: "The influence it would have on the minds of Indians surrounding it, who in their daily visits to their relations would daily be impressed with the importance. In fact sir, I conceive no place could be designated that would have a happier effect in promoting among those Indians the generous and humane policy pursued by our Government towards this whole people."[16] In 1841, Wisconsin Territorial Governor James Duane Doty wrote of mixed-ancestry Indians:

> Experience has shown that this class must be used in any attempt to civilize the Indians, they are the connecting link between the savage & civilized man, & ought to be employed by government as its agents, interpreters & teachers, when they possess, as they frequently do, the requisite qualifications. An opportunity will thus be given them to establish a character for themselves—to obtain a place in civilized life, I might say among human beings, for Indian Blood—and it will be for their interest to be faithful and give their best efforts in aid of the purposes of government—many of them are well educated, & the example of those who are farmers, and mechanics, as well as their teaching, will be most beneficial to the Indians.[17]

As these quotes demonstrate, American officials viewed putting land in the hands of mixed-ancestry Indians as a policy of assimilation. Writing in 1851, Superintendent of Indian Affairs D. D. Mitchell hoped to revive the practice of treaty provisions of land for mixed-ancestry Indians. He recommended the creation of two mixed-ancestry reservations: "I would recommend that a suitable section of the country, somewhere on the Missouri or its tributaries, be assigned to the half-breeds, who are becoming very numerous throughout the Indian country. . . . A half-breed colony, properly located in the midst of the Indians, would form a semi-civilized nucleus around which the wild Indians would soon be drawn by necessity to assemble."[18] Here Mitchell is taking the assumed assimilative influence of mixed-ancestry Indians a step further. Policymakers already envisioned landowning mixed-ancestry Indians as holding this assimilative influence, but Mitchell argued that even when mixed-ancestry Indians held land in common, such as reservations or "colonies," they still held this assimilative influence over their full-ancestry relatives. In Mitchell's view, mixed-ancestry landholding of any kind would aid in the assimilation of Indians. Mitchell and other policymakers perceived mixed-ancestry Indians as an integral part of the colonial efforts of the American government to assimilate Indians into American society.

Mitchell continued by recommending that Indian agencies and other government institutions should purposely be located near mixed-ancestry communities to aid in the assimilation of full-ancestry Indians. Mitchell continued that near mixed-ancestry communities "might be established the government agency, missionary, and trading establishments, where their physical wants could, to some extent be supplied. The example too, of the half-breeds, who would be compelled by want to turn their attention to agricultural and mechanical pursuits, would be of more advantage to the Indians, intermixed as they are with them, than all the government farmers that were ever sent among them."[19] Mitchell concludes that this is the best course of action to assimilate Indians. His recommendations would place mixed-ancestry Indians at the center of broader Indian communities. Not only did he believe that mixed-ancestry Indians could aid in assimilation, he believed they could do it better than any other so-called civilization policies of the federal government.

In 1851, Mitchell planned another "half-breed colony" on the Arkansas River and recorded the Indians' thoughts on his idea: "During the recent council at Fort Laramie I talked this matter over frequently with the half-breeds and Indians: both parties were delighted with the plan."[20] He confirmed the language of the treaties in which tribal leaders asked for reserving mixed-ancestry lands. Mitchell was serious about his plan, but by 1851, the federal government was no longer interested in putting land in the hands of mixed-ancestry Indians as a means of assimilation.

Beyond treaty negotiators, in a case of early scientific racism, early American thinkers argued for race mixing as a form of assimilation. Dr. Charles Caldwell, an early proponent of polygenism—the idea that different human races have different origins and traits, a hypothesis used in support of white supremacy—argued for assimilation through interbreeding. He argued that Indians of full ancestry could not be "civilized," but "of the *mixt*-bloods this is not true. Hence the only efficient scheme to civilize the Indians, is to *cross the breed*."[21] Such racist ideas were part of the American milieu at the time in thinking about Indians, but not all agreed. An opposing viewpoint, summed up by Rev. Berghold in speaking about the Dakota, that "the half-breeds generally practice the vices of both the white and the red man without possessing any of the virtues of either" was not an uncommon refrain.[22]

As part of these assimilation efforts, mixed-ancestry Dakota children began going to missionary schools and public schools, often sent there by their white fathers. Alfred Brunson believed that educating Indians of mixed ancestry was key and that they would be an assimilative influence on their full-ancestry relatives. He explained that mixed-ancestry Indian "advances in civilization, their kindred blood with the Indians & their adaption to services of the kind render them the most suitable persons to be educated for the purpose of Govt. interpreters & for missionaries whose business is to improve the condition of the Indians. It is among these people we wish to operate." Brunson hoped to build a mission church and a school near Fort Snelling in 1838 where there was a large population of Indians of mixed ancestry. Brunson explained that fur traders built their homes and trading posts on military land near Fort Snelling and the "traders brought into the country with them men of different bloods, some white, some half & some quarter bloods: some French & some Americans, &c. The most of these men married women of whole, half & quarter blood Indians of the Sioux & Chippewa nations." They built their homes on the military reservation near the trading houses and often maintained their residences there even after leaving the fur trade. Brunson claimed there were between four hundred and five hundred people in this community.[23]

In his quest to build a school, he requested the government allow him to build on military land, but Colonel William Davenport recommended the government not allow this because Brunson planned to specifically missionize mixed-ancestry Indians. Davenport explained that Brunson "wishes to establish his school, not to educate Indians, which I thought was the object in going into the country, but the half breeds for the purpose of making good Interpreters to the government." This was unnecessary, according to Davenport, because the mixed-ancestry children could attend the post school at Fort Snelling, if their parents so chose, or they could attend the missionary school at Lake Harriet eight miles to the west.[24]

Some mixed-ancestry Indians found disappointment in their lack of education. In his diary entries from 1838, Captain Frederick Marryat wrote of a conversation with Jack Fraser, claiming that Fraser wanted to kill his white father because of a broken promise: "He had promised to make a *white man* of him (that is to have educated him, and brought him up in a civilized manner), and that he had left him a Sioux."[25] A mixed-ancestry Odawa woman born in 1810, Elizabeth Thérèse Baird, lamented that she had not been educated like her mixed-ancestry mother. She claimed her grandfather taught her the rudiments of reading but that it was her husband who finally taught her to write and to speak English.[26] People like Baird and Fraser greatly felt their lack of a Euro-American education, and at the same time both Baird and Fraser expressed their affinity for their Native cultures.

While a handful of Dakota children received educations early on, such as Joseph Renville Sr., who was taken to Canada by his father for school in the 1790s, by the 1820s, the education of mixed-ancestry Dakota people began to increase significantly. Most attended missionary schools. Elisha Dorion, the mixed-ancestry Ioway and Dakota son of Martin Dorion, and grandson of Pierre Dorion Sr., went to a missionary boarding school: "In 1836 I was seven years old, my father sent me to the mission school at St. Joseph, Missouri, one hundred and fifty miles south of my home. For six years I remained at school, a part of the time in Pennsylvania."[27] Between 1826 and 1831, at least fifteen mixed-ancestry Dakota children—thirteen girls and two boys—attended a Protestant missionary school at Mackinac, although the vast majority of the students at the school were either Ojibwe or Odawa.[28] In his travels in 1829, Caleb Atwater wrote approvingly of mixed-ancestry Indian women, claiming "they make excellent wives." He raved about their cooking and asserted that "many of them have been well educated in some Catholic seminary, either in Canada or Missouri."[29] The 1838 census of mixed-ancestry Dakota listed several children attending school. Solomon W. D. Brown, the twelve-year-old son of Helen Dickson and Joseph R. Brown, attended Choctaw Academy in Kentucky. Five children attended the mission school at Lake Harriet, and two more attended Brunson's school in Little Crow's village.[30] The Hooe sisters, Josephine, Emily, and Harriet, attended a Catholic school near Dubuque, Iowa, in the 1840s and 1850s.[31] With the appearance of missionaries from the American Board of Commissioners for Foreign Missions in 1834 in Dakota country, many mixed-ancestry children attended these missionary schools in their own homeland.

Winúŋna (First Born Daughter), or Nancy McClure Faribault Huggan, born in Mendota in 1835, the daughter of Lt. James McClure of Fort Snelling and a Dakota woman, also named Winúŋna, recalled her school experiences in the 1840s and early 1850s. She first attended the missionary school at Lac qui Parle operated by Rev. Thomas Williamson and lived with Williamson's family. When the Williamson family moved away, she attended the school of Jonas Pettijohn at Lac qui Parle: "Here four of us mixed-blood girls boarded in the house. Rose Renville was one of them, and she was my roommate." She explained further, "At these mission

Figure 5. Winúŋna or Nancy McClure Faribault Huggan, 1835–1927. Drawn by Frank B. Mayer, 1851. The daughter of an army officer and a Bdewákhaŋthuŋwaŋ woman, Winúŋna was an eyewitness to the U.S.-Dakota War of 1862. Edward E. Ayer Digital Collection, Newberry Library, Chicago.

schools we girls were given religious instruction and taught reading, writing and something of the lower branches, and to sew, knit, and, as we grew older, to spin, weave, cook and do all kinds of housework. We were taught first in Indian, then in English."[32] She left school to take care of her sick mother, who died when Huggan was fourteen. She lamented that she had no one to care for her but her Dakota kin, with whom she did not want to reside. She explained that she wanted to live among white people rather than Indians: "How much I longed to be with some of my fathers' people then. . . . I was always more white than Indian in my tastes and sympathies." Upon her mother's death she decided to go back to school at Rev. Hopkin's school at Traverse des Sioux: "While here my intimate schoolmates were Victoria Auge and her sister, Julia La Framboise, three mixed-blood girls, and Martha Riggs," the daughter of missionary Stephen R. Riggs. "I learned very fast at this school, for I was now almost a woman. . . . I could do all kinds of housework, and was a pretty good seamstress."[33]

Unlike full-ancestry Dakota children, mixed-ancestry children could attend local public schools when they became available to them in the latter half of the nineteenth century. Jane Van Meter Waldron described attending a public school in Dakota Territory in the late 1860s. Before attending school at around age eight, approximately 1869, she only spoke Dakota. "I knew a few words [of English] but I couldn't carry on a conversation when I started school," Waldron explained, but she learned to speak English while in public school. Interacting with white children was a novelty to Waldron: "Up to the time I went to school I didn't know anything about playing with white children or talking with white children at all."[34] Sometimes their attendance in public schools was challenged by local white people, but many enjoyed the benefits of a public school education.[35]

Several mixed-ancestry Dakota left inventories of books that they owned, suggesting a high level of education. Ellen Brown owned many books in 1862, including history books such as *History of the Great Kings*, *History of the United States*, and *History of England*. She owned well-known novels like *Arabian Nights*, *Ivanhoe*, *Aesop's Fables*, and *The Count of Monte Cristo*. She also owned many Christian texts, French language books, and various other books. The same year, Antoine Frenier owned ten volumes of *The Congressional Globe,* three volumes of Charles Rollin's *Ancient History,* ten years of *Harper's Magazine,* six years of *Leslie's Monthly* and *Weekly,* and thirteen years of *Eclectic Magazine,* in addition to other texts. The fact that they owned these texts suggests that they were at least educated enough to read and that they held interests in far-flung topics.[36]

The mixed-ancestry Dakota also believed that they were entitled to "civilization" funds in treaties between the United States and the Dakota Nation set aside for education. In 1853, "at a meeting of the Half Breeds and other mixed Sioux blood Catholics," dozens of the mixed-ancestry Dakota, or their white fathers on their behalf, signed a petition to Governor Willis Gorman. My great-great-great-grandfather Francis Trudell signed on behalf of five of his children and the eldest, Frank Trudell, called "Hepí" (Thirdborn Son), signed in his own right, requesting that funds be used to establish Catholic schools for their children.[37] They believed that as Dakota people they had the right to take advantage of the education provisions in treaties. In the case of the Dakota, the government primarily spent those funds on Protestant missionary educators, but as many of the mixed-ancestry Dakota were Catholic, they hoped to have Catholic missionaries educate their children.

While attempts to assimilate mixed-ancestry Indians continued, not all government officials agreed that the assimilation of Indians through individual landownership would work. In 1816, a report by William Crawford, the secretary of war, asserted, "When every effort to introduce among [the Indians] ideas of exclusive property in things real as well as personal shall fail, let intermarriage between them and the whites be encouraged by the government. This cannot fail to preserve the race, with the modifications necessary to the enjoyment of civil liberty and social happiness."[38] A minority of American officials, like Crawford, still believed in Jefferson's conclusion that assimilation would come through intermarriage. However, assimilation through the exploitation of landed mixed-ancestry Indians remained in federal Indian policy for decades.

Just as in American culture, the Dakota people placed importance on individual property rights, but there were different conceptions of wealth and the purpose of acquiring property. William Laidlaw, a white fur trader, his wife, a full-ancestry Sisíthuŋwaŋ Dakota woman named Mary Ann, and their children gained prestige in American culture because Laidlaw accumulated significant property holdings through wealth he made in the fur trade. Amassing goods and property beyond what one needs is seen in Dakota culture as selfish. The Dakota prize generosity as one of the most important character traits. In the nineteenth century, people gained prestige in Dakota culture through generosity and how much they could give away. Gift giving was common; people regularly gave away their property without the expectation of return except in the general sense that their kin would provide for them if they were in need. Such generosity was so important that the Dakota held giveaways as part of ceremonies or important life events involving relatives. A Dakota family might hold a giveaway at the death or birth of a family member, to honor a child, or when a daughter reached puberty. Giveaways were a common component of the huŋká, or the making-of-relatives ceremony. Giveaways, gift giving, and the redistribution of wealth were deeply embedded in Dakota kinship practices.[39] These practices were so different from understandings of property and wealth in American society that the federal government chose to outlaw giveaways in 1883 in the Code of Indian Offenses. For Dakota people like Mary Ann Laidlaw, and her mixed-ancestry children who were raised in Dakota country, such extravagance probably had a very different meaning than for William Laidlaw.

Mary Ann, born about 1797, a daughter of the Sisíthuŋwaŋ chief Čhaŋté Tháŋka (Big Heart), married in the late 1810s to high-ranking Scottish-born fur trader William Laidlaw. Laidlaw was an employee of the Hudson's Bay Company and later a cofounder of the Columbia Fur Company; he worked early in his career at various posts at Lake Traverse in modern-day western Minnesota and later at posts on the Missouri River, especially Forts Pierre and Tecumseh. Later he became a partner in the American Fur Company. Having become wealthy in the trade, the family retired to Clay County, Missouri, near Kansas City in the mid-1830s, where Laidlaw retained his partnership in the American Fur Company. The settlement that became Kansas City was described as a "little settlement of Creoles and half-breeds" in 1823.[40] Mary Ann and William Laidlaw had at least ten children between 1823 and 1840, eight of whom were daughters, and for many years they raised a family at fur trade posts on the Missouri River.

Their large family is a good example of how mixed-ancestry families came to operate in American legal institutions. Their story demonstrates the depth and breadth of different kinds of legal conveyances that mixed-ancestry families participated in. The Clay County, Missouri Recorder of Deeds office documented how the Laidlaw family bought, sold, and mortgaged land and enslaved Black people and executed powers of attorney. They had civil marriages and divorces recorded in the local circuit court and had their property appraised and sold through the local probate court. Of course, this was only possible in places where the proper government apparatus was in place to do so, which was not the case where most mixed-ancestry Dakota people lived until the 1850s or later. Some exceptions are those that lived in Prairie du Chien, Wisconsin, or in Missouri. Mixed-ancestry Dakota people had access to individual landownership or fee simple ownership under American law. For instance, Augustin Rock sold his town lot in Prairie du Chien on the east bank of the Mississippi to Francois LaBathe in 1837 for $100.[41] Both men were Dakota and worked in the fur trade. Mixed-ancestry Indians had been recorded buying and selling land around Prairie du Chien since the county began recording deeds in 1820.

The Laidlaw family built a prosperous plantation called Hackberry Hall in Clay County, Missouri; William Laidlaw owned a plantation of several hundred acres and reportedly a large, opulent three-story house with twenty rooms decorated with Indian artifacts such as pipes and headdresses. The couple bought and sold numerous tracts of land in Clay County. William and Mary Ann Laidlaw sold 348 acres to William Dawson in 1838 for $2,450. The clerk of the Clay County Circuit Court, Samuel Tillery, examined the full-ancestry Dakota Mary Ann Laidlaw "separate and apart from her husband whether she executed the said instrument of writing freely voluntarily and without compulsion or undue influence of her said husband," to which she acknowledged that she "relinquishes her dower" in the lands.[42] This was a common property law practice in the United States called "inchoate dower," in which married women held an interest in the estates of their husbands while they were alive. A woman's right to the land was incomplete until the husband died, at which point it became a "life estate" that the widow enjoyed the use of until her death. Although Indian women were not explicitly written into such laws, by virtue of having a white husband with property, Mary Ann Laidlaw enjoyed these same rights. Such property could only be sold with her consent, although her husband could purchase land at will. Mary Ann Laidlaw's x-mark appears on numerous land sales in Clay County, including an 1844 deed to her son-in-law Moore Lurtey. Lurtey purchased an undivided half part in numerous tracts of land containing several hundred acres for $1,000. David Ferril, a justice of the peace, recorded the sale using the same boilerplate language as the previous deed, which acknowledged her consent to the sale.[43]

These American property practices included the Laidlaw family's involvement with chattel slavery. The Laidlaw family enslaved numerous African Americans by the 1830s. In 1840, the extended family enslaved nineteen people, and in 1850 they enslaved fourteen.[44] Son-in-law Moore Lurtey enslaved a thirteen-year-old "mulatto" girl.[45] William Laidlaw died in 1851 and his estate, both in land and enslaved people, passed to his family. But before he died, he gifted enslaved people to his mixed-ancestry Dakota children. William Laidlaw executed two deeds on September 4, 1848, "in consideration of the natural love and affection which I have." Daughter Mary, aged seventeen, received an enslaved girl also named Mary, aged thirteen. Elizabeth, aged nineteen, received Sam, aged twenty-three.[46] The same day he deeded to sixteen-year-old Jane a six-year-old boy named Josh and to daughter Julia a young African American boy, Perry, aged seven.[47]

Over time, the family became less prosperous, forcing the family to sell or mortgage their property. In retirement, Laidlaw remained a partner in the American Fur Company, and he and his wife regularly made trips up the Missouri to Indian country, but the decline of the fur trade destroyed their fortune.[48] By the time of Laidlaw's death he was deeply in debt, to the surprise of many who knew him.[49] In June of 1850, Laidlaw mortgaged John, a twenty-nine-year-old enslaved man, to his daughter Elizabeth Wallis. In addition, he mortgaged numerous other belongings to Elizabeth: a piano, three tables, two wardrobes, two pairs of glasses, two sets of silver spoons, a sideboard, a sofa, plus hogs and sheep for the sum of $1,500. He apparently managed to pay off his debt to his daughter Elizabeth for the enslaved John, as Laidlaw mortgaged him again two months later.[50] In August 1850, Laidlaw mortgaged a forty-year-old enslaved man named Mack, fifteen acres of hemp and forty acres of corn growing in his fields, six horses, and his entire stock of sixteen cattle to pay his debts owed to three men. The mortgage also promised $500 cash to pay off his debt in total. The day before, August 21, 1850, he once again mortgaged John for $450, which is probably where he got the cash needed to pay off his debts the following day.[51]

Although the practice of chattel slavery was rare among the Dakota, they had become acquainted with slavery through the practice of white army officers bringing enslaved people to army posts like Fort Snelling. Most notably, some Dakota people would have been familiar with Dred Scott while he was enslaved at Fort Snelling in the 1830s. Scott is famous for bringing a lawsuit against his enslaver in the 1840s, arguing that by bringing him to Wisconsin Territory, where slavery was illegal, his enslaved status was nullified. The U.S. Supreme Court ruled otherwise, arguing that he had no legal rights recognized by the United States, and Scott remained in bondage.

In addition to legal conveyances of land and enslaved people, the Laidlaw family also signed powers of attorney. In 1850, Mary Laidlaw Lurtey and her husband Moore Lurtey gave power of attorney to Henry Vanosdell to sell an enslaved girl also named Mary on their behalf. As was common practice, Mary Laidlaw Lurtey was examined by the clerk of the circuit court where she gave her consent for the power of attorney to sell the enslaved Mary.[52] The same day, the Lurteys executed another power of attorney to Vanosdell to receive in their name any money coming to them in a recent treaty in Minnesota with the Dakota, and in a separate examination, Mary Laidlaw Lurtey again consented.[53] Presumably this was the 1849 treaty to acquire the Lake Pepin Reservation, the subject of chapter 4, which the Senate refused to ratify.

After William Laidlaw's death in 1851, his full-ancestry Dakota widow Mary Ann bought and sold land in her own name. On October 3, 1853,

Mary Ann Laidlaw signed two quit claim deeds, one to L. W. Leavell for $66.33 and one to Nairy Cave for $133.67.[54] A month later she sold 749 acres to Joseph A. Sire for $250.[55] She paid $40 to Robert Gilmer and Hugh J. and Elizabeth C. Robertson for a town lot on the bluff in Richfield, Missouri, in 1854.[56] Mary Ann sold land again in 1868, a town lot on the hill in Missouri City to Robert G. Gilmer for $350.[57] Mary Ann Laidlaw and her children were able to navigate the Clay County Probate Court after William Laidlaw's death. Mary Ann placed her x-mark on several documents related to property she kept that was part of her husband's estate. An inventory of Laidlaw's property recorded many household goods, furniture, farm implements, and livestock, but only one enslaved person, a forty-five-year-old man named Mack.[58] Mary Ann's only son to survive childhood, William Laidlaw Jr., died in 1858, leaving a small estate. He owned no land, but his property included an enslaved man named Charley, aged twenty-four, a cow, a calf, a pony, and an old saddle. Charley was valued at $1,200, while his remaining belongings only amounted to $35.[59]

All eight of the Laidlaw daughters eventually married local white men and participated in the Euro-American institution of marriage. Their marriages founded kinship connections, as in Dakota culture, but through American legal marriages they also entered into legal contracts that carried with them certain legal duties and privileges.[60] Catherine and Barbara married brothers, Robert K. and Moore Lurtey. After Barbara died unexpectedly in 1849, Moore Lurtey remarried to another Laidlaw sister, Mary Ann. On May 2, 1857, sisters Mary Ann and Elizabeth filed for divorce from their husbands, Moore Lurtey and William Wallis, in the Clay County, Missouri, circuit court. Both men had apparently abandoned their wives, for neither man appeared for any of the court proceedings over the following years, despite the court-ordered announcements published in the local newspaper, the *Liberty Weekly Tribune*. Both sisters made several court appearances, with the court finally dissolving the marriage of Mary Ann Lurtey on October 29, 1858, and that of Elizabeth Wallis on April 28, 1860. Mary Ann Lurtey's divorce decree stated that "she is freely divorced from the said Moore K. Lurty and as fully released and acquitted from all duties and obligations of the marriage contract . . . as if such marriage had never been contracted or as if the said Moore K. Lurty had naturally died." In Elizabeth's divorce decree the court awarded her custody of her children but also absolved William Wallis of any financial obligations in the care of the children.[61] Euro-American families also placed high importance on kin ties, and as is evident with the Laidlaw family, they were codified in American law.[62] In American society, however, legal marriages were important for the legal rights and obligations they bestowed, most importantly the right to inherit property. Marriage and divorce were regulated by the court, as were property transfer and inheritance of property between kin.

The members of the mixed-ancestry Dakota Laidlaw family were deeply entrenched in Euro-American legal institutions after their move to Clay County, Missouri. From the historical record, it may appear that they fully acculturated into white American society. Indians of mixed ancestry learned to be astute in their legal dealings in these American institutions,

Figure 6. Michel Renville, 1825–1899. Renville was Waȟpéthuŋwaŋ and Bdewákhaŋthuŋwaŋ Dakota. Frank B. Mayer drew his likeness during treaty negotiations in 1851. He was a signer of the Constitution for the Hazelwood Republic in 1856 and served as an Indian scout during the U.S.-Dakota War. Edward E. Ayer Digital Collection, Newberry Library, Chicago.

but they did not give up their Dakotaness. Despite their move to Missouri, the Dakota language remained the common language of the household, at least until Mary Ann Laidlaw's death in 1870. By one account, Mary Ann preferred to speak Dakota and kept her grandson William C. Hodges, born in 1856, to help her interpret into English.[63] Mary Ann Laidlaw regularly returned to the Dakota homeland to visit relatives and ensured that the Dakota language endured in the family at least until her grandchildren's generation. Taking advantage of American legal practices or a Euro-American education did not mean that they gave up what it meant to be Dakota.

Like the Laidlaw family, the Dorion family also had similar practices, going back decades earlier. In fact, the families knew each other, as several Dorion family members served at fur trade posts like Fort Tecumseh at the same time the Laidlaws and famous fur traders like Hugh Glass and Jim Beckwourth were there. In their fur trade dealings, members of the Dorion family signed legal documents relating to their business. In 1808, Pierre Dorion Sr. and his sons Louis and Martin signed a document giving power of attorney to the prominent fur trader Pierre Chouteau. The power of attorney authorized Chouteau to acquire money on behalf of the Dorion men owed to them by the U.S. government. Such documents were common in New France and continued in culturally French places long after the end of the French regime. Another son, John Baptiste, signed a similar power of attorney to Pierre Chouteau the same year, so that Chouteau could procure funds owed him by the U.S. government. The following year, both Louis and John Baptiste signed additional powers of attorney on their own, again to Pierre Chouteau, to collect their salaries as government interpreters.[64] The Dorion men were savvy enough to use legal documents, as well as their connections to prominent men, such as Pierre Chouteau, to help them acquire salaries owed to them by the federal government.

Like many other mixed-ancestry Indians, the Dorion family also frequently worked as wage laborers for the federal government as interpreters. Starting in the first decade of the nineteenth century, Pierre Sr. worked as an Indian subagent while Louis, Martin, and John Baptiste Dorion were government interpreters. Martin Dorion was an accomplished government interpreter. As an Indian agent for the Upper Missouri Agency,

John Dougherty sought permission to hire Martin Dorion for his services as an interpreter in 1836. One of Dougherty's interpreters died, and he needed Martin to fill his place. "Mr. Dorion speaks the Otoe & Missouri, Ioway, Omahaw & Sioux languages fluently, understands all their characters well and has much influence over them."[65] Like the rest of his family, Martin was multilingual. Spending a lifetime in the fur trade gave mixed-ancestry Indians a linguistic advantage that made them ideal interpreters and gave them opportunities to earn wages. In addition, as Indians themselves, they understood the cultures they were engaging with, making them important diplomats too. Dougherty continued about Martin that "if employed as U.S. interpreter he could and would I think effect a great deal towards completing the reconciliation already commenced between the Omahaws & Ioways," suggesting Dougherty needed his services not only as an interpreter but also as a diplomat.[66]

Dougherty also wanted Martin for his assimilative influence and to keep peace between the Iháŋkthuŋwaŋ Dakota and the Potawatomi, or in Dougherty's words, "his services might be made valuable in preventing misunderstandings between these two tribes." Dougherty thought Martin's presence would be important in assimilating the Otoe by "aiding the farmers & others to instruct & encourage them in agriculture."[67] Martin continued to work as an interpreter and was listed as the official interpreter for the Otoe and Omaha on their visit to Washington, D.C., in 1837.[68] Martin was kin with the Ioway, having married a full-ancestry Ioway woman. The Iháŋkthuŋwaŋ Dakota and the Ioway were frequent trading partners in Iowa, which may have influenced his and his brother's marriages to Ioway women.[69] He had at least two children, one of them Elisha Dorion, born in 1829, who himself grew up to be a government interpreter for the Ioway from 1859 to 1871.[70]

In 1835, in desperate need of a good Lakota and Dakota interpreter for the Sioux subagency on the Missouri River, agent Joshua Pilcher requested additional funds to hire Martin's brother John Baptiste Dorion at a rate of $480 per year. William Clark, superintendent of Indian Affairs at Saint Louis, approved of the hire and recommended to the commissioner of Indian Affairs that he approve the hire and the necessary funds. Clark believed that the engagement of Dorion was "as advantageous a one as can be made." Dorion's ability to speak multiple languages convinced Clark of the necessity of hiring Dorion.[71] Pilcher wrote to Clark of his need. He found his work "very difficult, and the want of a good interpreter renders it more so than it would otherwise be. At no period during my intercourse with Indians have I labored under such a gauling embarrassment for want of one." The Indian Department had recently lowered the wages allowed for interpreters to $300 per year, but Pilcher wanted to engage him at the old salary of $480 per year. He told Clark, "This man I presume is known to you as the best interpreter in the Indian Country."[72] Both Pilcher and Clark thought highly of John Baptiste Dorion and his abilities as interpreter, so much so that they were willing to go through the trouble of paying him extra to retain his services. Dorion got the job, but it required an act of Congress to reimburse Pilcher a $100 advance he made to Dorion, and Clark had to pay the remaining salary out of contingent funds of the superintendency.[73]

Members of the Dorion family were deep in the fur trade and were coveted by American officials as interpreters, diplomats, and an assimilative influence because they retained prominence among their people. Several members of the Dorion family served as government interpreters during treaty negotiations. Louis Dorion was listed as a witness and interpreter for five treaties at Portage des Sioux, Missouri, in 1815—four with different bands of Lakota and Dakota, one with the Ioway Nation, and another away from Portage des Sioux with the Omaha Nation, demonstrating his ability to speak the Ioway and Omaha languages.[74] John Baptiste Dorion was a witness and interpreter for an 1825 treaty with the Lakota, Iháŋkthuŋwaŋ, and Iháŋkthuŋwaŋna, while his brother Martin worked as an interpreter for the Otoe Indians and was an interpreter for a treaty with the Otoe, Missouri, Omaha, and Dakota Nations in 1836.[75] Treaty negotiations during the period almost inevitably involved Indians of mixed ancestry acting as interpreters or go-betweens.

Treaty negotiations and mixed-ancestry Indians went hand in hand. It is no coincidence, then, that they were often mentioned in treaty provisions of land at the time. The two most significant treaties, in terms of solidifying the long-term notion of "mixed-blood" as a separate legal category, however, were with the Sac and Fox in 1824 and the Treaty of

Prairie du Chien in 1830, which created three Indian reservations between them. These Indian reservations were unlike other reservations. They were intended for the sole use of Indians of mixed ancestry and would be held in common by them. The Sac and Fox reservation only remained in common ownership for a decade, while the two reservations created by the 1830 Treaty of Prairie du Chien were eventually divided among individual claimants over twenty-five years after their creation. The division of these reservations into individual ownership had an extremely litigious result, ensuring that American officials would be forced to contend with this "mixed-blood" category for decades and were the primary spark for a mixed-blood history. In this moment, "half-breed" became codified into law as a legal and racial class of people with rights to land.

The land-based assimilation policy of the early nineteenth century had much in common with the assimilation policy of the turn of the twentieth century under the General Allotment Act, or Dawes Act, of 1887. Vine Deloria Jr. argues that the federal government intended to assimilate Indians through individual landownership, that the government believed that if "the Indian had his own piece of land, he would forsake his tribal ways."[76] While the land-based assimilation policy of the early nineteenth century was piecemeal in its focus on mixed-ancestry tribal members, the policymakers of the period intended these treaty provisions to be seeds that would eventually grow into entire tribal nations scrambling to adopt individual landownership. As we will see, this policy did not lead into wholesale assimilation. Instead, mixed-ancestry Indians acculturated to Euro-American practices of individual landownership, adapting new survival strategies but maintaining tribal connections.

In founding the mixed-ancestry reservations of Lake Pepin on the Mississippi and Great Nemaha on the Missouri, the 1830 Treaty of Prairie du Chien inaugurated a mixed-blood history and codified the legal term "half-breed," which racially delineated a group of Indians with their own set of legal rights. After 1830, the mixed-ancestry Dakota had their own land over which the mixed-ancestry Dakota began a relationship with the federal government resulting in numerous petitions, correspondence, and even treaties. The treaty created a new legal status that the federal government and local governments were forced to contend with. The reservation did not assimilate mixed-ancestry Dakota into American culture; rather, attending to their land interests over time simply made them into shrewd participants in the American legal system. The differentiation between those of mixed and full ancestry was colonially imposed and not something that necessarily carried great significance among Dakota people themselves.

As historian Berlin Basil Chapman concludes, the 1830 Treaty of Prairie du Chien was meant to complete the work of the 1825 Treaty of Prairie du Chien.[77] In negotiating the 1825 treaty, the United States intended to create a buffer zone between the tribes in the region to ensure peace. This was done by setting out concrete boundaries between tribes with the purpose of keeping people within their own borders. Gwen Westerman and Bruce White argue, "The purpose of establishing the boundaries may have been as much for facilitating treaties of cession for the lands as for establishing peace."[78] They continue, "Although the treaty contains no cessions, it was in effect a cessional treaty for all tribes who gave up claims to land. For the Dakota the line drawn would, for all practical purposes, 'cede' the northern portion of their ancestral homeland to the Ojibwe."[79] Indeed, forcing the tribes to draw on a map lines that had never existed in any definitive form before made it easier for the United States to coerce land cessions in subsequent treaties, and it erased any tribal claims to land outside those bounds. The 1825 treaty did not have the effect that American officials had hoped; violence between tribes continued, especially between the Dakota and Sac and Fox.

The Sac and Fox, Dakota, Omaha, Ioway, Otoe, and Missouri Nations negotiated the 1830 Treaty of Prairie du Chien with the United States to fix these problems. The American purpose of the treaty was to further the aims of peace between the tribes by cessions of land that would form buffer zones between them. The Dakota ceded a tract twenty miles in width between the Mississippi and Des Moines Rivers as a buffer between them and the Sac and Fox. In return, the "Sioux of the Mississippi" received $2,000 and the "Yancton and Santie Bands of Sioux" received $3,000, to be paid annually for ten years. In addition, each of the two named Dakota groups were to receive the use of a blacksmith, as well as agricultural tools. The Iháŋkthuŋwaŋ and "Santie Bands" mentioned were not present at the treaty council but gave their assent to the treaty on October 13 at Saint Louis. The Sac and Fox gave up a similar twenty-mile-wide section of ground to create a buffer zone forty miles wide.[80] Roy W. Meyer argues that the meager annuities in the 1830 treaty "were too small to have much effect, good or bad, on the Santee Sioux, but the blacksmith shop was a convenience for some."[81] The ceded territory and the annuities were small, but the major impact of this treaty was in articles 9 and 10, which created two reservations for the use of the mixed-ancestry members of the signing tribes.

During the negotiations, on the second day, the Dakota Chief Wápahaša said (as translated in the treaty accounts), "I have understood yesterday that you wished us to sell you a slip of our land. Before we do this I wish to say that it is our wish to give a small piece to our friends the half breeds. If this meets your approbation we will then speak of the other." Here, Chief Wápahaša is saying that this land is of the utmost importance, refusing to negotiate a land cession until the matter of the land for his mixed relatives was cleared up. Tribal leaders were often adamant that their mixed-ancestry relatives receive land. In the treaty with the Sac and Fox in 1824 that created a reservation for their mixed-ancestry relatives in Iowa, the chiefs reminded American officials that their "blood runs equal, yours & mine in their veins."[82] These chiefs expressed a sentiment similar to Wápahaša that mixed-ancestry land was important but with the additional implication that mixed-ancestry Indians were a kinship link between the two nations. During the negotiations with the Dakota, commissioner Colonel Morgan responded to Wápahaša's demand, "We agree to the request of the Sioux as respects their half breeds, provided the quantity be reasonable." The quantity that the commissioners ultimately found reasonable was a reservation of nearly six hundred square miles.

Wápahaša suggested the bounds of the Lake Pepin Reservation, which the U.S. negotiators accepted. Article 9 read, "The Sioux Bands in Council having earnestly solicited that they might have permission to bestow upon the half breeds of their Nation" a tract of land on the west bank of the Mississippi River. The boundaries of the reservation were "beginning at a place called the barn, below and near the village of the Red Wing

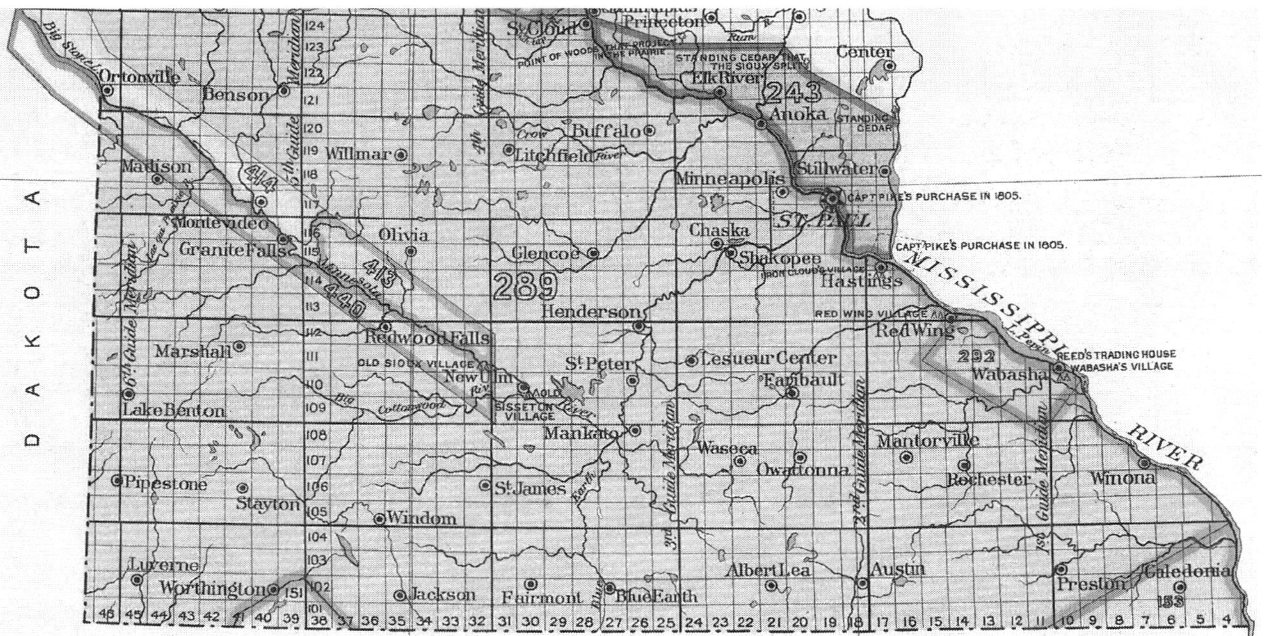

Map 1. Dakota reservations in Minnesota in the 1850s. The Lake Pepin Reservation is the rectangle marked 292 in the eastern part of the state. The reservation for the Dakota Nation created by the treaties of 1851 ran along both banks of the Minnesota River in western Minnesota. Charles C. Royce, *Indian Land Cessions in the United States: Eighteenth Annual Report of the Bureau of American Ethnology, 1896–1897, Part 2* (Government Printing Office, 1899).

Chief, and running back fifteen miles; thence in a parallel line with Lake Pepin and the Mississippi, about thirty-two miles to a point opposite Beef or O-Bouef River; thence fifteen miles to the Grand Encampment opposite the River aforesaid." For their part, the "United States agree to suffer said half Breeds to occupy said tract of country; they holding by the same title, and in the same manner that other Indian Titles are held."[83]

Article 10 used similar language: "The Omahas, Ioways and Ottoes, for themselves, and in behalf of the Yanckton and Santie Bands of Sioux [who consented later] having earnestly requested that they might be permitted to make some provision for their half-breeds, and particularly that they might bestow upon them" a tract of land on the Missouri River. The treaty described the bounds: "Beginning at the mouth of the Little Ne-mohaw River, and running up the main channel of said River to a point which will be ten miles from its mouth in a direct line; from thence in a direct line, to strike the Grand Ne-mohaw ten miles above its mouth, in a direct line (the distance between the two Ne-mohaws being about twenty miles)—thence down said River to its mouth; thence up, and with the Meanders of the Missouri River to the point of beginning." Like article 9, article 10 claimed that the United States would "suffer" the mixed-ancestry Indians to occupy the tract and "holding it in the same manner, and by the same title that other Indian titles are held." However, article 10 had an additional clause: "The President of the United States may hereafter assign to any of the said half-breeds, to be held by him or them in fee simple, any portion of said tract not exceeding a section, of six hundred and forty acres to each individual. And this provision shall extend to the cession made by the Sioux in the preceding Article."[84]

Despite the fact that both articles said that the United States would "suffer" the mixed-ancestry Indians to occupy these lands, from their previous policies, American officials believed that these reservations would be beneficial in their mission to assimilate Indians. This is also evidenced in the final clause of article 10, in which the treaty authorized the president to allot the lands of either reservation to individual mixed-ancestry Indians. This gave the United States the opportunity, if holding the reservations in common did not meet their expectations for assimilation, to allot the lands to individuals, which conformed to Euro-American practices of landownership. The federal government eventually extinguished common ownership of both reservations, as we will see in later chapters, and put land into the hands of individual claimants, but in different ways. By the time the Lake Pepin Reservation was divided in severalty a generation later, there were 680 mixed-ancestry Dakota claimants to the land. In the late 1850s, the Great Nemaha Reservation was allotted to 389 mixed-ancestry Indians, 173 of them Dakota.[85]

The Dakota gave up the strip of land between the Des Moines and Mississippi Rivers and the Lake Pepin Reservation with the understanding that they would retain hunting rights for both lands.[86] But because the Great Nemaha Reservation was on Otoe land, article 11 stated that the Omaha, Ioway, and "Yanckton and Santie Bands of Sioux" would pay $300 out of their annuities to the Otoe for ten years. The Dakota bands were to pay $100, a bargain considering that they made up almost half of the population of the claimants.[87]

This treaty encouraged mixed-ancestry Indians to think of landownership on an individual basis. The American assimilation project worked in the sense that after the Treaty of Prairie du Chien, many mixed-ancestry Dakota wanted to own their land as separate individuals. But one way in which they did not assimilate is in how mixed-ancestry women did not always conform to American coverture laws, instead controlling their own homes and property as they would in Dakota culture. Indeed, this mixed-blood history was more than a period when mixed-ancestry Indians acquired a separate legal status; it was a moment when they adapted to and challenged American cultural and legal practices, bending them to their own interests.

Pressing their claims to property was not unusual among mixed-ancestry Dakota women. In 1836, Margaret Hess of Prairie du Chien wrote to agent Lawrence Taliaferro, hoping to be recognized as a claimant to the Lake Pepin Reservation so that she could sell her share to support herself and "three little helpless children." Hess argued further: "We are poor, are certainly in a great need of that donation as any other individual to whom it has been given." She claimed, "I am sir the daughter of Charles Hess, who was himself a half Sioux & my mother a Sioux woman."[88] The mixed-ancestry Dakota were not permitted to sell shares

Figure 7. Julia Ann LaFramboise, 1842–1871, taken circa 1862. The daughter of a mixed-ancestry Odawa man and a full-ancestry Sisíthuŋwaŋ Dakota woman, LaFramboise became a teacher at missionary stations in Dakota country, teaching in both Dakota and English. Locator no. por 17818 p1, Minnesota Historical Society, Saint Paul.

of their reservation. Margaret Hess showed up on a roll of mixed-ancestry claimants in 1838 as Margaret Hess Campbell, aged thirty-five, receiving $500, now living at Saint Peter's Agency.[89] Taliaferro does mention her father in his journals, working as an interpreter in 1823.[90] It's unclear whether the three children were her own or were her younger half-siblings. As Lizzie Ehrenhalt argues, Hess's letter is not simply a plea for help, "it is also a savvy attempt to leverage a personal connection." Because she resided in Prairie du Chien, she could have spoken to the local Indian agent, Joseph Street; instead, however, she chose Taliaferro.[91] Hess appealed to Taliaferro on the grounds of this personal connection: "You I believe knew my Father and probably my Mother too, and I know of no one who can see me righted in this matter, or would probably take a greater interest than yourself."[92] Taliaferro replied on November 5, telling Hess he would look into the matter.[93] By writing, in English, to Taliaferro for help, she revealed a significant level of acculturation into American society, but by asserting her own land rights, she demonstrated a Dakota understanding of property ownership and business dealings.

These early treaties posited that putting land in the hands of Indians of mixed ancestry would quickly assimilate them and in turn provide an assimilative influence on their full-ancestry Indian relatives. The year 1833, however, marked a significant shift in this federal Indian policy. Beginning with a treaty between the United States and the "United Nation of Chippewa, Ottowa, and Potawatamie Indians" signed on September 26 of that year, treaty provisions shifted from providing land to providing money for mixed-ancestry Indians. The treaty set aside $100,000 to "satisfy sundry individuals, in behalf of whom reservations were asked, which the Commissioners refused to grant."[94] This shift in policy came in the wake of the passage of the Indian Removal Act of 1830, in which the federal government forcibly removed Indians from their homes and placed them on lands west of the Mississippi River. In essence, despite the perceived benefit of assimilation, the federal government was now in the business of removing Indians from their land, not keeping them on it.

Government officials, however, argued that this was a continuation of the assimilation policy; previous treaties set aside land for mixed-ancestry Indians, and the money distributed in subsequent treaties would allow Indians of mixed ancestry to develop their lands. In reality, however, most Indians of mixed ancestry quickly sold their lands after receiving full title and were cheated out of their treaty money. Other than an outlier treaty with the Wyandot in 1842, it was over twenty years, in 1854, that treaties between tribes and the federal government again began providing land explicitly for Indians of mixed ancestry.

This land-based assimilation policy, and the shift to the money-based assimilation policy, was to have major consequences in Indian country. First, the very act of treating Indians of mixed ancestry different from other Indians solidified the concept of "half-breed" or "mixed-blood" in American law as a separate legal and racial category. This confusion inherent in the assimilation policy permitted Indians of mixed ancestry to occupy a dual legal and racial category. This allowed them to respond to colonialism in unique ways, claiming rights to land specifically as mixed-ancestry Indians, but it also allowed them to benefit from subsequent treaties under their status as Indians. This, in turn, led to confusion over the land rights of Indians of mixed ancestry. As the Treaty of Prairie du Chien stated that Indians of mixed ancestry held their reservations "in the same manner that other Indian Titles are held," there was much confusion over what this meant. Did this mean that a treaty would have to be conducted in order for the federal government to acquire this land? In fact, the federal government negotiated two treaties explicitly with the mixed-ancestry Dakota to acquire their reservation at Lake Pepin in the 1840s. A third treaty was negotiated with the tribal chiefs whose mixed-ancestry members held the Great Nemaha Reservation, but the Senate refused to ratify the treaty on the grounds that the mixed-ancestry Indians did not give their consent in the treaty. The Senate refused to ratify all three of these treaties, but this demonstrates how the federal government viewed Indians of mixed ancestry as carrying a legal status separate from other Indians. The assimilation policy of the federal government, and the land and later money that mixed-ancestry Indians received because of it, had major consequences. The legal status and rights of Indians of mixed ancestry were uncertain. The federal government's colonial project to assimilate Indians through providing land to mixed-ancestry Indians was a failure, but it set in motion a series of mixed-blood histories, and, as we will see, this colonial project did contribute to lasting intratribal divisions and animosity.

Intermarriages created legal dilemmas for white Americans. Kinship in white American culture associated kinship with property rights. When fur traders died, their wives and children could inherit any property they owned under American law. In American culture, kinship was also expressed through law. Marriages were recorded by civil authorities and divorces had to be approved by courts or state and territorial legislatures. When a fur trader or a mixed-ancestry Indian with property died, their property was probated through the local courts, if they existed, so that the property, or its value after sale, went to the heirs. The buying and selling of property was also governed by American law and meticulously recorded. Mixed-ancestry Indians became embroiled in these American legal practices partly because of their kinship relationships with white men. But many mixed-ancestry Indians also chose to participate in this legal system because there was much to gain by doing so.

At the same time, white Americans perceived Indians of mixed ancestry as distinct from other Indians to the point that they put them within a separate racial and legal category. American officials, missionaries, and other white people who came into contact with them worked to create and prop up this new, invented legal category. When treaties between tribal nations and the U.S. government began incorporating separate provisions specifically for "half-breeds," it created a new legal category, a legal class of people that was ill-defined and whose legal rights were ambiguous. Americans worked to incorporate mixed-ancestry Indians into the American state through incorporating them into the legal system and through assimilation. At the same time, because incorporating them in this way would potentially bestow whiteness upon them, they created a new racial and legal category that also served to limit that incorporation and limit their access to whiteness.

Mixed-ancestry Indians learned to navigate the legal and property-based kinship system of Euro-Americans for their own gain, while also continuing to practice Dakota kinship. In their role as treaty negotiators, they influenced their full-ancestry relatives to ask for lands on their behalf in treaties; in the process, American officials used legal wordage that created "half-breed" as a legal and racial category of people entitled to land, separate from their full-ancestry relatives. Until the early 1850s, there was little in the way of legal institutions in Dakota country. Places like Saint Louis or Prairie du Chien, which were on the margins of Dakota country, saw these institutions early, or Dakota people might be shipped off to other places, like Choctaw Academy, Michilimackinac, or Green Bay for education. Western religious institutions in the form of missionaries moved ahead of political institutions. In Minnesota, most Dakota people did not encounter Christianity until the 1830s, and political institutions came fifteen to twenty years later. Despite this, they learned to take advantage of these institutions when the opportunity arose, but they also maintained their connection to the Dakota Nation.

CHAPTER 3

The Economics of Racial Mixedness and Kinship

The 1837 Treaty of Washington

The clash between the American capitalist economy and Indigenous kinship- and reciprocity-based economies, with mixed-ancestry Indians in the middle, fueled a new paradigm where Dakota people began to place a monetary value on kinship obligations and on mixed-ancestry status. The 1837 Treaty of Washington between the United States and the Bdewákhaŋthuŋwaŋ Dakota set aside $110,000 for the mixed-ancestry members of the tribe.[1] White fur traders, Dakota leaders, and mixed-ancestry Dakota people all pushed for this payment. The federal government distributed this money based on the criteria set by tribal leaders; those mixed-ancestry Dakota who had or were capable of performing their kinship obligations at a high level, particularly through gift giving and the sharing of resources, received the most money. American policymakers justified the expense by arguing that mixed-ancestry Indians had received land, and now they would receive money to develop those lands. Mixed-ancestry Indians were at the forefront of Dakota adaptation to and participation in the American economy; in the process, mixed-ancestry Dakota people began to perceive their participation in the kinship-based Dakota economy as having monetary value.

Mixed racial status was not a commodity in the sense that it could be bought and sold, but it carried with it a monetary value for themselves or often for their white fathers, husbands, or guardians.[2] Some local white men saw that they might benefit from singling out their mixed-ancestry wives and children for special payments. In a form of racial capitalism, they sought to financially exploit the mixed racial status of their families.[3] Considering many tribes in the region requested cash payments for their mixed-ancestry relatives in treaty stipulations, being a mixed-ancestry Indian in the 1830s and 1840s in the Midwest could be economically advantageous. In treaty negotiations, tribal leaders wished the government to provide for their mixed-ancestry kin, but the tribes wanted to make payments to their relatives in differing amounts, based on their perceived value and how well Indians of mixed ancestry carried out their kinship responsibilities to the tribe. In the 1830s, money, race, and kinship intersected; the federal government paid "half-breed" money to mixed-ancestry individuals owing to their racial mixedness, and tribal leaders distributed the money to their relatives based on the kinship value they placed on mixed-ancestry Indians. This value derived from the services rendered to the tribe, which mixed- and full-ancestry Indians understood as the fulfillment of kinship responsibilities, and for the Dakota, this also meant measuring to what degree the mixed-ancestry Indians were following the Dakota principle of being a good relative.

The Dakota, like other tribes in the region, had been participating to some degree in the Euro-American market economy through the fur trade since the mid-seventeenth century. Yet they were not victims of the market. They found their societies pulled ever deeper into the market economy year by year and made adaptations in ways that would benefit their communities.[4] Over time, as settlers and their business interests became more numerous, Indigenous people came to rely more on the cash economy, placing importance on an object controlled by the settler colonial state rather than products, such as furs, that they produced in their own lands. Reliance on cash gave the state more power and, as Brian Gettler argues, aided settler colonial states like the United States and Canada in the dispossession of Indigenous land.[5] Settler colonial governments relied on the continuous dispossession of Indigenous land to grow their own economies, in the process weakening Indigenous nations and their economies. Land cession treaties like the 1837 Treaty of Washington increased Indigenous dependence on cash payments while also building the economy of the settler state.[6] Indigenous nations grew ever closer to the settler colonial market economy, with Indians of mixed ancestry at the forefront. As the nineteenth century progressed and the fur trade faded, mixed-ancestry Indians increasingly practiced wage labor, bought and sold land, including lands ceded by their respective nations, received annuity goods and moneys from the federal government, and paid taxes. At the same time, they continued to participate in the Dakota kinship-based economy.

A good example of the Dakota kinship-based economy appears in the 1819–1821 post journals of John Palmer Bourke at a trading post near Lake Traverse. Bourke, an Irishman, appeared in the fall of 1819 at the Hudson's Bay Company post run by Duncan Graham, a Scottish fur trader married to a Dakota woman, and a mixed-ancestry Dakota man named Joseph Renville. Graham and Renville held reciprocal kinship obligations with the Dakota based on marriage and ancestry. In one of his first entries, Bourke complained, "Messrs Graham & Renville have evidently squandered away the Goods of the Company without attempting to make a profitable trade. In fact they were surrounded by their Indian relations, and the goods seem to have been distributed among them more as presents, than anything else."[7] Over the course of his journal, Bourke regularly noted his exasperation with Graham and Renville allowing their relatives to have the goods at the post. What Bourke did not understand is that Graham and Renville were actively engaging in the Dakota economy. By gifting goods to their relatives, they ensured that those Indians were indebted to them in a reciprocal relationship that would obligate them to trade with Graham and Renville for years to come. When he wintered among the Dakota in 1808–1809, fur trader Thomas G. Anderson refused to give goods on credit, resulting in bad feelings and death threats from the local Dakota. Soon after, "following the custom of the country, which I had hitherto resisted, I took to live with me a little half-breed" Dakota woman. His fur trade activities ran more smoothly after becoming kin to the Dakota with this marriage, but he did not stay in the fur trade long, with his wife taking their children and abandoning him by 1814.[8]

After Duncan Graham left the post in October 1820, Bourke complained that "Renville [is] squandering goods upon his relations." The next spring

Figure 8. The mixed-ancestry Bdewákhaŋthuŋwaŋ daughters of fur trader Duncan Graham. Left to right: Elizabeth Graham Faribault, 1805–1875, the wife of a member of the Minnesota legislature, mixed-ancestry Alexander Faribault; Nancy Graham Buisson, 1810–1888; and Jane Graham Wells, 1818–1881, also the wife of a Minnesota legislator, James "Bully" Wells. Item 0170, collection B, State Historical Society of North Dakota, Bismarck.

when Bourke confronted Renville about giving goods to his relatives, Renville threatened to have his relatives hurt Bourke.[9] The relationship between Bourke and Renville soured; he wrote, "Renville keeps at a distance, he passes the day with his relations and at night returns to partake of our supper."[10] Renville again threatened Bourke with his relatives in March of 1821.[11] When Renville's mother-in-law died in April 1821, Bourke complained about the quart of liquor that Renville gave to his relatives, but he felt consolation in the fact that "had she lived it would cost us much more in the provisions way."[12] In these examples, we can see the Dakota economy working in several ways. Renville supplied his relatives with goods. In Dakota communities, members were expected to share game and agricultural products that had been grown or gathered. By sharing trade goods, Renville was simply continuing this practice, but in the process, it obligated his relatives to bring him furs in the future. The post journals also demonstrate how Renville relied on his relatives for protection and intimidation.

By November of 1820, Renville claimed that only his relations could be trusted to pay their debts; subsequently, Renville offered them more credit. Bourke did not trust the Indians near the post, complaining that they never hunted for furs because Graham, Renville, and Robert Dickson, a fur trader from a nearby post, constantly provided their kin with necessary goods.[13] When Renville gave credit to three of his cousins, Renville told Bourke not to worry for they would immediately leave to hunt and pay their debt. When Bourke confronted one of the cousins, the cousin was surprised to hear of his imminent departure, stating he was staying there to take care of another cousin whose mother died.[14] Bourke wrote about the mixed-ancestry interpreter, Narcisse Frenier, and how he was "in the habit when sent to cut trees for the Horses to go and cut firewood for his mother in law, however we are scarce of Hatchets, frequently lends his to his Indian connections."[15] Bourke misunderstood the nature of the Dakota economy. He saw Renville, Frenier, and others regularly provide goods for their relatives, but he rarely saw those provide furs, which was the purpose of the trading post. Bourke expected immediate payment, in the form of furs, for the goods that Indians received in this way. However, the Dakota economy did not work this way. Immediate payment was not expected; instead, it was understood that, in this reciprocal relationship, at some point in the future the relatives of Renville and the other traders would provide them with furs.[16]

After the Hudson's Bay Company absorbed the North West Company in 1821, the company began retreating northward to more economically viable locales, closing the Lake Traverse post in 1823. Renville moved on to work for the Columbia Fur Company. Bourke must have come to understand the importance of Dakota kinship in their economy, for he soon married a mixed-ancestry Dakota woman, Margaret Campbell, and moved to the Selkirk Colony where they raised a large mixed-ancestry family.[17] These brief journals of John Bourke provide a window into the Dakota economic and kinship systems and how mixed-ancestry Indians fit within them. As demonstrated in the post journals, economics and kinship were inseparable from each other and inseparable from Dakota life. Despite their mixed heritage and their participation in the Euro-American capitalist economy, Joseph Renville and Narcisse Frenier continued to maintain their Dakota kinship obligations and continued to recognize the economic aspects of those kinship connections. As they recognized, their practices may not have yielded economic success in the short term, but by maintaining their kinship connections, they could retain their kin as trade partners for life.

Like many other Dakota children of mixed ancestry, the children of my great-great-great-grandparents Francis Trudell and Ičíyapiwiŋ grew up engaging with the American capitalist economy, the Dakota economy based on kinship and reciprocity, and the fur trade economy, which included elements of both American and Indigenous economies. Their lives in Minnesota, from the 1830s to the 1870s, coincided with the creation of American governmental apparatus and courts in the region and the eventual removal of most Dakota people from the state. As late as 1835, Trudell worked for Hercules Dousman, the head of the "Western Outfit" of the American Fur Company, but in 1841, fur trader Henry H. Sibley gave testimony that Trudell had been discharged from service.[18] Trudell had become indebted to the American Fur Company multiple times during and after his service with the company. In July of 1835, Trudell owed $20.12 to the "Sioux Outfit," and as late as 1852 he owed $99.57. Sibley sued Trudell in 1841 to recover another debt, which he paid out of court.[19] From the 1830s to the 1860s, Trudell became indebted to Indian traders, labored for traders and Indian agents to pay his debts, paid property taxes, and worked as a farmer. At the same time, Ičíyapiwiŋ and her children occasionally received annuities and other treaty-guaranteed moneys. This mix of American and Native economic practices was typical of mixed-ancestry families in the early Midwest; at the same time, mixed-ancestry families continued traditional kinship practices in their economic lives. The historical record of the Trudell family is rich with their economic activities, but by reading between the lines, we can discern the role that kinship played in their economic lives and how the economy changed over time.

The fur trade was the catalyst that brought most mixed-race couples together and perpetuated the mixed-ancestry population. Trudell was probably the same Francois Perron dit Trudelle that contracted for three years with ten other men as a voyageur with William Wallace Matthews of Montreal in February 1827. He added his x-mark to a contract worth 1,200 livres and received 36 livres as a signing bonus.[20] In 1855, Trudell claimed June 1828 as his arrival in Minnesota; he was out of the fur trade before 1841. During his time with the American Fur Company, he probably worked along the Mississippi and the eastern reaches of the Minnesota River; his occupation with the company was listed as "baker."[21] He likely married Ičíyapiwiŋ about 1835 to gain economic access to her kin as part of his fur trade activities. The Trudell family's foray into the fur trade was short-lived, but other mixed Dakota families had worked in the fur trade for generations and continued to build a stronger and broader economic base through the additional kinship connections brought on by marriage.

By the 1830s, fur trade companies were in rapid decline as demand for furs decreased and Indian land cessions resulted in fewer Indians laboring in the fur trade on ever-shrinking territories.[22] Many former fur traders became Indian traders. While Indian traders continued to occasionally accept furs from Indians in exchange for goods, the main difference between fur traders and Indian traders was that the latter began to expect cash payments from Indians for debts, usually in the form of annuity payments from the federal government. I use the term "Indian trade" or "Indian trader" to differentiate them from the earlier fur traders.[23]

The 1830s to the 1860s was a period of extreme economic change and turmoil for the Dakota and other Indigenous nations in the region. Like their Lakota relatives farther west, the Dakota had relied on the buffalo for their meat and hides, although with the presence of other game animals, not to the same extent as their western relatives. After years of dwindling bison populations, the buffalo were nearly nonexistent in Wisconsin by the 1820s and were a rarity in most of Minnesota and Iowa by the 1830s; their population began to decline in the Dakotas soon after.[24] As buffalo hunts became less and less productive each year, this forced Dakota people to adapt and find other sources of food and other materials for tipi covers and blankets. With the encouragement of missionaries and American officials, some Dakota bands began to expand their agricultural activities in the 1830s and 1840s, but the majority of Dakota people were resistant to this expansion beyond the typical corn crops they grew each year. Frequent land cessions resulted in the loss of access to hunting, fishing, and gathering grounds, and the cash payments that were often included in land cession treaties changed trade patterns. Competition from a swarm of settlers and squatters as well as the American state exerting greater control over the region all worked to dramatically change Dakota subsistence patterns and economic activities and make them reliant on the federal government and traders.[25]

Members of the Trudell family regularly engaged with local Indian traders, both as customers and laborers. As early as November 19, 1833, Francis Trudell appeared in the ledger books of the fur traders and Indian traders in the region. Between March 17 and June 13, 1834, Trudell appeared fifteen times in the books of fur trader Alexis Bailly, a mixed-ancestry Odawa, purchasing numerous items. He bought clothing such as moccasins, palm leaf hats, a calico shirt, trousers, handkerchiefs, and cotton and calico cloth. The food items he purchased included sugar, flour, and salt. In the fall of 1838, he purchased twenty-two pounds of pork from Henry Sibley at his New Hope trading post.[26] He also purchased pipes, tobacco, whiskey, fish hooks, a comb, gunpowder, and a pocket knife.[27] In the winter of 1843–1844, Trudell purchased soap, clothing, candles, cloth, tobacco, suspenders, numerous pipes, and a comb from Alexis Bailly.

Francis Trudell's purchase of cloth, needles, and buttons reveals how he clothed his closest relatives. He bought boots and socks in October 1840.[28] Trudell bought a large quantity of cloth in late 1843, presumably so that Ičíyapiwiŋ could produce clothing for the family. On December 29, he purchased six yards of cotton cloth, four yards of ribbon, five yards of calico cloth, two and one-half yards of satin, and one dozen buttons.[29] He made a similar purchase of two yards of cotton cloth, two yards of flannel, two yards of ribbon, and needles on July 22, 1844.[30] These measures of cloth matched the typical size for making garments. About two yards was sufficient for a blouse or shirt, and one would typically use about five yards to make a long-sleeved dress. Judging from his purchases, Ičíyapiwiŋ likely made a calico dress, a satin shirt or blouse, and three cotton shirts with the purchase on December 29, 1843, and two shirts, one of cotton and one of flannel, in the summer of 1844, all trimmed in ribbon. Between June and October 1852, he made numerous purchases from Sibley, including many yards of several different cloths, a shawl, shirts, moccasins, boys' boots, and boys' socks.[31] These purchases demonstrate the familial or kinship obligations of Trudell in purchasing the cloth and Ičíyapiwiŋ in making clothing for her family.

Women of mixed and full ancestry also purchased goods from Indian traders. Ičíyapiwiŋ was listed in Bailly's books by her kinship relation, as "Trudell's Wife," when she purchased a trunk, two blankets, a pair of scarlet leggings, and ribbon in the winter of 1844–1845. Bailly transferred the $12.00 owed for these goods to Francis Trudell's account.[32] White men and Dakota men and women of mixed and full ancestry regularly appeared in the trade books of Bailly and other Indian traders in the region.

The books of Indian traders also revealed how families offered their labor to pay their debts. Bailly's trade books credit Francis Trudell $12.50 on February 1, 1844, for his work for Bailly of one month and seventeen days, but he still owed a balance of $29.31 several months later on June 12, 1844. He was credited with an additional month on June 12, 1844, for $15.00. He was listed in Bailly's books on July 22, 1844, as paying off his remaining debt of $19.13 by working one and one-third months. On that same day, he racked up additional charges of $21.93 by purchasing cloth, clothing, tobacco, needles, and a blanket, but he was credited $8.90 for supplying Bailly with four cords of wood.[33] Beside supplying firewood, the books of Alexis Bailly do not mention the kind of labor Trudell conducted, but it shows that Trudell was directly involved in the American capitalist economy. Similarly, the books reveal Trudell's Dakota kinship connections. He worked to feed and clothe his family, while Ičíyapiwiŋ used her skills to make clothing for the family.

Trudell, like other Indian and white men in the region, often contracted for labor for short periods to pay debts or acquire small sums of money. Besides the wages he received as a member of the American Fur Company and the debts he paid through his labor to Alexis Bailly in 1844, Francis Trudell earned money for the family through other forms of labor. He was paid $6.66 by Indian Agent Charles Flandrau for ten days of unspecified work as a laborer at the Lower Sioux Agency on May 20,

1857.[34] On October 26, the family was listed in the 1857 Minnesota Territorial Census as living 140 miles straight east of the agency in Red Wing; only nineteen-year-old Frank Trudell, oldest living son of Francis Trudell and Ičíyapiwiŋ, was listed with an occupation, that of laborer.[35] By 1860, the federal census enumerated Trudell as a farmer, and the older sons Frank and Joseph were recorded as laborers, living in Hastings.[36] Francis Trudell's occupation was still listed as farmer when he enlisted in the U.S. Army on August 21, 1862, while residing in Wabasha.[37] He received an enlistment bounty of $27 and received $13 a month in pay. Trudell later claimed he had been disabled during his military service and unsuccessfully filed for a military pension in 1877. After the death of Trudell in 1881, Ičíyapiwiŋ's only subsistence was her weekly ration of 3 1/2 pounds of flour, 1/2 pound of sugar, 1/4 pound of coffee, and 5 pounds of beef supplied by the Indian agent at Santee, and according to Charles Mitchell, "all else she gets is furnished at irregular intervals by her relatives."[38] In 1894, she began receiving a widow's pension of $8 per month for Trudell's military service. Francis Trudell's work history entails a long list of labor in the American capitalist economy, but there is evidence of kinship in this economic history. Ičíyapiwiŋ took advantage of Euro-American kinship conventions to receive a pension for the remaining seventeen years of her life as the widow of an American soldier, while Mitchell's testimony shows how Ičíyapiwiŋ's kin, in keeping with Dakota cultural values, provided her with food and supplies when they could.

An undated slip of paper in the records of Indian Agent Charles Flandrau documents an example of Francis Trudell's involvement in the Dakota economy. At some point Trudell provided a stove to Maȟpíǧi, a member of Šákpe's band. Because the Dakota economy was based in ongoing reciprocal relations between kin, Trudell did not expect to be remunerated immediately for providing the stove, anticipating that he could count on Maȟpíǧi in the future. Flandrau recorded that Maȟpíǧi wanted to give Trudell $21.00 out of his next annuity payment. Trudell did not want the money, instead directing Flandrau to forward the money to a man named Miller, whom Trudell was presumably indebted to.

Considering the mobility of the family, Trudell and his sons probably worked in various other occupations and engaged in the American economy in other ways. Members of the Trudell family had worked as farm laborers, but by the 1880s they primarily earned a living working for the Office of Indian Affairs as Indian policemen, government interpreters, reservation farmers, and laborers at the Santee Boarding School. Family members engaged in the American economy in other ways, such as when Trudell paid a small tax in 1848 on his personal property in Prescott, Wisconsin, valued at $50, tied with W. C. Copley for the lowest-valued property in Prescott that year.[39] Along with the family's labor in the market economy and property tax payments, Trudell's deal with Agent Flandrau over a stove he gave to Maȟpíǧi and the food Ičíyapiwiŋ received from her relatives are examples of the Dakota reciprocity-based economy, where kin shared goods with each other and expected a reciprocal relationship in which they might receive goods in the future if needed. As we will see, by the mid-nineteenth century, the Dakota economy was increasingly intermeshed with the American cash economy. But these changes were not an example of Dakota people giving up their cultural practices; rather, as Chantal Norrgard argues, "Indians integrated new forms of labor into the social, political, and economic structures in place in their communities in ways that enabled their survival."[40] When mixed- or full-ancestry Dakota performed wage labor or paid cash for goods, they were simply exploiting the opportunities available to them. Mixed-ancestry Indians were more likely to be deeply engaged with both economies than were white Americans or Indians of full ancestry.

Because of their kinship connections with the Dakota, the family received cash payments guaranteed through treaties between the federal government and the Dakota Nation. Ičíyapiwiŋ collected substantial sums of cash in 1854 when she received $23.50 per person, for a total of $164.50 in annuities for herself and six children, as members of Šákpe's band of Bdewákhaŋthuŋwaŋ Dakota.[41] Under the 1837 treaty with the Dakota, the family received a share of the $110,000 that the treaty set aside explicitly for Dakota people of mixed ancestry. In 1838, the couple received $500 for their firstborn son, two-year-old Baptiste Trudell, who probably passed away soon after, considering he does not appear in subsequent documents. As the head of household, Trudell gained control of the $500, which was intended for his mixed-ancestry son. In the 1830s, $500 was the equivalent of two to three years' wages for the average American laborer and represented a substantial sum of money. The family received $500 simply because Baptiste was of mixed ancestry and held a kinship connection to the Dakota; in essence, Baptiste's mixed ancestry and kinship status held monetary value, which allowed the family to receive a large windfall of money.

The Trudell family's economic experiences were similar to many other mixed-ancestry Dakota families. The Trudells engaged in the American wage-based labor economy and the Dakota reciprocity- and kinship-based economy. Like other mixed-ancestry families in the Midwest, they found that their status as mixed-ancestry Indians and their kinship connections to the Dakota people held monetary value—an important source of funds that other Indians did not have access to.

The kinship that had evolved between white traders and Dakota people was evident in the 1837 Treaty of Washington, which set aside money for the offspring of intermarriages between the Dakota and white people. A Dakota delegation of twenty-six chiefs and headmen, accompanied by nine of their mixed-ancestry relatives, arrived in Washington, D.C., on September 15, 1837, to negotiate a treaty. The treaty set aside $110,000 to be divided among the Dakota of mixed ancestry "having not less than one quarter of Sioux blood."[42] In exchange for the tribe's five million acres of land east of the Mississippi River, the treaty also offered money to the remainder of the tribe, but this primarily came in the form of the payment of debts, goods, services, and small cash payments spread over twenty years. The 1837 Treaty of Washington marked the convergence of the Dakota economic system centered on kinship and reciprocity and the American capitalist economy, with the mixed-ancestry Dakota at the center. As evidenced by this and other treaties with similar provisions of money for mixed-ancestry Indians, mixed-ancestry status held monetary value. Mixed-ancestry Indians regularly engaged in both economies and acted as a bridge between the two; at the same time, the economies gradually became more fluid. Mixed-ancestry Indians often availed themselves of their kinship connections to make a living, occasionally exploited American wage labor, but held additional economic benefits, because of their mixed racial and legal status, that other Indians did not have.

The Dakota principle of being a good relative played out in multiple ways in the 1837 Treaty of Washington. First, the chiefs were fulfilling their kinship obligations by demanding $110,000 be disbursed among their mixed-ancestry relatives. Second, the chiefs delineated the value of individual mixed-ancestry Indians by giving them different amounts based on their perceived record of being a good relative, primarily determined by their residence on tribal land and their rank in the fur trade. Finally, three mixed-ancestry women—Margaret Campbell, Pelagie Faribault, and Pelagie LaChapelle—each requested $1,500 from the tribe in a separate provision in the treaty meant to cover the tribe's debts. These women felt the tribe was indebted to them for the extensive kinship services they performed, such as providing meals, caring for the sick, and burying the dead.

By the time of the 1837 treaty, many mixed-ancestry Dakota had been involved in the local fur trade and the American economy for generations, while still participating in the reciprocity-based Dakota economy. William Davenport claimed in 1838 that "the half Breeds & others who have settled about Fort Snelling with a very trifling exception, are all in the employment of the Traders. This place is a sort of depot for their families, while the men are out on the trading expeditions."[43] Claiming that four hundred to five hundred mixed-ancestry Indians lived near Fort Snelling, Alfred Brunson wrote, "Of the mixed bloods I found nine out of ten are mere voyageurs & laborers, & derive but a scanty hard earned living."[44] Despite Brunson's claim that most mixed-ancestry Indians earned a hard living, some Indians of mixed ancestry grew wealthy in the Indian trade, served in political offices, or worked other important jobs in early Minnesota. Several Dakota men worked on riverboats on the Mississippi; Frank Trudell gave testimony that he met the mixed-ancestry Dakota Joseph Young in 1866 "on a Steamboat on the Mississippi River on which he [Young] was acting as pilot."[45] Whether they were laborers in the Indian trade or made a living in some other manner, unlike their full-ancestry relatives, most mixed-ancestry Dakota performed wage labor, earned wages, and participated in the American economy.

Federal Indian Policy and Payments to Mixed-Ancestry Indians

The payment of $110,000 to the mixed-ancestry Dakota was representative of a shift in federal Indian policy away from setting aside land to cash payments for mixed-ancestry Indians. The earlier federal assimilation policy posited that putting land in the hands of Indians of mixed ancestry would more quickly assimilate them, and in turn mixed-ancestry Indians would be an assimilative influence on their full-ancestry relatives. A shift in policy came in the wake of the passage of the Indian Removal Act of 1830, in which the federal government forcibly removed Indians from their homes and placed them on lands west of the Mississippi River. Given this, it is not surprising that the federal government no longer wanted to set aside land for mixed-ancestry Indians. Since the federal government was more concerned with removing Indians from land rather than securing land for them, when tribal leaders asked for that land to be set aside for their mixed-ancestry relatives, the federal government now offered them cash payments instead.

Government officials argued that this was a continuation of the assimilation policy; previous treaties set aside land for mixed-ancestry Indians, and the money distributed in subsequent treaties would allow them to develop their lands. The federal government was particularly interested in providing cash payments to mixed-ancestry Indians in 1836 and 1837, with six treaties offering funds to mixed-ancestry Indians in the Midwest. The Indian agent to the Dakota and Ojibwe at Saint Peters Agency, Lawrence Taliaferro, argued in 1837 that payments to mixed-ancestry Indians was crucial: "If ever we shall accomplish anything of a beneficial tendency in regards to the Indian tribes we shall in all time to come have to approach them through the medium of their connections properly supported and rewarded—our loss will be nothing, our gain beyond all calculation."[46] Taliaferro not only believed that tribes wanted to provide for their mixed-ancestry relatives but also asserted that in doing so, through the influence that mixed-ancestry Indians had within their tribes, the payments to mixed-ancestry Indians would cause them to use that influence to the federal government's gain.

Although a handful of treaties provided money for mixed-ancestry Indians in the 1840s and 1850s, American officials understood by the early 1840s that the money-based assimilation policy had failed. Some American officials argued that because many mixed-ancestry Indians squandered their money or had been cheated out of it and few had used the money to improve lands, the payments to mixed-ancestry Indians were a waste of money and had not aided the government's assimilation efforts. Alfred Brunson, while an Indian agent at La Pointe, carried on an extensive correspondence with various American officials in the Midwest over the lack of separate payments to mixed-ancestry Indians in the 1842 treaty with the Ojibwe. Brunson feared violence might ensue if the demands of the mixed-ancestry Indians were not met. He claimed that "the commissioner was prohibited from allowing anything to the half breeds or relatives of the Indians, in the way of remuneration for their lands. This was displeasing to the Indians, & highly offensive to their relatives." Brunson argued further, "The claim of half breeds to indemnity for their lands is based upon identically the same ground as that of the Indians or whole bloods: that is, of blood, birth upon & occupancy of the soil."[47] Brunson tried to convince the Office of Indian Affairs that mixed-ancestry Indians were also owners of the land and that when tribes ceded lands, the mixed-ancestry members of the tribe also deserved compensation.

Superintendent of Indian Affairs Robert Stuart disagreed with Brunson, arguing that the policy of providing cash payments to mixed-ancestry Indians had failed: "Large sums of money have been allowed them under different treaties, and not one in ten is this day the better for it; but many have thereby been rendered worthless; of this the Government have for some time been aware, and are determined to put a stop to the system. But the half breeds have so long been accustomed to receive these gratuities, that they look upon them now as their positive right."[48] Stuart explained further, "The Govt. has for the last ten or twelve years (out of an over flowing treasury) made large donations to half-breeds in nearly all the Indian treaties, so that these precedents have now acquired almost the force of law." Stuart characterized payments as "gratuities" or "donations," yet many mixed- and full-ancestry Indians perceived them as recompense for land cessions. He said Brunson should have told the Indians "that the policy of the Govt was now changed in regard to making donations to half breeds."[49] Indeed, after this time American officials rarely spoke of money as a tool of assimilation.

Like Brunson, however, tribal chiefs felt that their mixed-ancestry relatives should receive payments in treaties. The Ojibwe Chief Buffalo said in 1843, "I shall now say a few words to you in regard to my half breeds. They grow from my soil. My blood flows in their veins. I pity them, for in this treaty nothing is given them. My grandfather gives them nothing—my heart aches on their account."[50] Chief Martin of the Lac Courte Oreilles Ojibwe made a similar point and argued that the government should make separate payments to the mixed-ancestry Indians, not the tribe: "Our half breeds must be paid if we give up our own pay. But our grandfather can better afford to pay them than we can. He is rich & has plenty of money."[51]

Treaties with Midwestern Indians in the 1830s attest to this desire of tribal leaders to provide their mixed-ancestry relatives with cash payments. Article 6 of a treaty with the Odawa and Ojibwe in 1836 stated: "The said Indians being desirous of making provision for their half-breed relatives, and the President having determined, that individual reservation shall not be granted, it is agreed, than in lieu thereof" the government would provide the mixed-ancestry members of the tribes with $150,000.[52] This treaty revealed that like the Dakota, the Ojibwe placed monetary value on the fulfillment of kinship obligations by their mixed-ancestry relatives based on how well they had fulfilled those obligations. The treaty continued that a census of eligible claimants would be made, and "as the Indians hold in higher consideration, some of their half-breeds than others," the chiefs would designate three classes of claimants, each class to receive a different amount.[53] Article 2 of a similar treaty with the Menominee the same year claimed that the "Indians are desirous of making some provision and allowance to their relatives and friends of mixed blood." The Menominee and the United States agreed to pay their mixed-ancestry relatives $80,000, but it would be divided among them at the direction of the chiefs.[54]

The American policy of providing cash payments to mixed-ancestry Indians for assimilative purposes was short-lived because of its perceived failure, but it demonstrates how during this mixed-blood history Indians placed monetary value on mixed-ancestry status and mixed-ancestry kinship obligations, and American officials used cash payments to exploit the influence of mixed-ancestry Indians.

Mixed-Ancestry Indians and the Dakota Delegation to Washington

The federal government invited delegations from several Midwestern tribes to Washington, D.C., in 1837 to negotiate land cessions and to awe the tribes with American culture, technology, and power. The Dakota delegation, composed of twenty-six chiefs and at least nine mixed-ancestry members of the tribe, began their trip on a steamboat heading south on the Mississippi then east on the Ohio River to Pittsburgh. In an attempt to demonstrate the grandeur of American society, officials then escorted the delegation by train to Boston, New York, Philadelphia, and Baltimore, completing the final leg of the journey by sea. The Dakota delegation arrived in Washington, D.C., on September 15, 1837, where they stayed at the Globe Hotel on Pennsylvania Avenue. They stayed for nearly a month, finally leaving Washington on October 9 and arriving home about a month later.[55]

The negotiations began on September 21 at Rev. Dr. James Laurie's Presbyterian church on New York Avenue, where the negotiations culminated with the treaty's signing on September 29.[56] Each day the session started with the Dakota passing a pipe. Chauncey Bush, secretary to the commissioner of Indian Affairs, kept a journal of the proceedings; each day he wrote that the chiefs were "accompanied by their Interpreters and half breeds," who were an influential part of the delegation. Nearly all the mixed-ancestry men worked for the American Fur Company and were likely representing the interests of the company in addition to their own interests. Scott Campbell, Indian agent Taliaferro's interpreter at Saint Peters Agency, was also present, acting as the primary interpreter for the tribe in the treaty negotiations. As their voices are not recorded in the council minutes, it is not possible to ascertain to what degree the mixed-ancestry Indians influenced the chiefs, but their influence was probably significant.[57] Of the mixed-ancestry Indians present, only Scott Campbell's name appears on the treaty, signing as the interpreter for the tribe. Certainly, these men accompanied the delegation to secure their own interests, which were intertwined with those of the American Fur Company. Yet they were an important part of the delegation, acting as additional interpreters and councillors for the chiefs. According to Taliaferro, "some of the blood relations of the tribes" accompanied the delegation "at the special request of the Indians themselves." Taliaferro continued that "the government will find it advisable to notice in an equal manner all those of the half blood, & other connections of the Sioux."[58] The mixed-ancestry Dakota were not simply hangers-on or solely individuals selfishly looking after their own interests; as Taliaferro notes, they were an important segment of the delegation that came at the request of their chiefs, and, as Taliaferro asserts, they were equal members of the delegation. Indeed, the Dakota delegation of chiefs sent a communication to the American negotiators that they wanted a treaty that "will satisfy our brothers at home, our wives and our children, and our relations of mixed blood," demonstrating that they saw Dakota people of mixed ancestry as their relatives and as part of the tribe.[59]

The Dakota and the U.S. government negotiated a cession of all Dakota land east of the Mississippi River. The Dakota asked for $1.6 million for the five million acres they owned east of the Mississippi, but when the government countered with $1 million on September 25 and refused to go higher, the delegation reluctantly agreed to accept $1 million for their land. At the September 25 council, Bush recorded the government's offer and set out a plan for how the $1 million would be paid.[60] The Chief He That Comes Last simply responded that they wanted to talk it over among themselves. Two days later, the delegation responded with its own design on how the money should be divided.[61]

The chiefs made several major changes to the government's proposal, including changes that would prove favorable to the mixed-ancestry Dakota.[62] On day six of the council, Chief Waŋbdí Phá (Eagle Head) told the commission, "It is the wish of the Chiefs and braves now here that our relations should receive $110,000" instead of the proposed $100,000. The chiefs also wished an additional $20,000 to pay debts, most of which would go to traders of the American Fur Company. Indeed, at least four of the nine mixed-ancestry Indians in Washington received payments for debts, including Augustin Rock, Scott Campbell, Alexander Faribault, and Alexis Bailly. Many of their relatives would also make claims that the tribe was indebted to them. Scott Campbell's wife Margaret and brother Duncan made claims for payments, as did Alexander Faribault's father, mother, and brother-in-law.[63] The final change was a proposed payment to Scott Campbell of twenty annual payments of $450, totaling $9,000. The mixed-ancestry Dakota pushed for these provisions on their own behalf, to benefit their relatives, and to benefit their employer, the American Fur Company.[64] There is no record of the internal debate among the tribe concerning how the $1 million would be paid, and it is impossible to ascertain the level of pressure that the mixed-ancestry Dakota applied to their full-ancestry relatives in Washington. They unquestionably exerted some pressure, but their full-ancestry relatives wanted to provide for their mixed-ancestry relatives; this was part of their desire to be a good relative.

American negotiators accepted all of the tribe's counterproposals except the payment to Scott Campbell. The Senate struck this provision from the treaty and ratified it without it. Campbell never received the money, and the tribe only received $991,000 instead of the agreed-upon $1 million. The Dakota proposed to pay Campbell "in consideration of valuable services rendered by him to the Sioux."[65] The valuable services Campbell rendered were as an interpreter at Saint Peter's Agency under agent Lawrence Taliaferro since 1822. Taliaferro called him "a man of great worth and efficiency, a true friend of the Americans," revealing how Campbell was valued both by his tribe and American officials.[66] In essence, the tribe agreed to pay Campbell this money because his "valuable services" demonstrated that Campbell had been a good relative and that he had observed his kinship obligations exceedingly well. Campbell probably used his important position as interpreter to ask for this money, but considering the tribe agreed to it, they must have acknowledged that the way he carried out his kinship obligations deserved monetary compensation.

Earlier that year, when asked if the Dakota would like to receive their annuities under the 1830 Treaty of Prairie du Chien in money or goods, the chiefs responded, "We all prefer goods decidedly as we know not the use of money."[67] However, they probably knew more about money than they let on. Because of the exorbitant prices for goods in cash or furs demanded by the traders, acquiring goods directly from the government meant that they would receive more provisions for the same price. The Dakota increased the investment in stocks from $200,000 to $300,000. The Dakota were to receive an annual income, forever, of a minimum of 5 percent on this investment. The treaty permitted the president to direct one-third of the usage of this income as he saw fit, but "the residue [was] to be paid in specie, or in such other manner, and for such objects, as the proper authorities of the tribe may designate."[68] Under this provision, the chiefs could elect to receive the remaining two-thirds of this income in goods. This was a savvy move on their part. The money for the increase of this provision came from the section on goods, originally set at $360,000, to which they decreased to $200,000. This section was limited to payments in goods split over twenty years; by moving much of this money to the investment in stocks, it ensured they would receive a greater amount of goods in perpetuity rather than for simply twenty years. Additionally, they increased the section on provisions by $40,000 and added an additional $6,000 in goods that they would receive on their way home. This last provision would allow the chiefs to give their relatives gifts upon their return and help smooth over any ill feelings about the treaty.

Most of the terms of the 1837 treaty ensured that the Dakota would receive goods and services rather than money, but despite their contestations to the contrary, the treaty reveals that they had some proficiency with the use of cash. When they did receive cash payments, the chiefs demanded that they be paid in small denominations—only in silver dollars and half dollars and not in gold coin. This would make it easier for the tribe to disseminate cash payments and to pay traders in exact change.[69] The importance of silver as currency became the Dakota definition for "money." The Dakota word "mázaska," which translates to "white metal," is used to mean "money," "dollar," and "silver." Full-ancestry Indians probably became acquainted with the uses of money through their mixed-ancestry relatives who regularly engaged in the American cash economy. Lucius Lyon wrote of the mixed-ancestry Ojibwe who also received payments in a treaty with their tribe in 1837 that "they are nearly all the descendants of traders, in the country, and are well acquainted with the value of money and its uses."[70] Despite the chiefs proclaiming that they "know not the use of money," the final treaty provisions reveal a monetary adroitness, possibly the influence of the mixed-ancestry Dakota present. Mixed-ancestry Indians acted as a kind of conduit between Native and American economies; at the same time, mixed-ancestry Indians, through their knowledge of both economies, received monetary benefits by acting as this conduit.

Distribution of the "Half-Breed" Money

Commissioner of Indian Affairs Carey A. Harris appointed Judge Lorrain T. Pease and General William L. D. Ewing to act as commissioners and go to Fort Snelling to distribute the money to the mixed-ancestry Dakota and pay the rightful debts of the tribe. The commissioners had the task "to pay to the Relatives & friends of the Chiefs and Braves as aforesaid having not less than one quarter of Sioux blood one hundred and ten thousand dollars to be distributed, by the proper authorities of the tribes upon principles to be determined by the Chiefs and Braves."[71] As we will see, the principles determined by the leaders of the tribe were based on how well the mixed-ancestry Dakota had fulfilled, or had the potential to fulfill, their kinship obligations.

These payments to mixed-ancestry Indians were often subject to fraud. A treaty with the Ho-Chunk, also in 1837, offered $100,000 to the mixed-ancestry members of the tribe. With the delay in payment and shady dealings by the commissioners appointed to distribute the money, many of the mixed-ancestry Ho-Chunk became uneasy. The distribution occurred at Prairie du Chien, where mixed-ancestry Ho-Chunk arrived from as far away as Green Bay and Saint Louis to receive their treaty money. As Joseph Montfort Street stated, as agent for the Ho-Chunk, many of the claimants paid up to a dollar a day to stay in Prairie du Chien while they awaited payment. Delays were costly, by design, prompting many of the claimants to sell their shares in the payment at half or even less of the value. However, initial suggestions that the mixed-ancestry Ho-Chunk sell their claims came from Simon Cameron, one of the commissioners delaying the payment.[72]

To disperse the funds for mixed-ancestry Indians, the chiefs had to agree on a list of claimants. Indian agent Lawrence Taliaferro tasked Jean

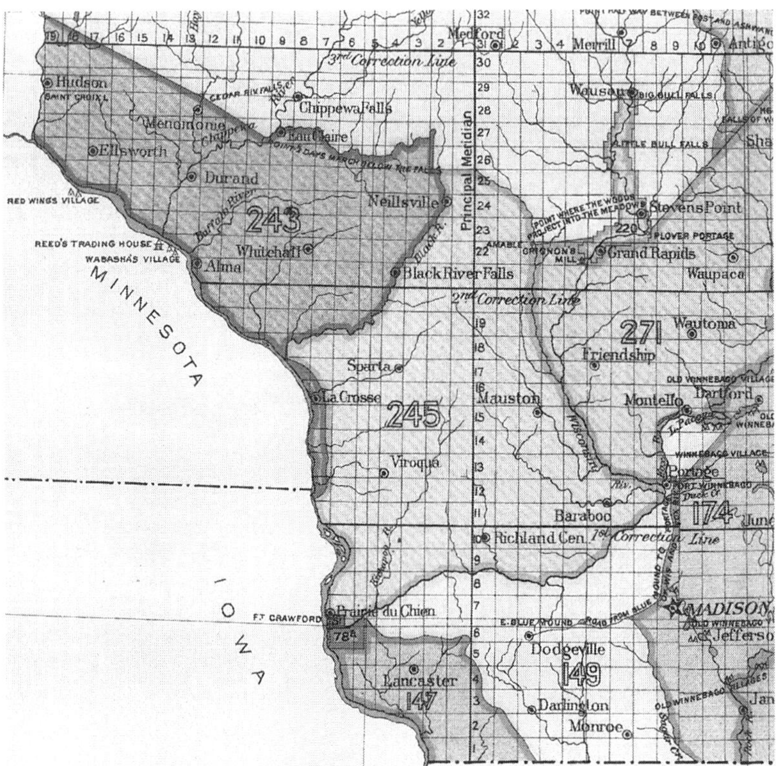

Map 2. Dakota presence in Wisconsin. The Dakota ceded the section marked 243 in the Treaty of Washington in 1837. Notice the settlement of Prairie du Chien in the southwestern part of the state. Charles C. Royce, *Indian Land Cessions in the United States, Eighteenth Annual Report of the Bureau of American Ethnology, 1896–1897, Part 2* (Government Printing Office, 1899).

Baptist Faribault, a white fur trader and patriarch of the large mixed-ancestry Faribault family, with constructing a list of mixed-ancestry Dakota of one-quarter blood quantum or more. By August 17, he had 143 names. On August 26, Chief Wakíŋyaŋ Tháŋka (Big Thunder) told the agent that the list was not well received and gave him twenty more names to add to the list.[73] By September, the commissioners, under the direction of the chiefs, finalized the list. The list contains the age, sex, blood quantum, and residence of two hundred people, although the commissioners rejected thirteen because they resided in Canada or the commissioners determined that they were not Dakota.

The commissioners, at the behest of the chiefs, paid the Dakota of mixed ancestry relative to their perceived usefulness to the tribe or, in other words, paid according to their willingness to fulfill kinship obligations. In distributing the money, the commissioners used four criteria, based "upon principles to be determined by the chiefs and braves signing the Treaty, and the War Department." The first principle stated "that all their relations aforesaid who at the date of said Treaty resided with or near said Indians and who still reside with or near them, with whom they hold frequent intercourse shall each be awarded not less than five hundred dollars." The first principle revealed a preference for those mixed-ancestry Indians with whom the tribe had regular association and who therefore continued to engage in the Dakota kinship-based economy. This was certainly criteria emphasized by the chiefs, who wanted to reward and reciprocate with "their relations" who remained close to the tribe.[74]

The second principle also reflects the wishes of the chiefs: "that their relations aforesaid residing at a distance from said Indians but within the Territorial limits of the United States shall each be awarded a sum less than five hundred dollars." Twelve of the mixed-ancestry Dakota received less than $500. Six lived in Missouri, one lived in Green Bay, Wisconsin, and two lived far to the west at Fort Pierre on the Missouri River in Lakota country, in the center of present-day South Dakota. All of these received $400. Because they lived far away from the Dakota, they were unable to participate in the reciprocal obligations of the Dakota kinship economy. Therefore, the chiefs valued them lower than they did their relatives who resided among them. But the chiefs still felt their own kinship obligations to these relatives, providing them with $400. Three others, all members of the Hurtibise family, received smaller sums despite residing in Red Wing's village in 1838. It is possible they received smaller sums because of their relation to the Ojibwe. Pierre Hurtibise Sr., born in 1801, received $400, while his two children, Pierre Jr. and Theresa, received only $250, the lowest-paid of the claimants. Pierre Sr. had married an Ojibwe woman and the children had more Ojibwe ancestry than Dakota. Because of ill feeling toward the Ojibwe at the time, the chiefs may have awarded them a reduced sum.[75]

Commissioners Pease and Ewing demanded a third principle: excluding those residing in British Canada. The commissioners struck six of the seven mixed-ancestry members of the Bourke family from the list because they had all been born in the Red River Colony, north of the U.S. border. The entire family continued to live on the British side of the border. Only their mother, Nancy Campbell Bourke, received payment. Despite living away from the tribe, she received $500. As far as the Dakota were concerned, the international border between British Canada and the United States meant little. The Dakota put them on the list because they perceived them as relatives; it did not matter that they lived across a colonially imposed border. Similarly, the commissioners disallowed four members of the Rock family, who also lived at Red River.[76]

The intent of the chiefs is best exemplified in the final principle. They awarded the remaining funds "to such persons among them, as by themselves or their friends of the mixed or white blood have rendered to said Indians extraordinary services or supplies and who are in a condition to continue to afford such services or supplies in the future. And in proportion to the extent of such services and supplies, no one person to be awarded a sum exceeding fifteen hundred dollars." All the mixed-ancestry Dakota who lived among them received $500, but some received additional sums because they had shared services and supplies to their full-ancestry relatives. Additionally, the chiefs wanted to continue this reciprocal relationship, awarding money to those who could continue to provide for them in the future. An important distinction here reveals the importance of kinship connections to Euro-American traders. Many of the recipients of these sums obtained money because of their own actions, but others received funds from the tribe because of the importance of their white relatives in the Dakota kinship economy.[77]

Of the thirty-one individuals who received more than $500, all were, or had connections to, prominent people in the Dakota world. Of the eleven recipients who received the maximum of $1,500, five were men prominent in the fur trade, one was Scott Campbell, the Dakota interpreter, and the remaining five recipients were women married to prominent men. Many of these women were well-respected members of the Dakota community, and Pelagie LaChapelle had briefly worked as a trader herself, but these women received money primarily because of their kinship connections to prominent non-Dakota men. The Dakota honored these kinship connections but could not award those men money directly because they were not Dakota.[78]

The eight men and women who received $1,000 and the twelve who received $750 accepted funds based on the same principles, except eleven-year-old Mary Taliaferro, a recipient of $750, who was the daughter of Indian agent Lawrence Taliaferro. Nearly all of the thirty-one recipients of funds over $500 were connected to the American Fur Company, and twenty of them came from just seven families, including five from the Faribault family, four from the Campbell family, and three from the Graham family, all prominent fur trade families. The recipients of extra funds were also the wealthiest among the mixed-ancestry Dakota. Through their connection to the American Fur Company, they had acquired nominal wealth, but more importantly, this wealth permitted them to share more goods, earning them prestige among the Dakota. By sharing goods, this had made them good relatives in the eyes of the Dakota, in turn causing the chiefs to reciprocate with the additional funds in the provision of money for the tribe's mixed-ancestry relatives in the 1837 treaty.[79]

The vast majority of the mixed-ancestry Dakota, 144, or 72 percent, received $500, but some extended families made out extremely well. Again, the Campbell and Faribault families received a significant proportion of the $110,000. The members of the extended Campbell family received $15,150, and the large Faribault family received $11,500. These two families alone collected over 24 percent of the total. Other families did not fare nearly so well. The Trudell family collected a total of $500 for their oldest son, Baptiste, born two years before the distribution. But even this amount was the equivalent of two or three years of wages for a common laborer in the 1830s.[80]

The distribution of the $110,000 in the 1837 treaty between the Dakota and the United States illustrates how the clash between the Dakota kinship- and reciprocity-based economy with the American capitalist economy had resulted in the fusion of some elements of both economies.

The Dakota continued to place a premium on kinship and the concept of being a good relative; at the same time, when it came to mixed-ancestry Indians, monetary value became attached to these doctrines. The disbursement of the $110,000 revealed how full-ancestry Indians placed monetary value on the kinship practices of their mixed-ancestry relatives, but another article in the 1837 treaty revealed how some mixed-ancestry Dakota placed a value on their own economic activities in the kinship economy of the Dakota.

Mixed-Ancestry Women and the Payment of Tribal Debts

After distributing the treaty funds to the mixed-ancestry Dakota, commissioners Pease and Ewing then determined and paid the debts of the tribe. The commissioners heard claims from twenty-nine individuals, amounting to over $247,000, but under the treaty, the government would only pay $90,000, meaning they prorated all accepted debts, some going back as far as 1805. The majority of the twenty-nine claimants worked in the fur trade and were hoping to collect debts related to their work. Nine were mixed-ancestry Dakota Indians, and most of the others were mixed-ancestry Indians of other tribes or married to Dakota women. Most significantly, Pelagie LaChapelle, Pelagie Faribault, and Margaret Campbell were the only women to request payment for debts.

All three women hoped to recover $1,500 each for services rendered and provisions given to tribal members. Their attempt to receive compensation was an expression of them placing a monetary value on their kinship practices. Because they went above and beyond in their performance as good relatives, they felt entitled to reciprocal compensation from their people. Linda M. Waggoner argues that kinship ties were "invisibly anchored by wives, mothers, and sisters."[81] These women were kinship anchors in their respective communities; their homes were focal points where visiting Dakota people expected and received hospitality.

They garnered support for their claims and turned over affidavits to the commissioners. Pelagie LaChapelle was the first of the three women to enter a claim. She was born Pelagie LaPointe in 1786, the daughter of a French Canadian fur trader named Pierre LaPointe and a sister of Chief Wápahaša whose name is unknown. Pelagie's first marriage was to a fur trader, Louis Crawford, about 1803; she had three children by this marriage. Crawford abandoned his family, and soon after Pelagie married Antoine LaChapelle. They had a large family of eight children. Pelagie had briefly worked in the fur trade. She was in charge of her own outfit during the winter of 1825–1826, employed by James H. Lockwood.[82] She lived most of her life in Prairie du Chien, her residence at the time of her claim. Through an interpreter she claimed "that since her residence in Prairie du Chien for thirty years she has been in the habit of administering to the wants of the Indians particularly to Wabasha's band who claimed relationship & would call on deponent for relief of their wants, two of whom died at Deponent's house of small pox & that she attended others at their lodges afflicted with small pox, & administered to their wants, and that she conscientiously believes the account rendered to her just and true for the services which she rendered to the Sioux Indians thro a long series of years."[83] In her claim, LaChapelle asserted that Wabasha's band "claimed relationship" to her, recognizing the reciprocal kinship obligations she had with that band. She emphasized that she had provided band members hospitality and that she had nursed many of her kin afflicted with smallpox. LaChapelle made claims for thirty years of fulfilling her kinship obligations to a degree that she felt the tribe was indebted to her. Pelagie Faribault and Margaret Campbell made claims very similar to LaChapelle's.

Born in 1783 to Joseph Ainse and a Dakota woman, Pelagie married Jean Baptiste Faribault in 1805. Like LaChapelle, her husband and father were white fur traders, and she too had a large family. At the time of her claim, she lived with her family at the Saint Peter's Agency, near Fort Snelling. Faribault signed her x-mark to a brief affidavit on September 1, 1838, making claim "for services rendered, care taken of them when sick, clothing given them, provisions given them, feeding them daily &c. &c. &c. for the last 25 years. $1500.00."[84] Her son-in-law Alexis Bailly gave longer testimony on her behalf: "He has known Pelagie Farrebault for nineteen years and has known her to be in the constant practice of rendering services, taking care of, giving Provisions and daily feeding the Indians of the Sioux Nation. . . . She has often to his knowledge covered the dead, which according to the Sioux customs is expensive."[85] Like LaChapelle,

Faribault took care of the sick, provided food and clothing, and, according to Bailly, buried the dead according to Dakota tradition if they died under her care.

Finally, Margaret Campbell, called "Madeline" in her claim, also filed for $1,500 for her services to the tribe. Younger than the other women, Margaret was born in 1799 as Margaret Menager, probably the daughter of Louis Fromm dit Menagre. Campbell was not Dakota by birth; her mother was a Menominee woman. She was married to Scott Campbell, the interpreter at Saint Peter's Agency, by the early 1820s. Like LaChapelle and Faribault, Campbell was the mother of a large family, and twenty-five years later her sons fought on both sides of the U.S.-Dakota War. Hazen Mooers interpreted Campbell's testimony: "Says when she furnished the provisions she did not make a charge, she furnished more provisions in the year 1837 than any other years, she says that she is satisfied during these fifteen years she did furnish at least the amount charged."[86] A Mr. Quin gave more details: "She fed & lodged Indians at her house, has seen from 20 to 30 Indians at a time, at her house, provisions were high & thinks Mrs. Campbell has expended as much as $2000 since wit[ness] knew her."[87] Testifying on her behalf, Taliaferro said he had known her since 1822 when he hired her husband Scott Campbell to be the agency interpreter. He revealed that Campbell showed hospitality and shared goods at the request of Taliaferro, who told her she would be remunerated for her services by the government. He argued further that Campbell deserved money for "losses sustained by Indians in borrowing pans, pots &c. which were never returned."[88] Although she was a Menominee Indian, because she married a Dakota man and lived among them, the tribe considered Campbell to be kin and recognized the same reciprocal kinship obligations that they did with Faribault and LaChapelle. Campbell appealed to the commissioners on the same grounds—that she deserved a monetary award from the tribe for the exceptional fulfillment of her kinship obligations.

All three women performed similar duties, providing food and lodging, taking care of the sick, and burying the dead. But these were not simply services; these women held kinship bonds with the Dakota, and their work was in fulfillment of those kinship obligations. When they fed and lodged their kin, they were good relatives. These women were not simply asking for money; these women tied monetary compensation to their performance of kinship responsibilities.

In all three cases, the commissioners denied their claims because they did not perceive the kinship labor of Indian women as valid economic activity worthy of remuneration. Faribault and LaChapelle had each already received $1,500 under article 2 of the 1837 treaty as mixed-ancestry members of the tribe; the commissioners felt that this was payment enough. In the claim of Pelagie LaChapelle, commissioners Pease and Ewing ruled: "This claim is for charities and kind offices rendered to the Indians through a long series of years during the claimant's intercourse with them. The commissioners are of opinion that such a claim constitutes no legitimate indebtedness against the Indians especially as the claimant is a principal participant in the distribution of the half breed fund. The claim is therefore disallowed."[89]

These women were unusual in American society, which held an explicit gender distinction—men were the sole breadwinners, at least in the social imaginary rather than practice, while the labor that women conducted in the home did not hold monetary value in the eyes of male Americans in the early nineteenth century. Other mixed-ancestry Dakota women went further and petitioned Congress concerning payments from this treaty. Mary Taliaferro Woodbury and Elizabeth Williams Odell petitioned Congress in 1851 and again in 1862 claiming they had never received their payments in full.[90] In addition to her attempt to acquire additional funds under the 1837 treaty, Pelagie Faribault and her family fought for decades to receive land promised her in an unratified 1820 treaty.[91] Women in American society, however, who perceived the devaluation of their work as a form of gender inequality, likely would have sided with women like LaChapelle, Faribault, and Campbell.[92] Mixed-ancestry Dakota women were willing to fight for their rights and used whatever means at their disposal to do so.

The commissioners denied the claims of LaChapelle, Faribault, and Campbell because they did not perceive women's labor as deserving of a wage. To Pelagie Faribault's claim, the commissioners responded, "The claimant is one of the Half Breed relations of the Indians interested in the

Treaty and one of the largest participants in the distribution of the money set apart in the treaty for their use. The claimant has thus been compensated and very suitably compensated for the services charged and her claim is disallowed."[93] Several mixed-ancestry Dakota men received payment for the debts due to them without any mention of the fact that they had already received money as mixed-ancestry Dakota. Faribault's son Alexander received $334, and Campbell's husband Scott and brother-in-law Duncan Campbell both received payments. Francois Labathe received $3,760.30, Augustin Rock $1,444.50, and Joseph Renville Jr. received $699.[94]

Essentially, these three women provided many of the same goods that the mixed-ancestry men provided, the primary difference being that the men had provided goods to their full-ancestry relatives as formal participants in the American economy while the commissioners perceived the labor and goods shared by the women as informal. The failure of the commissioners to compensate the women illustrates the differences in the American and Dakota economies. From the Dakota perspective, both the men and women had been good relatives, performing their kinship obligations at an extraordinary level. Tribal leaders perceived the relationship with these men and women as important kinship connections and were willing to pay their relatives for the mutually beneficial way they engaged in the kinship-based Dakota economy. Americans did not recognize the significance of kinship, simply seeing the business transactions on the books of the mixed-ancestry traders.

In the distribution of the $110,000 and payment of debts allowed in the 1837 treaty, we see the ways that mixed-ancestry status became monetized and how Dakota people perceived the kinship obligations of mixed-ancestry Indians as holding monetary value. The mixed-ancestry Dakota received money simply because of their mixed race, but they also received money because they were a channel between the American and Dakota economic systems. As the Dakota economy increasingly merged with the American wage-based economy, the Dakota began incorporating the American monetary system into their economic practices. The mixed-ancestry Dakota were at the center and were the driving force of this fusion.

This idea of placing monetary value on the kinship practices of mixed-ancestry Dakota people was not a one-off. Two decades later, article 6 of

Figure 9. Three Iháŋkthuŋwaŋ Dakota men: Chief Phadáni Aphápi, 1804–1888; Charles Felix Picotte, 1829–1896; and Chief Mathȟó Sabʼíčʼiye, circa 1790–1865. Chief Phadáni Aphápi was the half brother of Paul Dorion. Charles Picotte served as sergeant-at-arms in the Dakota Territorial legislature. All three men signed the 1858 Yankton treaty as chiefs. Edward E. Ayer Digital Collection, Newberry Library, Chicago.

a treaty with the Iháŋkthuŋwaŋ Dakota offered $150,000 to pay the tribe's debts and to "provide for such of their half-breed relations as do not live with them" on the Yankton Reservation.[95] The chiefs decided that $107,000 of this money would go to their mixed-ancestry relatives.[96] Rather than a lump sum, the Iháŋkthuŋwaŋ chiefs gave annual payments to their mixed-ancestry relatives, again in different amounts based on how they had fulfilled their kinship obligations. In deliberating on specific amounts, Chief Phadáni Aphápi (better known as Struck by the Ree) referred to several people: "Alexie Guion and Cardinal have been liberal to us—we will look out for them. Bruguier and Traversie have saved many of our lives, they gave us much when we were in want. Rulo also was our friend and assisted us." Phadáni Aphápi did not see all mixed-ancestry Dakota as fulfilling their obligations: "We have a great many worthless half breed relations," he claimed, "and one of them is my brother," referring to his half brother, my ancestor Paul Dorion. Despite this, Dorion and four of his children each received $170 per year under the treaty. In contrast, each of the eleven Bruguier children received $2,550 per year, largely for the help their white father had given the people.[97]

Being an Indian of mixed ancestry in the Upper Midwest in the nineteenth century could mean acquiring cash because of their mixed racial status. Through this process, mixed racial status held monetary value. For white men like Theophilus Bruguier, who received money for his eleven mixed-ancestry children, this was a form of racial capitalism that allowed white men to make money off the race of their children. For Indians of full ancestry, they saw the payments as a fulfillment of their kinship obligations but distributed funds based on their ideas of how well their mixed-ancestry relatives had fulfilled their own kinship obligations.

CHAPTER 4

An Unintended Nation

The Mixed-Ancestry Dakota Treaties, 1838–1849

Theophilus LaChapelle added his signature to a treaty on August 27, 1841, alongside the names of twenty-three other Dakota Indian residents of the village of Prairie du Chien, Wisconsin Territory. The treaty had been negotiated a month earlier, July 31, at Traverse des Sioux, Iowa Territory, modern-day Minnesota, between the United States and "the half breeds of the Dakota or Sioux nation."[1] The treaty commissioners collected additional signatures at Mendota and Lake Pepin, and after the signing at Prairie du Chien, the treaty contained the names of nearly 120 mixed-ancestry Dakota people, signed in their own right or by a relative or guardian on their behalf. A citizen of the Dakota Nation, LaChapelle also belonged to the American nation. The voters of Saint Croix and Crawford Counties elected him to represent them in the Wisconsin Territorial Legislature in 1840, although he was not seated until 1842, given the disputed nature of the contest. How could a citizen of the Dakota Nation sign a treaty with the U.S. government when he was also a citizen of the United States? Treaties are nation-to-nation agreements, and a government cannot make a treaty with its own citizens. LaChapelle was caught between and intertwined with two nations. Indeed, Indians are members of sovereign nations, not simply racial or ethnic minorities.[2] However, the United States negotiated this treaty directly with the "half-breeds" of the Dakota Nation, who, as we saw in chapter 2, held a legal status as something apart from Indians, leaving LaChapelle a potential subject of a third possible nation, one made up solely of mixed-ancestry Dakota Indians.

As the United States continued to press into the territory of the Dakota Nation, Americans sought to exert control over Dakota land and people. Indians of mixed ancestry were a natural target of assimilation into the American nation, considering many of them saw the benefits of playing both sides of the fence. Yet, there might have been a third side to this fence. The 1841 treaty and another with the mixed-ancestry Dakota negotiated in 1849 would have had the consequence of solidifying the nationhood status of the mixed-ancestry Dakota through a nation-to-nation treaty relationship with the United States, had the Senate ratified either treaty. The Senate refused to ratify an 1838 treaty with the various tribal nations interested in the mixed-ancestry reservation at Great Nemaha in southeastern Nebraska on the grounds that the treaty did not have the consent of the mixed-ancestry owners. Although unratified, the two treaties conducted directly with mixed-ancestry Dakota in the 1840s contributed to a sense of mixed-ancestry nationhood. There is no evidence that any of them saw themselves as belonging to a separate mixed-ancestry nation, nor did white American officials perceive mixed-ancestry Indians as holding nationhood status, but, if ratified, because only nations have treaty-making power, these treaties would have had the consequence of creating a mixed-ancestry Dakota Nation with a treaty relationship with the United States. Over the course of the 1840s and 1850s, the mixed-ancestry Dakota had become active in politics in Wisconsin Territory and Minnesota Territory. As we will see in chapter 5, they participated in the American nation as citizens and public servants. At the same time, they retained their Dakota kinship connections and sense of Dakotaness. There was never a conscious effort on the part of the mixed-ancestry Dakota to create a separate nation; this was an unusual case in which a treaty would have created a sovereign nation out of a people who did not perceive themselves as such.

This situation gets to the methods and structures of recognition and nation creation in U.S.–Indian relations. Indigenous nations within the United States are not created by the federal government, nor is federal recognition necessary for an Indigenous group to identify as an Indian nation or polity. In this case, because "half-breeds" had been accorded a separate, albeit indistinct, legal and racial status, government officials were willing to experiment with treaties with the mixed-ancestry Dakota. In the process, the federal government nearly established an unintended nation, one with a nation-to-nation relationship with the federal government, possessing treaty-making power. Despite the Senate's failure to ratify these treaties, I argue that they reflect how in this moment, mixed-ancestry Dakota Indians occupied a revolutionary position in American Indian law, one in which the federal government was willing to entertain the possibility of mixed-ancestry nationhood that could have had major repercussions in U.S.–Indian relations. Indeed, other mixed-race Indigenous communities could have used this precedent to assert their own sovereignty. Moreover, these treaties provided a moment of reflection for the mixed-ancestry community to consider notions of race, mixedness, and nationhood. In these treaties, the mixed-ancestry Dakota themselves, using categories of blood quantum, race, residence, and acculturation, contemplated who fit this classification, which gives us a glimpse into mixed-ancestry perspectives on race and belonging.

The 1841 and 1849 treaties were parts of larger negotiations with the Dakota, which had much broader implications for the Dakota Nation, and in 1841, broader implications for all Indian nations in the United States. The mixed-ancestry Dakota treaty of 1841 was one of three treaties signed by the Dakota that summer that together would have created a radical shift in federal Indian policy, as well as a new Indian Territory in the northwest, to which the government would remove northern Indians. An Indian Territory, or Indian Country, was created as a concept by American officials as a place of removal, yet the concept was rather short-lived, as settlers soon invaded Indian Country within a generation.[3] These treaties also provided a relatively quick and simple pathway to U.S. citizenship and had provisions for a territorial government to incorporate the residents of this new Indian Territory into the American settler colonial nation. The 1849 treaty was also part of larger negotiations with the Dakota, but officials found that, because of the federal government's failure to follow through with stipulations in the 1837 treaty, only the mixed-ancestry Dakota were willing to treat with the federal government. Although for different purposes, the 1841 and 1849 mixed-ancestry Dakota treaties were land cession treaties meant to acquire the mixed-ancestry reservation at Lake Pepin, founded in 1830 by the Treaty of Prairie du Chien.

Federal Indian law scholar David E. Wilkins defines a "nation" as "a social group which share a common ideology, common institutions and customs, and a sense of homogeneity; controls a territory viewed as a national homeland; and has a belief in common ancestry." Wilkins continues that nationhood also requires a belief "that one's group is unique," therefore a "nation is not tangible but psychological, a matter of attitude rather than of fact."[4] Edward H. Spicer adds that "a people's boundaries" could be fluid and shift and change over time.[5] Métis scholar Chris Andersen cautions that nationhood is different from racialization and that Indigenous nations do not fit modern notions of state building. As today, nineteenth-century American officials typically perceived Indians as members of a racialized group, a "problem" that needed to be solved, and only reluctantly as sovereign nations with which the U.S. government was on an equal footing.[6] The Dakota term "oyáte" is translated as "nation" or "a people," and they recognized separate Indigenous and European nationalities. But for the Dakota, the concept of nationhood is more expansive to include the animal world, so they might speak of the "waŋbdí oyáte" (the eagle people) or the "thatháŋka oyáte" (the buffalo nation).

Common understandings of nationhood are Eurocentric, and Indigenous nations often defy those understandings.[7] Ella Cara Deloria argues that members of the Očhéthi Šakówiŋ or the Seven Council Fires see themselves as a single people but notes that "'nation' is not the most apt designation," as divisions of the people acted as nations in their own right and they maintained some cultural and linguistic distinctiveness, while occupying separate lands.[8] The Očhéthi Šakówiŋ never had a central government, and its seven constituent "tribes," for lack of a better term, also operated as nations. In turn bands or other subdivisions of those tribes sometimes acted as nations too. The various divisions of the Očhéthi Šakówiŋ held the authority to make war or alliances, carry out diplomacy, or negotiate treaties as they saw fit, essentially each acting as a nation.[9] But two or more of these divisions could band together at any time for military, trade, or diplomatic purposes. The smallest political division was the thiyóšpaye, an extended family or village community with its own chief. Euro-American observers perceived Očhéthi Šakówiŋ political structures as simplistic and ineffective. While government was decentralized, this was deliberate to allow smaller units to make important decisions for themselves. When the need arose, different divisions might unite to elect temporary chiefs or decision-makers; otherwise, small autonomous bands or villages relied on careful deliberation and consensus and placed importance on good oratory and kinship responsibilities. This system confused American officials and often served to thwart American attempts to take advantage of individual leaders.[10]

A common myth about Native Americans is that they historically had no concept of landownership and that, therefore, Indigenous understandings of nationhood were not rooted in bounded spaces with specific borders.[11] Philander Prescott debunked this in 1853, writing that the Dakota say that "they believe the Great Spirit gave them their land, and that no other nation has a right to hunt" on their land and that "each nation should stay within their hunting boundaries."[12] For the Dakota, understandings of nationhood were tied to kinship, land, a common ethnic and cultural identity, and the will to act politically as a nation, either collectively or in smaller groups as necessity dictated.

The 1838 Treaty and Mixed-Ancestry Sovereignty

At Bellevue in modern-day Nebraska, members of the Omaha, Ioway, and Otoe tribes met, "for themselves and in behalf of the half-breeds of their respective tribes or nations," with American officials to negotiate a treaty on May 5, 1838. The Dakota chiefs of the Iháŋkthuŋwaŋ and Isáŋyati (a collective term for the four eastern Dakota groups) tribes were not present, but they consented to be included in all provisions of the treaty on October 31. The Senate refused to ratify the treaty.[13] Government officials argued that the chiefs did not have the authority to cede the land on behalf of the mixed-ancestry members of their tribes, asserting that they could only ratify the treaty with the consent of the mixed-ancestry Indians, essentially arguing that any treaty for the cession of the Great Nemaha Reservation needed to be negotiated directly with the Indians of mixed ancestry.[14]

The treaty contained four articles for the purpose of ceding the Great Nemaha Reservation to the federal government in exchange for cash payments to the mixed-ancestry members of the tribes.[15] Article 1 stated that the chiefs and headmen were "desirous to relieve the distress of their respective half-breeds, many of whom are orphans and totally destitute of the necessaries of life." The article went on to express that the chiefs felt that the reservation "has not, and never will afford that aid and relief to the said half breeds which was intended" when the Treaty of Prairie du Chien created it in 1830. Therefore, the tribal leaders agreed to cede the land to the federal government in exchange for payments to the mixed-ancestry claimants.[16]

Article 1 stated that the chiefs ceded "all our right or interest, and also the right or interest of the said half breeds in the above mentioned reservation." When the Dakota signed the treaty on October 31, the treaty noted, "The undersigned chiefs, headmen, and half breeds for their tribe and on behalf of the other half breeds thereof" agreed to all articles in the treaty. In these statements, the chiefs signed on behalf of the mixed-ancestry Indians of their tribes, confirming that they were full members of their respective tribal nations. In article 2, the federal government agreed to survey the land to determine the number of acres and pay the mixed-ancestry Indians one dollar per acre. Instead of paying the mixed-ancestry Indians directly, the government would invest these funds and pay out an annual income of no less than 5 percent of the investment, to be distributed equally during the lifetime of all eligible mixed-ancestry Indians born before the signing of the Treaty of Prairie du Chien on July 15, 1830. Those who wished to could withdraw their entire share from the investment only if the government found them competent to manage their money. Finally, the government would hire a commissioner to determine the number and names of eligible claimants. Articles 3 and 4 simply stated that the "Yancton and Santie bands of Sioux" would be bound by the treaty if they agreed to sign it and that the treaty would be fully binding if the Senate agreed to ratification.[17]

The momentum for this treaty came two years earlier. Concerned about their mixed-ancestry relatives' land on the Great Nemaha Reservation, four chiefs from four different tribes, including Wakšíčana (Little Dish) of the Iháŋkthuŋwaŋ, wrote a letter to William Clark in 1836. They expressed their exasperation that the government had not yet surveyed the lands, explaining, "Many of those persons are now growing up and anxious to settle upon those lands; but are at the same time unwilling to attempt any improvement without some guarantee that they will be permitted to hold them." The chiefs asked that the federal government solve the problem as soon as possible.[18] The mixed-ancestry Indians feared the uncertainty of common ownership of the Great Nemaha Reservation; in this case, the chiefs pressed the claims of their mixed-ancestry relatives like they did later in the 1838 treaty.

Of the signatories to the 1838 treaty, only two were of mixed-ancestry: Joseph Brazeau Jr. and Baptiste Brazeau, both Iháŋkthuŋwaŋ Dakota. Agent John Dougherty of the Council Bluffs subagency expressed his thoughts that as the owners of the reservation, the treaty should have been made with the mixed-ancestry Indians: "It appears to me that the real parties in interest have had no part in making this treaty, except the two Sioux." Dougherty continued that the mixed-ancestry Indians' "full and voluntary assent thereto" needed to be obtained: "It follows that the treaty in its present form is not entitled to the ratification of the President and Senate; but it might be confirmed on the condition that the half-breeds shall give their assent thereto. This, it is supposed they will readily do, as the provisions appear to be favorable to their future comfort and interests."[19] Even President Martin Van Buren, when forwarding the treaty to the Senate, agreed that the treaty needed the consent of the mixed-ancestry Indians.[20]

By refusing to ratify the treaty because of the lack of consent of the mixed-ancestry Indians, the federal government denied that the chiefs of these tribes had full authority over their mixed-ancestry relatives. When the federal government made other land cession treaties in this period, they only sought the consent of tribal leaders, not individual Indians. American officials argued that it was the mixed-ancestry Dakota that held sovereignty over the Great Nemaha Reservation, not the tribes. In so doing, the government inadvertently expressed the national sovereignty of mixed-ancestry Indians and declined to ratify the treaty to uphold that national sovereignty. Agent Dougherty argued that a treaty should be made with the mixed-ancestry Indians; Dougherty resigned in exasperation soon after the federal government did not attempt to acquire their consent and refused to ratify the treaty.

The 1841 Treaties with the Dakota and Federal Indian Policy

Cynthia Cumfer notes how state and local governments were often the driving force behind the creation of federal Indian policy.[21] Tense differences between local notions of nationhood, race, Indian sovereignty, and federal policy led to the influence of states and territories on federal Indian policy and affected how the federal government perceived the sovereign status of Indian nations, or lack thereof. In this case, James Duane Doty, governor of Wisconsin Territory, used his local understandings of the situation on the ground in the Upper Midwest to introduce a new federal Indian policy. Doty, a longtime resident of the region, previously was judge of Michigan Territory's additional court at Prairie du Chien from 1823 to 1832, where he regularly heard cases involving Indians of full and mixed ancestry.[22] Doty and Secretary of War John Bell of Tennessee came up with the plan to create a northern Indian Territory, with the approval of Thomas Hartley Crawford, commissioner of Indian Affairs. This new territory in the heart of Dakota country would require both the mixed- and full-ancestry Dakota to cede their lands and agree to these terms.[23]

In the words of Governor Doty, a series of three treaties negotiated with the Dakota in 1841 represented "a radical change in the policy of the United States towards the Indians."[24] Doty and the Office of Indian Affairs intended these treaties—one with the Bdewákhaŋthuŋwaŋ band, another with the Sisíthuŋwaŋ, Wahpéthuŋwaŋ, and Wahpékute bands, and one directly with the mixed-ancestry Dakota—to found a new "Indian Territory" in the north. This region would act as another Indian Territory, similar to that on the central Great Plains. Here, the government would remove many northern Indian nations; the treaties provided for the creation of a territorial government and a plan for incorporating Indians into the American nation through providing a path to U.S. citizenship for individual Indians living there.[25]

This entire policy hinged on these three treaties, putting the Dakota, as well as those of mixed ancestry, at the center of federal Indian policy. Federal negotiators proposed to carve this new Indian Territory out of Dakota land and the mixed-ancestry reservation at Lake Pepin. The Dakota and their mixed-ancestry relatives agreed to the terms in the treaties and were willing to participate in this radical new policy. Of utmost importance to the government in negotiating these treaties was the removal of Indians from the territory that would become the state of Iowa in order to make way for white settlement, but Bell gave further instructions to Governor Doty to acquire significantly more land to make room for the removal of other Indigenous nations to the new Indian Territory. Doty was to use his discretion in the negotiation of compensation in exchange for these Dakota land cessions.

In the summer of 1841, Doty traveled first to Traverse des Sioux on the Minnesota River then Mendota on the Mississippi to negotiate with the Dakota. The first treaty, signed July 31, 1841, was with the Sisíthuŋwaŋ, Wah̆péthuŋwaŋ, and Wah̆pékute bands of Dakota. In this treaty, the bands agreed to cede all of their land to the federal government for the creation of the Indian Territory of the north, amounting to 21.9 million acres. In return, these bands were to receive numerous concessions. In the second treaty, signed on August 11, the Bdewákhaŋthuŋwaŋ agreed to cede an additional 2.5 million acres, and both treaties were meant to operate in conjunction.[26]

Because the government wanted to remove many other tribes to the region, the Dakota were only to retain a small fraction of the total twenty-five million acres ceded in the three treaties of 1841. The two treaties with the Dakota Nation proposed reservations for each band north of the Minnesota River, ranging from fifty thousand to two hundred thousand acres. Those Indians that wished to become farmers would receive one hundred acres, and after two years of continued residence and cultivation, they would receive a fee simple patent from the federal government, with the right to sell or transfer their land. However, the treaty provided that transfers of land could only be to those "of the Indian blood," which was intended to guard against the dispossession of Indian lands.[27]

In a radical departure from previous treaties, in addition to these reservations, the treaties would create seven settlements along the Minnesota River and offer a generous package of improvements intended to assimilate Indians and incorporate them into the American nation. The government would furnish each settlement with a sawmill, grist mill, blacksmith shop, a school, and other necessities built at government expense. For any person that chose to reside at any one of the settlements, the government would pay to have a house built and provide them with ten acres of fenced and plowed land and each family would receive "farming utensils, spinning wheels, and looms, as may be necessary." In addition, families would receive garden seeds and seeds to produce crops of corn, potatoes, and wheat, as well as livestock, consisting of two pigs, five sheep, one cow, and one yoke of oxen. Millers, farmers, teachers, blacksmiths, mechanics, doctors, and other necessary workmen would be employed at each settlement, paid for by the government. Further, the government would hire female teachers "to teach the Indian women the arts of domestic life," and the government would pay for these employees for twenty years. Each band would have an agent to help fulfill treaty stipulations.[28]

One of the most significant stipulations in the treaties provided for the creation of an organized government. The federal government would appoint a governor or superintendent for the territory, and all residents of the territory would "be subject to such government, rules, and regulations, as shall be established by the Government of the United States therein." Agents would be under the authority of the governor, and the governor would be responsible for hiring the teachers and other employees and would appoint a trader for each of the bands, who would reside at the settlements or another place selected by the governor.[29] This too was a radical departure from most previous treaties and would have guaranteed a level of autonomy and political power to the Indian residents of the territory, while at the same time absorbing them into the American political system.

A path to U.S. citizenship for Indian residents of the proposed northern Indian Territory was one of the most radical provisions in the treaties.

The treaty framers tied citizenship to the cultivation of land, for those Indians that took the one-hundred-acre allotment and received a patent after two years would be incorporated into the American nation through the rights of citizenship. To acquire citizenship, Indians would have to personally apply to the governor of the territory, and if the governor felt the applicant was "civilized," that person would become a citizen of the United States.[30] The treaties would have quickly brought Indian people into the fold of American nationhood.

Doty negotiated yet a third treaty directly with the mixed-ancestry Dakota. Although the treaty is dated July 31, 1841, at Traverse des Sioux, additional signatures were appended at Mendota on August 13, Lake Pepin on August 22, and Prairie du Chien on August 27. The preamble of the treaty affirmed that the mixed-ancestry reservation at Lake Pepin "is or may be required by the Government of the United States as a part of the Indian Territory to be established." For the consideration of $200,000, the mixed-ancestry Dakota agreed to cede their reservation of 384,000 acres to the federal government. To those mixed-ancestry Dakota who had built houses and other improvements on the reservation, the government would reimburse them the value. Finally, the mixed-ancestry Dakota requested that the government appoint a commissioner "to ascertain and determine the individuals who were entitled . . . and to pay them or their representatives their equal proportion" of the sum.[31]

The treaty did not refer to the mixed-ancestry Dakota as a nation; rather, the preamble of the treaty stated that the treaty was negotiated between the United States "and the half-breeds of the Dakota or Sioux nation." This phrase implies that the federal government did not see the mixed-ancestry Dakota as their own nation but rather as a part of the Dakota Nation, yet only mixed-ancestry Dakota negotiated and signed the treaty. It also implies that through an equal distribution of funds, the mixed-ancestry Dakota were not interested in using kinship as a determinant in dividing the money. The treaty stated that the federal government would appoint a commissioner "on the particular request of the said half-breeds." In this case, the mixed-ancestry Dakota left it in the hands of the federal government to decide who was a "citizen" of this potential mixed-ancestry nation. Because of this, authority to sign the treaty did not necessarily make one a claimant to the $200,000 in the treaty, as a commissioner would make such decisions later.[32]

This cession of the mixed-ancestry Dakota contributed to the nearly twenty-five million acres ceded by the Dakota treaties of 1841; however, this would not make the mixed-ancestry Dakota homeless. The treaty permitted "the half-breeds, or persons of the Indian or mixed-blood," to reside at any of the seven settlements on the Minnesota River. All three of these treaties coalesced and all three needed to be ratified by the Senate in order for the new Indian policy to take shape, putting the full- and mixed-ancestry Dakota at the center of a radical new federal Indian policy.

Secretary of War Bell estimated that the government would remove over thirty-five thousand Indians from Ohio, New York, Michigan, Wisconsin, Indiana, Iowa Territory, and the lands north and south of the proposed Indian Territory to Dakota country.[33] Not only would the government remove these Indian nations, but Doty also envisioned the new Indian Territory to be the home of all the mixed-ancestry Indians of the Midwest. Doty asserted:

> This treaty also provides a permanent home for the Half Breeds, or persons of the Indian Blood, of the North West, who number about two thousand, and who are now floating between savage & civilized life, without being attached to either. In other Treaties, provision in money has been made for them, but this has been of no real advantage to them, as the money has either been immediately squandered, or given into the hands of white men who have been unable to return it.
>
> Experience has shown that this class must be used in any attempt to civilize the Indians, they are the connecting link between the savage & civilized man, & ought to be employed by government as its agents, interpreters & teachers, when they possess, as they frequently do, the requisite qualifications.
>
> An opportunity will thus be given them to establish a character for themselves—to obtain a place in civilized life, I might say among human beings, for Indian Blood—and it will be for their interest to be faithful and give their best efforts in aid of the purposes of government—many of them are well

> educated, & the example of those who are farmers, and mechanics, as well as their teaching, will be most beneficial to the Indians.[34]

On top of the thirty-five thousand Indians, Doty estimated that two thousand additional mixed-ancestry Indians of various tribes (although presumably several hundred were Dakota of mixed ancestry) would also call the new Indian Territory home. Like previous American officials, Doty attested to the civilizing benefits the mixed-ancestry Indians would have on their full-ancestry relatives but advanced this idea further than previous officials had. He recognized that the policy of providing cash payments to mixed-ancestry Indians as part of an assimilation policy had failed; as we saw in chapter 3, the mixed-ancestry Dakota simply incorporated aspects of the cash-based American economy into the Dakota kinship-based economy. Despite this, he still perceived that mixed-ancestry Indians were crucial to the assimilation of full-ancestry Indians. He further suggested the mixed-ancestry Indians would form a kind of liminal class between Indians and white people that would work as interpreters, teachers, and Indian agents. Not only was the new Indian policy a radical departure from previous federal Indian policy, but this idea of mixed-ancestry removal and their employment as Indian agents was equally radical. In addition, Doty offered jobs in the proposed territory to several prominent mixed-ancestry Dakota people, specifically as Indian agents and traders.[35] In creating this new federal Indian policy, Doty perceived mixed-ancestry Indians as central actors in administrating the new Indian Territory and its success.

The treaty with the mixed-ancestry Dakota did not come out of nowhere. They had their own political interests separate from those of the Dakota Nation, demonstrated that they were adept at participating in the American political system, and used petitions as a form of political activism. The mixed-ancestry Dakota wrote these petitions as political instruments primarily to protect their land rights in the Lake Pepin and Great Nemaha Reservations or to get a fair price for their lands. The petitions also reveal anxieties and political divisions over blood quantum among the mixed-ancestry Dakota, in which "half-breeds" and "quarter-breeds" occasionally competed over legal rights to land based on blood quantum. Most of these petitions mentioned some kind of division of the land into individual landownership, and one of the provisions of the 1830 treaty permitted the president to have the land surveyed and divided into 640-acre allotments at his discretion.

These kinds of petitions are certainly not unique to the Dakota of mixed ancestry. Dakota leaders frequently sent petitions of their own to the federal government, as did leaders of other Indigenous nations. Probably the most famous of such petitions was that of the Cherokee Nation protesting their impending removal by the federal government, signed by thousands of Cherokee citizens in the 1830s. What was unusual was that the mixed-ancestry Dakota banded together based on their racial mixedness and worked to secure their rights, separate from the Dakota Nation.

The mixed-ancestry Dakota wrote a petition for the first time on July 25, 1836, sending it to Indian agent Lawrence Taliaferro at Saint Peter's Agency, concerning their lands at Lake Pepin. Taliaferro forwarded the petition, with the names of sixty-four mixed-ancestry Dakota affixed, to Superintendent of Indian Affairs William Clark in Saint Louis. Taliaferro wrote that the mixed-ancestry Dakota "ask the protection of the President and of the Congress of the United States in a matter of so much importance to them, and their families."[36] The mixed-ancestry Dakota feared that a small minority among them were colluding with white land speculators to cheat the majority out of their share in the reservation. The petitioners offered to cede the entire reservation to the government for a fair price or to have the government survey and allot the land to individuals. As nothing came of this petition, the mixed-ancestry Dakota sent another to Henry Dodge, the governor of Wisconsin Territory, a year later.

This petition, signed by eighty-one mixed-ancestry Dakota on August 15, 1837, brought to light the contentious nature of the term "half-breed" used in the 1830 treaty. While some Dakota of mixed ancestry and some government officials felt that "half-breed" was a precise term, meant to refer to people of one-half blood quantum, others felt it was a general term designed to encompass all those with any mixture of European and Indian ancestry. The mixed-ancestry framers of this petition challenged the one-half blood quantum definition, writing: "We are also usually denominated half breeds, but we are in fact only quarter breeds, and many of us cannot say more than that we know that we are of Sioux blood and consequently relations of those tribes of Indians."[37] They asserted that when a mixed-ancestry Dakota was asked, "What are you?," they would inevitably "reply Sioux half breeds. Indeed, any other description was entirely unknown until the anxiety of some of our friends to grasp an immense tract instead of being satisfied with little more than a section conjured up the terms quarter breed."[38] The signers of this petition argued that it was the "half-breeds" that introduced the idea of fractionated categories of mixedness to the Dakota. It was certainly Euro-Americans who introduced the concept of blood quantum, but this quarrel between the "half-breeds" and "quarter-breeds" reveals how some Indians were complicit in perpetuating blood quantum, and they used it for exclusionary purposes to acquire more land.

The petitioners argued further that, because the tribal leaders had gifted the reservation to their mixed-ancestry relatives, only the Dakota Nation had the authority to define who fit the definition of "half-breed" in the 1830 treaty. The true intention of the chiefs, they believed, was the English term "relations," which was probably a more accurate view of the original intent.[39] Instead of pressing their claims further, the petitioners wanted the government to appoint a well-informed commissioner to make the decisions of eligibility. Again, the government took no action, but a group of mixed-ancestry Dakota of one-half blood quanta sent a memorial in 1839.

Addressing their memorial to the secretary of war, Joel R. Poinsett, the seventeen signers of the 1839 memorial revealed their fears that land speculators and "quarter-breeds" were interfering with the reservation and said that they wanted the government to leave the land as it was: "Your memorialists have viewed with sincere regret the efforts of some of our connections (who have been led astray by designing speculators) to bring in the quarter blood relatives who are not and never have been acknowledged by the proper authorities of the tribe, participators in the grant of land to the half breeds."[40] This divide between those of one-half and one-quarter blood quanta was one of legal definition for economic gain rather than any deep-seated belief in racial difference between the two groups. Like the "quarter-breeds," the memorialists felt that the question of eligibility should fall on the tribe, but in this case, they believed the chiefs supported their claim. As their memorial reveals, white land speculators were a real threat, and powerful white men, particularly Henry H. Sibley, worked behind the scenes with the mixed-ancestry Indians and the government to affect some disposition of the reservation.[41] As soon as the federal government extinguished the title of the mixed-ancestry Indians, these speculators were poised to swoop in and acquire the land at cheap prices. The Wisconsin Territorial Legislature also tried to push Congress to allot the land by passing a resolution and sending it to their delegate in Congress.[42] This too was ignored by the federal government.

After the 1841 treaty was negotiated, the so-called half-breed contingent complained one last time that the reservation was intended solely for their use in a petition sent to the commissioner of Indian Affairs in November of that year. After a flurry of seven petitions between 1836 and 1841 on behalf of the mixed-ancestry Dakota to press their various land claims at Lake Pepin, they sent no more petitions until 1853. As we will see in chapter 6, by this time, with the influx of white squatters on their reservation, and their situation becoming more desperate, the mixed-ancestry Dakota worked together to press their land rights.

These petitions were acts of political collectivity on the part of the mixed-ancestry Dakota, but rather than coming from a place of a common perception of nationhood, their cooperation stemmed from the hopes of economic gain. They were politically savvy and understood that sending petitions to political leaders as a collective body with a common political goal, also a common political tactic among white Americans, might just achieve their aims. Similarly, what appeared to be racial anxiety over blood quantum was simply an economic tactic by the "half-breeds" to acquire more land for themselves and their families while the "quarter-breed" faction simply sought to retain their rights in the land.

The treaty with the mixed-ancestry Dakota prompted many questions by officials as to blood quantum and other forms of eligibility. Lawrence Taliaferro, agent to the Dakota, sent a letter to the new secretary of war, John C. Spencer, on November 27, 1841, telling him some of his race-related concerns. Relating to the confusion that many American officials had with the term "half-breed" and its one-half blood quantum implications, he asked questions about blood quantum. He asked if mixed-ancestry Indians of one-fourth blood quantum would be eligible participants in the treaties and proposed hypothetical situations when mixed-ancestry Indians of more or less than one-half Dakota blood quantum were to be eligible. First, he asked if the children of "quarter-breeds" who married full-ancestry Indians, who would be five-eighths Dakota, would be eligible. He then asked if the children of a Dakota of one-quarter blood quantum who married a one-half blood quantum Odawa Indian, who would be one-eighth Dakota but three-eighths Indian, would be eligible. He also asked if those mixed-ancestry Dakota who were fully acculturated into Dakota society would be able to receive a share of the $200,000 offered in the treaty.[43] Taliaferro's questions reflected the realities of the diverse nature of mixed-ancestry Dakota. By 1841, the blood quantum of mixed-ancestry Dakota ranged anywhere from one-sixteenth to seven-eighths, and many mixed-ancestry Dakota had heritage from other tribes, such as the Ojibwe, Odawa, Cree, Assiniboine, Sac, Fox, Ho-Chunk, and Ioway. They also ranged in cultural practices from completely Euro-American to completely Dakota. The mixed-ancestry Dakota were not a monolithic group, but their kinship connections to each other, as well as their kinship connections to the Dakota Nation, served as a common bond that held them together.

Doty himself believed that "the term Half Breed I have always understood to embrace every person of the Indian Blood. It is used to designate a race and not the quantity of the blood of the red or white man in the veins of the individuals." Doty further commented that the majority of the mixed-ancestry Dakota wanted to include those of one-half and one-quarter blood quantum but to exclude those of one-eighth or less.[44] His classification of the mixed-ancestry Dakota as a "race" further represents how white Americans classified mixed-ancestry Indians as an Indigenous group separate from Indians.

Darren O'Toole argues that the mixed-ancestry people in the Great Lakes region never developed a common identity or sense of nationhood like the Métis did at the Red River settlement in modern-day southern

Manitoba. O'Toole outlines different steps toward nationhood. Beginning with simply an entity, he characterizes them as "a group that is defined as such by outsiders based on objective criteria, but lacks the subjective perception of itself as a distinct group."[45] He describes the second step, identity, as collective self-ascription as a distinct group, but a group that is prepolitical. The final step is nationhood, which involves a collective identity with a political consciousness "where political action is both motivated by a strong desire and capacity to maintain the objective and subjective aspects that distinguish it from other groups." The mixed-ancestry Dakota certainly fit the category of entity, but they never fully achieved the second step of a collective identity, let alone nationhood, even though they did act collectively in political ways on occasion when there was clear economic benefit to them individually when doing so.[46] But this gets muddied considering they did have a common identity as members of the Dakota Nation, and many of them also considered themselves as belonging to the American nation.

Other officials had major misgivings about the Dakota treaties. Because the treaties also stipulated the formation of a government for the proposed Indian Territory, many in Congress felt that this went beyond the scope of a treaty. They argued that a government could only be created by legislative action and that this treaty sidestepped Congress and usurped their authority. Further, other officials feared the proximity of the Indian Territory to the influence of the Métis and the Hudson's Bay Company at the Canadian border.[47] Although Doty clearly delineated the boundaries of the proposed Indian Territory in his correspondence accompanying the treaty, the treaty itself did not. The eastern boundary was to be the Mississippi and the western boundary the Missouri, but the treaty simply said the southern boundary would be the modern boundary between Iowa and Minnesota and stated no northern boundary. His correspondence set the forty-sixth parallel as the northern boundary, 180 miles from the international border. However, Doty's failure to explicitly state the northern boundary in the treaty would leave it open to interpretation, and if the territory were to stretch to the Canadian border, officials feared the British or the Métis would foment rebellion among the Indians in the region.[48] Ultimately, Congress refused to ratify the first treaty of July 31, and considering the policy required the ratification of the additional treaties with the Bdewákhaŋthuŋwaŋ and the mixed-ancestry Dakota, these treaties never received consideration.

The 1849 Treaty with the Mixed-Ancestry Dakota

Talks of ceding the land lay dormant until 1849, when, because of the imminent creation of Minnesota Territory, the federal government wanted to extinguish the title of the Dakota to their land and the mixed-ancestry Dakota to their reservation at Lake Pepin to make way for white settlers. In 1849, Alexander Ramsey, the first governor of Minnesota Territory, and John Chambers, the former governor of Iowa Territory, began negotiations on September 29 at Mendota with the Dakota to acquire as much Dakota land as possible. The government's proposal does not appear in the treaty journal, but they evidently made an offer on the tribe's land on October 3. The Dakota "requested that their relations, the half-breeds, should be permitted to come into council with them, which was assented to by the commissioners." Just like in the 1837 Treaty of Washington, the Dakota saw their mixed-ancestry relatives as important members of the Dakota Nation and wanted them there to help advise them and negotiate any potential treaty. Immediately following the consent of the commissioners, Chief Wápahaša ended the treaty council for the day, telling the commissioners that the delegation wanted time to consult together on the government's proposal. On the morning of October 4, the council resumed. Wápahaša spoke: "We and these my friends and relations, the half breeds, have listened to what you have said," again revealing the important counsel of the mixed-ancestry Dakota. He then pointed out that the government had not fulfilled the government's obligations and had misrepresented some provisions in the 1837 Treaty of Washington. Wápahaša told the commissioners that the tribe had no interest in a treaty at this time. The council ended on October 5, but before leaving, Wápahaša handed the commissioners a paper in Henry Sibley's handwriting, listing in detail their complaints over the 1837 treaty.[49]

Commissioner of Indian Affairs Orlando Brown authorized the treaty negotiators to negotiate directly with the mixed-ancestry Dakota, and three days later, on October 8, the commissioners began negotiating at

Mendota.[50] When the commissioners asked if all of the eligible mixed-ancestry claimants to the Lake Pepin Reservation were present, trader Philander Prescott responded that two-thirds of the claimants "were present by themselves or their authorized representatives." The previous day, the mixed-ancestry Dakota had met at the home of Henry Sibley and appointed a committee of five men, with Prescott as a member and Sibley as the chairman, to determine who was eligible and to negotiate on behalf of the mixed-ancestry Dakota. Commissioners Ramsey and Chambers were willing to negotiate with Sibley and the committee but wanted the mixed-ancestry Dakota to be present and participate in the treaty council. Prescott and Sibley told the commissioners "many of the Half-breeds were poor, and needed money to establish themselves, purchase stock, &c." and they simply wanted the government to purchase the reservation.[51]

The commissioners had hoped to secure a large land cession from the Dakota, but when that was not possible, they decided to treat with the mixed-ancestry Dakota separately. They told the mixed-ancestry Dakota that the Senate refused to ratify the 1841 treaty because the purchase price of $200,000 was too high. In consequence, the commissioners offered $150,000, or what they reckoned to be almost fifty cents per acre. However, the commissioners said that the mixed-ancestry Dakota "would have the opportunity of making preemption rights upon the very best portions of it." Despite the lower offer, fifty cents per acre was far more than the government typically offered to Indian tribes in land cession treaties. Indeed, in 1837, the Dakota had received only $1 million for ceding five million acres, or twenty cents per acre.[52]

Sibley countered that this was considerably less than the value that the mixed-ancestry Dakota placed on their lands. He claimed that since 1841 "the value of the land had increased as it had been ascertained that a great deal of it was mineral land of great value," containing lead and copper. Sibley asked that the commissioners raise their offer, insisting on $250,000. The commissioners countered with $200,000 and refused to go higher. The next day, based on this offer, Sibley accepted and the treaty "was signed by the commissioners and by Mr. Sibley, as the representative of the Half breeds generally, and by such of the half breeds themselves as were present, and by the fathers of some who were not present on behalf of their children."[53] From this description, it may seem that white men dominated the treaty negotiations, and they did have an inordinate amount of power in the negotiations, but dozens of mixed-ancestry Dakota had signed for themselves and on behalf of their families a power of attorney to Sibley on October 8 to negotiate on their behalf. Many of these mixed-ancestry Dakota, along with dozens of others, signed a similar document a year previous, on November 7, 1848, putting authority in Sibley to negotiate a sale of the land and, if a sale was not possible, to petition the president to divide the land among the claimants.[54] This document was annexed to the treaty, which the commissioners accepted. Many of the mixed-ancestry Dakota had worked for Sibley at the American Fur Company and trusted him to negotiate on their behalf. Sibley probably hoped to acquire much of this money, but despite this conflict of interest, the mixed-ancestry Dakota felt he could get them a good deal, which he did by convincing the commissioners to raise their offer by $50,000. Even though tribal leaders often relied on the mixed-ancestry Dakota as councillors in treaty negotiations, the mixed-ancestry Dakota did not include any full-ancestry Dakota in their negotiation. Instead, they appointed Sibley to see to their "national" interests.

In their report to Secretary of Interior Thomas Ewing on October 15, Ramsey and Chambers noted that the mixed-ancestry Dakota were not willing to make a treaty in conjunction with the tribe, claiming that "those of mixed blood are totally averse to being charged with the Indians, and could not be induced to unite with them in any treaty by which their interests might be affected."[55] It's likely that the mixed-ancestry Dakota believed that the chiefs would not be able to satisfactorily negotiate a treaty on their behalf, instead relying on Sibley. By insisting that a treaty be made separately with them, the mixed-ancestry Dakota were exerting a sense of national sovereignty. The treaty was negotiated on their terms by a surrogate they chose and trusted to negotiate on their behalf.

Unlike the 1841 treaties, the 1849 treaty was simple, with three brief articles. Article 1 stated that the mixed-ancestry Dakota agreed to cede their land. Article 2 offered the mixed-ancestry Dakota $200,000 for their land. Article 3 stipulated that the president would appoint commissioners

Figure 10. Joseph LaBatte, 1825–1914, photographed circa 1910. A mixed-ancestry Bdewákhaŋthuŋwaŋ man, his French Canadian fur trader father was killed by the Dakota in the U.S.-Dakota War in 1862. Locator no. por 27701 r1, Minnesota Historical Society, Saint Paul.

to ascertain who the eligible claimants were and distribute the money to them. This was a unique treaty. Unlike other treaties between Indian nations and the United States, there were no recognized national leaders and the majority of the mixed-ancestry signers signed powers of attorney, assigning Sibley to negotiate on their behalf.

Like the 1841 treaty, questions arose as to which mixed-ancestry Dakota were to be eligible to participate in the treaty. During the negotiations, a commission of five appointed by the mixed-ancestry Dakota sought to find who was eligible to take part in the treaty. The mixed-ancestry Dakota appointed Sibley the chairman of the committee, Joseph R. Brown was appointed secretary, and Alexis Bailly and Philander Prescott were also members of the committee. A mixed-ancestry Dakota trader, Francois Labathe, was the fifth committee member, but he soon asked to be relieved; his successor was not recorded. To the question "Shall the mixed blood Sioux other than with white Blood be participants in the distribution?" the commission decided in the negative.[56] This decision excluded mixed-ancestry Dakota people with African ancestry and delineated mixed-ancestry Dakota as those of mixed Indian and white "blood." Next, the committee decided that those "who have been brought up as Indians and always lived as Indians" would not be considered for the purposes of this treaty.[57] This definition of being mixed-ancestry Dakota was based on acculturation; those who were fully acculturated into Dakota society were not considered mixed-ancestry Dakota, but those acculturated into Euro-American society or those that occupied a cultural space in between were considered mixed-ancestry Indians. For those mixed-ancestry Dakota who resided outside the territory, it was determined that they were eligible. The committee next looked at blood quantum. The question was asked if those of less than one-fourth blood quantum were to be eligible to partake in this treaty, to which the committee answered in the affirmative. The American negotiators explained further "that they [the Dakota] understand our term, half breed as including all of mixed blood. A number of the half breed women have intermarried with white men and to exclude their children would be considered by the half breeds generally, as great injustice, your commissioners would therefore respectfully recommend that their views be adopted in any future designation of persons entitled to participate in the benefits of the treaty."[58] The committee considered four criteria for defining the eligibility of mixed-ancestry Dakota. First, the committee defined them as of mixed Indian and European ancestry only, excluding those of African ancestry. Second, the committee excluded mixed-ancestry Dakota fully acculturated into Dakota society. The committee next declined to exclude mixed-ancestry Dakota based on residency. Finally, they decided there would be no blood quantum standards and wanted to include all of their kin, suggesting that the participants in the treaty viewed the racial and cultural makeup of mixed-ancestry Dakota to be more significant than residency or blood quantum.

The decisions of the five-person committee appointed by the mixed-ancestry Dakota offers a window into how the mixed-ancestry Dakota perceived themselves and reckoned membership in their potential nation. The committee made their decisions based on the input of the mixed-ancestry Dakota present at the meeting. Despite the fact that two African American men, formerly enslaved Joseph Godfrey and James Thompson, signed the 1848 power of attorney to Sibley on behalf of their wives and children, the committee decided to exclude their families from the treaty. It is uncertain what motivated the mixed-ancestry Dakota to exclude them, but it was probably, at least in part, because they had internalized the anti-Black racism they witnessed from the white populous of the region. They rejected blood quantum as a valid measure of eligibility; the quarrel between the "half-breed" and "quarter-breed" factions in 1841 had apparently been quashed by 1849.

The Senate voted on the ratification of the treaty nearly a year later, on September 24, 1850. Minnesota politicians strongly supported the treaty. Indeed, the Senate voted 27 to 17 in favor of ratification, but this failed to meet the two-thirds threshold of present senators set in the constitution for the ratification of treaties. While both the "Yea" and "Nay" votes featured a mix of Democrat and Whig senators, the votes were split between Northerners and Southerners rather than between parties. Among the "Yea" voters were twenty-one senators from northern states and seven from southern states. In this vote count I include the two votes from Missouri as southern votes, but I argue that in matters of mixed-ancestry

Indian policy, Missourians were more aligned with Midwesterners. The "Nays" featured fifteen from southern states and only two from northern states. The treaty was especially popular among senators from the Midwestern states of Iowa, Missouri, Wisconsin, Michigan, Illinois, Indiana, and Ohio. Of these fourteen senators, eleven voted for ratification and only one against (a Democrat from Indiana) and two others failed to vote (Democrats from Indiana and Illinois).[59] Given the growing tensions between North and South over the issue of slavery and the Compromise of 1850 earlier that year, it is not surprising that the vote fell along these lines.

By the time of the Senate vote in September of 1850, most of the mixed-ancestry Dakota had been enfranchised as American citizens by law in Minnesota Territory, undermining the possibility of a mixed-ancestry nation. After the creation of Minnesota Territory in 1849, one of the first acts of the new territorial legislature was to enfranchise people who were "a mixture of white and Indian blood."[60] A nation cannot sign a treaty with a people, regardless of perceived nationhood status, if that people comprises that nation's own citizens. And the fact that the mixed-ancestry Dakota closely intertwined themselves with both the Dakota and American nations essentially ended any possibility of creating a mixed-ancestry Dakota Nation. The Wisconsin state constitution offered citizenship, albeit in a circumscribed manner, to mixed-ancestry Indians upon the achievement of statehood on May 29, 1848. This meant that many of the seventy mixed-ancestry Dakota from Prairie du Chien who signed the treaty were already citizens nearly seventeen months before signing the treaty on October 9, 1849. Minnesota Territory followed suit less than a month after the treaty, granting a less restrictive form of citizenship to mixed-ancestry Indians in the territory on November 1. This meant that the majority of the Dakota of mixed ancestry were citizens of the United States ten months before the Senate voted on the treaty on September 9, 1850. Having failed to acquire the land of the mixed-ancestry Indians in the 1840s, the U.S. government, in negotiating a treaty with the Dakota in 1851, made provisions to purchase the Lake Pepin Reservation from the mixed-ancestry Dakota. Like the 1849 treaty, the 1851 treaty did not employ blood quantum. The treaty offered the mixed-ancestry Dakota

Figure 11. Frank Deloria, also known as Saswe, 1816–1876. A mixed-ancestry Iháŋkthuŋwaŋ Dakota who served as a chief, was a signatory to the 1858 Yankton treaty, and was known as a fearsome warrior and medicine man. Photo taken in 1868. Edward E. Ayer Digital Collection, Newberry Library, Chicago.

$150,000 for the reservation; however, the Senate struck this provision from the treaty before its ratification.[61]

Much had changed in the eleven years between the failed treaties of 1838, 1841, and 1849. The Senate refused to ratify the treaty of 1838 because American officials argued that the treaty should include the consent of the mixed-ancestry Indians or a treaty should be made explicitly with them. This belief by American officials had not changed by 1841, when they negotiated a treaty directly with the mixed-ancestry Dakota. In 1841, the federal government contemplated a radical shift in federal Indian policy that would have incorporated Indians into the American nation and placed mixed-ancestry Indians in powerful positions in the proposed Indian Territory of the north. Again in 1849, the federal government negotiated a treaty directly with the mixed-ancestry Dakota that had significant support in the Senate. By not ratifying the 1838 treaty, the federal government recognized that mixed-ancestry Indians held sovereignty over their land. However, ratifying the 1841 or 1849 treaties would have created a nation-to-nation relationship between the United States and the mixed-ancestry Dakota.

A group of mixed-ancestry Dakota acting as a distinct band or political unit was not without precedent. For instance, after the 1858 treaty with the Iháŋkthuŋwaŋ, a new band arose in the 1860s, the Wašíču Číŋčapi (White Men's Children) band with Saswe, or Frank Deloria, ancestor of the famous Dakota scholar Vine Deloria Jr., as chief. Similarly, among the Oglála of Red Cloud Agency and the Sičháŋǧu of Spotted Tail Agency, new Iyéska Číŋčapi (literally "Translator's Children") bands arose on the Great Sioux Reservation by the 1870s.[62] However, while there might have been some internal momentum to create these bands, their creation was primarily the work of the federal government. No formal mixed-ancestry political units within the Dakota political organization are known to exist before then.

Among mixed-ancestry Indians, notions of belonging to a nation were often fluid and changed as needed. Major Joseph Plympton wrote, while at Fort Snelling in 1838, "I presume the Government cannot be aware fully of the great number of persons who are constantly wandering through the Indian Country, and who call themselves White, but who are in fact half breeds, and who acknowledge allegiance to no Nation, but who are when an object is presented for them to accomplish, American Citizens, or British Subjects, as may best suit their momentary views."[63] Given the chaotic nature of the American nation on the ground in the ever-changing territorial boundaries and the diverse nature of the Midwest, mixed-ancestry families could slip into different national identities without any nefarious intent.

During this period, some mixed-ancestry Dakota too toyed with the idea of mixed-ancestry Dakota nationhood. In the 1841 and 1849 treaties they did not seek the council of their chiefs, and they explicitly stated in 1849 that they did not want their land to be included in any treaty negotiated with the tribe. While they never fully recognized a national status, they did have their own land base and exhibited a sense of homogeneity and group identity. The Dakota kinship obligations that the mixed-ancestry Dakota retained ensured that they continued their connection to the Dakota Nation. Nicole St-Onge argues that the mixed-ancestry Dakota never developed a national identity like the Métis because they retained their kinship and cultural connections to the Dakota and to the French Canadian culture of the region.[64] Had the mixed-ancestry Dakota severed ties with the Dakota Nation, they would have had much to lose. They acquired the land at Lake Pepin in the 1830 treaty and the $110,000 in the 1837 treaty as mixed-ancestry *Dakota,* not as a separate people. In order to gain from these treaty provisions, they had to proclaim their mixedness as well as their Dakotaness. They also profited from other provisions in Dakota treaties, such as annuity goods. There was little to gain by insisting on a national identity that they did not feel but much to gain by maintaining their connection to the Dakota Nation.

Treaties between Indian tribes and the U.S. government usually meant a loss of autonomy or land or both for the tribe, but treaty provisions in the Dakota treaties of 1830 and 1837 resulted in land and money for mixed-ancestry Dakota people. The unratified treaties of 1841 and 1849 with the mixed-ancestry Dakota would have resulted in the loss of their land but a guarantee of their autonomy and status as a nation. As law scholar Matthew L. M. Fletcher argues, "Under foundational American law, no president and no Senate may enter into or ratify a treaty with a group that is not a nation. In short, each treaty is an explicit recognition of the sovereign governmental status of an Indian Tribe."[65] Fletcher contends that the United States cannot ratify a treaty with a nonnation, nor can it "enter into" a treaty with a nonnation. Yet in this case, the federal government entered into a treaty, which essentially gave the mixed-ancestry Dakota federal recognition as an Indigenous nation.

Duane Champagne, in acknowledging that the federal government bases federal recognition of tribes in their treaty relationship with those tribes, argues that even nations whose treaties went unratified should be federally recognized as Indigenous nations. At least 150 treaties went unratified, but Champagne asserts, "treaty commissioners entered into negotiations with Indian tribes with the understanding and recognition that the Indian nations had the power and rights to make treaties." Champagne makes his point by revealing that if the United States fails to ratify a treaty with any non-Indigenous nation, that does not erase the sovereign or nationhood status of those nations.[66] The fact that the U.S. government negotiated with the mixed-ancestry Dakota as a separate nation on two different occasions suggests that the federal government was willing to create a nation-to-nation relationship with them. If the federal government simply perceived them as racial minorities, they could have treated with leaders of the Dakota Nation. American negotiators felt the need to get the consent of the mixed-ancestry Dakota to acquire their reservation at Lake Pepin, not the leaders of the Dakota Nation, with whom the United States negotiated in 1830 to create the reservation. They agreed to acquire that consent through treaty-making.

The story of Theophilus LaChapelle, who ran for delegate to the Wisconsin Territorial Legislature in 1840, and of my ancestor Francis Trudell, who voted in the election, illustrate the complexities and murkiness of the nationhood status of Indians of mixed ancestry. On September 28, 1840, Francis Trudell visited the home of his neighbor Joseph Monjeau, a white man with a Dakota family, where an election was held for residents of the Red Rock voter precinct for representatives of Saint Croix and Crawford Counties, Wisconsin Territory. This was an election where voters chose two out of the three candidates running for the position. Trudell and the other thirteen men who voted at Monjeau's house in

Saint Croix County that day voted for Joseph R. Brown and Alfred Brunson. The third candidate in the election was Theophilus LaChapelle, a mixed-ancestry Dakota Indian born in Prairie du Chien in 1816 to French Canadian fur trader Antoine LaChapelle and Pelagie LaPointe, the niece of Chief Wápahaša. LaChapelle continued to live in Prairie du Chien in Crawford County, where he had served as register of deeds in the 1830s. The residents of Crawford County voted for LaChapelle in large numbers, but he came in third in the election, with Brown and Brunson winning the seats in the territorial legislature. The total votes were 168 for Brown, 106 for Brunson, and 88 for LaChapelle.[67] However, at least twenty of the voters, including Trudell, were not citizens of the United States; they were French Canadians and subjects of the British Empire. Francis Trudell and at least seven of the fourteen voters at Monjeau's had spouses who belonged to the Dakota Nation. This election illustrates the problematic understandings of nation and nationhood in the early Upper Midwest.

Brown and Brunson had connections to the Dakota and Ojibwe Nations. Over his lifetime, Brown had three wives. First, he married Helen Dickson, a mixed-ancestry Dakota woman. Brown and Dickson divorced in 1832 and Brown married Margaret McCoy soon after, an Ojibwe woman of mixed ancestry. After divorcing McCoy in 1840 by an act of the Wisconsin Territorial Legislature, Brown remarried, again to a mixed-ancestry Dakota woman, named Susan Frenier.[68] Brown was a fur trader, and through these marriages Brown acquired important kinship connections to both the Dakota and Ojibwe Nations, which permitted him to trade with his wives' kin groups. Brunson worked briefly as a Methodist missionary to the Dakota in the 1830s, finding little success in converting them. By the 1840s, Brunson was an Indian agent to the Ojibwe at LaPointe. Brunson's son Ira B. Brunson was married to LaChapelle's sister Pauline at the time of the 1840 election, but they divorced by the early 1850s. All three candidates in this election and most of the voters at the Red Rock precinct had connections to multiple nations, either by themselves or through marriages with Indian women.

LaChapelle contested the election, and the court threw out the votes of the twenty noncitizens, leaving LaChapelle ahead of Brunson by two votes; he was finally seated in the Wisconsin Territorial Legislature in 1842.[69] In the legislature's hearings to clear up the voter issue, Henry Sibley traveled to Madison, the capital of Wisconsin Territory, to give testimony. LaChapelle questioned Sibley about the election at Red Rock, mentioning Francis Trudell and three other men by name. When asked about their nationality, Sibley responded, "I cannot say positively to the place of their birth—but they have been long in our employ, engaged by us in Canada, and brought by us from there, and we have always considered them as aliens."[70] LaChapelle belonged to the Dakota Nation of Indians, at the same time he served in political office as a member of the American nation. This belonging to two nations was typical of Indians of mixed ancestry. But for many mixed-ancestry families, this was more complicated. Although Francis Trudell failed in his attempt to exercise the electoral franchise as a member of the American nation, he did succeed in subsequent elections, even before he filed his naturalization papers in 1855. Before 1855, Trudell was a subject of the British Empire, but occasionally he was able to exercise the rights of a member of the American nation. He also served in the U.S. Army in Company K of the Ninth Minnesota Infantry Regiment from 1862 to 1863 with LaChapelle's younger brother Frederick LaChapelle. His wife, Ičíyapiwiŋ, was a member of the Dakota Nation and acquired the additional citizenship status of her husband. The Trudell children were enrolled members of the Dakota Nation their entire lives, but as we will see in chapter 5, they acquired, lost, and reacquired U.S. citizenship. Many mixed-ancestry Indians of this period had dual citizenship in the United States and their tribal nation. However, among the Dakota in the 1840s, the possibility of a third nation emerged—that of the mixed-ancestry Dakota.

In a letter to the *Wisconsin Herald* in 1845, Theophilus LaChapelle wrote of his experiences in the Wisconsin Territorial Legislature and his role in the 1841 treaties. LaChapelle portrayed himself as a reluctant legislator, complaining that being sent to Madison, the capital of Wisconsin Territory, was "contrary to my wish and inclination."[71] "Among the many questions upon which I was required to vote during the first session that I attended the assembly," he wrote, "there is one which I wish to notice in this letter. It is that in relation to Gov. Doty's Treaty with the Dakota

Indians." LaChapelle continued, "When I speak of Gov. Doty's Treaty, I do not mean the Treaty for the purchase of the Sioux Half Breed tract on Lake Pepin—for I am interested in the latter"; rather, he explained that he voted against the legislature's memorial to Congress to ratify the treaties. He explained that he regretted his vote against the memorial: "I have been pursued by the unceasing complaints of my friends who are made to suffer incessantly, who dread the consequences of a refusal to treat with the United States, and who are threatened with vengeance and extermination on account of my political opinions. It is on their account that I wish this Treaty were ratified." In his reckoning, his "friends," the mixed-ancestry Dakota, suffered real consequences because of the failure to ratify the 1841 treaties. LaChapelle resigned his seat in the legislature in March 1844.[72]

In this period, Indians of mixed ancestry were often political pawns that the federal and local governments used for their own ends. For example, enumerators for federal and territorial censuses frequently recorded Indigenous people of mixed ancestry in territories to inflate population numbers, while Indians of full ancestry were explicitly excluded and rarely recorded in federal or local censuses before 1900. Of course, census forms in the nineteenth century were not designed for racial mixedness or racial complexities, but census enumerators would sometimes use their own ingenuity to record mixed-race people.[73] Most often they simply left the racial box for mixed-ancestry Indians blank or marked them as white. Under the Northwest Ordinance of 1787, a region could acquire territorial status if its population reached 5,000 free males, and counting mixed-ancestry Indians was a way of achieving this. The 1849 census of Minnesota Territory recorded over 4,500 residents, but William P. Murray, a resident of early Minnesota, claimed that the white population was little more than 1,000; the rest were Métis or Indians of mixed ancestry. The acquisition of territorial status for Minnesota was primarily due to Indigenous people rather than white American residents.[74] The Trudell family first appeared in the 1840 federal census, along with many other mixed-ancestry families, living near Fort Snelling. The family also appeared in early local censuses of Wisconsin Territory in 1846 and 1847 and in Minnesota Territory in 1849 and 1857.

This was a complex situation made possible by marriage and kinship; the vast majority of mixed-ancestry Indians and Métis in the Upper

Midwest held the names of their Euro-American fathers, grandfathers, or husbands. This made them appear white in the census and other documents. But Catherine J. Denial attests to the "nation-shaping power of marital acts" and how Indigenous people, while being used by the state, simultaneously resisted "the vision of family or government that Americans imported, and in their resistance to the gender and familial roles" promoted by Euro-Americans, "the Native and mixed-heritage inhabitants of the Upper Midwest frustrated American attempts to transform Indian country into a state." Marriage and Indigeneity in the Upper Midwest shaped individual property rights and the nationhood status of mixed-ancestry families in ways that were counter to common practice for white Americans.[75]

Marriage was not only an important nation-shaping power under U.S. law; Christina Gish Hill argues that kinship connections, including marriages, were central to Indigenous sovereignty and nationhood. Native leaders made national decisions based on kinship obligations, and national belonging was determined through kinship. These marriages, like those of Francis Trudell to Ičíyapiwiŋ, served to extend and strengthen Dakota sovereignty, while such marriages in American circles were sometimes exploited, as in the case of the census, but often they threw a wrench in the gears of American law and state formation.[76] At the same time, these interracial marriages created a new category of people that were thrust into a situation where they flirted with nationhood status akin to that of the Métis.

This mixed-blood history exhibited conditions where American officials and mixed-ancestry Dakota nearly created a mixed-ancestry Indigenous nation. The mixed-ancestry Dakota were at the center of radical plans to change Indigenous–white relations. The United States failed to ratify all of these treaties between 1838 and 1849; nonetheless, as Duane Champagne argues, even unratified treaties have consequences.[77] The very fact that the United States was willing to negotiate directly with the mixed-ancestry Dakota reflects an American willingness to treat the mixed-ancestry Dakota as a nation. The ratification of either the 1841 or the 1849 treaty would have had major consequences for federal Indian law and Indian–white relations, permitting mixed-ancestry groups of any tribe to claim nationhood status.

CHAPTER 5

Native Suffrage

Mixed-Ancestry Indians in the Midwest

Of 108 citizens from the Mendota, Minnesota Territory, voting precinct that cast their votes on October 12, 1852, at least nineteen were Indians of mixed ancestry: one Odawa, two Ojibwe, and sixteen Dakota.[1] At least nineteen more voters in Mendota were white men with Dakota families and two more with Ojibwe and Cree families, meaning more than one-third of the voters in this election were Indians or were the heads of Indian households. One of the voters was my great-great-great-grandfather Francis Trudell, although he did not file his naturalization papers until the following year. The poll list for an election held at Mendota the previous year, April 14, 1851, recorded an even higher percentage, with fully half of the fifty-four voters connected to Indian households.[2] This racial and political situation did not fit the typical mold of Jacksonian America. Yet some mixed-ancestry Dakota men and other Indians had enjoyed U.S. citizenship and the right to vote in the Upper Midwest since at least 1823 when two Dakota men, Augustin Rocque and Etienne Dubois, alongside Ottawa, Cree, Ho-Chunk, and Meskwaki men, voted in Prairie Du Chien in Michigan Territory's election for delegate to Congress.[3]

As early as 1840, when the Dakota Indian Theophilus LaChapelle was elected to the Wisconsin Territorial Legislature, Indians of mixed ancestry enjoyed the rights of U.S. citizenship and exercised political power in the Upper Midwest. Especially after Minnesota Territory's 1849 law explicitly granted citizenship to Indians of mixed ancestry, there was a brief period when Indians could vote and hold public office. Baptiste Campbell—a citizen, a voter in the Mendota election, and a farmer—was most famous for his role on the side of the Dakota in the U.S.-Dakota War in 1862, for which he was hanged by the U.S. Army with thirty-seven other Dakota men on December 26. With him on that cold day in 1862 the ability of most mixed-ancestry Indians to exercise their citizenship in Minnesota also died. Despite the fact that Indigenous people served in each session of the Minnesota State and Territorial Legislatures between 1849 and 1862, the war soured white Midwesterners toward Indian citizenship and Indians in public office. Indeed, after 1862, no other person of Indian ancestry served in the Minnesota legislature for over seventy years.

The 1840s to the 1860s was a moment in the Upper Midwest when mixed-ancestry Indians held a modicum of political influence. In this moment, local white people conflated whiteness with citizenship and the concept of being "civilized," and politicians exploited the loyalty of mixed-ancestry Indians to the Democratic Party. As local American legal and political institutions were in their infancy, they relied on the mixed-ancestry population to fill local political offices and to vote until there were enough white settlers to take their place.[4] At the same time, Indians of mixed ancestry used this opportunity to consolidate political power and to demonstrate their political sophistication in the American political system, while retaining their citizenship in the Dakota Nation.

Indians of mixed ancestry had voted in elections in the Upper Midwest since at least 1823, but it was not until 1848—when the new state of Wisconsin's constitution permitted citizenship for "civilized persons of Indian descent," soon followed by similar laws in Michigan and Minnesota—that Indians had an explicit right to citizenship.[5] Under these laws, however, American lawmakers limited Indian citizenship based on race or their status as "civilized." Indeed, for many lawmakers, "citizen" was synonymous with "white and civilized," often leading to contorted logic. This chapter examines three manifestations of the fight for citizenship for Indian people. First, I investigate the participation of mixed-ancestry Dakota Indians in American political institutions through voting and how they easily took up American leadership and decision-making roles that were foreign to Dakota political practices. Second, I analyze state constitutions and other laws that secured Indian citizenship and the contemporary race-based debates over Indian citizenship. Finally, I examine how one Dakota community, the Hazelwood Republic, tried to acquire American citizenship en masse on their own terms.

Before the Indian Citizenship Act of 1924 granted American citizenship to all Native Americans born in the United States, the citizenship status of Indians was in a state of flux and uncertainty. The U.S. Constitution made it clear that Indian tribes existed outside of American jurisdiction. The famous Marshall Trilogy, a set of three U.S. Supreme Court decisions between 1823 and 1832, muddied understandings of tribal sovereignty and the relationship between Indians and federal and state governments.[6] The U.S. Supreme Court ruled in *Elk v. Wilkins* in 1884 that Indians were ineligible for citizenship under the birthright Citizenship Clause of the Fourteenth Amendment. Additionally, there was no naturalization process for Indians.[7] Before 1924, Indians attained citizenship in piecemeal fashion, through local laws, treaties, or congressional acts. But Indians also lost citizenship in various ways: if they moved to a different state or territory without provisions for Native suffrage, laws changed, or if local officials simply refused to recognize the citizenship rights of Indians.

Most of the scholarly literature on American Indian suffrage focuses on the twentieth and twenty-first centuries.[8] A notable exception is two chapters in Deborah A. Rosen's *American Indians and State Law,* with a particular focus on post–Civil War Massachusetts and New Mexico Territory.[9] Historical analysis of Indian lawmakers is nearly nonexistent, although William Unrau's biography of U.S. Vice President Charles Curtis, a mixed-ancestry Kaw Indian born in Kansas in 1860, reveals how Curtis used his Indianness and mixed ancestry for economic and political gain, often to the detriment of Indian people.[10]

For the purposes of this chapter, I use the concepts of suffrage and citizenship interchangeably. This is not meant to minimize either institution or assume that they are interdependent; rather, I recognize that the right to vote is the most fundamental of citizenship rights and is required to protect all other rights of citizenship. Without the right to vote, one cannot exercise the full rights of citizenship. In addition, local officials frequently conflated the two concepts, making it difficult to parse out different perceptions of the two institutions. As a practical matter, poll lists are often the sole or at least the most accessible evidence for determining the citizenship status of Indians in the nineteenth century.

Historians characterize the Jacksonian era as an expansion of democratic participation to the common citizenry of the United States, but the era also saw the declension in the legal rights of African Americans and many Indians. The era's widening racial inequality did not emerge with the same vigor in every corner of the nation.[11] Andrew Jackson's thinking on American Indians was summed up in his fifth annual message, December 3, 1833, in which he argued that Indians were racially inferior to whites and that Indians would become extinct unless they were forcibly removed west of the Mississippi, far from Euro-American settlement. Despite his push for Indian removal, Jackson signed at least two treaties as president—one with the Choctaw in 1830 and another with the Cherokee in 1835—that offered U.S. citizenship to individual Indians, yet few accepted.

This history of citizenship and involvement of mixed-ancestry Indians in the American political system was due to settler colonial expansion of the United States into Indigenous territories, bringing with them American political and legal institutions. These were settler colonial institutions of white supremacy that usually worked to alienate Indigenous people from their land and to limit the rights of nonwhite people. The federal government often extended nominal control of a region through the creation of a U.S. Army fort (such as Fort Crawford or Fort Snelling), later followed by settlers who founded local governments, courts, and churches. However, this was a brief mixed-blood history when mixed-ancestry Indians were able to operate within these institutions while maintaining an Indigenous identity.[12]

Like many other Indian families of mixed ancestry in the Midwest, the American citizenship status of the Trudell family was in a frequent state of flux and uncertainty. Members of the Trudell family acquired, lost, and reacquired citizenship at different times under different legal means. In the nineteenth-century United States, wives and children carried the citizenship status of the father or husband. Francis Trudell, an immigrant from Canada, was a subject of the British Empire, and after his marriage to Ičíyapiwiŋ in 1835 and the birth of his children, his family should also have been considered citizens of the British Empire, although their race made it unlikely that they could have exercised their citizenship, even if it had been acknowledged. However, Ičíyapiwiŋ and her children retained their connection to and citizenship in the Dakota Nation and were enrolled tribal members their entire lives.

In 1849, the Minnesota Territorial Legislature passed an act granting citizenship to people of "a mixture of white and Indian blood."[13] This act alone should have secured citizenship for the Trudell children, and when Francis Trudell filed his naturalization papers in 1853, this should have further solidified the American citizenship of the Trudell children. However, as late as 1905, Henry Trudell, the second-oldest surviving child of Francis and Ičíyapiwiŋ, wrote a letter to the commissioner of Indian Affairs inquiring into the fate of a petition he and fifteen other members of the Santee Sioux Tribe of Nebraska wrote, requesting American citizenship.[14] Just two years previous, the Indian agent at Santee, W. E. Meagley, wrote to the then–Commissioner of Indian Affairs William Arthur Jones, describing Henry as a "citizen Indian," leaving Henry's citizenship status unclear. Henry also tied citizenship to the fact that the petitioners did not fight against the United States, arguing, "All the signers to said are loyals, and was not near or took part in the outbreak of the massacre in Minnesota in the year of 1862."[15] For Henry, citizenship was tied to loyalty, while most white Americans tied citizenship to race.

While white Americans of the nineteenth century held their own conceptions of what made one a citizen, Dakota people held their own understandings of both American and Dakota citizenship. In the nineteenth century, the Dakota, with the help of missionaries, developed language to accommodate the Eurocentric concept of civilization and language that attempted to approximate how white Americans understood notions of citizenship. These concepts, published by white missionaries, reflected both the lexical interpretations of these products of Euro-American society and the Indians that taught them and contributed to their dictionaries. It can be difficult to parse the contributions of Indians in these entries, but often significant numbers of Indians participated in the construction of these language dictionaries. Catholic missionary Eugene Buechel began recording Lakota words for his manuscript dictionary as early as 1910. Buechel documented nearly two hundred Lakota and Dakota contributors for his dictionary, including the youngest Trudell brother, Antoine, and my great-great-grandmother's brother John Colombe Jr.[16]

The first published uses of the word "citizen" appear in missionary Stephen R. Riggs's *Grammar and Dictionary of the Dakota Language* and the anonymous *An English and Dakota Vocabulary, by a Member of the Dakota Mission,* both published in 1852.[17] Both works use the term "wóžuti," meaning literally "farmer," to approximate the concept of citizen. This represents the influence of the missionaries in their use of the Jeffersonian concept of the yeoman farmer at the center of American democracy. In nineteenth-century Dakota culture, women were at the center of agricultural production, which stood in contrast to male-dominated agriculture in American society. Americans restricted suffrage explicitly to males; in order for Dakota men to become citizens, they would have to take up American gender roles.[18] Only Riggs's 1890 edition of his dictionary continued to use "wóžuti" for "citizen"; instead, most other documents and publications of the nineteenth century used variations of the Dakota verb "yuhá" ("to have or to possess") to express the concept of citizenship.

Riggs's 1890 *A Dakota-English Dictionary* uses two variations of "yuhá" to approximate the American concept of citizenship.[19] The first of these, "aíhduha," means "to provide for one's self," suggesting a concept of citizenship rooted in self-reliance and still retaining a Jeffersonian influence. Another variation is "oíhduha," which translates to "to own one's self." "Oíhduha" probably came as a response to the institution of American chattel slavery. With the establishment of Fort Snelling in the heart of Dakota country in 1820, officers regularly brought enslaved African Americans with them. By the 1850s, the Dakota had been exposed to slavery for decades and likely developed "oíhduha" as a concept of citizenship in opposition to slavery. One who owned one's self was a citizen, while those who did not were enslaved and noncitizens. A similar concept appears in John P. Williamson's *An English-Dakota School Dictionary* of 1886. Williamson uses the term "wičášta táwaičiya," "to be a free man," to mean "citizen."[20] Yet in Williamson's 1902 edition of his dictionary, he uses the phrase "oyáte ópa," or "to be a member of a nation" to mean citizen.[21] This is probably the most accurate and least problematic iteration of the concept of citizenship, but it only appears in this dictionary. "Oyáte" is an important Dakota word that can mean "nation," "a people," "tribe," or "band." Nineteenth-century Dakota held a clear understanding of nationhood and "oyáte ópa" builds on that understanding to provide a concise definition of citizenship.

The fact that there were so many terms used to approximate the concept of citizenship reveals that this was a concept in flux and not easy to nail down in Dakota. At various points "citizen" became equated with "farmer," self-sufficiency, and being a member of a nation, and in contrast to slavery. The Eurocentric term "civilization," however, came to be equated to whiteness, just as it was in English.

Despite its constant usage in discussions of Indian citizenship from the 1840s to the 1860s, variations of "civilization" do not appear in the early dictionaries. John P. Williamson's 1886 dictionary defines "civilization" as "wówašiču," meaning "whiteness" (always referring to the race, not the color).[22] Williamson's 1902 edition defines "civilization" as "wašíču ič'íyapi," meaning "to cause one's self to be white."[23] These definitions clearly draw on white American notions that equate civilization with whiteness. The authors of these dictionaries expressed similar racial language in the verb "to civilize." Williamson used the term "wašíčuya" or "to regard as white."[24] However, other terms appear that were more in keeping with Dakota understandings of civilization based in assimilation. Fred Hans uses the phrase "wičóȟaŋ uŋspékiya," meaning "to teach someone culture or customs."[25] In addition to "wašíčuya," Williamson uses "kaúŋspe," "to train or teach someone."[26] An additional form of "civilization" is the adjective "civilized." Only Williamson attempted to translate this concept, using the racial term "wašíču" but also "kaúŋspepi," "those who have been taught."[27]

The language used to translate "civilization," "to civilize," and "civilized" couched these terms either in whiteness or assimilation. These words regularly retained their Eurocentricity when translated into Dakota. For white Americans, the white racial category, "citizenship," and "civilization" were synonymous, while the Dakota perceived "civilization" and "citizenship" as synonymous with Euro-American culture.

Minnesota white people were apprehensive of the citizenship of mixed-ancestry Indians. The *St. Cloud Democrat* ran a story in 1858 that appeared repeatedly for months on their pages. With the founding of the town in the 1850s, the paper hoped to attract settlement. The paper reported that there were 332 votes polled in the Saint Cloud precinct and bragged that they were "not the votes of Indians or Half Breeds, for there are none here," as a way to attract white settlers.[28] A correspondent for the *Madison Journal,* reprinted in the *Stillwater Messenger,* claimed that half of the votes in an 1858 election in Douglas County, Wisconsin, just over the Mississippi from Minnesota, were cast by mixed-ancestry Indians and wrongly asserted "they are not citizens of the United States."[29] An article in the *Rochester City Post* in 1860 wrote of the race for the speakership of the Minnesota House of Representatives: "Whoever is in the Speaker's chair, let him by all means be a *thorough and uncompromising Republican.* The day for soft shells and half breeds has passed."[30] Many newspapers around the country reported on the complaints of Republicans who lamented close elections because of mixed-ancestry voters. For example, in Douglas County, Wisconsin, thirty mixed-ancestry Indians voted, all for the same candidate, who only won his seat by forty-six votes.[31] Republicans in 1859 complained of "Indian voting" in prior elections and proclaimed that "the swindling game was effectually blocked . . . and repudiated the breech-clout Democracy" when they won many state elections.[32] In a proposed constitution for the state of Kansas, some Republican voters were against Indian suffrage because "like all other ignorant, half-civilized, and barbarous beings, [they] would become the tools of the Democratic party."[33] These articles reveal that many white people in the Midwest did not want mixed-ancestry voters and denied that they were citizens, despite the constitutions of states like Minnesota and Wisconsin guaranteeing their suffrage.

While some white Midwesterners opposed mixed-ancestry suffrage, some mixed-ancestry Indians had a role in making U.S. citizens through the naturalization process. Before 1906, standards for naturalization varied widely, and it was done on a local level. The usual process involved the immigrant filing a declaration of intention to become a U.S. citizen, called an immigrant's "first papers." After meeting their residency requirement, usually five years, potential citizens would file a petition for naturalization, or final papers, after which time a court would grant the petitioner U.S. citizenship upon giving an oath of allegiance to the United States. In Minnesota Territory, the final papers included the signatures of two witnesses, U.S. citizens, who could attest to the petitioner's residence in the territory for five years. In Dakota County in the 1850s, occasionally mixed-ancestry Indians, who were themselves citizens, acted as witnesses for potential citizens. Alexis Bailly served as a witness for Hypolite Provost and John Rousseau. Samuel Findley was a witness for Amable Dufont. Alexander Duncan Campbell was a witness for Claud Cournoyer, Louis Martin, Hypolite Dupuis, Francois Gammel, and Pierre Felix. Many of these witnesses were white men married to Dakota women.[34] These men only served as witnesses for French Canadian men, and some gave witness for each other. All the men that Alexander Duncan Campbell witnessed, except Claud Cournoyer, were married to Dakota women

Figure 12. Samuel J. Findley, 1818–1855. Findley was a mixed-ancestry Bdewákhaŋthuŋwaŋ Dakota and served in the Minnesota Territorial Legislature. Locator no. por 22941 r1, Minnesota Historical Society, Saint Paul.

and had been in the region for years. The American naturalization process gave a handful of mixed-ancestry men power in the Dakota Nation. This process permitted mixed-ancestry Dakota to fulfill kinship obligations by helping white men who had married into Dakota kinship groups acquire U.S. citizenship. Indeed, two of these men, Alexis Bailly and Samuel Findley, also held political power in the American nation as legislators in the Minnesota Territorial Legislature.

Mixed-Ancestry Dakota Lawmakers

There is substantial evidence for the participation of mixed-ancestry Dakota Indians in Minnesota both as voters and as public servants. From the 1820s to the 1850s, many of the local legal officials in Minnesota Territory and western Wisconsin Territory were fur traders, and often their mixed-ancestry Indian sons followed in their footsteps.[35] Elections were sometimes held at the homes of mixed-ancestry Dakota people. The territorial government authorized the 1852 election to be held at the homes of Henry Bailly and Augustine Rock, in their respective precincts.[36] At least eight Dakota Indians of mixed ancestry were among the Democratic voters of Le Sueur and Nicollet Counties that appealed to Martin McLeod in a public letter to run for the territorial council in 1853.[37] Pierre St. Antoine, a mixed-ancestry Dakota, ran unopposed as a Democrat for road supervisor of Dakota County in 1854, receiving 105 votes.[38]

Mixed-ancestry Dakota Indians also flexed their political muscle in party politics. A convention of Democrats met in Hastings on July 10–11, 1855, to oppose the nomination of Henry Rice as the Minnesota territorial representative to Congress. Mixed-ancestry Dakota Henry G. Bailly chaired the convention. After hearing about the upcoming meeting, a group of mixed-ancestry Dakota met at Wabasha on July 7 to appoint a delegation to go to the Democratic convention and "to act to the best of their abilities, in behalf of the Half Breeds and others interested in the Half Breed Tract."[39] The meeting appointed Augustine Roque, Oliver Cratte, Oliver Rasico, Alexis Bailly, Joseph LaChapelle, and Peter Larivie as delegates to the convention in Hastings. At the convention three days later, the delegates proposed eight resolutions, passed by the convention, all with the purpose of protecting their land at Lake Pepin and asserting their legal rights over their land. They used strong language, declaring that their right in their reservation was "indefeasible and absolute, and that no power exists either in the Government of the United States or in individuals to divest them of that right." They continued using strong language in defense of their rights: "This Convention protests most solemnly against the assumption of any power either by the Government or its agents, whereby any part or portion of said Half Breed tract shall be recognized as open to pre-emption or sale, to squatters or other persons not allied by blood to the Sioux nation."[40]

The 1855 democratic convention and the role of mixed-ancestry Dakota people revealed their political power. The meeting was chaired by a mixed-ancestry Dakota, and the convention heard a delegation from the Lake Pepin Reservation who included language in the strongest possible terms asserting their rights over their land. Mixed-ancestry Dakota were a strong part of the Democratic base, and they also exerted significant political power within the party.

Mixed-ancestry Indians used this political power to serve in high political offices, such as the Wisconsin and Minnesota legislatures. At least five mixed-ancestry Indians served in the Wisconsin legislature, including three Brothertown Indians, one Ottawa man, and one Dakota man. At least nine Indigenous men served in the Minnesota legislature between 1849 and 1862: three Dakota men, one Ottawa, three Métis, and two Ojibwe men. At least ten white men with Indigenous wives and children served in the Wisconsin and Minnesota legislatures, including Joseph R. Brown, who served in both. Charles F. Picotte, a mixed-ancestry Iháŋkthuŋwaŋ Dakota and nephew of Chief Phadáni Aphápi (Struck by the Ree), served as sergeant-at-arms of the council of Dakota Territory during its inaugural session in 1862 until his retirement in 1877.[41] All of these men were members of the Democratic Party and had a stake in the legal rights of mixed-ancestry Indians either on their own behalf or that of their children. Additionally, two Dakota men, brothers Edwin and Andrew Bourke, served in the Manitoba legislature in the 1870s, less than ten years after their first cousin Baptiste Campbell had been executed with thirty-seven other Dakota men in 1862 for his part in the U.S.-Dakota War.

The service of mixed-ancestry Indian men in public offices in the Upper Midwest attests to the political sophistication of mixed-ancestry Indians. Mixed-ancestry legislators quickly and easily took to American politics and political leadership. Their presence and power on the political landscape could not be ignored, and the influence of the mixed-ancestry Indians as a substantial potential voting block led directly to Indian citizenship in the Upper Midwest.

Not only did Dakota people associate kinship with citizenship, but kinship also played a role in the public service of Dakota men. When it came to citizenship in the Dakota Nation, kinship was the key factor in belonging. As explained in chapter 1, the concept of "being a good relative" was paramount; striving to be a good relative and having kinship connections to members of the tribe was all that was needed to be a citizen of the nation. Through the documentation of the prominent Wápahaša family, kinship connections between numerous legislators are revealed. A granddaughter of Wápahaša I, Házaȟotawiŋ (Gray Huckleberry Woman), married a prominent fur trader, Alexander Graham, around the turn of the nineteenth century. Házaȟotawiŋ was the matriarch of a family that sent several members to the Minnesota Territorial Legislature. One daughter, Jane Graham, married James "Bully" Wells, a white man who served in three of the first four sessions of the Minnesota Territorial Legislature. Another daughter, Mary Graham, married a mixed-ancestry Dakota in the fur trade, Alexander Faribault, who served in the second session of the territorial legislature. Mary Graham Faribault's daughter Agnes married a white man named William Henry Forbes, who served in the first four sessions of the legislature, while her son George worked as a messenger during the third session.

The Faribault family was yet another mixed-ancestry Dakota family with strong ties to the Minnesota legislature. Alexander was the son of Jean Baptiste Faribault and a mixed-ancestry Dakota woman, Pelagie Kinie. Alexander's sister Lucy Faribault married a mixed-ancestry Ottawa Indian, Alexis Bailly, who served in the first session of the territorial legislature. Their son Henry G. Bailly was prominent in territorial politics. As mentioned above, he served as chair of the democratic convention held in Hastings in 1855. He was elected to the Minnesota Constitutional

Convention of 1857 and served in the last two sessions of the territorial legislature and the first session of the Minnesota state legislature before leaving the state to serve as an officer in the Fifth Minnesota Infantry Regiment during the Civil War and dying in service in 1865. The Graham and Faribault families were prominent mixed-ancestry Dakota families who had been in Minnesota since the late 1790s. Because of their significance among both the Dakota and white Minnesotans, marriage into these families often resulted in the creation of wealth through employment in the Indian service and political power in the Minnesota Territorial Legislature.

Taking a broader view, even more connections of the Wápahaša family served in the Wisconsin and Minnesota legislatures. Another granddaughter of Wápahaša I, Pelagie LaPointe, was an important matriarch. Her son Theophilus LaChapelle was elected to the Wisconsin Territorial Legislature in 1840. Two of Theophilus's siblings married siblings in the mixed-ancestry Ottawa Brisbois family of Prairie du Chien; another

Figure 13. Lucy Faribault Bailly, 1809–1855. A mixed-ancestry Bdewákhaŋthuŋwaŋ woman married to fur trader Alexis Bailly, a mixed-ancestry Odawa Indian and a member of the Minnesota Territorial Legislature. Her son Henry Bailly also served in the legislature before his death in the Civil War. Locator no. por 20467 p1, Minnesota Historical Society, Saint Paul.

Brisbois sibling, Joseph Brisbois, served in the Wisconsin Territorial Legislature. Another daughter of Pelagie LaPointe, Pauline LaChapelle, married Ira Brunson, a white man who served in the Wisconsin Territorial Legislature. Brunson's father, Alfred, ran against Theophilus in the 1840 election, and Brunson's brother Benjamin served in the Minnesota legislature. Although indirectly related, yet another granddaughter of Wápahaša I, Margaret Dubois, had kinship connections to men who served in Minnesota and Wisconsin long after her death. She married a fur trader of Ottawa descent, Joseph Rolette, whose brother-in-law Jean Brunet later served in the Wisconsin Territorial Legislature. Rolette's son through his second marriage, Joseph Rolette Jr., served in the Minnesota Territorial Legislature, while Joseph Jr.'s brother-in-law, a Métis man named Jerome Jerome, served in the Minnesota Constitutional Convention of 1857.

Strong women were the hinges in these powerful kinship connections. "Bully" Wells, the husband of Jane Graham, was able to benefit from Jane's kinship connections within the Dakota Nation to become a successful Indian trader. When he served in the legislature, Jane was a conduit through which she could lobby her husband on behalf of her Dakota kin or her own interests. Similarly, Lucy Faribault, the wife of an Odawa Indian of mixed ancestry, Alexis Bailly, offered her powerful kinship connections to make her husband a wealthy Indian trader among the Dakota. Like Jane, Lucy could use her influence on her husband in the legislature. Pelagie LaPointe lived to see her son, Theophilus Lachapelle, son-in-law Ira B. Brunson, and her daughter Therese's brother-in-law Joseph Brisbois serve in the Wisconsin Territorial Legislature. Unfortunately, Dakota women are largely invisible in the colonial archive, but through family history and an analysis of kinship we can uncover the significance of mixed-ancestry Dakota women. Women and their valuable kinship connections were at the center of belonging and citizenship in the Dakota Nation; they were also pivotal to both Indian and white men who wanted to acquire wealth and political power in early Minnesota.

The Hazelwood Republic

In 1856, the year before the Minnesota Constitutional Convention, the Indians of the Hazelwood Mission, on the Dakota Nation's reservation in western Minnesota, had declared themselves the Hazelwood Republic.[42] They elected a president and officers and drew up their own constitution. This was not a declaration of independence; rather, their constitution proclaimed their desire to become citizens of the United States en masse, on their own terms. Following Dakota understandings of citizenship, the members of the Hazelwood Republic wanted American citizenship for their entire kin group rather than in piecemeal fashion. Like the mixed-ancestry Indian men who served in public office, the mixed- and full-ancestry Dakota members of the Hazelwood Republic had political influence in Minnesota and used that power to influence the Minnesota Constitutional Convention of 1857 to include citizenship rights for Indians.

In his report to the commissioner of Indian Affairs in 1860, Joseph R. Brown, agent at Yellow Medicine, wrote of the Dakota view of the members of the Hazelwood Republic and other Dakota people "who desire to adopt the dress and habits of the whites." Brown wrote that the government needed to protect the members of the republic from other Dakota people in "opposition to the 'white Indians,' as they are termed in derision." He further argued that this derision led to intimidation and occasional violence "to discourage those who have joined the civilization bands, and to prevent others from joining."[43] Here Brown reveals how the Dakota also fused the concepts of "civilization," "citizenship," and "whiteness," although, as Brown notes, the Dakota may have seen whiteness as a performance where they "adopt the dress and habits of the whites."[44]

The Hazelwood constitution, written in both Dakota and English and dated July 29, 1856, had seven basic premises. They intended sections 1 through 4 to demonstrate that they were assimilated into American culture and ready for citizenship. Section 5 attested to their obedience to the U.S. government, while in section 7, the framers of the constitution expressed their wish to be treated as white people.[45] Of the seventeen signers of the constitution, eight were Dakota people of mixed ancestry, seven of them from the extended Renville family, who had long been influential among the Sisíthuŋwaŋ and Waȟpéthuŋwaŋ Dakota.

The intention of the writers in their appeal to whiteness was in both the legal and the racial sense. The members of the Hazelwood Republic wanted to be citizens, which, they understood from white Minnesotans, was the equivalent of whiteness. In 1857, the republic sent a petition to the constitutional convention to ensure that the Minnesota state constitution would include provisions for Indian citizenship. The petition read that the members of the republic were

> composed of half-bloods of the Dakota nation, who, by the Organic Act of the Territory, are constituted citizens; and full-blood Dakotas who have not been thus invested. That their Republic has been formed on the principles of education and labor; in other words, they have learned to read and write their own language, and some of them have obtained a partial knowledge of the English language, and they have adopted the dress and habits of civilized men. Your petitioners therefore desire that all who are civilized and educated among the Indians, whether part or full blood, may be recognized by the Constitution as citizens of the State of Minnesota.[46]

The petitioners succeeded, and the 1858 Minnesota state constitution included separate provisions for mixed- and full-ancestry Indians to acquire citizenship. The Hazelwood Republic, as did the Republican and Democratic members of the Minnesota Constitutional Convention, all tied Indian citizenship to whiteness and civilization. The tie to whiteness was both literal and figurative. Indians of mixed ancestry held Euro-American heritage, but Democrats went further to claim that citizenship bestowed whiteness. The Democrats and Republicans, as well as the members of the Hazelwood Republic, further tied Indian citizenship to civilization. The contemporary understandings of "civilization" fit what we would call "assimilated" today. Being civilized simply meant being assimilated into Western culture.

After the ratification of the Minnesota state constitution, the Hazelwood Republic had it published in Dakota so that its members could easily access the document. However, the Dakota translation of the section on the elective franchise is different from the English version and reflects a Dakota perspective. In the English version of the constitution, part 3 states, "Persons of mixed white and Indian blood, who have adopted the customs and habits of civilization." In Dakota it reads, "Tona hanke

Waxicun qa hanke Ikcewicaxta Waxicun ihduzapi qa Waxicun wicoran opapi kin hena."[47] However, translating the Dakota back into English, it reads, "Those that are part White and part Indian, that dress White and follow White customs." The Eurocentric term "civilization" has no equivalent in Dakota, instead using the term "wašíču," the Dakota word for the white race. This also reflects the Dakota perspective on the coalescence of citizenship, civilization, and whiteness. The Dakota translation replaces the word "civilized" with "white," demonstrating that they understood "civilized" to be the equivalent of Euro-American culture. Further, while the English version contains the language of "blood," the Dakota version did not use the discourse of blood when discussing race. The Dakota translation reflects a perception of race different from white Minnesotans' but gives a more forthright translation of "civilized" to "white," which matched how white Minnesotans understood "civilization."

Similarly, part 4 of the section on the elective franchise was also different in Dakota. In the original English, it read: "Persons of Indian blood residing in this State, who have adopted the language, customs and habits of civilization, after an examination before any District Court of the State, in such manner as may be provided by law, and shall have been pronounced by said court capable of enjoying the rights of citizenship within the State." Translated back into English, the Dakota version reads, "Those that follow the way of life of Indian Land, those who have language and dress and customs of Civilization, in the Minnesota District Court, according to the law the judge will ask them questions, when it is decreed, in that manner he will have proper citizenship in this Land." Although the original English in both the third and fourth sections mentions the word "civilization," only the fourth part in the Dakota translation uses this word and uses it in English. While part 3 uses "white" in place of "civilized," part 4 carries no racial language. Part 4 is also different in that it bases citizenship in the land, while part 3 never mentions the word "citizenship."

The mixed-ancestry clause in the state constitution simply read that mixed-ancestry Indians who "adopted the customs and habits of civilization" would be citizens. However, the full-ancestry clause required not only that Indians be "civilized" but also that they should adopt the language of civilization, and they had to prove in court that they were civilized.

This added burden of legally proving that Indians had adopted the "language of civilization" became a point of contention. Many Dakota people were literate in Dakota but not English and argued that because Dakota was a written language, it was a language of civilization. The courts disagreed, interpreting the clause in the constitution to mean that full-ancestry Indians had to speak English. While mixed-ancestry Indians could easily gain citizenship, simply by adopting Euro-American clothing and performing "whiteness," the English-language requirement effectively barred most full-ancestry Dakota from citizenship.[48]

The Minnesota constitution worded the full-ancestry citizenship clause in such a way—"in such manner as may be provided by law"—that an additional law was necessary to fully flesh out the process by which full-ancestry Indians could acquire citizenship. The legislature showed little interest in passing the necessary legislation to provide a means of legal citizenship to full-ancestry Indians. Indeed, it was in 1861, three years after Minnesota gained statehood, that the legislature finally passed this law. The law specified that full-ancestry Indians must produce at least two witnesses, "one of whom shall be a white man," to prove that they possessed five qualifications. First, candidates for citizenship had to understand what an oath was. Second, he must live in "a fixed residence in a house, as distinguished from a teepee or wigwam." Third, the candidate for citizenship must show that he had been employed for at least the previous two years in farming "or in the trades or in any other strictly civilized pursuit." Fourth, he must have "assumed the habits and worn the dress of civilization" during the previous two years. Finally, the full-ancestry Indian must possess "good moral character" and be a man "of correct general demeanor." If the courts accepted the man's request for citizenship, the court would deem him "a full citizen of the State, with the right to sue and be sued in any of the courts of this State in like manner and with the same effect as other inhabitants thereof, and shall be entitled to the same civil rights as other citizens."[49]

This act revealed that full-ancestry Indians were held to an extreme standard that was nearly impossible to meet. The act also imposed numerous additional limiting factors that the Minnesota constitution did not enumerate. Potential citizens had to prove that they had assimilated into

Euro-American culture. While mixed-ancestry Indians simply had to appear "civilized," full-ancestry Indians had to prove in court that they lived in Euro-American houses, were employed in Euro-American occupations or styles of agriculture, and wore Euro-American clothes. In addition, while not specified in the 1861 law, the state constitution included the language requirement. The full-ancestry uncle of the Trudell children, the brother of Ičíyapiwiŋ, Henry Waŋbdíšuŋ, may also have been interested in acquiring American citizenship. In a Works Progress Administration interview in 1936, Henry's daughter Susan reported that her parents were members of the Hazelwood mission at the Upper Sioux Agency before the U.S.-Dakota War.[50] As an Indian of full ancestry, Henry Waŋbdíšuŋ likely never acquired U.S. citizenship before his death in 1898.

The performance of whiteness through clothing was also a performance of citizenship. In the nineteenth century, American officials, when speaking of clothing, regularly referred to Euro-American clothing as "citizens' clothing" when contrasting with American Indian clothing. In a report to the military commander of the U.S. Army's Sioux Expedition of 1864, Captain Charles E. Flandrau wrote of discovering Dakota Indians "dressed in citizens' clothing" near a church.[51] Twenty-five years later, General S. C. Armstrong had similar sentiments, arguing that "citizens' clothing is now the rule among the Sioux, where a half dozen years ago it was the exception, and marks an affiliation between them and the whites, which is only second to importance to using the same language."[52] Flandrau and Armstrong demonstrate the importance of clothing in how white Americans perceived Indians. Euro-American clothing was not only tied to whiteness but also equated to citizenship, at least when used to describe Indians. Armstrong further notes the significance of the English language in incorporating Indians into the American nation.

Race and Citizenship in the Midwest

Wisconsin was the first state in the Midwest to explicitly permit the suffrage of Indians. On February 1, 1848, Wisconsin officially adopted their state constitution, which provided suffrage to "Persons of Indian blood who shall have once been declared by law of Congress to be citizens of the United States," referring to the Brothertown Indians who had accepted

U.S. citizenship as a tribe in 1839. The Wisconsin constitution section on suffrage also included "civilized persons of Indian descent not members of any tribe."[53] This brief sentence enfranchised numerous Indians in the State of Wisconsin. As a legal statement, two parts of this sentence, "civilized" and "not members of any tribe," would be difficult to prove or disprove legally.

The Wisconsin constitution did not go on to give a legal definition of "civilized" or "not members of any tribe." As mixed-ancestry Indians voted and served in the legislature both before and after statehood, certainly some Indians fit the criteria of citizenship. It is uncertain if officials ever challenged the citizenship of Indian voters, but these concepts would be difficult to legally prove or disprove in court. Despite the clause stating that potential voters could not be members of tribes, voters like Theophilus LaChapelle, although living away from his tribe, continued a connection with his people. Even while serving in the territorial legislature, LaChapelle wrote a letter to the *Wisconsin Herald* where he spoke of voting on issues relating to the Lake Pepin Reservation, in which he explicitly stated he had an interest as a mixed-ancestry Dakota.[54] Many mixed-ancestry Indians lived away from their tribes but continued to retain some connection to their tribes, or at least identified as members or descendants of their tribes, but this did not exclude them from citizenship.

Similarly, "civilized" was a term not defined in law and usually meant simply performing whiteness by wearing short hair and Euro-American clothing. An 1857 newspaper article about the Hazelwood Republic revealed the ways that white Americans tied civilization to clothing and short hair. Calling the republic a "civilized community," the article explained, "the ordeal which they pass through, being the cutting off of their jet and flowing locks, and the donning of pantaloons, jacket, &c., like the white man."[55] Another article a year later drew this connection more clearly, "The Sioux Indians have signified their intention of adopting the dress of their pale-faced brethren and pursuing an agricultural life. . . . But the greatest step towards civilization is in their requesting Superintendent Cullen to bring a pair of shears to their settlement in order to cut off their hair."[56] White Americans in the Midwest placed high value on Indians cutting their hair and wearing Euro-American clothing. Yet this was a superficial measure of "civilization" that merely required that Indians look the part by changing their clothes and cutting their hair.

Two years after Wisconsin adopted its constitution, the state of Michigan adopted a new constitution, in 1850, which included Indian suffrage. The Michigan constitution used similar language as that of Wisconsin: "Civilized male inhabitants of Indian descent, native of the United States, and not members of any tribe, shall be an elector and entitled to vote."[57] Indian suffrage in the Michigan constitution was nearly indistinguishable from that in the Wisconsin constitution, simply including the statement "native of the United States" to ensure Indians born in Canada could not acquire citizenship in Michigan. Although Wisconsin and Michigan provided citizenship for Indians without any mention of ancestry or blood quantum, it was primarily Indians of mixed ancestry who, because of their greater mobility outside their tribal lands, could benefit from these provisions. Although these provisions of citizenship seem stark and highly limited, without additional legal language to define "civilized" and "not members of any tribe," citizenship was easier to acquire in Wisconsin and Michigan than it appeared. It also demonstrates the importance placed on Indian citizenship in the Upper Midwest at mid-century.

In November of 1849, the newly created legislature of Minnesota Territory met for the first time. The Organic Act, passed earlier that year by the U.S. Congress, created the Territory of Minnesota. It stated, "Every free white male inhabitant above the age of twenty-one years, who shall have been a resident of said territory at the time of the passage of this act, shall be entitled to vote at the first election, and shall be eligible to any office within the said territory." The act went on: "But the qualifications of voters and of holding office, at all subsequent elections, shall be such as shall be prescribed by the legislative assembly."[58] One of the first acts of the territorial legislature was to define which of the territory's inhabitants were to be considered citizens, with the right to vote and hold office. The legislature upheld the language of the Organic Act, limiting suffrage to white males who had reached the age of twenty-one. Although, in a section that appears hastily tacked on, the legislature enfranchised another set of territorial inhabitants, declaring, "All persons of a mixture of white and Indian blood, and who shall have adopted the habits and customs of civilized men, are hereby declared to be entitled to all the rights and privileges granted by the provisions of this act."[59] This law specified that only those Indians with a mixture of white and Indian blood were enfranchised, meaning that the citizenship of mixed-ancestry Indians was based in their whiteness and despite their Indianness.

Unlike the provisions for Indian suffrage in the Wisconsin and Michigan constitutions, the law in Minnesota Territory specified a racial requirement and made no mention to connection to tribe. The Minnesota law was explicit that suffrage was only for mixed-ancestry Indians and based citizenship in race. However, the law was more permissive in that there was no requirement that prospective citizens be disconnected from their tribal nations. This meant that even mixed-ancestry Dakota that lived on the Dakota reservation along the Minnesota River or that appeared on tribal rolls could vote. The law also specified that they adopt the "habits and customs of civilized men," but, like in Wisconsin and Michigan, this meant that they simply had to perform "civilization" by cutting their hair and wearing Euro-American clothing. The law entirely disregarded Indians of African ancestry. In other parts of the country, the boundaries of whiteness were limited and heavily policed, but in Minnesota in the first half of the 1800s, where Euro-Americans were heavily outnumbered by nonwhite people, whiteness was fluid. Because of their small population, white Americans did not have the power to exclude in early Minnesota, which meant that Indians of mixed and full ancestry, and a small handful of African Americans, were able to hold power and status. For instance, the laxity of the racial hierarchy in the Upper Midwest led George Bonga, born in Minnesota in 1802 to an African American father and an Ojibwe Indian mother, to famously call himself one of the first white men born in Minnesota. This came not from an internalized identity as white but rather from the conflation, in Minnesota, of three concepts: whiteness, citizenship, and being civilized.[60]

But Bonga's experience as a respected fur trader and interpreter was atypical after statehood. As William D. Green argues, before Minnesota acquired statehood in 1858, African Americans and mixed-ancestry Indians were treated comparably to white residents of the region. After statehood, the Upper Midwest largely adopted the anti-Black legal measures common in the rest of the United States but permitted mixed-ancestry Indians to continue to participate in state politics.[61]

The debates over the citizenship of Indians during the Minnesota Constitutional Convention of 1857 provide the most extensive window into how lawmakers in the Upper Midwest perceived Indian citizenship.[62] When the citizens of a territory wished to obtain statehood, they must first have ratified a state constitution. The Republican and Democrat members refused to work together, meeting separately to construct their own constitutions, and later convened a joint session in order to merge the two documents. Both bodies debated whom would be eligible for suffrage within the state, and although they came to the same conclusion that mixed-ancestry Indians should be considered citizens, their arguments for and against enfranchisement differed in significant ways.

Two main points arose in the Republican side of the convention pertaining to Indians of mixed ancestry and citizenship. First, the Republicans were more concerned with African American citizenship than Indian citizenship and hoped to exploit the popularity for the enfranchisement of mixed-ancestry Indians to include suffrage for African Americans. Second, the Republicans demonstrated that they understood citizenship as tied to whiteness and being civilized. Many members of the Republican convention argued that if mixed-ancestry Indians were to be included as citizens based on their white ancestry, then African Americans with white ancestry should also be included. John Wesley North argued that "it does not become men to admit the rights of the Indians and half-breeds of this Territory, and at the same time despise the mixed blood of the other race. I hold that the blood of the first families of Virginia, running in the veins of mulattoes is as elevating and whitening in its influence as the blood of the Indian traders, whisky sellers and gamblers running in the veins of the half-breed Sioux."[63] Here North is explicit in his belief that citizenship should be tied to whiteness, as it was perceived in early Minnesota, and should be made to include Indians and African Americans. Members of the Republican convention treated citizenship for mixed-ancestry Indians as a given and spent most of their energy fighting for African American citizenship—a fight they ultimately lost.

Many Republicans felt that the enfranchisement of mixed-ancestry Indians could be abused and would result in fraudulent elections. Thomas Wilson, although he believed in mixed-ancestry suffrage, argued that there had been fraudulent votes in the past when noncitizen Indians had been dressed in so-called civilized clothing, taken to the polls, and were paid to vote for particular candidates. "I know some half-breeds I would vote for as soon as for any man I know," he claimed, but he argued further that the constitution should "throw a guard around the right [to vote] so that it cannot be abused."[64] Another member, Amos Coggswell, went a step further, stating, "I am decidedly opposed to half-blood Indians, or half-breeds, or quarter-breeds, or any other kind of breeds voting, unless it is under restrictions which fully provide against abuses of that right."[65] Coggswell proposed a long list of potential restrictions, but in the end, the Republican version of the proposed state constitution left it to the legislature to regulate mixed-ancestry citizenship.

Unlike the Republican side of the convention, the Democrats completely opposed African American citizenship but argued that mixed-ancestry Indians should be considered "white." A lengthy debate among the Democrats concluded that mixed-ancestry Indians should enjoy white racial status. Missionary Stephen R. Riggs summed up these efforts in the Democratic convention: "They propose to make a new dictionary meaning of the word white so that it shall include all mixed bloods of Indian descent and civilized Indians."[66] This was not totally without precedent; as Lucy Eldersveld Murphy notes, many mixed-ancestry Indians in the Midwest were able to avoid racialization as nonwhite even when they were not permitted to fully participate in the white American world.[67] The Democrats perceived whiteness and citizenship as so intertwined that they agreed to not only overlook but essentially erase the Indianness of mixed-ancestry citizens.

The members continued to debate whether mixed-ancestry Indians were white or if citizenship bestowed whiteness upon them while at the same time expressing their wish to exclude African Americans. This inconsistency was best exhibited by Lafayette Emmett: "Now, I am willing that the word 'white' shall be inserted in the proper place, and that it shall be made to include persons of mixed Indian blood. I doubt whether there is a man on this floor who would exclude them from that privilege. But I want to exclude mulattoes; I want to exclude even those with one-eighth African blood."[68] Minnesota Democrats were willing to make the boundaries of whiteness permeable, allowing mixed-ancestry Indians into the fold of the white race. This was to acquire the patronage of mixed-ancestry voters who would help keep the Democrats in power. Proclaiming mixed-ancestry Indians to be white, however, allowed the Democrats to uphold the idea that "citizen" equaled "white."

The Minnesota Democrats were so deeply invested in mixed-ancestry suffrage not from a moral sense of racial equality but rather for the political boon mixed-ancestry citizens would be to their party. All of the Indigenous people that served in the Minnesota territorial and state legislatures between 1849 and 1862 were Democrats. Further, all of the white members of the legislature who were married to Indian women were also Democrats. These members were known as the "Moccasin Democrats" and were a powerful faction of the Democratic Party in Minnesota. Democrats had long been connected to the Indian service in the Upper Midwest and had worked as Indian traders and Indian agents or held lucrative supply contracts with the Office of Indian Affairs. The white men who held these positions were allied with prominent mixed-ancestry men, cemented through their kinship connections cultivated through intermarriage.[69] The Republicans, a party in its infancy in the 1850s, did not hold the political patronage that the Democrats did, leaving Indians of mixed ancestry to align with the Democrats because they understood that the Democrats held political influence in Indian affairs.

Meanwhile, some mixed-ancestry Indians connected to the Great Nemaha and Yankton Reservations voted in Nebraska Territory, although there was no law explicitly enfranchising them. Republican abolitionist Samuel G. Daily, running for Nebraska Territory's delegate to Congress in 1860 against Democrat J. Sterling Morton, alleged numerous frauds and contested the election. Morton, later the founder of the Arbor Day holiday, won the election by a slim margin of fourteen votes, but in the end, the U.S. House of Representatives reversed enough votes to give Daily the victory by 150 votes. In response to Daily's allegations, Morton served a countercomplaint that it was Daily who benefited the most from irregularities and frauds. In his complaint, many of Daily's allegations centered on Indian reservations. He argued that residents of the various Indian reservations in the territory (without mentioning their race) were ineligible to vote in the territorial election because Indian reservations were federal lands outside the jurisdiction of the territory and claimed that these residents were paid to vote for Morton.[70] Morton's countercomplaint made no mention of Indians or Indian reservations; instead, he repeatedly blamed "itinerant abolitionists and negro thieves" of stealing votes.[71]

Witnesses testified that there were only about forty voters that appeared to vote at the northern precinct of L'Eau Qui Court County, but the poll list names 122 voters. At least twelve of the badly misspelled names are of mixed-ancestry Dakota men, but as witnesses said that some voters voted more than once under false names or were claiming to cast a vote for somebody else, it's unclear how many mixed-ancestry Indians actually voted in the election and which names were fictitious. Witnesses claimed that the mixed- and full-ancestry Indians present were from the nearby Yankton Agency. A group of about eight full-ancestry Iháŋkthuŋwaŋ Dakota were apparently working for Charles Booge, a sutler at Yankton Agency, and guarded the door of the polling place with swords and refused to let anyone in or out except at Booge's orders. At least one of the full-ancestry Indians also voted, and the final tally had all 122 votes go to the Democrat, Morton.[72] Their votes were eventually discarded, but Dakota people played a significant role in the election at this polling place.

At the same election, residents of the Great Nemaha Reservation also voted in the election in Richardson and Nemaha Counties. Lawyers who deposed witnesses in the Daily–Morton dispute were most interested in voters in Rulo, Arago, and Saint Stephen precincts, all associated with the Great Nemaha Reservation. Witnesses testified that as many as one-third to one-half of the residents of Rulo and Saint Stephen were Indians of mixed ancestry, while only about 5 to 10 percent of the residents of Arago were of Indian ancestry. In addition, most of the white men living in Rulo and Saint Stephen were French Canadians married to Indian women, and most had never been naturalized or declared their intention to become citizens. Most of the residents of Arago were German immigrants who had been naturalized or declared their intentions. It is unclear how many Indians of mixed ancestry voted from those precincts, but one witness identified five or six on the poll book for Rulo, and the vast majority of the votes in these three precincts went to the Democrat Morton.[73] There were almost certainly other mixed-ancestry voters on the reservation, and numerous white men with Indian families voted. My mixed-ancestry Iháŋkthuŋwaŋ Langdeau ancestors were residents of Saint Stephen in 1860, and my French Canadian great-great-great-grandfather Maurice Langdeau may have voted in the election.

A mixed-ancestry Otoe woman, Fillisita Beddow, a resident of the Great Nemaha Reservation, inquired into the rights of mixed-ancestry Indians and the right to vote. She asked, if there is civil law in Nemaha County, "why is it the half breeds is not a loud there oath or to vote[?]" She further complained that the county made them pay taxes on their land but did not allow them to vote. "Tha can sue me and take my land and Property for det and yet I am not a loud my oath in court."[74] Beddow tied her complaint over suffrage to landownership. As mixed-ancestry Indians could have their property taxed and could be sued in court, she believed they should have the right to give oaths in court and to vote in the local elections.

The next year, Congress created Dakota Territory, carving it out of Nebraska Territory and much of what had been Minnesota Territory just a few years earlier. The new territory had a similar political terrain as Minnesota, with the Moccasin Democrats composing a significant faction of the territory's Democratic Party, although the party was more factionalized than it was in Minnesota. Like Minnesota, Dakota Territory had a significant population of mixed-ancestry Dakota, mostly Iháŋkthuŋwaŋ Dakota and Sičháŋǧu Lakota but also some mixed-ancestry members of the Minnesota bands and from other Lakota bands, most of whom were willing to follow the Democrats. Unlike Minnesota, however, the territorial legislature was made up solely of white men, except Charles F. Picotte, a mixed-ancestry Iháŋkthuŋwaŋ Dakota who served as sergeant-at-arms of the territorial council.

In May 1862, a year after the creation of the territory, the Moccasin Democrats in the legislature proposed the General Half-Breed Bill, intended to provide citizenship for mixed-ancestry Indians in the territory.

Moses K. Armstrong, a Democrat in the legislature and later the territorial delegate to Congress, explained that the "bill provided that all mixed bloods who could read, write or speak the English language should be entitled to the right of citizenship."[75] This law went further than the Minnesota constitution's implication that full-ancestry Indians should be literate by explicitly laying out that potential citizens had to be literate in English or at least speak English. Unlike the Minnesota constitution, it limited citizenship to mixed-ancestry Indians only.

Perhaps learning from the debacle of the Minnesota Constitutional Convention of 1857, legislators in Dakota Territory held different racial politics than their counterparts in Minnesota. The Republicans of Dakota Territory, like those in Minnesota, wanted African American suffrage but were sternly opposed to the suffrage of mixed-ancestry Indians, understanding that enfranchising mixed-ancestry Indians would be a gift to the Democrats. For their part, the Democrats were so strongly against the African American vote that they wished to ban all African Americans from entering the territory. Because the mixed-ancestry population, among whom legislators counted the large Métis population, was larger in proportion to the non-Indian population than in Minnesota, mixed-ancestry suffrage would have given the Democrats an unbeatable coalition in the territory. However, given the factionalized nature of the Democrats in the territory, the bill failed to pass by one vote.[76] Armstrong explained, "Under this act the half-breeds would have outvoted the rest of the territory."[77] Armstrong and some other Democrats feared that enfranchising mixed-ancestry Indians would give the numerous Métis people, whom lawmakers lumped with mixed-ancestry Indians as half-breeds, too much power in the territory, leading to some Democrats voting against the bill.

The failure of the General Half-Breed Bill did not discourage Democrats; instead, they bestowed citizenship on a handful of mixed-ancestry Dakota men to acquire their patronage. Days after the defeat of the bill, the territorial governor, William Jayne, signed bills into law enfranchising fourteen mixed-ancestry Dakota in May 1862. This included Charles F. Picotte, who was already serving as sergeant-at-arms of the territorial council. The legislature enfranchised six more in 1863 and an additional ten mixed-ancestry Dakota between 1864 and 1868.[78] Thirty mixed-ancestry Dakota people acquired citizenship in Dakota Territory, and as many as one-third of those enfranchised were minors; Democratic lawmakers probably enfranchised them at the request of their white fathers or to gain their influence.

By 1864, if not before, there were already electoral issues with the mixed-ancestry Dakota. In an 1864 election in Charles Mix County, which included the Yankton Reservation within its bounds, the poll was reduced to sixty-nine total votes for the county. As many as sixteen mixed-ancestry Indians voted in the county, but a committee found that only four had been made citizens by statute, resulting in the remaining votes being discarded. With such a small voter base, mixed-ancestry Indians had the power to sway elections, especially if they voted illegally, which they often did.[79]

The first Dakota man to acquire U.S. citizenship in Dakota Territory was Walter Arconge. He was the son of a French Canadian, Moses Arconge, and Ellen Dixon, a mixed-ancestry Dakota from the Bdewákhaŋthuŋwaŋ band and ex-wife of trader and Indian agent Joseph R. Brown. Born in Mendota in 1843, he grew up there, but by 1860 he was living with his mother in a small mixed-ancestry Dakota community west of the Minnesota border, just west of Big Stone Lake. By the late 1860s, he was married to an Iháŋkthuŋwaŋ Dakota woman named Tašína and living on the Yankton Reservation. Arconge was only eighteen when he acquired citizenship in 1862, but by 1866 the citizens of Bon Homme County elected him constable, and in the years following, he engaged in some unsavory political tactics.[80]

My great-great-great-grandfather John Baptiste Colombe revealed the ways that politicians in Dakota Territory exploited Indians of mixed ancestry. John, a French Canadian, was named by his wife's relatives Wašíču Huŋská, or White Man's Leggings. John had lived among the Sičháŋǧu Lakota and Iháŋkthuŋwaŋ Dakota since 1847. By 1855, he married Josette Dorion, a mixed-ancestry woman of Sičháŋǧu and Iháŋkthuŋwaŋ descent. Josette was a descendant of the old Dorion family, who had been trading and intermarrying with the Indians of the Missouri River since the 1770s. Born about 1825, John's obituary claimed that "he was successively a hunter and trapper for the Hudson Bay Company, Indian trader, government interpreter, scout for the army, farrier for a cavalry regiment, steamboat-man and later engaged in raising horses."[81] Adeline S. Gnirk claimed he was also a wood chopper and freighter and was appointed town marshal of Denver, Colorado Territory, in 1862.[82] While some of his activities have been recorded, many have not been documented. By 1864, the family lived near Fort Laramie in present-day Wyoming, where one observer claimed of John that "I have known him to have no permanent residence, nowheres, he roaming about like an Indian with his lodge and is not a native of the United States but of Canada."[83] The family moved east in 1869 to Whetstone Agency after the Treaty of Fort Laramie. John was a boss farmer at the agency from 1869 to 1870, a federal position with the responsibility of acculturating Indians into Euro-American forms of agriculture and animal husbandry and overseeing the distribution and use of seeds, animals, and agricultural implements.

On April 27, 1871, John gave testimony about the 1870 election for the Dakota territorial delegate to the U.S. House of Representatives. The election, between Republican Walter Burleigh and Democrat Moses Armstrong, saw the Republican candidate exploit mixed-ancestry Indians on the Great Sioux Reservation and Yankton Reservation in order to gain political power. Burleigh was closely connected to the Indians on the Yankton Reservation as he had served as an Indian agent there from 1861 to 1865. John, who did not vote in the election, viewed the poll list for the Campbell Ranch precinct, near Fort Randall on the Dakota–Nebraska border, and was asked by Burleigh's council to designate "all persons he recognizes as half-breed Indians, and to state which ones were under the age of twenty-one years."[84] John named eighteen voters that were mixed-ancestry Indians, ten of whom were under age twenty-one and as young as sixteen. While John did not witness the Indians being paid for their votes, he testified that they all voted for the Republican, Burleigh, and that "a majority of them were so much under the influence of liquor that I do not think they knew who they were voting for; in fact, I do not think they cared."[85] An anecdote between Burleigh and Abraham Lincoln gives some insight into Burleigh's character. He campaigned for Lincoln in Pennsylvania in 1860 and visited the new president in Washington in 1861 where

Lincoln offered him the job of Indian agent at Yankton Agency. When told that the pay was $2,000 per year, he answered that at that rate he "would have to starve or steal." Lincoln allegedly responded, "If I am any judge of human nature, you won't starve," suggesting that theft was part of the job.[86] According to the Ihá̧ŋkthuŋwaŋ Dakota, as an Indian agent, Burleigh cheated them out of thousands of dollars of cash and goods.[87]

Other witnesses gave damning testimony against the Democrat, Armstrong. R. W. Andrews testified that he witnessed at least fourteen mixed-ancestry Dakota from the Yankton Reservation illegally vote for Armstrong at the Emmanuel Creek precinct in Bon Homme County. He claimed that Alexander Keeler told him he worked for Armstrong and that the mixed-ancestry Dakota would only come to vote if they were paid.[88] John L. Turner corroborated Andrews's testimony, saying that he gave whiskey from his store to voters at Armstrong's orders. Turner could not name how many mixed-ancestry Indians he supplied with liquor, stating, "I cannot always tell a half-breed from a white man."[89] In his testimony, Lester E. Wood claimed that Alexander Keeler and Walter Arconge were responsible for bringing these noncitizen Indians to the polls.[90]

Walter Arconge, a mixed-ancestry citizen of Dakota Territory, played both sides of the political field for personal gain. Before the election, as Ray D. Andrews testified, the Republican, Burleigh, paid Arconge twenty dollars to electioneer for him.[91] However, Arconge led a party of mixed-ancestry Dakota from the Yankton Reservation who all voted for the Democrat, Armstrong, including Arconge. Armstrong's man, Captain R. W. Andrews, paid Arconge twenty dollars to electioneer for the Democrats. After voting, Arconge demanded an additional twenty dollars from Andrews, asserting that the deal for getting the mixed-ancestry Indians to the polls was forty dollars. Andrews refused to pay, asserting the deal was only for twenty dollars.[92] Arconge participated in the dirty politics of the day, accepting money from both candidates to commit voter fraud by means of bringing noncitizen Indians to the polls. Although a handful of the men he brought to the election precinct were enfranchised by the legislature like himself, most were not citizens.

The case of mixed-ancestry citizenship in Dakota Territory reveals how white American politicians exploited mixed-ancestry Indians for their own political purposes. In Minnesota, Republicans only wanted to enfranchise mixed-ancestry Indians in hopes of using their citizenship as a springboard to enfranchise African Americans. A few years later in Dakota Territory, Republican lawmakers opposed Indian citizenship because they knew it would work against them politically. The Democrats wanted to manipulate the mixed-ancestry vote to achieve their political goals but failed to pass the General Half-Breed Bill for fear it would give Indians too much power. This did not stop them from enfranchising a small number of mixed-ancestry Indians to bolster their numbers, and they turned to more nefarious means by paying noncitizen Indians to vote for them. However, by 1870, the noncitizen Indian vote could be manipulated to vote for either Democrats or Republicans. As John Colombe testified, the mixed-ancestry Indians of the Whetstone Agency were induced to vote for the Republican Burleigh, while Arconge persuaded the mixed-ancestry Indians of the Yankton Reservation to vote for the Democratic candidate, Armstrong.

The Dakota Territorial Civil Code made certain that Indians in the territory held limited legal rights. The civil code asserted that "Indians resident within this territory have the same rights and duties as other persons" but "they cannot vote or hold office" and "they cannot grant, lease or incumber Indian lands, except in the cases provided by special laws."[93] The territory also restricted militia service and jury duty to citizens, meaning that the rights and duties of Indians in the territory were virtually nonexistent.

The territorial legislature also enacted laws with specific language limiting the rights of mixed-ancestry Indians. When it appeared to a "probate judge that a half-breed minor, or an infant of mixed blood" resided in the territory and owned property "or is entitled to, an annuity from the United States, or has script for an amount of land," the court would appoint a guardian. However, the law continued, "an Indian woman, or a half-breed woman, cannot be lawful guardian of the property of their children."[94] Mixed-ancestry children who had received an allotment of land on the Great Nemaha Reservation or who had received land scrip from the relinquishment of the Lake Pepin Reservation would likely have a white man assigned to them as guardian by the probate court. This law put Indian land into the hands of white men of the territory who then had the right to dispose of these lands as they saw fit, ostensibly for the benefit of their mixed-ancestry wards.

The citizenship of mixed-ancestry Indians in Minnesota, as well as their public service, was short-lived. The U.S.-Dakota War erupted in the summer of 1862, ending with the mass execution of thirty-eight Dakota men on December 26, 1862—the largest mass execution in American history. Despite Indians of mixed ancestry having served in every session of the Minnesota territorial and state legislatures between 1849 and 1862, it was not until 1933 that another person of Indian ancestry served in the Minnesota legislature. The racial language permitting the enfranchisement of mixed- and full-ancestry Indians remained in the Minnesota constitution until 1960. The war also put an end to the Hazelwood Republic. Indians of full ancestry perceived the Hazelwood community as a threat to the Dakota way of life and destroyed all of the buildings in the community.

Following the war, the state House of Representatives posed the Bill to Outlaw Indians, which "provides that any Indian, who shall be found off the reservation, shall be deemed to be an outlaw, and not under the protection or entitled to any of the benefits and privileges, which the Constitution and laws of the State provide or secure to persons, and that no action or prosecution shall be had or entertained in any court of this State, for any violation of the person or property of such Indian committed during the time he shall be off the reservation." The bill also provided "that half-breeds shall be considered as Indians, and in the same manner."[95] The bill never passed, but it was part of a broader movement to restrict the civil liberties of Indian people in Minnesota in the wake of the war. It was no coincidence that bills to restrict Indians to reservations would arise at the same moment when states began denying suffrage to Indians based on the fact that they resided on reservations, which were outside the jurisdiction of the state. In Minnesota, this was a form of legislative revenge against the Dakota to punish those few who remained in the state.

When the U.S. Army executed the thirty-eight Dakota men for their participation in the war, so too died Indian citizenship in Minnesota and the special legal rights afforded to Indians of mixed ancestry. Among those executed were three Dakota men of mixed ancestry who were American citizens. One of these men was Baptiste Campbell, a citizen who voted ten years earlier, beside Francis Trudell, at an election in Mendota, Minnesota, on October 12, 1852. Despite Campbell's U.S. citizenship and his decade-long voting record, the U.S. Army tried Campbell by military tribunal, finding him guilty and sentencing him to death in mere minutes, without benefit of council. Campbell and the other thirty-seven executed Dakota were not afforded the rights of enemy combatants from a sovereign nation but were treated as criminals. Likewise, Campbell and the others did not receive due process as U.S. citizens.

In later years, my great-great grandfather Levi Trudell was politically active in the Democratic Party and served in public office, although according to his reckoning, he did not become a U.S. citizen until 1885, when he was in his thirties.[96] Despite the *Knox County Democrat*'s declaration in 1887 that "Levi Truedell will be the first member of the Sioux nation that ever sat in a state convention," Dakota people had previously attended political conventions in Minnesota and Wisconsin. Levi was probably the first Indian to attend a political convention in Nebraska, where, just three years earlier, the U.S. Supreme Court denied that John Elk, an Indian from Nebraska, was eligible for U.S. citizenship under the Fourteenth Amendment. Levi Trudell served as a delegate from Knox County, where, according to the *Omaha World-Herald,* "he represents some 200 Indians in that county who have become citizens."[97] He was elected a constable in Knox County in 1898 and was appointed a postmaster in the same county in 1906. Despite his public service, white Americans, according to the *Democrat* article, were more concerned about the novelty of an Indian attending the state convention: "Lincoln's name is honored and revered as the emancipator of the negro race from the bonds of slavery. To Grover Cleveland belongs the honor of conferring the right of suffrage upon the more intelligent, braver native American race—the Indians."[98] Despite the triumphant nature of the article, it illuminated a hierarchy of citizenship based in race, with Indians above African Americans and the implication that Euro-Americans were at the top.

This brief moment of citizenship from the 1840s to the 1860s was a climax for Indians of mixed ancestry in the Midwest, ending with the virtual loss of their citizenship rights in Minnesota in the wake of the U.S.-Dakota War and the loss of their separate legal rights. In the aftermath of the war, government officials began using blood quantum against Indians of mixed ancestry to define them out of existence. As the debates in the Minnesota Constitutional Convention and the Hazelwood Republic's constitution reveal, Indian citizenship was understood by both lawmakers and Indians as based in whiteness and civilization. Although the Hazelwood Republic succeeded in having a pathway for full-ancestry citizenship included in the Minnesota constitution, Indian citizenship was effectively limited to those of mixed ancestry. Mixed-ancestry Indians held political power and exerted this power to achieve American citizenship and serve in both the Wisconsin and Minnesota legislatures. They quickly adapted to and succeeded in American politics, which were dramatically different from Indian consensus-based political systems.

CHAPTER 6

Land Scrip and Allotment

Mixed-Ancestry Indians and Land Dispossession

Mary Wacouta, a mixed-ancestry neighbor of the Trudell family, filed a lawsuit in 1864 with the Wabasha County Minnesota District Court, alleging that Artemas Sharpe, a prominent Connecticut-born farmer, planted fields on her land and had stolen hundreds of dollars' worth of crops that had been stored in her house. Through a Dakota interpreter, Wacouta testified that she built the house and farm on her land on the Lake Pepin Reservation in 1853. "I have forbidden him in Sioux probably 10 times" from plowing her lands, she said, eventually asking Frank Trudell to confront Sharpe in English about his attempt to take over Wacouta's land. Sharpe testified that Trudell never forbade him from plowing her land. In Frank Trudell's testimony, corroborated by his brother August, also called Thatóheya (Against the Wind), however, he testified, "I told Sharp at his house that Pl[ainti]ff said he must not plow there." Wacouta's lawyer asked Frank Trudell, "What if anything did D[e]f[endan]t Sharp offer you at the time you forbid Sharp, if he [Frank] would get Plff out of possession of [her] property[?]" Trudell responded, "Sharp said if I would get Plff out of [her] house he would give me $50."[1] In this case, Sharpe attempted to dispossess Mary Wacouta out of her land. Indians of mixed ancestry were not exempt from land dispossession, but unlike Dakota tribal lands that the American government acquired through dishonest and coercive treaties, Dakota people of mixed ancestry experienced an array of individually based dispossessive practices at the hands of non-Indian squatters, settlers, and land speculators.

After the 1830s failed attempts of the mixed-ancestry Dakota to have the government divide and allot their lands at Lake Pepin, and after the Senate refused to ratify the land cession treaties of the 1840s, the Dakota of mixed ancestry once again began an intense petition campaign to have their reservation surveyed and allotted among them in 1853.[2] This campaign resulted in an act of Congress in 1854, which, in exchange for their reservation, provided land scrip to the mixed-ancestry Dakota. Land scrip is simply a legal document stating that the bearer is eligible to claim land; in this case, the mixed-ancestry Dakota could claim 480 acres of land on the reservation or anywhere in the public domain. As a result, the Dakota people of mixed ancestry experienced two distinct dispossessive events: from the white settlers who squatted on their reservation and devalued their land by stealing their timber and, on an individual scale, when many mixed-ancestry Dakota were defrauded, coerced, or swindled out of their individual lands.

In this chapter, I argue that Indians of mixed ancestry held different property rights from other Indians and from other U.S. citizens. Just like other Indians, however, non-Indians dispossessed them of their lands in ways sometimes reminiscent of other Indigenous dispossessions and sometimes in unusual ways at the individual level. The mixed-ancestry Dakota owners of the Lake Pepin Reservation experienced dispossession before the federal government divided their land and again on an individual level after receiving their land scrip. Despite their status as U.S. citizens, as "half-breeds" with a distinct legal and racial status, the mixed-ancestry Dakota, who held their land "in the same manner that other Indian Titles are held," also endured land dispossession.[3] With their newfound fictitious whiteness through the acquisition of U.S. citizenship, the property of mixed-ancestry Indians was also subject to American legal jurisdiction. In many respects, it was this landownership that provided them legal legitimacy. The settler colonial legal apparatus was obligated to regulate mixed-ancestry land dealings, which, in part, made it possible for the mixed-ancestry Dakota to enjoy the rights of U.S. citizenship.[4]

Cheryl I. Harris argues that the "rights in property are contingent on, intertwined with, and conflated with race."[5] Landownership, citizenship, and whiteness became inextricably linked; this is demonstrated in the very foundation of federal Indian law, the foundation of which is the belief that white Americans had a fundamental right to Indian land. Harris asserts that "only whites possessed whiteness, a highly valued and exclusive form of property," but in this case, Indians of mixed ancestry held a kind of "fictive" whiteness but later experienced dispossession because of their Indianness.[6] The racial ambiguity of mixed-ancestry Dakota enabled them to own individual lands and exercise their legal rights in the American legal system through a form of white privilege while at the same time suffering under the racist American machinery of Indian land dispossession. For mixed-ancestry Indians, their whiteness made them eligible to own additional lands in ways that their full-ancestry relatives could not under American law. Indeed, Harris asserts that the "courts established whiteness as a prerequisite to the exercise of enforceable property rights."[7]

The dispossession of Indian land in the nineteenth century took many different forms. I interpret "dispossession" in the broadest sense to include not only large-scale dispossession through treaties, military conquest, removal, or congressional acts but also small-scale tactics of dispossession that affected small communities and individuals. The loss of land is not necessary for dispossession; dispossession could occur by taking the land's resources, thereby reducing its value. Dispossession occurred when local land speculators colluded to only pay a fraction of what the land was worth or when local white people coerced Indians into selling their lands or selling them at reduced prices. As members of the Dakota Nation, mixed-ancestry Dakota lost land through treaties and other broad tactics of dispossession, but they lost their lands on the Lake Pepin Reservation as a community and as individuals.

Most works on Indian land dispossession focus on the broad strategies of dispossession used by the federal government, such as through treaties or legislative acts like the General Allotment Act of 1887.[8] The dispossession of the mixed-ancestry Dakota, however, happened on a smaller scale as a community rather than as a tribal nation, and as individuals. Mixed-ancestry Dakota tried different strategies to protect their land, including owning land in severalty. Brad D. E. Jarvis notes how the Brothertown Indians adapted to U.S. citizenship and individual landownership in the mid-nineteenth century as a survival strategy that they used to acquire land and foster a communal identity.[9] Unfortunately for the mixed-ancestry Dakota, they were less successful in holding on to both their citizenship and their land. Jean M. O'Brien writes in *Dispossession by Degrees* about how Indian dispossession in the town of Natick, Massachusetts, occurred through the "slow but steady displacement of Indians by English landowners" and how it was "through the excruciating workings of business as usual."[10] Although most mixed-ancestry Dakota land was lost within five years, like in Natick, their dispossession continued for decades, at least until the 1930s. For the mixed-ancestry Dakota, race played a role in their dispossession. Melissa L. Meyer argues in her study of the White Earth Reservation in Minnesota that mixed-ancestry Ojibwe, in conjunction with policies that favored them, played a significant role in the dispossession of the tribe through their extensive accumulation of wealth and resources to such a degree that it hurt the tribe.[11] Meyer reveals the internal racial politics of dispossession within tribes, while David A. Chang argues that white Americans used race to dispossess Indians and African Americans and that property owners in Oklahoma continuously revised conceptions of race based in landownership.[12] As we can see with the Trudell family, mixed-race families had some access to remedies to dispossession, such as Francis Trudell's membership in the Dakota County Association, or how, because of their race, the family was able to briefly maintain a residence and land near the Dakota sacred sites of Bdóte and Ȟemníčaŋ.

The mixed-ancestry Dakota of the Bdewákhaŋthuŋwaŋ band met in Wabasha on October 14, 1853, to sign a petition to Minnesota Territorial Governor Willis A. Gorman to protect their land interests. The petitioners complained that white squatters were trespassing on their reservation and asked the governor to aid them by "removing all and every person or persons now trespassing on our lands, contrary to our rights, and the laws, regulations, trade and intercourse with Indian tribes . . . and put a stop to any further encroachments. The present white settlers on this our tract have made permanent establishments and bid defiance to your petitioners, and have absorbed some of the most important points. They are destroying our best timber, and laying out a portion of our land, into a town plat and offering lots for sale."[13] The petitioners here asserted their rights as Indians, arguing that their reservation was subject to the Indian Intercourse Acts. They compared their plight to the mixed-ancestry Sac and Fox and the dispossession of their reservation in Iowa. The mixed-ancestry Dakota "have had an eye on a similar grant made by the Sac and Fox Indians . . . and have viewed with regret the disastrous results."[14] The signers of this petition perceived that they were being dispossessed in two ways: by the theft of land and through the theft of timber, which was where the main value of the land resided.

The signers of this and other petitions were not solely Dakota people of mixed ancestry. Many signers were white men, signing on behalf of their wives or children. White men married into Dakota families had much to gain through treaty provisions or other laws that furnished land, money, or other goods to their families. Indeed, Francis Trudell signed the petition on behalf of five of his children, and the signatures of other white men appear on this and other petitions. Many white husbands, despite being non-Indians, were also able to interject themselves into petitions, giving them an inordinate amount of power over Indian land. Additionally, mixed-ancestry women married to white men were subject to local coverture laws that gave husbands full rights over their wives' lands. For Indian women, American coverture laws collided with Indian custom, leading to uncertain property rights for Indian women married to white men.[15]

The mixed-ancestry Dakota at Redwood Agency signed another petition to Governor Gorman on November 5, 1853, to help them achieve a conveyance of the Lake Pepin Reservation to the federal government in exchange for land scrip. The petitioners noted that they had made three attempts to sell the reservation to the federal government, but all failed, "the last on a general principal, that the Half breeds being citizens cannot be treated with as a separate nation." In this case, U.S. citizenship worked against the mixed-ancestry Dakota. They made note of the fact that squatters were taking their land and creating an untenable legal situation with the confusion over landownership. "To obviate this difficulty," the mixed-ancestry Dakota "suggest that a conveyance be made of the whole tract to the U. States, in consideration of Land Warrants, to be granted to each of the parties for as much land as they would be entitled to individually." They argued that the territorial delegate to Congress, Henry Rice, "can no doubt but accomplish what is desired." The petition was signed by, or on behalf of, over four hundred claimants, including Frank, Joseph, August, Henry, and Elizabeth Trudell, who affixed their x-marks to the petition.[16]

Governor Gorman quickly acted, requesting information from U.S. District Attorney D. H. Dustin. Dustin responded with a December 8 letter, saying that the white squatters were committing a crime by trespassing on the Lake Pepin Reservation and cutting timber. "Any person making a settlement on such lands," he argued, "or engaged in designating any of the boundaries, by marking trees, or otherwise, is subject to indictment and a fine of one thousand dollars." He asserted that any trespassers were subject to civil suits to recover damages caused by their actions. Dustin further claimed that cutting or removing timbers "is also liable to indictment and a fine imposed of not less than three times the value of said timber & imprisonment of not less than 12 months" and were subject to be sued in civil court. Dustin informed the governor that the reservation was also subject to the Indian Intercourse Acts, which gave the governor, as the superintendent of Indian Affairs of Minnesota Territory, the right "to employ the military force of the country to drive off all persons found upon the territory in question contrary to the law."[17] Although armed with this information, there is no evidence that Governor Gorman exerted any energy to curtail these intrusions onto the reservation. As early as 1850, Governor Alexander Ramsey gave notice to white squatters to leave the reservation or face the penalty of law, but little action was ever taken to remove them.[18]

The Minnesota Territorial Delegate Henry Rice, who had been mentioned in the November 5 petition, did accomplish what was desired with the passage of a congressional act on July 17, 1854, offering land scrip to the mixed-ancestry Dakota in exchange for their reservation at Lake Pepin, just as they had asked in their petition. The act provided that each mixed-ancestry Dakota would receive land scrip equivalent in acreage to what they would receive if the reservation were to be divided equally among them and could be located on any of the unoccupied lands on the reservation or any unoccupied public lands in the United States. The act forbade the conveyance of the scrip and authorized the government to "cause to be ascertained the number and names of the half-breeds or mixed-bloods who are entitled to participate in the benefits of said grant . . . before the issue of the certificates or scrip."[19] This legislation set in motion a series of events that dissolved the Lake Pepin Reservation and put the land into the hands of individuals.

The April 28, 1854, report accompanying this bill reveals the role that race, citizenship, and civilization played in Congress's passage of the act. The author of the report, Daniel Wright, wrote, "The term 'half-breed,' as applied by some to them, is a misnomer, for it was intended to include all those having an admixture of white and Indian blood in their veins, in whatsoever degree." Wright continued that many of the mixed-ancestry Dakota had "become citizens of Minnesota and of the adjoining States. Some of them have served in the legislature and filled offices of honor and trust in the Territory." Wright continued that for these individuals, at least, "the object of the fostering of policy of the government has been attained, in fitting them for civilized life; for, in point of intelligence and civilization, many of them would compare favorably with their white brethren."[20] However, he argued that some mixed-ancestry Dakota were uncivilized and wished to sell their interests and join their relatives to the west. Wright asserted that dividing the land would serve the purposes of both groups: those "uncivilized" Dakota could sell their interests and rejoin their tribe in the west, while the "civilized" group would prefer to own their land as individuals.[21]

The report maintained that the Lake Pepin Reservation was fully Indian land, not a novelty or a piece of land of ambiguous ownership. Wright wrote, "The actual title of those persons to the reservation in question is that of Indians, although many of them have a preponderance of white blood." He continued by upholding the Nonintercourse Acts, which strictly held that only the federal government could purchase their land, "nor is any white citizen authorized to settle upon the same."[22] Despite the strong affirmation of the rights of mixed-ancestry

Indians from the federal government, Governor Gorman failed to protect their rights, even with the garrison at Fort Snelling nearby to enforce them and arrest squatters.

In preparation for carrying out the act of 1854, which ultimately took three years from the passage of the act to the time the land scrip was delivered, there was some question among government officials as to who was eligible and how to carry out the act. The commissioner of Indian Affairs, George Manypenny, wrote to the secretary of the interior, Robert McClelland, to clear up some of the issues of eligibility. Manypenny wrote, "I would call your attention to the language of the law [of 1854] wherein the term 'mixed-bloods' is inserted in addition to the term 'half-breed,' which is employed in the treaty of Prairie du Chien, and upon which the question may arise whether it was intended by the act to enlarge the number of beneficiaries or not?" Here Manypenny noted that the 1830 Treaty of Prairie du Chien simply used the term "half-breed," which some American officials and some mixed-ancestry Dakota took to mean literally that only those of one-half blood quantum were to enjoy the benefits of the reservation. The law, however, specified "half-breeds" and "mixed-bloods," leading to some confusion. Manypenny asserted, "In my opinion a liberal construction should prevail in the assignment of this land," arguing that all Dakota of mixed ancestry, regardless of blood quanta, should benefit from the act.[23]

Responding to Manypenny, McClellan noted the monumental task of fulfilling the act of 1854, which required the cooperation of the Department of the Interior, Office of Indian Affairs (OIA), and the General Land Office (GLO). The Department of the Interior had the ultimate responsibility to carry out the act but tasked the OIA to determine eligibility. Because the mixed-ancestry Dakota had to officially relinquish their claims to the Lake Pepin Reservation before receiving land scrip, the GLO had the responsibility to survey the reservation and ascertain the means of relinquishment. When the GLO determined the means of relinquishment, the OIA then had to obtain the relinquishments from each individual, then issue the scrip. After the scrip had been located, the GLO would then issue a land patent in the name of the individual mixed-ancestry Dakota.[24]

Since the passage of the act, the mixed-ancestry Dakota had not been idle and wished to know how the land would be divided. At Hastings, Minnesota, in the summer of 1855, the mixed-ancestry Dakota appointed a committee of three—Henry H. Sibley, Alexis Bailly, and Alexander Faribault—to query the commissioner of Indian Affairs. They asked how the Office of Indian Affairs planned to divide the land and requested copies of all instructions related to the division of the Lake Pepin Reservation and dispersal of land scrip so that they could inform the mixed-ancestry Dakota.[25]

C. Billinghurst claimed that since the passage of the act in 1854 and the writing of his letter March 1, 1856, hundreds if not thousands of white squatters settled on the Lake Pepin Reservation. The squatters assumed they would have preemption rights as soon as the government surveyed the land.[26] Many white people mistakenly believed that the 1854 act opened the Lake Pepin Reservation to white settlement, leading to numerous land disputes. In protest, a group of white squatters sent a petition to President James Buchanan complaining that mixed-ancestry Dakota used their scrip to expel whites and take over their improved lands. They complained further, "Already do we see many busy Speculators prowling about buying Scrip, and trying to procure the best portions of the Tract, irrespective of Settlers improvements, development, progress, humanity, honor, moral obligations, or any other considerations. . . . Shall they be ousted from their homes and driven elsewhere merely to satiate the avaricious cravings of ambitious, designing, unprincipled speculators?"[27] The white squatters failed to see the irony in their plight; they complained that land speculators were dispossessing them of their land, while at the same time they themselves were dispossessing the mixed-ancestry Dakota and while the federal government was in the business of dispossessing Indians in general.

Because of the slow process of dividing their land and the continued depredations of white people, the mixed-ancestry Dakota continued to use petitions to lobby for their interests and bring attention to the fact that the provisions of the 1854 law needed to be carried out as soon as possible to avoid further dispossession. In the spring of 1856, a group of mixed-ancestry Dakota elders, self-described as "among the oldest of the class," petitioned President Franklin Pierce to take action concerning the dispossession of their timber and land on the Lake Pepin Reservation. They argued that since the passage of the 1854 law, "the most desirable portion of the tract, belonging to your petitioners and others, is taken possession of and is now occupied by persons who have no shadow of right to settle thereon. That the destruction and waste of the most valuable timber on said tract, by those persons, is so great, that there is scarcely a valuable tree left standing the whole length of the tract for miles back [from the river], a circumstance much regretted by your petitioners, as they had up to this time preserved said timber as indispensable to their future wants." They feared that if the government did not issue the scrip soon, there would be very little public land left in the region for the mixed-ancestry Dakota to claim.[28]

In the meantime, on April 10, 1855, upon the recommendation of Commissioner of Indian Affairs George Manypenny, Secretary of the Interior Robert McClelland appointed Harvey H. Johnson and William Ashley Jones as commissioners to determine the names and numbers of eligible claimants to the Lake Pepin Reservation. The commissioners determined the best course of action was to publish notices in the newspapers in the region—in Minnesota Territory, Wisconsin, Missouri, and Nebraska Territory—stating their intentions to collect the affidavits of mixed-ancestry Dakota and their guardians.[29] The affidavits required that claimants give their name, age, blood quantum, residence, parentage, and tribe, and a witness affidavit was required to corroborate their testimony.

The commissioners began their work on August 1, 1855, and traveled to several destinations to collect the affidavits of potential claimants, which was explained in the published notices. Jones and Johnson started at Prairie du Chien, Wisconsin, where they collected sixteen affidavits between August 1 and August 16. Next, they moved to the town of Wabasha, Minnesota Territory, near the Lake Pepin Reservation, collecting thirty-eight affidavits between August 20 and 25. At Saint Paul, between August 29 and September 18, the commissioners collected eighty-three affidavits. The commissioners completed their journey, collecting over one hundred affidavits at the Indian Agency on the reservation on the

Minnesota River from September 24 to October 8.[30] Dozens of other claimants sent notarized affidavits, signed by their local justices of the peace, to the commissioners.

Despite only going to four locations, as evidenced by the affidavits, mixed-ancestry Dakota came from many different locations to give testimony. Most came from points in Minnesota, but others traveled from the surrounding region to have their claims heard. Charlotte Mercier traveled from Dubuque, Iowa, to give testimony at Wabasha, a distance of approximately 175 miles.[31] Theophile Bruguier, a white man married to two Dakota sisters, traveled a similar distance from Sioux City, Iowa, to the Lower Sioux Agency, to give testimony for his ten surviving children.[32] In most cases, when claimants lived far away, such as Vienna, Indiana, at Fort Douglass near modern-day Winnipeg, Manitoba, San Francisco, or New York City, their kin would give testimony on their behalf or they would send notarized affidavits.

Francis Trudell only traveled a few miles from his home in Mendota to Saint Paul in September to have the claims of his children recorded. As they corroborated each other's testimony and their affidavits were in succession, Francis probably traveled with his friend George H. Faribault, the son of Alexander Faribault. Francis Trudell placed his x-mark on an affidavit for his children:

> I, Francis Trudell of Dacotah County Min[nesota] Terr[itory] (near Mendota) do solemnly swear that I am a Canadian Frenchman. About twenty years ago I was married by Indian custom to a Sioux woman of the Medawahkanton band. At her baptism she was called Mary. She is now about thirty six year of age and I am forty eight. We live together and have seven children now living, viz: Francis aged seventeen years; Joseph aged ten years; Augustin aged seven; Henry aged five years; Elizabeth aged four years; Peter aged two years and Leon [Levi] aged one month. They are Half Breeds, & all live with us.[33]

The commissioners also required that a third party vouch for the person signing the affidavit. In this case, George Faribault vouched for Francis Trudell, and vice versa.

> I, George H. Farribault of Mendota Min Terry do solemnly swear that I well know the above Francis Trudell, also his wife and all his children, seven in number as stated by him, and believe his affidavit true in all respects. His wife is a full blood Sioux & he is a Frenchman. He is a man of irreproachable character & his affidavit entitled to full credit. I have known this family from my earliest recollection. I am now twenty nine years of age.[34]

Francis replied with a similar affidavit:

> I, Francis Trudell of Dacotah County M. Terry do solemnly swear that I have known the above Geo. H. Farribault twenty six years and have during that time been well acquainted with the Farribault family. That I have examined the above affidavit of said George H. Farribault and have good reason for believing it to be true in all respects.[35]

Figure 14. George H. Faribault, 1826–1890. Photo circa 1880. He was Waȟpéthuŋwaŋ and Bdewákhaŋthuŋwaŋ, was a friend of the Trudell family, and later served as a chief clerk at the Standing Rock Agency. Collection 00036, item 00097, State Historical Society of North Dakota, Bismarck.

These affidavits provide invaluable ethnographic data on race and kinship. In Francis Trudell's testimony about his family, he delineates three different ethnic or racial identities in one family—French Canadian, Dakota, and "half-breed." This demonstrates how in mixed-ancestry families, multiple racial and ethnic identities existed, setting them apart from most white and full-ancestry families in the region. George Faribault explained his family this way: "I George H. Farribault, of Mendota Min. Terry. being duly sworn do say that I am the son of Alexander Farribault & grandson of J. B. Farribault. The latter is a Frenchman and my grandmother was half white & half Sioux of the Medawahkanton & Wahpaton Bands. My father is therefore one fourth Sioux & three fourths white. My mother is half Scotch & half Sioux of the Medawahkanton Band. I am therefore strictly speaking three eighths Sioux and five eighths white, but am of that blood commonly called 'quarter bloods.'"[36] Faribault describes several different identities in his family: He describes his paternal grandfather as a Frenchman and his paternal grandmother as a member of two Dakota bands, the Bdewákhaŋthuŋwaŋ and Waȟpékute. He describes his mother as half Bdewákhaŋthuŋwaŋ and half Scotch. In this family, Faribault describes two different European ethnicities, two different Dakota bands, and identities tied to blood quantum. He describes himself as three-eighths Dakota but says he belongs to the group called "quarter bloods," suggesting identity differences among mixed-ancestry Dakota based in blood quantum. Such diverse families were common among mixed-ancestry Dakota, who often claimed multiple descent from European ethnicities, multiple tribes and bands, and a variety of blood quanta.

With their work of collecting affidavits completed on October 8, 1855, commissioners Jones and Johnson set about the task of wading through the affidavits to compile a census of mixed-ancestry Dakota eligible to receive scrip under the 1854 act. They completed a census on February 9, 1856, admitting 613, rejecting 1, and suspending 9.[37] On June 20, 15 additional names had been added, bringing the total to 628 accepted claimants.[38] The commissioner of Indian Affairs added additional claimants, numbering 642 by November.[39]

Adequate evidence exists, however, for the omission of some claimants. Some people claimed they or their family members had been missed and hoped to be added to the enrollment of those to receive scrip. Baptiste DeLoney, a mixed-ancestry Ojibwe, had married Mary, a full-ancestry member of Táoyateduta's (Little Crow's) band, in 1848. She and DeLoney had three children, but the eldest child died in 1852 and Mary died in 1854. He claimed that he was sick and thirty miles from Yellow Medicine Agency when the commissioners came to enroll the mixed-ancestry Dakota and he had no relatives to alert the commissioners of the surviving children.[40] The DeLoney children did not receive scrip. Amable Morrin complained that while his children received scrip, his wife Angelique Bailly Morrin was overlooked by the commissioners.[41] Like the DeLoney children, Angelique Morrin did not receive scrip. Although the commissioners did well to enumerate so many Dakota people of mixed ancestry, due to various circumstances many were left off and not enumerated on the list of scrip recipients. In 1860, the commissioner of Indian Affairs accepted an additional thirty-eight claimants that had been left off the original enumeration for various reasons.[42] These were subsequently accepted and issued scrip.

While the commissioners did their duty, through 1855 and 1856, white squatters continued to threaten Dakota land and commit depredations. On November 15, 1856, twenty-two mixed-ancestry heads of families signed another petition to Commissioner of Indian Affairs George Manypenny complaining of white squatters and the destruction of their timber. Their petition began, "The acts of the white settlers on our Sioux half breed tract is becoming so outrageous, so unreasonable, that we have decided once more to call your attention to the following facts," then explained how white squatters were dispossessing their timber and land. Not only were the squatters cutting the timber for fuel, "which could be borne," they claimed, but they were cutting timber for use by steamboats and for "supplying innumerable steam mills erected all over the tract." They perceived the cutting of their timber itself as an act of dispossession because they were stealing a valuable resource and the loss of the timber dramatically decreased the value of the land.[43]

In their second complaint, they argued that white squatters, in collusion with the local courts that they set up, were also dispossessing the mixed-ancestry Dakota of their land itself. They explained that the white squatters were "settling so rapidly and in such numbers as to leave scarcely a corner for the Half Breeds to live on, suits at law are brought by those White Settlers (who partition the tract among themselves) against the Half Breeds for using their own timber and a court of justice & juris composed of those White Settlers invariably decide against the Half Breed, and throw them into costs and damages. Their daily acts, are acts of aggression and our position is really deplorable and becoming intolerable." They complained that Thomas H. Ford, lieutenant governor of Ohio, purchased the claims of two white squatters with the plan of laying out a townsite. "Such example coming from such a High source," they argued, "cannot but be of serious injury to us as it encourages others more ignorant to commit similar acts."[44]

The petitioners brought up the problem of white squatters receiving preemption certificates for land on the Lake Pepin Reservation from the local land offices at Red Wing and Winona. They complained that nothing had been done about the matter and compared their issues with squatters with the mixed-ancestry Indians on the Great Nemaha Reservation in southeastern Nebraska. The commissioner of Indian Affairs had had the squatters kicked off the land, and the mixed-ancestry Dakota petitioners hoped the commissioner would do the same in their case. They punctuated their request by arguing that the Great Nemaha case involved "Indian interest, in this case it involves the interest of American Citizens entitled to the protection of the Government."[45] The mixed-ancestry Dakota were in the unusual position of asserting their land rights both as Indians and as American citizens, yet neither status availed them in the quest to protect their land and their timber.

On May 31, 1856, six months before this latest petition, white squatters at Lake Pepin formed the Settlers' Protection Society to ensure that white squatters would continue to hold the land they claimed. Their constitution permitted each member of the society to claim a maximum of 160 acres, while article 7 stated, "We pledge ourselves to respect the rights of the so called Half Breeds or Mixed Bloods as citizens of the United States, equally with the white settlers." These two articles in the constitution of the Settlers' Protection Society were contradictory: On one hand, the members could claim 160 acres of land to which they had no right,

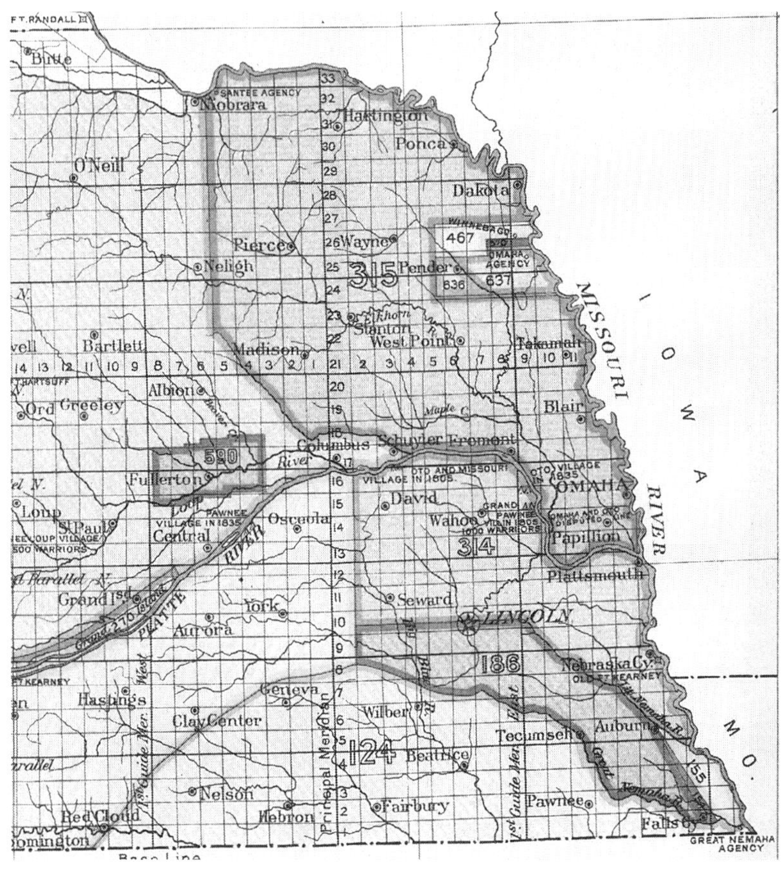

Map 3. The Dakota Nation in eastern Nebraska. The small wedge marked 155 in the southeastern part of the state was the Great Nemaha Reservation. The Santee Agency, founded in 1866, is visible in the northern reaches of the state. Charles C. Royce, *Indian Land Cessions in the United States, Eighteenth Annual Report of the Bureau of American Ethnology, 1896–1897, Part 2* (Government Printing Office, 1899).

and on the other hand, it stated that they would respect the rights of the mixed-ancestry Dakota.[46] Alexis Bailly sent a copy of the Settlers' Protection Society constitution in a newspaper clipping to Secretary of the Interior Robert McClelland in hopes that this would speed up the process of dispersing the land scrip. Bailly, however, had faith in the mixed-ancestry Dakota: "Does the Dept. of the Interior expect that they the Mixed Bloods will surrender their rights like sheep to be robbed by a set of miserable devils, no Sir. They will defeat the machinations of their relentless enemies & in the end obtain justice."[47] Bailly's feeling in the matter may have been tempered by his rejection when he attempted to acquire money as a mixed-ancestry Ottawa under an 1836 treaty with that tribe. His claim was denied because he did not reside among his people; instead, he lived among the Dakota. Perhaps this experience prompted him to ensure the same did not happen to his wife and children.[48]

After the 1854 law, a problem arose when white squatters assumed that the passage of the law dissolved the reservation, throwing it open to white settlement. Alexis Bailly alerted Commissioner of Indian Affairs Manypenny that the land offices at Winona and Red Wing had been granting preemptions to white settlers on the Lake Pepin Reservation, arguing that they would have to be rescinded to avoid land disputes.[49] Manypenny cited this letter in his own letter to Secretary of the Interior Robert McClelland, arguing that if true, the certificates of preemption should be rescinded, asserting that "the half-breed Sioux have an unquestionable priority of right" to claim land on the reservation.[50] Commissioner of the General Land Office Thomas A. Hendricks wrote to Acting Commissioner of Indian Affairs Charles Mix noting a petition from white settlers that there were about five thousand white settlers living on the reservation by June 12, 1857.[51] While the Office of Indian Affairs and the secretary of the interior worked to uphold the rights of the mixed-ancestry Dakota, members of Congress began work on a bill to protect the white squatters at Lake Pepin who had obtained certificates of preemption from the local land offices. Alexis Bailly alerted Commissioner of Indian Affairs Manypenny to the existence of this bill, hoping that Manypenny could put a stop to it.[52] Because the process dragged out so long, the mixed-ancestry Dakota were losing their battle to white squatters. Some felt that if the commissioners immediately issued the scrip, the loss of land to squatters could be mitigated.[53] However, even after the Office of Indian Affairs agreed on the final names and numbers of mixed-ancestry claimants, they had to wait to issue land scrip until the General Land Office had completed their survey of the reservation.

On February 5, 1857, Commissioner Manypenny had a notice published in local newspapers stating that James Shields would take the relinquishments and distribute the scrip at Wabasha beginning on March 23, 1857. The notice said that the entitled mixed-ancestry Dakota themselves should come to collect their scrip, except in the cases of minors the father or, if he were dead, the mother could collect the scrip. Or if living at a great distance, a white or mixed-ancestry husband could receive scrip on behalf of his wife. The notice reiterated that the scrip was "not to be assignable or transferable."[54]

In Washington, D.C., James Shields received fifteen books containing scrip for 640 mixed-ancestry claimants on March 7, 1857. He also received "a form for the relinquishment by the claimants with the names of the claimants appended thereto," signatures to which he was responsible for getting. He received two additional forms, including the form of a power of attorney "authorizing the attorney of the claimant to relinquish in his behalf in certain cases" and a blank book of receipts to be filled out upon distribution of the land scrip.[55] By June 8, 1857, Shields uneventfully delivered most of the scrip, except to those living at a great distance, such as those at Red River or in Missouri.[56] Francis Trudell signed the relinquishment documents at Saint Paul on May 25, 1857.[57] Immediately following the relinquishment, Shields issued thirty-five pieces of land scrip to Francis Trudell as guardian of the seven Trudell children.[58]

On December 1, 1857, James Shields reported to the commissioner of Indian Affairs that he had completed his work in acquiring the relinquishments and distributing the scrip. He reported several difficulties. He appeared in Wabasha on March 23 to distribute the scrip, but due to the winter weather, many mixed-ancestry Dakota were unable to appear to receive their scrip. "The next difficulty arose from the condition and character of the halfbreeds themselves. They lived dispersed over the Western Country, some in Missouri, some in Iowa and some in Wisconsin, and some of them resided on the territorial frontiers, beyond the limits of civilization. In addition to this, many of them were unacquainted with the English language and the usage of civilized life. It became necessary therefore to publish notices and address circulars to them and visit a variety of places . . . to enable them to obtain their scrip." Another problem, he explained, were the white squatters who "had made very valuable improvements upon it embracing houses, farms, mills and even villages and towns." The squatters were "alarmed for their improvements which were all liable to be taken by the halfbreed [scrip] locations," prompting them to, "peacefully" in Shields's terms, intimidate the mixed-ancestry claimants. However, Shields reported, "both parties came to an understanding and adjusted upon equitable terms a satisfactory compromise which enabled the halfbreeds with the consent of the Settlers to make locations on their improvements." This was less likely a compromise and more likely the mixed-ancestry claimants settling for what they could realistically get, considering the government repeatedly refused to protect their land from squatters.[59]

Despite the Trudell family collectively acquiring 3,360 acres of "halfbreed" land, most of that land was lost within a year of obtaining it in 1857. On May 25, 1857, on behalf of the children, Francis Trudell placed his x-mark next to his children's names, relinquishing their right to the Lake Pepin Reservation.[60] This relinquishment was necessary under the 1854 law granting mixed-ancestry Dakota land scrip in exchange for their reservation. The seven living Trudell children—Frank, Joseph, Henry, Elizabeth, August, Peter, and Levi—received their scrip on the same day as the relinquishment from the Office of Indian Affairs. Shields signed over the scrip to their father, as was typical in the case of minors.[61] All of the 680 mixed-ancestry Dakota who were eligible received five pieces of land scrip, or legal documents entitling them to land, totaling 480 acres. Each recipient's scrip was labeled A through E: scrips A and B were worth 40 acres each, scrip C was worth 80 acres, and scrips D and E were worth 160 acres each. Since each mixed-ancestry Dakota received five pieces of scrip, the federal government issued 3,400 pieces of scrip. The Trudell family received 35, for a total of 3,360 acres.

Starting just two weeks after accepting his children's scrip, from June 11 to December 14, 1857, Francis Trudell appeared before Judge Lemon Bates

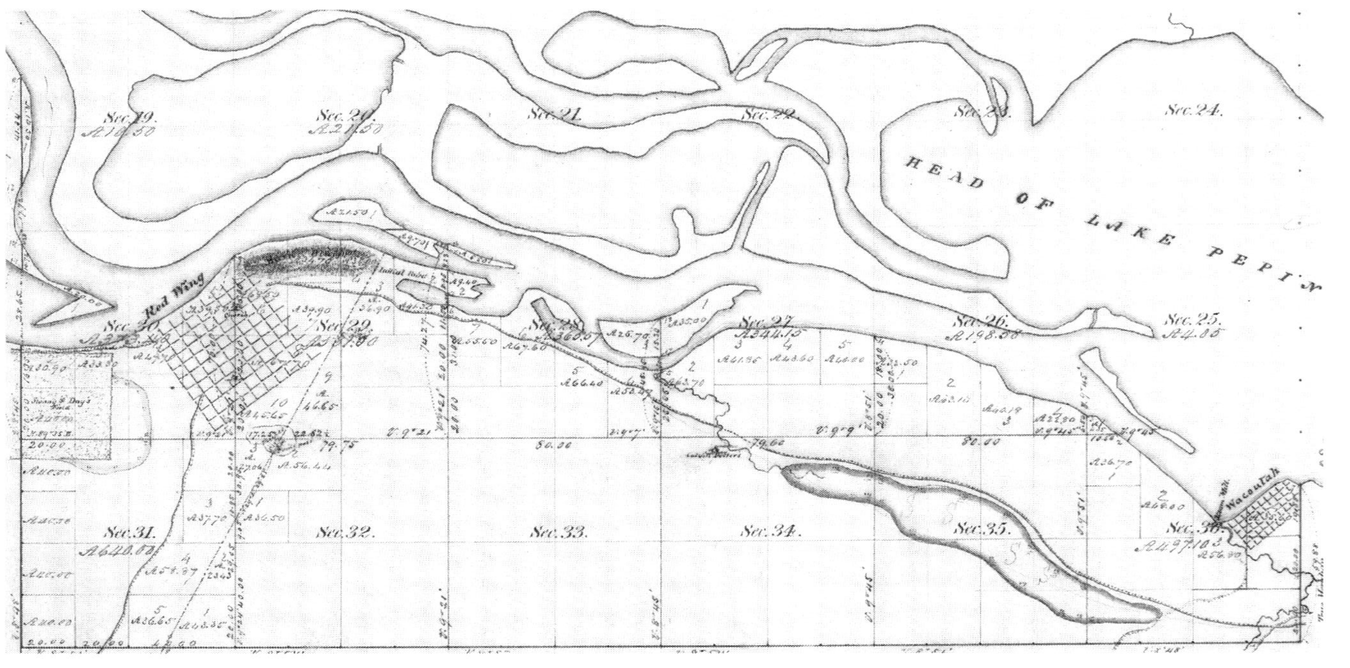

Figure 15. Map showing the northwestern boundary of the Lake Pepin Reservation, the town of Red Wing, and Ȟemníčaŋ, or Barn Bluff, in 1856. Township 113 North Range 14 West, Dakota County, Minnesota. "General Land Office Records," Bureau of Land Management, accessed November 15, 2024, https://glorecords.blm.gov.

of the Goodhue County Probate Court eight times to legally complete the sale of his children's lands. On June 11, Francis requested that the court appoint him guardian of his sons Joseph, Peter, Levi, Henry, and August, with the intent to sell their land. The court declared Trudell to be the children's guardian on July 10 with authority to sell their real estate and ordered that a notice be published in the *Red Wing Sentinel* to all who may have an interest in their land that Trudell intended to sell it for the "maintenance and education" of the children. His daughter Isabella, anglicized to Elizabeth in the scrip documents, was dead by this time and the court declared Trudell heir to Elizabeth's "half-breed" land on July 21. On August 11, the court ordered Francis Trudell to sell the lands, and on August 20 he swore to sell the land "in such manner as will be most for the advantage of all persons interested therein." Trudell sold the land on September 14 at auction at the Real Estate Office of Smith, Towne, & Co. in Red Wing, Minnesota. He appeared in court on September 23, where the sales of the children's lands were recorded. George Wilkinson purchased 320 acres of Joseph's land for $400 and Levi's 480 acres for $600. Joshua C. Pierce bought August's land for $600, 360 acres of Peter's land sold to Thomas F. Town for $450, and Otis F. Smith acquired Henry's land for $600. Joseph had an additional 160 acres and Peter 120 acres that did not sell that day because those lands were in Wabasha County, and since proper notice of the sale had not been given in that county, the lands could not yet be sold. Trudell petitioned the Goodhue County Probate Court again on November 5 for permission to sell the remainder of his children's land in Wabasha County, which the court ordered. He returned to court a final time on December 14 to record the sale of the remaining land. Trudell reported that at an auction at the Lake City Hotel in Wabasha on November 30, he sold Joseph's 160 acres to George Wilkinson for $200 and Wilkinson purchased Peter's 120 acres for $150.[62] Francis Trudell made a small fortune of $2,600 on September 14 and acquired an additional $350 on November 30. This money was probably squandered soon after considering in the 1860 U.S. Federal Census, unlike for his neighbors, the enumerator did not list a monetary value for any real estate or personal property that he might have owned.[63]

The Trudell children, however, maintained a different story of their dispossession. August Trudell, or Thatóheya, wrote to Judge Ammiel Jenkins Willard of the newly founded National Indian Defense Association in 1886, inquiring about the "half-breed" land scrip that the Trudell children had received in the 1850s. Thatóheya wrote, "Our mother is a full blood Sioux and cannot talk English, and our father was a full blood Frenchman and could not speak English. Our scrip was given him. He is dead and [we] don't know where it is. White people made him drunk and while they had him in this condition they induced him to sell some of our lands located by this scrip." Thatóheya continued, "We do not know if all the lands allowed us by the scrip was ever located. The white people there are not our friends and we cannot get its description and boundaries of these lands." Thatóheya hoped that if the Office of Indian Affairs could discover exactly where the lands were, they might be returned to the Trudell family.[64] Levi Trudell claimed in 1886 that some of his land was now under the city of Red Wing. Levi "left there when young but was back about seven years ago, when the possessor of the 160 acres outside of town offered him $500, to sign a deed for him. Says he was then young and wild and did not sign the paper."[65] While they acquired the needed information, it did not help them regain their land in Minnesota. Indeed, as the records of the Goodhue County Probate Court reveal, their father sold all of their land in 1857, conflicting with their stories of how their land was lost. Because they were children at the time, and in the confusion of the U.S.-Dakota War a few years later in 1862, they may have been uncertain as to the disposition of their lands.

The Trudell brothers were still interested in their land scrip in 1897 when they hired attorney D. H. Talbot to inquire to the commissioner of Indian Affairs on their behalf. In the fall of 1897, Talbot asked for information on the scrip and asked "if any time a claim has been filed asking for a reissue" to inform him.[66] It was not uncommon for scrip to be lost and a request for duplicate scrip to be fulfilled by the government. Talbot argued that the government had no right to issue the scrip of the children to their father and that Francis Trudell had no right to sell it, and he demanded that the Indian Office issue new scrip to the living Trudell claimants.[67] From these documents it is unclear whether the children knew that their father had sold their land through the Goodhue County Probate Court in 1857. Regardless, the family perceived that the Office of Indian Affairs was wrong to issue "half-breed" land scrip to non-Indian fathers, and they felt that their father did not have any right to sell what was essentially Indian land. Despite their confusion over how their land had been lost, they perceived the loss of their land as illegal and as a form of Indian land dispossession.

Francis Trudell only sold five of his children's lands in this way. His daughter Elizabeth was dead by the time he went to the Goodhue County Probate Court and half of her scrip was located by Clinton Gurnee Jr., as attorney of Francis Trudell, in northern Wisconsin a few miles south of the Bad River Reservation.[68] It is unclear how this land transaction occurred, but the land was used for mining interests and was quickly out of the hands of the Trudell family.[69]

The oldest surviving child, Frank Trudell, or Hepí, was about eighteen when he located his own scrip on June 15, 1857.[70] While he held his land longer than his brothers, he too was under pressures of dispossession. After acquiring their land, mixed-ancestry Indians were subject to local property taxes and to having their land confiscated and sold for failure to pay. The imposition of property taxes, a foreign concept in Dakota culture, was a form of dispossession, nor was it explained to mixed-ancestry Dakota in the 1830 Treaty of Prairie du Chien or the 1854 act. Numerous Dakota landowners appear in Minnesota county tax books. Hepí had a tax of $2.04 assessed on his eighty-acre plot in Penn Township, McLeod County, in 1861. The notation "sold" appears in the tax book; it is unclear if he or the new owner paid the tax. Several of Hepí's mixed-ancestry neighbors in Penn Township were also assessed property taxes in 1861. Isaac Renville owed $5.24 on two hundred acres. Siblings Janet, Isabella, Walter, and Mary McLeod owed $4.34, $5.48, $1.44, and $4.34, respectively. The county assessed Louisa Forcier $5.24, while Pierre Provencalle owed $14.33. Many mixed-ancestry Dakota appeared in the tax assessment for McLeod County in 1863, but significantly fewer than in 1861.[71] The Dakota who sold their land had many reasons for doing so, some of them personally beneficial, but many probably felt pressure to sell in order to pay or avoid property taxes, some of which may have been fraudulently assessed.

The Trudell children may have felt that they had been cheated out of their lands, but they also used a strategy of shady land deals to make money. The family sold several parcels of the scrip land more than once. As the guardian of his son Joseph, Francis Trudell sold his land to George Wilkinson in 1857. Ten years later, Joseph was dead, and in a deed in 1867, Francis and Ičíyapiwiŋ were listed as Joseph's heirs when they sold 280 acres of the same land to William H. Grant for $500.[72] August Trudell resold the entirety of his 480 acres in 1871 to Daniel G. Shillock for $300, which his father had sold in 1857 to Joshua Pierce for $600.[73] Apparently the family practiced several shady deals that same year as George Wilkinson filed a lawsuit against August, Henry, and Peter Trudell in 1867 concerning over 1,000 acres of land he purchased from the Trudell family a decade earlier. The judge ordered that Wilkinson be "quieted in his possession," meaning the Trudell family were to allow him to own his property without the family causing further difficulties.[74]

Frank Trudell, particularly, used this tactic, selling his lands at least three times. In 1867, Hepí sold 240 acres of his "half-breed" land in Sibley County to Joshua Egbert for $200.[75] Four years later, Hepí sold these same lands and the remainder of his 480 acres of "half-breed" lands in Sibley and McLeod Counties to Daniel G. Shillock for $500, the same day his brother August sold his lands to Shillock.[76] Years later, Frank Trudell and his wife Maggie, now residents of the Santee Reservation in Nebraska, again sold the same 240 acres of land in Sibley County that he had already sold twice. Frank and Maggie acquired a tidy sum of $1,250, paid by J. B. Lucas in 1897, around the same time that the Trudell children said they had been dispossessed of their lands.[77] It is unclear whether the family faced any significant legal repercussions for repeatedly selling their land. Nor is it clear whether they intended to defraud people or if buyers like Shillock hoped to acquire land at below-market prices. When Francis Trudell had sold his children's lands in 1857, he received $1.25 per acre, a standard price of land at the time. But when the Trudell family resold land, it was usually at either a significantly lower or significantly higher price.

The Trudell family had other legal episodes over land, and like other mixed-ancestry families, they had multiple means by which to acquire land that full-ancestry Indians did not have access to. In the 1850s, Francis Trudell purchased a 151.2-acre parcel of land from the federal government under authority of the Land Act of 1820.[78] This act permitted Trudell to purchase public land if the buyer paid $1.25 per acre up front, a total of $189 in this case. In the summer of 1855, Francis and Ičíyapiwiŋ mortgaged the land to Henry Sibley, and six months later they sold it to Sibley for $1,000.[79] The General Land Office finally sent a land patent to Trudell dated March 10, 1856, signed by President Franklin Pierce, six weeks after he had sold the land to Sibley.[80] This was a narrow strip of land between the Minnesota River and Gun Club Lake in modern-day Mendota Heights, about one mile south and on the opposite bank from Fort Snelling, which is at the confluence of the Mississippi and Minnesota Rivers. The land was only a few hundred yards from the sacred site of Ohéyawahi, or Pilot Knob, where Dakota people buried their dead for generations. Before the 1850s, a Dakota village site was on or very near Trudell's purchase. This land was part of the larger sacred region known as Bdóte—the confluence of the Minnesota and Mississippi Rivers—the place of creation for Dakota people. It is unclear if or how long the family lived on this parcel of land, but the family did live in the town of Mendota, an anglicized version of Bdóte, on this sacred site. The family would have known the creation story of Bdóte and it is likely that the family had friends and relatives buried at Ohéyawahi. Trudell purchased the land after the 1851 Treaty of Mendota forced the Dakota bands in the region to move hundreds of miles westward to the Dakota reservation on the Minnesota River. Being a mixed-ancestry family afforded the Trudell children opportunities that full-ancestry Dakota did not have. Their white father took advantage of the Land Act of 1820, and because mixed-ancestry Dakota were not forced to move to the reservation, the family was permitted to own part of and to continue living in this sacred Dakota place.

Not only did the Trudell family have the opportunity to continue to live at the sacred Dakota site of Bdóte after their full-ancestry relatives were obligated to move to the reservation in western Minnesota, but also the family later lived in the shadow of yet another sacred Dakota site, Ȟemníčaŋ, or Barn Bluff, in the city of Red Wing. The eldest son, Frank Trudell, purchased a town lot in Red Wing from William and Esther

Curtis and David Hughes for $700 in the fall of 1857. Less than a month later he sold the same lot to Arne Henrickson for a major loss, receiving only $400 in return.[81] Francis Trudell and Ičíyapiwiŋ also bought and sold land in Red Wing. On October 14, 1858, Trudell purchased a lot in Red Wing from George and Hannah Wilkinson for $800, but Francis and Ičíyapiwiŋ sold the land the next day to Edward Kiernan for the same price.[82] The deed stated, "Francis Trudell and Mary Trudell his wife the signers and sealers of the foregoing deed . . . acknowledge the same to be their own free act and deed." The document continued, "And the said Mary Trudell on an examination separate and apart from her said husband acknowledged that she executed the deed without any fear or compulsion from any one."[83] While coverture laws, in which men assumed the land and legal rights of their wives upon marriage, were beginning to be challenged at mid-century, there were no laws in Minnesota that protected the property rights of married women in Minnesota at this time. Yet the county recorder sought the consent of Mary or Ičíyapiwiŋ, a full-ancestry Dakota woman, in the sale of the land. As explained in chapter 2, married women did have the right of "inchoate dower," an interest in the property of their husbands. This was boilerplate language often used in deeds, but it meant that county officials needed to affirm the consent of Indian women when their white husbands sold land.

The Trudell family also had their own legal troubles over land. John Kennedy made a complaint in the Dakota County District Court in July of 1861 alleging that since January members of the Trudell family had been cutting and hauling away timber from Kennedy's alleged property in Dakota County. The land was located on Mud Hen Island in the Mississippi River near the modern-day Prairie Island Indian Community. In the complaint, Kennedy requested an injunction from the court to direct the family to cease cutting and hauling away timber, which Kennedy perceived to be the main value of the land. Kennedy claimed to have made numerous requests for them to stop felling trees; the family, with their own claim to the land, simply ignored Kennedy's requests, hired men and teams of horses, and continued cutting until the time of his complaint.[84] Further legal documents of this case do not exist; the outcome of the case is unknown, and the Trudell family's claim to the land is uncertain. From this evidence, it is unknown if the family was committing a criminal act or asserting their land rights. What is known from this case is that the family was not intimidated by Kennedy or his threats to go to the local courts and that the family aggressively exploited land that they believed they had a right to.

Francis Trudell was one of fifty-nine members who revived a defunct land association, the Dakota County Association, in March of 1855. They revived the association to combat the "trespassers and outrages [that] are almost daily committed upon the lands and property of some of the peaceful and honest citizens of Dakota County by unprincipled villains." The association resolved to "protect each other in our rights and property." The members elected John Kennedy, who sued the Trudell family in 1861, to be the secretary of the association.[85] These kinds of local settler land associations were common in the nineteenth century, intended to protect against squatters and land speculators, but their intentions were to protect settler lands, which resulted in a vested interest against the preservation of Indian title.

Thomas Walker, a young and ambitious Minnesota businessman, wrote of his acquisition of Dakota and Ojibwe "mixed-blood" scrip. In the 1860s, he met prominent businessmen from Minneapolis, Henry T. Welles and William S. Chapman, for whom he worked to secure scrip. He claimed it was his idea that Chapman purchase scrip and that Walker offered to locate it for him. Chapman liked the idea and began buying Dakota scrip, "which he was obtaining at the very modest price of 50 cents to 75 cents an acre." Chapman, Welles, and Franklin Steele soon extended their land dealings to Nevada and California. Chapman asked Walker to "go with him to California, where he said the Sioux scrip was worth from $5 to $10 an acre to locate on redwood timber."[86] Between them, Chapman, Welles, and Steele purchased tens of thousands of acres of Dakota scrip and were directly involved in fraud and bribery over the scrip. After locating thousands of acres of scrip land in Minnesota, Chapman moved on to Nevada and California. Chapman located nearly fifteen thousand acres of scrip in Nevada and more than fifteen thousand acres in California on valuable mining or timber lands, and he sold the scrip to others at high prices. Chapman employed or bribed a host of people to help him acquire and push the land scrip through the government. He had help from Minnesota judge Isaac Atwater "to ensure favorable rulings from the Secretary of the Interior" concerning the scrip.

According to historian William Millikan, Chapman had Senator Henry Rice and Representative Cyrus Aldrich, both from Minnesota, in his pocket to help him push through the land scrip. Chapman also paid for the services of the law firm of Van Arman, Britton & Gray in Washington, D.C., to smooth over any problems with the scrip. He had employees in Minnesota to expedite the power of attorney process and complete the documents to acquire land scrip from mixed-ancestry Dakota people.[87] Franklin Steele acquired tens of thousands of acres of Dakota scrip in his own right; his papers at the Minnesota Historical Society are full of powers of attorney, receipts, and various documents relating to his speculation in scrip.[88]

The land scrip created fortunes for American businessmen but did little for individual mixed-ancestry Dakota. Ninety percent of the Dakota land scrip was used in Minnesota; the rest was used all over the west, primarily by speculators and businessmen, especially for mining and lumber interests. California and Nevada were the states where most mixed-ancestry Dakota scrip was used outside of Minnesota, totaling over thirty thousand acres.[89] The next two states, South Dakota and Wisconsin, saw the use of over nine thousand acres each. North Dakota was the next most common state with over five thousand acres of mixed-ancestry Dakota land scrip used there. Not all of those who exploited the scrip were wealthy businessmen like Chapman or Steele; many others speculated in smaller amounts of scrip in Minnesota. In 1863, C. S. Rice wrote to mixed-ancestry Dakota Samuel Brown asking him to acquire scrip on his behalf: "Purchase for me all the adult half breed scrip you can for $1.00 per acre—let me know the amount you purchase & I will send money & papers & is there a Notary Public at the agency?"[90] Despite the proscriptions on the sale of scrip, speculators and businessmen easily found ways around the law to purchase all the scrip they wished.

Like the Lake Pepin Reservation, the Great Nemaha Reservation in southeastern Nebraska was created by the 1830 Treaty of Prairie du Chien for the use of mixed-ancestry Indians of the Iháŋkthuŋwaŋ Dakota,

Isáŋyati Dakota, Omaha, Otoe, and Ioway tribes. Of the 389 eventual allottees on the Great Nemaha Reservation, 173 were Dakota. The claimants at Great Nemaha experienced many individually based dispossession tactics after acquiring the land through allotment, reminiscent of that under the General Allotment Act of 1887. Also like the claimants at Lake Pepin, the mixed-ancestry Indians of the Great Nemaha Reservation also petitioned the government. Seventeen mixed-ancestry men from the reservation sent a petition to Commissioner of Indian Affairs George Manypenny in order to persuade Congress to have the reservation allotted to the individual claimants.[91] Congress quickly answered their petition of March 1, 1854, appropriating $11,000 on July 24 to cover the cost of a survey, a commissioner to determine the rightful claimants, and other costs related to allotment.[92] This act set in motion a flurry of affidavits and correspondence as the mixed-ancestry Indians attempted to provide evidence for their claims. Over the next several years, the commissioner collected evidence, and in a process reminiscent of that under the later Dawes Act, the reservation was surveyed and divided into 320-acre tracts.

Two branches of my family were claimants to the Great Nemaha Reservation. The matriarchs of these families were my great-great-great-grandmothers Margaret Hart Langdeau, or Wápaha Ȟóta Wíŋ (Gray Hat Woman), a mixed-ancestry Iháŋkthuŋwaŋ Dakota woman born in 1832 and a member of the Wagmúha Owíŋ (Pumpkin Rind Earrings) band, and Josette Dorion Colombe, of Iháŋkthuŋwaŋ Dakota and Sičháŋǧu Lakota ancestry born about 1834. Josette was the daughter of Paul Dorion, whose father, Pierre Dorion Jr., had met Meriwether Lewis and William Clark and was a guide for the ill-fated Astor expedition to the Pacific from 1810 to 1813. Josette married a French Canadian, John Baptiste Colombe, about 1855 by Iháŋkthuŋwaŋ custom, at which time John was working for the U.S. Army as a guide at Fort Pierre on the Missouri River during the First Sioux War.[93] Colombe, born about 1824, came to the Northern Great Plains in 1847 to work in the Indian trade.

Margaret was the daughter of a white fur trade employee, Benjamin Hart, who was possibly a member of the prominent Jewish Hart family of Montreal, and an unknown Iháŋkthuŋwaŋ woman. Like Josette Dorion and Ičíyapiwiŋ, Wápaha Ȟóta Wíŋ married a French Canadian

Figure 16. Alex C. Guion or Guyon. A mixed-ancestry Iháŋkthuŋwaŋ Dakota, he served as an interpreter and testified to Congress. Edward E. Ayer Digital Collection, Newberry Library, Chicago.

man. Born in 1820 in Montreal, Maurice Langdeau married Margaret by Iháŋkthuŋwaŋ custom about 1848, but they had a second marriage recorded in Fremont County, Iowa, in 1856. Maurice worked on the Great Plains hauling freight by wagon train.

Josette Dorion and Wápaha Ȟóta Wíŋ were active in trying to acquire land for themselves and their children on the Great Nemaha Reservation. Only Wápaha Ȟóta Wíŋ was successful. Their stories reveal the role of gender in the history of mixed-ancestry Dakota. Although limited, those women who obtained allotments exercised some level of property rights, while those who did not relied even more on their white husbands for their livelihoods. Unlike unmarried American women or Indian women married to Indian men, these married mixed-ancestry women quickly found that they were subject to coverture laws. Under Nebraska law, married women could not legally control their property or their earnings until the Nebraska legislature passed laws in 1881 permitting these rights to married women. Their white husbands and local governments that taxed mixed-ancestry lands held an inordinate amount of power in regulating what was essentially Indian land held in the name of Indian women, but in some situations, women successfully employed power in their land dealings. Some of these women were able to exert their property rights because they lived outside of any organized territory, and in their own cultures, women often controlled family property. For Indian women, American coverture laws collided with Indian custom, leading to uncertain property rights for Indian women married to white men.

On June 2, 1860, a white man named William Kinsler gave testimony for Josette's father Paul Dorion and several of her younger unmarried siblings who still lived with her father. In an affidavit for Josette's sister Sophia Dorion, Kinsler claimed that he had "resided among the Yancton Band of Sioux Indians for thirty five or six years, and has known the said Paul Dorian for that period and knows that [he] is about one fourth white and three fourths Indian of said Band. Deponent further says that he has known the wife of the said Paul Dorian, and mother of the said Sophia for eighteen or twenty years, and always understood her to be a full blood woman."[94] He went on to say that he knew that Paul Dorion was the half brother of Chief Phadáni Aphápi (Struck by the Ree) and that "Paul Dorian and his children have always been recognized and regarded as mixed bloods of the Yancton Band of Sioux Indians."[95] Paul and two of his daughters received allotments of land on the Great Nemaha Reservation.

Josette Dorion probably never lived on the reservation and never produced evidence adequate to satisfy the commissioner of her right to claim an allotment. On June 19, 1858, three Iháŋkthuŋwaŋ men—Chiefs Phadáni Aphápi, Tȟatháŋka Witkó (Crazy Bull), and Siháŋske (Long Foot)—appeared in front of N. C. Hudson, a notary public for Woodbury County, Iowa, to attest to the mixed-ancestry status and tribal connection of several mixed-ancestry Dakota. Among others, the chiefs claimed Josette and her young daughter Emma Colombe as mixed-ancestry members of the tribe.[96] For unknown reasons, the testimony of these men was not enough to secure Josette's claim, yet, the testimony of a white man, William Kinsler, on behalf of her father and siblings was enough for them to acquire allotments. Kinsler did not give testimony for Josette, but despite the testimony of chiefs of the tribe, one of whom was her uncle, Josette did not receive an allotment. Yet, on the word of a white man, Josette's father and younger siblings were admitted to the roll of allottees. Kinsler was married to a full-ancestry Iháŋkthuŋwaŋ woman and had several mixed-ancestry children who received allotments. In this process, through their testimony, white men apparently held greater influence than chiefs in the determination of which mixed-ancestry Indians would or would not be included.

The allotment of lands at Great Nemaha happened after the distribution of land scrip at Lake Pepin, and numerous mixed-ancestry Dakota tried to acquire an allotment at Great Nemaha after having already received land scrip. After comparing the list of mixed-ancestry Dakota admitted at Great Nemaha to the Lake Pepin list, J. Sharp, the commissioner responsible for creating a list of claimants, struck forty-two from the list who tried to acquire land both at Great Nemaha and Lake Pepin. American commissioners were also adamant that those Indians with African ancestry also be struck from the list, reducing the number of claimants by twelve. This came about because Thomas Sloan, a white man with a mixed-ancestry Omaha family, complained to the commissioner of Indian Affairs that Sharp was enrolling "Negroes, Molattoes, and anyone else who chose to represent themselves as claimants."[97] However, at Lake Pepin, James Thompson, a previously enslaved man from Virginia, successfully acquired land scrip for his two children at Lake Pepin.[98]

During the period of allotment, mixed-ancestry Indians wrote numerous petitions to government officials concerning issues on the reservation. Most of these petitions exhibit the signatures of men or sometimes both men and women, but the sole signatories to an 1856 petition were three Otoe and Omaha women—Margaret Sloan, Pelagie Ritter, and Mary Rodgers. The women were residents of the reservation and feared the entire reservation would be sold without their consent. They wrote to Commissioner of Indian Affairs George Manypenny to ensure they would retain the rights to the allotments they had chosen.[99] All three women were married to white men, and their petition in their own names was an expression of their control over their property.

Many white husbands, including those of Josette Dorion Colombe and Margaret Hart Langdeau, despite being non-Indians, were also able to interject themselves into petitions concerning Indian land to the commissioner of Indian Affairs. However, Margaret herself was one of forty-eight signers of a petition to the commissioner of Indian Affairs in 1858, protesting that a survey of the western boundary of the reservation was faulty. This resulted in a loss of nearly twenty thousand acres of land, and they requested that Congress conduct an impartial investigation and establish a new line more favorable to their interests.[100] That same year, a treaty with the Iháŋkthuŋwaŋ Dakota set aside money for the mixed-ancestry members for the tribe. Four years later, in 1862, a group of all men, both white and mixed, including Maurice Langdeau, petitioned the commissioner of Indian Affairs, asserting that the rightful recipients were not paid their share of the money. In this case, Maurice Langdeau appropriated control of his wife's property, signing a petition on behalf of his wife.

Similarly, John Colombe was one of 154 white and mixed-ancestry male signers of a petition to Congress and the commissioner of Indian Affairs in 1867. Because Josette had been unable to secure allotments for herself and her children at Great Nemaha, John Colombe took matters into his own hands to try to acquire a parcel of Indian land for his family. The petitioners, residents in the vicinity of Fort Laramie, Wyoming, who supported themselves by "accommodating the overland trail to the mining regions west," claimed to have lost their livelihoods due to the recent construction of the transcontinental railroad. All 154 men married Indian women and asserted that these "families and their half breed children now number on the Platte and Missouri Rivers more than two thousand souls." They requested that a tract of land be set aside for themselves and their Indian relations as a permanent home.[101] In this case, John Colombe was not just working for the good of his family; he and the other men circumvented their Indian wives and tried to acquire Indian land for their own purposes as well.

Paul Dorion worked diligently to acquire land. While working as a guide and interpreter at Fort Randall in 1857, he paid Charles Rulo to make his claim and put improvements on the land he claimed at Great Nemaha.[102] While waiting for American commissioners in the town of Rulo, Nebraska, who were supposed to arrive the previous week to finalize the distribution of allotments, Dorion wrote, "We half breeds are all here, waiting for our rights on this land." He complained that "we half-breeds are poor, and have to sell our horse to pay our board, and some of us are getting in debt."[103] In 1858, he signed a treaty between the federal government and the Iháŋkthuŋwaŋ as a witness, which created the Yankton Reservation on the east bank of the Missouri River in modern southern South Dakota. Paul was named in article 7 of the treaty, with several other mixed-ancestry Dakota. They received land "on account of their valuable services and liberality to the Yanctons."[104] Dorion finally received his allotment at Great Nemaha, but he also received land under the 1858 treaty in Dakota Territory to the north.

Back at Great Nemaha, the mixed-ancestry Indians began receiving allotment certificates in 1857 for the land they had chosen, officially putting the land into mixed-ancestry hands, although the government did not issue patents for the land until 1860, at which point the land became taxable and could be sold. It is unclear whether after allotment this Indian land was legally taxable; however, after 1860, numerous mixed-ancestry Indians, including men, women, and children, appear on the tax rolls of Richardson and Nemaha Counties in Nebraska Territory. The tax rolls were inconsistent, sometimes naming the mixed-ancestry Indians themselves as owners, while at other times naming the white husbands or fathers of mixed-ancestry children as owners. For instance, Wápaha Ȟóta Wíŋ and her three oldest children who received allotments show up on the tax rolls of Richardson County for 1861, with Margaret owing $12.43 for her lands. The next two years, her husband Maurice Langdeau appears on the rolls as the sole owner of the family's lands, but Wápaha Ȟóta Wíŋ and her children reappear on the rolls in 1864 and 1866.[105] Whether or not the local governments had the right to tax these lands is murky, leading Charles Rouleau, a white man married to a Dakota woman, to write a letter to the commissioner of Indian Affairs in 1864, complaining that the lands on the reservation were being taxed. He argued that "there is not 1/8 of those who have lands allotted to them here that know the nature of taxation nor can they be made to know the policy of such, as they do not find it consistent with their ideas or Indian customs."[106] Taxing the lands of Indians was a colonial measure intended as a means by which American officials could dispossess Indians of their land. As the tax records simply read "paid," it is unclear whether Wápaha Ȟóta Wíŋ paid the taxes assessed on her land herself, but that the land appeared in the rolls in her name attests to the fact that local officials acknowledged that she was the owner of these lands, not her husband.

Over the next decade, Wápaha Ȟóta Wíŋ and her family continued to reside on the reservation, gradually selling off their land. Like the tax rolls, it is sometimes Wápaha Ȟóta Wíŋ and her children that show up in the Richardson County Deed Books as owners and sometimes Maurice Langdeau.[107] Over time, the family sold their landholdings to a German American mutual aid organization called the German Emigration Society.[108] The deed books mostly list Maurice as the grantor, but some entries list "Morris Langdo & wife" or simply list Wápaha Ȟóta Wíŋ as the grantor. Lewis Allgewahr, president of the organization, purchased much of Wápaha Ȟóta Wíŋ's land.[109]

This inconsistent representation of landownership also appeared in the U.S. federal census. In the 1860 Census of Richardson County, Nebraska Territory, Maurice Langdeau is listed as owning no land but simply owning personal property of $500. Maurice and Wápaha Ȟóta Wíŋ sold twenty-five acres of land they owned in Fremont County, Iowa, to Thomas Harrison for $200 that same year.[110] Wápaha Ȟóta Wíŋ, however, is listed with $1,600 worth of real estate in the census, and her children are also represented as owning a substantial amount of real estate. By 1870, Maurice Langdeau is listed as the sole owner of real estate in the family, with $4,000 worth. Sometime after 1871, most of the family moved to the Yankton Reservation in Dakota Territory, where Maurice Langdeau died in 1876. By 1891, Wápaha Ȟóta Wíŋ moved on to the Rosebud Reservation, where she lived until 1928.

The experiences of the mixed-ancestry Dakota at Great Nemaha and Lake Pepin reveal important similarities and contrasts. Instead of scrip, claimants on the Great Nemaha Reservation received a 320-acre allotment of land on the reservation. But like the Lake Pepin claimants, they experienced similar dispossessions both before and after the allotment of their land. The same treaty created both reservations, but the federal government distributed the lands in very different ways, and the end result and the tactics of dispossession were much the same.

Despite their advantageous position in receiving land, the mixed-ancestry Dakota soon found that they too were cheated out of their lands, but unlike their full-ancestry relatives, dispossession occurred on an individual level. In the following decades, mixed-ancestry Dakota made numerous complaints to the Office of Indian Affairs about the tactics used to cheat them out of land, such as forged powers of attorney, fraudulent applications for duplicate scrip to replace that which was lost, or, with the case of Wápaha Ȟóta Wíŋ in Nebraska or Frank Trudell in Minnesota, prohibitive local property taxes that forced many mixed-ancestry Dakota to sell their land or face seizure for delinquent taxes. Mary Taliaferro Woodbury claimed that her white husband was "practically insane" and that "some swindlers . . . , operating in Sioux Half Breed Scrip, took advantage of the said condition of her husband, and deprived him of nearly all the scrip of this deponent as well as of her children, so that this deponent and her children have received no benefit of said scrip."[111] She asked that the Office of Indian Affairs issue duplicate scrip so that her family could benefit.

In order to sell their land, many mixed-ancestry Dakota sold powers of attorney to buyers who would then transfer the land into their name once located, but this practice was severely abused. Louis Rock told of how Dennis Moore fraudulently claimed a power of attorney from him. Rock's affidavit stated that he denied "all authority of Dennis Moore his pretended attorney, & declaring that he has no knowledge of the existence of such a man, and that he believes him to be a fictitious person, and that the power under which he pretended to act was a forgery."[112] In Rock's case, in 1865, his scrip was located by F. W. Andrews, "the professed attorney in fact of the scripee," but because he never produced a valid power of attorney, the location was suspended until the scrip was canceled by Dennis Moore in 1872. Moore accompanied his request for cancelation with what the land office believed to be a valid power of attorney from Rock. Soon after, duplicate scrip was sent to Moore and Rock lost his land.[113] Upon learning that, William M. B. Hartley, a land speculator, located her scrip in 1860, Angelique Boyer accused Hartley of fraud. In her affidavit, she claimed that "Hartley got hold of her said scrip in a manner not known to this deponent for the purpose of locating the same for his own benefit by means of some forged power of attorney."[114]

Given the large extent to which duplicate scrip had been applied for, the commissioner of the General Land Office, Willis Drummond, wrote to Secretary of the Interior Columbus Delano complaining about applications for duplicate scrip: "The business of this office relating to Sioux Half-Breed Scrip is at best exceedingly involved and difficult of adjustment." He further argued that, as was often the case in his opinion, when both the original scrip and duplicate scrip had been located, "the complications and difficulties are greatly increased, as the locator of each strenuously claims that his authority from the Scripee is superior to that of the other, and each submits a mass of testimony in support of his claim, thereby involving a protracted suspension of the cases and a voluminous correspondence." Drummond argued against the issuance of duplicate scrip, as he believed it was usually to the benefit of land speculators rather than the mixed-ancestry Dakota.[115] In these disputes over scrip, many of the legal battles went on between white people because the mixed-ancestry

Dakota were not directly involved. They had signed powers of attorney or sold their lands.

Walter Bourke complained to the commissioner of Indian Affairs on November 29, 1870, when he learned that Henry S. Welles requested duplicate scrip in Bourke's name as Bourke's attorney. Bourke argued that Welles had no authority from him to request or receive duplicate scrip.[116] In an affidavit soon after, Welles produced from his possession a signed power of attorney from Bourke, notarized in Pembina County, Minnesota, from October 26, 1870. He explained further that the scrip was lost while in the possession of Henry A. Lambert, a Saint Paul attorney. Bourke had left the scrip with Lambert in 1857, but when Lambert died several years later, the scrip was nowhere to be found. Welles claimed that Bourke hired him to recover the scrip.[117] In response to Bourke's letter, Commissioner of Indian Affairs Ely S. Parker wrote to Joseph Wilson, the commissioner of the General Land Office, to see if there was any record of this scrip in his office. In reply, Wilson noted that two pieces of Bourke's scrip had been filed for land in Dakota Territory by Byron M. Smith of Saint Paul in 1860 but that the scrip location was never completed and no patents had been issued.[118] These kinds of disputes often led to years of investigations and correspondence between mixed-ancestry claimants, their attorneys or alleged attorneys, local land offices, and the GLO and OIA. In his case, it took Bourke several years to finally receive the benefit of his scrip; the final three were not patented until 1881.

Between 1875 and 1901, dozens of mixed-ancestry Dakota, including John Baptiste Dorion, the son of Pierre Dorion Jr. and an Ioway woman, and at least thirty-four of John's descendants, received "half-breed" land scrip in Canada as Métis people. The oldest of these was Nancy Campbell Bourke, the matriarch of the mixed-ancestry Bourke family in Manitoba, born in 1800. Nancy and nineteen of her children and grandchildren received Métis scrip in 1875. Nancy and six of her children also received mixed-ancestry Dakota scrip in the United States under the 1854 law, despite the fact she moved to Canada in the 1820s and her children were born and raised in what became Manitoba.[119] Métis scrip was much like the Dakota scrip; provincial governments issued it to Métis who could use it to acquire Crown land in the province in which it was issued.

Nicole C. O'Byrne argues that the Canadian government issued the scrip "for the purpose of extinguishing the Métis share of Indian title" and that, unlike the United States, Canada recognized Métis people as having coexistent claims to Native land.[120]

Being a mixed-ancestry family afforded the Trudell children opportunities that full-ancestry Dakota did not have. Their white father sometimes took actions that furthered makhóčhe khípi, or Dakota land dispossession. But he also bought land in two sacred places, allowing the children to continue living there while their full-ancestry relatives were forcibly held on a reservation far to the west. Yet these pieces of Bdóte and Ȟemníčaŋ were in the hands of their white father, and these lands were only available for purchase because their full-ancestry relatives had been forced off by the Treaty of Mendota. As with many benefits enjoyed by mixed-ancestry Indians, the Trudell family possessed this right at the expense of their kin. Like other mixed-ancestry Dakota families, the Trudell children experienced the dispossession of their land but also benefited from the dispossession of their full-ancestry relatives. Two Trudell brothers, Hepí and Thatóheya, served as go-betweens in *Wacouta v. Sharpe,* in which Mary Wacouta sought their help to keep Artemas Sharpe off her land. At the same time, Sharpe tried to bribe the Trudell brothers to help him dispossess Wacouta of her land. They were allowed to live at sacred Dakota sites only because of their white father. At every turn, the Trudell family found themselves deeply involved in the divergent and often conflicting land interests of full-ancestry Indians, mixed-ancestry Indians, and white Americans who forced their own unfamiliar land practices on Indians in the Midwest. Cheryl I. Harris argues that "whiteness as property" endures, but it was a short-lived phenomenon for the Trudells and other mixed-ancestry families; they were able to engage in fictive whiteness, and therefore white property rights, only for a brief period in the nineteenth century.

CHAPTER 7

The U.S.-Dakota War of 1862

After decades of American encroachment on Dakota land, the theft of Dakota resources, and confinement on an ever-shrinking reservation, a segment of the Dakota Nation decided to go to war against American settlers in Minnesota. The catalyst for the war was an action by a small, hungry Bdewákhaŋthuŋwaŋ Dakota hunting party from Redwood Agency that murdered five white settlers on August 17, 1862, in Acton, Minnesota. Dakota warriors believed that war would inevitably come to them due to these killings and concluded that they should attack while they still possessed an element of surprise, beginning a concerted attack on white settlers and American soldiers the following morning. That night, Chief Táoyateduta, commonly called "Little Crow," reluctantly agreed to lead the Dakota in a war against the white settlers of Minnesota.[1] Soon, both men and women began preparing for impending attacks the next morning. This event also spurred numerous white settlers and mixed-ancestry Dakota men to join state militias and army units to defend against Dakota attacks and initiate an offensive war against the Dakota. This was a consequential war, resulting in at least six hundred settlers dead, hundreds of Dakota people killed, including the execution of forty Dakota men, as many as forty thousand non-Native refugees, and six thousand Dakota people either incarcerated, removed from Minnesota, or forced to flee.[2]

The American response to the U.S.-Dakota War was catastrophic; this moment dramatically changed the trajectory of Dakota history, and the traumas of the war are still felt by Dakota people today. The war also laid bare the divisions and animosities that had grown between Dakota people of mixed and full ancestry. After the war, with the settler state placing more restrictions on Indians, Dakota people of mixed ancestry found it difficult to vote and exercise their rights of citizenship. Scholars have produced an extensive literature on various aspects of the U.S.-Dakota War, but these works pay little attention to the mixed-ancestry Dakota and their role in the war and its aftermath.[3] Dakota people of mixed ancestry fought on both sides in the war, feared that they would be massacred by their full-ancestry relatives, and acted as go-betweens to bring about a cessation to the hostilities.[4]

After years of mixed-ancestry Dakota Indians receiving separate provisions of land and money in treaties, access to American citizenship and other legal rights, and taking economic advantage of the full-ancestry Dakota, animosities between the groups erupted into violence. During the war, the full-ancestry Dakota captured and threatened to kill over 160 of their mixed-ancestry relatives, while dozens of mixed-ancestry Dakota joined the U.S. military to fight against them. While Americans continued to treat full- and mixed-ancestry Indians differently after the war, due to the war, many mixed-ancestry Indians found it more difficult to exercise their legal rights, prompting most mixed-ancestry Indians to eventually move to reservations with their relatives. There was a deeper racialization and division present during the U.S.-Dakota War, and the traditional binary narrative of a war between white people and Indians fails to portray the true complexity of those whose lives were disrupted by the war. The Dakota were vehemently divided between war and peace with the white settlers of Minnesota. But these divisions went further, creating a lasting rift between mixed- and full-ancestry Dakota Indians that still exists today.

Before the start of the U.S.-Dakota War in August of 1862, because so many Dakota were destitute and short of provisions, there were grumblings of a possible fight against white Minnesotans to acquire food. At the same time, many of the full-ancestry Dakota voiced their displeasure with the mixed-ancestry Dakota. Speaking of the summer of 1862, Robert

Hakéwašte noted, "We were in a starving condition and desperate state of mind."[5] Some thought that the distraction of the Civil War would provide an opportunity to go on the offensive. Waŋbdíthaŋka, also known as Jerome Big Eagle, a full-ancestry Dakota, argued that because U.S. Army officials began recruiting Dakota of mixed ancestry, the Union must have been desperate. Major Thomas Galbraith, Waŋbdíthaŋka noted, had recruited a company of men from the Dakota Indian agencies at Yellow Medicine and Redwood: "His men were nearly all half-breeds. The Indians now thought the whites must be pretty hard up for men to fight the South, or they would not come so far out on the frontier and take half-breeds or anything to help them."[6] Chief Wápahaša, in a speech he made before the war to a council of Dakota about potential resistance to paying Indian traders, asserted, "I did not want the half-breeds to be admitted to our councils; that they had always been the tools of the traders, and aided them to deceive the Indians."[7] Waŋbdíthaŋka and Wápahaša summed up the feeling of many Dakota people in the summer of 1862: their poverty and lack of food due to late treaty-guaranteed annuities and building animosities toward mixed-ancestry Dakota people might result in war and the splintering of the Dakota Nation between those of mixed and full ancestry.

The U.S.-Dakota War is usually viewed as a brief conflict, beginning on August 17, 1862, with the killing of white settlers at Acton, Minnesota, and ending with the surrender of approximately 1,200 Dakota on September 26, after the Battle of Wood Lake. However, hostilities continued for years in western Minnesota and Dakota Territory. Thousands of Dakota fled westward and northward, hoping to escape the wrath of American soldiers. Summer expeditions, led by Henry Sibley in 1863 and by Alfred Sully in 1864 and 1865, continued to press the Dakota and engaged various tribes of the Očhéthi Šakówiŋ in pitched battles, many of whom were not involved in the war in Minnesota. The Massacre of Whitestone Hill, October 3–5, 1863, was particularly costly. American troops murdered hundreds of Dakota and Lakota Indians, mostly women and children. The Dakota conducted periodic small raids into Minnesota, but after 1862, the war was one-sided, with the Dakota sustaining most of the casualties. During these years, the army continuously manned forts in western Minnesota and in Dakota Territory, often with the help of Dakota scouts.

The first major attack was on the Redwood Agency, where many mixed-ancestry and white Indian traders and government employees lived with their families. A mixed-ancestry Dakota, Cecilia Campbell, recalled her family's ordeal at the agency. A group of full-ancestry warriors entered a store where her father and uncle—Antoine J. and Baptiste Campbell—were talking to two white men, who the warriors killed in front of them. One of the warriors "levelled his gun at father's breast and told him now was the time to take revenge" but she explains how eight full-ancestry men protected the Campbell brothers, "men [who] were related by blood to Grandfather Scott Campbell."[8] There was great fear not just among the white settlers; mixed-ancestry Dakota also feared they would be killed by their relatives. A mixed-ancestry Indian at Redwood Agency, Joseph Coursolle, wondered if he would be killed: "But they have been my friends for years. My French father married a Sioux woman. I am as much Indian as white. Surely they will not kill."[9] These accounts demonstrate the danger and fear that mixed-ancestry Dakota experienced during the war.

While few mixed-ancestry Dakota were killed in the initial onslaught, many were taken captive and threatened with violence. Nancy McClure Faribault, who lived near Redwood Agency with her mixed-ancestry husband David Faribault Jr. and their daughter, reminisced about her capture. When the attack came, her family fled to the woods, followed by another mixed-ancestry family. "Just as we started for the woods, Louis Brisbois and his wife and two children, mixed-blood people, came up and went with us," she wrote. A group of Dakota warriors observed their flight to the woods and demanded that they come out. When David Faribault asked what was happening, one of the warriors replied, "We have killed all the white people at the agency; all the Indians are on the warpath; we are going to kill all the white people in Minnesota; we are not going to hurt you, for you have trusted us with goods, but we are going to kill these Brisbois." When two wagons full of settlers sped by, the warriors were momentarily distracted, allowing the Brisbois family to escape, but Nancy and her family were captured and forced to go to Táoyateduta's camp. "We stayed that night with the Indians that brought us," she said, and "soon other prisoners, many of them half-bloods like ourselves, were brought in."[10] David Faribault Jr. explained, "I always remained while a prisoner with those related to me. They treated me well."[11] The war party, led by Táoyateduta, captured about 160 mixed-ancestry Dakota and held them prisoner for the remainder of the war.

Some mixed-ancestry Dakota, however, sympathized with the war party's views and joined in the fight. He was only nineteen at the start of the war, but George Quinn explained, "I am half white and half Indian. . . . When the outbreak came I went with my people against the whites. . . . I was in the attack on Captain (John S.) Marsh's company at Redwood Ferry, the first day of the outbreak at the agency, and helped to destroy the command."[12] Another mixed-ancestry Indian, George LeBlanc, a.k.a. George Provencial, was killed at the Battle of New Ulm while fighting for

Figure 17. Baptiste Campbell, 1831–1862. Drawn by Robert O. Sweeny, 1862. A mixed-ancestry Waȟpéthuŋwaŋ Dakota, he was also of Menominee descent. He was a voter and citizen of the United States. The military tribunal found Campbell guilty and he was subsequently hanged with thirty-seven other Dakota men on December 26, 1862. Accession no. AV2017.203.8, Minnesota Historical Society, Saint Paul.

the Dakota.[13] During the subsequent trials by the military tribunal, at least nineteen mixed-ancestry Dakota were tried, fourteen of whom the tribunal found guilty, and three were executed. Some of these claimed that the full-ancestry Dakota forced them to fight. In his trial, Baptiste Campbell claimed that Táoyateduta threatened him and two other mixed-ancestry men, Hypolite Auge and Henry Milord: "If you don't help to kill some white people you will be killed." "Wouldn't hurt a man if we hadn't been pushed," Campbell argued.[14] The tribunal did not distinguish between those who had fought voluntarily or involuntarily, finding Campbell guilty and executing him.

Many other mixed-ancestry men chose to fight against the Dakota Nation, joining local militias and army regiments. Among the militia regiments, at least fifteen mixed-ancestry Dakota served in the Renville Rangers, at least four in Major Alfred Brackett's Battalion, at least three in the Rice County Rangers, and one more in Major E. A. C. Hatch's Independent Battalion. Dozens of Dakota men had already enlisted in the army and been sent south to fight the Confederacy. At least a dozen served in the Fifth Minnesota Infantry, eight of them in Company G and at least ten more served in the Sixth Minnesota Infantry. Mixed-ancestry Dakota served in many other Minnesota regiments, as well as Wisconsin, Dakota Territory, and Iowa regiments.

Many mixed-ancestry Dakota, particularly those in the Renville Rangers, had the unlucky timing of joining just days before the outbreak of war and were forced to fight against their own people. Peter Boyer, who enlisted four days before the start of the war, was killed in battle fighting against his people at Birch Coulee just two weeks later.[15] Many others joined the army specifically because of the war: Baptiste Campbell's first cousin Jeremiah Campbell joined the Tenth Minnesota Infantry Regiment on September 2, while a Dakota friend of Francis Trudell, Frederick LaChapelle, joined the same company as Francis on August 20, Company K of the Ninth Minnesota Infantry. At least sixty-five other mixed-ancestry Dakota served as scouts during the war, many joining Henry Sibley's and Alfred Sully's punitive expeditions against the Dakota who fled Minnesota.

At least thirty-five mixed-ancestry Dakota had joined the army on or before August 18, 1862, thirteen of whom had joined just days before the start of the war with the intention of fighting the Confederacy in the Civil War. At least seven more enlisted within days after the start of the war. In all, at least eighty Dakota men, all but two or three of whom were of mixed ancestry, joined the army between 1861 and 1865. At least sixty-five additional mixed-ancestry Dakota served as scouts between 1862 and 1866. Hundreds of full-ancestry Dakota also served as scouts during this same period. All of the scouts served in Minnesota or Dakota Territory, but of the more than eighty Dakota who enlisted in the army, many saw action in the South after fighting their own people. Charles Clewett was wounded in the arm at Chickamauga. Pierre Felix contracted dysentery in Alabama in 1864, after fighting his own people as a member of the Sixth Minnesota Infantry Regiment. Alexander McLeod, also a member of the Sixth Minnesota Infantry, who had enlisted two days before the start of the war, died of chronic diarrhea November 14, 1864. Mixed-ancestry Dakota men took their duty to the U.S. Army seriously and never balked at engaging in hostilities with Dakota warriors.

Many white men with Dakota families also enlisted to fight against their wives' people. On August 21, just four days after the Dakota attack at Acton, Francis Trudell enlisted as a private in Company K, Ninth Minnesota Infantry Regiment, to serve three years. Despite being over sixty years of age, physician F. H. Milligan of Wabasha, Minnesota, husband of a mixed-ancestry Dakota woman, "considered him to be a man of a good constitution, with great powers of endurance particularly free from disease," and persuaded him to enlist.[16] His enlistment papers list him as aged forty-five, a necessary fiction considering that was the cut-off age to enlist in the U.S. Army at the time.[17] Upon enlistment, Trudell received a bounty of twenty-seven dollars. This bonus and the promise of the wages of a private, thirteen dollars per month, was probably a welcomed economic boost for the family.

Despite his three-year enlistment, Trudell's military career was short-lived. He was healthy and on duty with his company at Fort Snelling as late as October 31. During this time, on September 11, 1862, Trudell was promoted to wagoner, with the responsibility to transport military cargo and supplies as needed, as well as maintain the wagon and take care of the horses and mules. The muster rolls for November and December, however, show he was in the hospital at Fort Snelling. Sometime in December, he moved with his company to Mankato, Minnesota, where his company was tasked with guarding Dakota prisoners. By April, he was in a hospital at Saint Peter, Minnesota, where he was discharged for disability on July 2, 1863.[18] Surgeon R. H. Bingham of the Ninth Minnesota Infantry Regiment wrote of Trudell's health upon his discharge on July 2: "Chronic Bronchitis, complicated with functional derangement of the Heart. The said Trudell is sixty years of age—has been a man of intemperate habits producing great nervous prostration. He has been unable to perform any duty for the past six months."[19]

One Dakota soldier summed up his motivations for serving in the army. Joseph Allord, a private in Company A, Sixth Minnesota Infantry Regiment, wrote to his commanding officer, General Dodge, while in the Myrtle Street Military Prison in Saint Louis, Missouri, on January 6, 1865. Unable to speak English, Allord wrote his letter in Dakota, but a Dakota friend in the regiment translated the letter for him. Allord was serving a brief sentence for being absent without leave. He was writing to Dodge to secure a discharge so that he could go home.

> Sir Permit me to inform you that I am a "Sioux Indian" enlisted in the Service of [the] Great father the President at Washington and have served him two years and six months with my white brothers against my own people who were wrong. I left my own land at the command of the great father and came down here to help him fight my white brothers who were wrong. I want to tell you if my father the President has no more need of me I want to go home for I can do him no more good in here. I have had my trial some time ago and do not know what is to be done with me.[20]

Allord asserted that his relatives were wrong for making war on the white settlers, prompting him to enlist and fight against them. He used the same logic in explaining his motivation for fighting against the Confederacy, calling them his "white brothers" but arguing that they were wrong for making war on the Union.

Allord not only served in the war but also was put on trial November 2, 1862, for his part in the war. The tribunal accused him of participating in the battles at the Fort, New Ulm, Birch Coolie, and Wood Lake. In defense, he testified, "I was not at the Fort, Birch Coolie, or New Ulm. I was at Wood Lake. I was where the Indian was shot by the cannon. I was not near where they were firing. I was out at the Big Woods at the other battles. I went out there before the outbreak. I killed a Chippewa squaw out there. The Indians gave me what I have on."[21] The tribunal found Allord not guilty. His admission of killing an Ojibwe woman did not phase the tribunal, who had sentenced hundreds of men to death on thin evidence that they fired on white settlers. The tribunals were simply meant to punish the Dakota for any perceived transgressions toward white settlers; Indian lives were inconsequential. Two days after his acquittal, he enlisted in Company A, Sixth Minnesota Infantry Regiment.

Even though dozens of mixed-ancestry men enlisted to fight against their own people, they did not disregard the importance of kinship. Indeed, in many families, multiple family members served. Among the extended Faribault family, three served in a militia unit, the Rice County Rangers, recruited at the start of the war. David Faribault Sr. served as a scout. All three Bailly brothers, Alexis, Daniel, and Henry, served as officers. Cousins of the Faribaults and Baillys, brothers Henry, Mark, and Norman Wells, all served, two of whom had the unlucky distinction of receiving discharges for testicle injuries. Brothers Dennis and Pierre Felix served in Company A of the Sixth Minnesota Infantry Regiment with Joseph Allord. Four members of the LaChapelle family served in the army, as did their cousins, brothers Arthur, Duff, and Theophilus Brunson. White observers often wrote of their surprise at the loyalty of the mixed-ancestry soldiers to the United States.[22] Several members of the extended Campbell family served, including Antoine, Alex, and Scott Campbell as scouts; father and son, both named George Campbell, served in the army, as did Jeremiah and John Campbell. At least ten members of the Renville family served as scouts between 1862 and 1866. A handful of mixed-ancestry Iháŋkthuŋwaŋ also served, including brothers Charles and Rousseau Papin and brothers Alexis and Paul Traversie, who both enlisted in Company A of the First Dakota Territory Cavalry Regiment. For mixed-ancestry Dakota, service in the military as either scouts or soldiers was often a family affair.

After the initial onslaught of the Dakota warriors at Redwood Agency, the Dakota sent messengers to the Yellow Medicine Agency to convince the Sisíthuŋwaŋ and Waȟpéthuŋwaŋ bands to join them in the war. When they arrived, rumors of their treatment of the mixed-ancestry Dakota at Redwood Agency followed them. A mixed-ancestry Dakota at Yellow Medicine, Gabriel Renville, relayed to missionary Thomas Williamson that "it is reported that even the mixed-bloods who are Dakota have been killed, and the only thing for you to do is to flee."[23] Renville's son, Victor, remembered that Wičáŋȟpinuŋpa had told him that these were simply rumors.[24]

The Dakota at the Yellow Medicine Agency were much less receptive to the idea of killing or imprisoning their mixed-ancestry kin. Mixed-ancestry Dakota Joseph LaFramboise Jr. recalled a council among the Yellow Medicine bands when three messengers from the Bdewákhaŋthuŋwaŋ band came to acquire their support: "These three men told all that had been done at the lower agency in regard to mixed bloods also, and wanted to know what the feeling of these people was in regard to the mixed bloods. One man got up and said that he had no relatives among the mixed bloods, but that they were all his friends, and that he had no desire to injure the mixed bloods or the white men." Another man spoke in council, "I am a mixed blood, but was raised among the Indians, dressed in breech clout, and my name is Ma-rpi-oi-car-mani. . . . If anybody tries to injure the mixed-bloods, I will stand by them as long as I stand alive." LaFramboise reflected, "When we first heard them consulting about the mixed bloods myself and brother-in-law had intended to shoot these men who had come from the Medawakantons, but after these two men spoke we knew we had friends there, therefore did not do anything."[25] This council illustrates the difference in feeling the different tribes held toward their mixed-ancestry relatives. The Dakota at Yellow Medicine were disgusted with the rumors that mixed-ancestry Dakota had been killed, so much so that they viewed the full-ancestry Bdewákhaŋthuŋwaŋ messengers as in the wrong and considered killing them. While certainly animosities existed between the mixed- and full-ancestry Dakota at Yellow Medicine, relations had not degraded to the point that they had among the Bdewákhaŋthuŋwaŋ.

There were multiple reasons for the difference in feeling toward mixed-ancestry Dakota among the Yellow Medicine tribes and the Redwood tribes. The Redwood tribes, the Bdewákhaŋthuŋwaŋ and Waȟpékute, were from eastern Minnesota, having made their homes on both sides of the Mississippi for centuries. Because of this, these bands had had much earlier and prolonged contact with white fur traders, soldiers, and settlers. The mixed-ancestry population was much older and larger among these bands. Looking back to the 680 mixed-ancestry Dakota who received land scrip, the vast majority were descendants of the eastern bands. A whopping 465 were Bdewákhaŋthuŋwaŋ and another 16 were members of the Waȟpékute band. Only 162 were from the Sisíthuŋwaŋ and Waȟpéthuŋwaŋ bands of the Yellow Medicine Agency. An additional 47 more were from two or more bands, but for all 47, the Bdewákhaŋthuŋwaŋ was one of those bands, meaning almost 78 percent of the mixed-ancestry population who received land scrip were from the eastern Dakota tribes. The mixed-ancestry Dakota population at Yellow Medicine Agency was of a much smaller proportion, and because they had largely grown up away from white settlement, they maintained closer ties to their full-ancestry relatives than had those of the eastern tribes. Not coincidentally, the Bdewákhaŋthuŋwaŋ tribe were the most desperate to prosecute the war, and the vast majority of warriors came from this tribe.

During their captivity, the mixed-ancestry prisoners heard their full-ancestry captors debate whether or not to kill the captives. Nancy McClure Faribault wrote that the warriors were so enraged after the Battle of Fort Ridgely on August 20 that some of their mixed-ancestry relatives were fighting against them. "This made them very bitter against us," she wrote, "for they said we were worse than the whites, and that they are going to kill all of us," although the mixed-ancestry Dakota remained unharmed. Táoyateduta threatened the mixed-ancestry prisoners that if any decided to escape, they would kill those that remained, although Faribault called this a hollow threat. She recorded an event several days later, when "the cry was raised that the half-breeds were all to be killed. Little Crow held a council and would allow no Indians to attend it that had half-breed relatives." During the council, Faribault's full-ancestry uncle Ȟdémani arrived to rescue Faribault and her family. Táoyateduta confronted Ȟdémani and forbid anyone from taking mixed-ancestry Dakota from the camp. Ȟdémani stood his ground and took Faribault and her family with him, nearly inciting a fight.[26] Many full-ancestry Dakota had hard feelings toward those of mixed ancestry, but as Faribault's story demonstrates, many had full-ancestry relatives willing to protect them. Throughout the war, the full-ancestry Dakota debated the "mixed-blood" question, and the mixed-ancestry Dakota were often in danger, but in the end, through the protection of their full-ancestry relatives and the peace faction, the mixed-ancestry captives survived the war.

Over the course of the war in Minnesota, white officials had hard feelings toward the Dakota, so much so that they debated their legal status and whether or not to negotiate a peace treaty with them. General John Pope regularly used the most vicious and genocidal language when discussing the Dakota: "It is idle and wicked, in view of the atrocious murders these Indians have committed . . . to make treaties, or talk about keeping faith with them." He explained further, "It is my purpose utterly to exterminate the Sioux, if I have the power to do so, and even if it require a campaign lasting the whole of next year. Destroy everything belonging to them, and force them out on to the plains. . . . They are to be treated as maniacs, or wild beasts, and by no means as people, with whom treaties or compromises should be made."[27] Pope did not want the Dakota treated as a sovereign nation; he went so far as to assert the Dakota were not people, suggesting their total annihilation. In expressing his hatred for the Dakota, Pope suggested punishments that would curtail the legal rights of the Dakota. Sibley wanted to ensure that they not receive the legal rights of enemy combatants, while Pope went further, opining on the immorality of making any kind of peace treaty with the Dakota. Both denied the sovereignty of the Dakota Nation.

Pope wanted to use brutal tactics even among Dakota tribes that had not taken part in the war. Pope proposed sending five hundred cavalry soldiers and two cannons to the Yankton Reservation in Dakota Territory and to "make prisoners of all that tribe" and round up and execute any who had taken part in the war. He also recommended rounding up "at least forty of the principle Indians" and chiefs and holding them as hostages. In case any Iháŋkthuŋwaŋ Indians committed "any sort of outrages upon the whites," he would immediately hang all of the hostages.[28] Pope was exceptionally brutal in his ideas for prosecuting the war and retribution to the Dakota.

During the course of the war, the full- and mixed-ancestry Dakota found themselves on different sides of the battlefield. Despite their threats to the mixed-ancestry captives, the warriors wanted to give their mixed-ancestry relatives a chance to change sides. At the Battle of Birch Coulee on September 3, Charles Flandrau, commander of a militia regiment, ex-Indian agent at Redwood Agency, and former Minnesota legislator, recorded a conversation between the hostile Dakota and his mixed-ancestry troops. Under a white flag, a warrior rode up and carried on a conversation in Dakota with Flandrau's mixed-ancestry interpreter, Corporal James Auge. The warrior told Auge "that they were now going to charge the camp and should take no prisoners, but if the half-breeds and all those who had Indian blood in them would march out and give themselves up, they would be protected." Flandrau wrote that the eight or ten Dakota members of the regiment gathered around Auge to discuss what they would do. After some time, Auge told Flandrau, "We are going to stay with you, captain." Auge told this to the messenger from the Dakota camp and followed it with an insult: "You fight like Chippewas!" The battle soon commenced, resulting in a defeat of the American forces.[29]

Despite his dehumanization of the Dakota, General Pope recommended enlisting mixed-ancestry Indians and Métis into the army to fight against the Dakota: "I desire much to get a force of five or six hundred men or more, of the half breeds of Pembina, to come down as soon as possible and join in an attack of the Sioux." He wrote to Norman Kittson, a white Indian trader in the region, to communicate his desires to the Métis on his behalf so that they could aid "in exterminating the Sioux."[30] This was not an expression of altruism toward Indigenous people; Pope saw the enlistment of Métis and mixed-ancestry Indians to fight in the U.S.-Dakota War and the Civil War as a way to control them and tamp down any unrest among them. Pope wrote to Edward Salomon, governor of Wisconsin, about matters among the Red Cliff Ojibwe in northwestern Wisconsin. Pope had sent a company of soldiers to the region to quell a disturbance among the mixed-ancestry Ojibwe there. "It seems that many of them have enlisted," he wrote, "received subsistence, and now refuse to obey the call of the State" to move to their designated meeting point. Pope supported the proposal of Judge McCloud, who wanted to raise several more companies of mixed-ancestry Ojibwe and argued that "if he can do so and get those men out of that region, it would greatly tend to quiet apprehension."[31] Pope saw enlisting Métis and mixed-ancestry Indians in the military as a tactic to bring some semblance of peace to the region, while at the same time exploiting their service for the war effort.

Fighting on the Dakota side, mixed-ancestry Dakota George Quinn recounted his encounter with a mixed-ancestry Indian fighting with the U.S. forces. Quinn was with a small squad of warriors to scout Fort Ridgely, when "old Jack Frazer, a well-known half-breed who had made his escape from Wacouta's village the day before, leaving his family behind, was standing picket in plain view of us. He called out to us to get right away from there or he would shoot us, and he said that if he did not know our fathers and mothers so well he would shoot us anyhow."[32] Frazier called on kinship connections to justify not killing the warriors. Waŋbdíthaŋka recalled a similar incident at Birch Coulee: "There were some half-breeds with the whites who could speak Sioux well, and they heard us arranging to assault them. Jack Frazer told me afterward that he heard us talking about it plainly. Alex[ander] Faribault was there and heard the talk and called out to us: 'You do very wrong to fire on us. We did not come to fight; we only came out to bury the bodies of the white people you killed.'"[33] Again, Faribault asserted that the Dakota should not be fighting each other. These peaceful exchanges recorded by Quinn, Flandrau, and Waŋbdíthaŋka did not always end so well.

At other times, mixed- and full-ancestry Dakota were involved in ferocious battles against each other. Several mixed-ancestry Dakota were wounded or killed in battles against their relatives. Peter Boyer was killed at Birch Coulee; brothers Alexis and Francis Demars, members of the Renville Rangers, both received gunshot wounds to the pelvis, but survived. Francis was shot in the left hand and in the groin, fracturing his pelvis at the Battle of New Ulm. Alexis received his wound at the Battle of Wood Lake.[34] Frank LeClair was shot through the arm during the second siege of New Ulm on August 22, but he took "a handkerchief from his pocket, he bound it around his arm, and remained unflinchingly at his post."[35] Some mixed-ancestry Dakota recorded their exploits in battle against their full-ancestry relatives. Joseph Coursolle joined a militia regiment because his young daughters had been captured. He feared they had been killed, but he fought in hopes of rescuing them. Recounting his exploits at the Battle of Birch Coulee, he told how he killed a Dakota sniper, then "I heard a loud voice calling in Sioux, 'Hear me, Hinhankaga. We saw you shoot. You killed the son of Chief Traveling Hail. Now we kill your little girls!'" Coursolle was relieved to hear that his daughters were still alive but instantly dreaded they would be killed. His daughters survived the war and Coursolle soon reunited with them.[36] These examples illustrate the ferocity of the fighting between the mixed- and full-ancestry Dakota, but mixed-ancestry Dakota also served in other capacities to bring an end to the war.

Henry Sibley, commander of the American forces, left a note on the Birch Coulee battlefield, where it would be found by the Dakota, suggesting that Sibley and Táoyateduta use mixed-ancestry Dakota as messengers between the warring parties in order to negotiate a peace. When this note was found, Táoyateduta had several mixed-ancestry Dakota who could read English—including Antoine J. Campbell and David Faribault—translate it for him. However, Táoyateduta did not trust these men and called for Thomas A. Robertson, a mixed-ancestry man he could trust, to be brought to him. Robertson translated the letter the same as the others. Sibley asked that two mixed-ancestry men be sent to parlay with him under a white flag, then he would allow them to return to the Dakota. Táoyateduta asked Thomas Robinson, not to be confused with Thomas A. Robertson, to find another mixed-ancestry man to go with him on this mission. Robertson was the only man that would agree to go, but Táoyateduta saw Robertson as a relative and did not want him to go for fear he might be killed. After pleading with Táoyateduta, he allowed the two similarly named men to ride to Fort Ridgely to deliver a message to Sibley. However, as Robertson explained, "while we were ostensibly messengers from Little Crow and the hostiles, I was, in secret, a messenger in the interests of the friendly element and the release of over 150 prisoners in the hostile camp." Robertson was working as a double agent as a messenger for Táoyateduta but also secretly to rescue the white and mixed-ancestry captives.[37]

As the war continued, coinciding with a request from Sibley that the peace faction form their own camp, the Dakota split into two camps. Sibley wrote "to those of the Half Breeds and the Sioux Indians" who had not been involved in killing white settlers that he wanted to protect them. He wrote, "I have not come into this upper country to injure any innocent person, but to punish those who have committed the cruel murders upon innocent men women & children. I therefore write to you to withdraw from these guilty people, you must when you see my troops approaching take up a separate position and hoist a flag of Truce and send a small party to me when I have a flag of Truce in answer, and I will then take you under my protection."[38] The Dakota did separate themselves, one camp composed of the Bdewákhaŋthuŋwaŋ who wanted to

Figure 18. George LeBlanc, alias George Provencial, 1820–1862. He was a mixed-ancestry Bdewákhaŋthuŋwaŋ Dakota. Provencial fought on the side of the Dakota during the U.S.-Dakota War and was killed at the Battle of New Ulm. Drawn in 1851 by Frank B. Mayer. Edward E. Ayer Digital Collection, Newberry Library, Chicago.

continue to prosecute the war and hold the mixed-ancestry Dakota captive, led by Táoyateduta, and the peace faction, made up of the Sisíthuŋwaŋ and Wahpéthuŋwaŋ tribes, who wished to end the war and protect the captives, primarily led by leaders of the Hazelwood Republic. Several of these mixed-ancestry-led peace missions occurred, in each case passing messages from Táoyateduta but also secretly passing messages from the peace faction. As Gabriel Renville noted, "There were other letters written to General Sibley, but all unknown to the hostile Indians."[39] The peace faction saw their most important task as securing and protecting the prisoners.

Leaders of the peace faction organized a soldiers' lodge, headed by four men, comprising two full-ancestry Dakota and two of mixed ancestry—Gabriel Renville and Joseph LaFramboise Jr.—tasked with getting the prisoners out of Táoyateduta's camp. "After these four had been duly installed and authority given them," Renville recalled: "The first question discussed was the release of the prisoners, both whites and mixed-bloods. . . . Then we had a consultation in regard to the mixed-bloods, who, though they were white, were children of the Indians. It was thought to be wrong that their property should be taken from them, and that therefore their horses and wagons should be returned to them. After we had discussed the matter, it was decided to demand the property, and Little Paul was chosen as spokesman to present the matter to the hostile Indians."[40] Renville claimed they prepared for battle, arming themselves and painting their faces. When they delivered their demands, a spokesman for the Bdewákhaŋthuŋwaŋ responded, "The mixed-bloods ought not to be alive, they should have been killed. But now you say their property should be returned to them. We will never do so."[41] Tensions between the two factions ran high; they nearly went to war with each other over the disposition of their mixed-ancestry kin and their property.

Despite the threats by members of the Bdewákhaŋthuŋwaŋ camp, members of the soldiers' lodge secured the prisoners and held them in their own camp. One of the leaders of the soldiers' lodge, Joseph LaFramboise Jr., wrote, "When we got to Little Crow's camp, we asked these mixed bloods where the property was—horses and other things that had been taken away from us. We took them through the camp and they pointed out the property that belonged to us, and we took this property away from Little Crow and returned it to those to whom it belonged."[42]

Although the mixed-ancestry captives were now in the camp of the peace faction, they were not out of danger. They continued to fear that members of Táoyateduta's faction would come to kill them. In the aftermath of the Dakota defeat at the Battle of Wood Lake, Nancy McClure Faribault wrote of the renewed threat toward the mixed-ancestry Dakota. She was happy to hear the cannons of the army: "To us captives in the Indian camp the sound of Gen. Sibley's guns were as sweet as the chimes of wedding bells." However, when the defeated warriors returned, "They were cursing the half-breeds, saying that Gen. Sibley had numbers of them with him in the battle, and that every shot that one of them fired had hit an Indian. It did me real good to learn that so many of my race had stood loyal and true and had done such good service. . . . But then came the word that the defeated Indians would take vengeance on the half-breed captives and the whites, too, as soon as they got back."[43] To protect themselves, Faribault and others began to dig pits as a safeguard from errant gunfire if war erupted between the two factions. A Dakota woman who dug one of these pits, Wičáŋȟpiwaštewiŋ, explained that these pits were traditional defenses for Dakota women and children.[44]

Despite these renewed threats, Faribault felt a wave of relief of their impending rescue. She wrote, "The soldiers were near, the half-bloods were in the saddle and I felt that I would soon be safe." By this point, she had had enough of these death threats. "An Indian woman near me began abusing us. She said: 'When we talk of killing these half-breeds they drop their heads and sneak around like a bird-dog.'" Faribault would have none of it: "I flew at that woman and routed her so completely that she bore the marks for some time."[45] Faribault noted the racial differences between mixed- and full-ancestry Indians in her account. She referred to "half-breeds" as members of her race, yet she made a differentiation between herself and an Indian woman. This gets to the heart of the animosities between mixed- and full-ancestry Dakota; many had begun to think of themselves as a separate people, from different races. The day after the battle, the prisoners finally enjoyed safety and the site of their liberation was named Camp Release by the American soldiers. At the lowest point in Dakota history, after years of mistreatment by the federal government, Indian traders, and white settlers, after a season of starvation and being forced out of their homeland, after the defeat of the Dakota Nation at the Battle of Wood Lake, the mixed-ancestry Dakota instead found reason to rejoice in this moment.

In the aftermath of the battle, Táoyateduta's band fled, while the camp of the peace faction, with the prisoners, remained. The next day, American soldiers arrived and first took away the approximately one hundred white prisoners. Only the white prisoners were taken, as Nancy McClure Faribault explained, because "the soldiers were greatly enraged at some of the half-bloods, and their officers were afraid they could not 'hold them.'"[46] Another day passed before the approximately 160 mixed-ancestry prisoners were finally taken to Camp Release. In the final tally, Sibley wrote on October 3, "I have 107 white captives and 162 Half Breeds rescued from the Indians."[47] Just two days after the Battle of Wood Lake, Sibley appointed a commission of military officers to try Dakota men accused of participating in the war; the mixed-ancestry Dakota were heavily involved in these trials, some as defendants but especially as witnesses. The military commission had the duty "to try summarily the Mulatto and Indians or Mixed bloods, now prisoners, or who may be brought before them," demonstrating how the white settlers racially delineated the prisoners.[48]

Sibley wanted to use mixed-ancestry Indians as witnesses in the military tribunals happening at Camp Release against the Dakota participants in the war, writing a flurry of letters on October 17. To Thomas Galbraith, twenty miles away at Yellow Medicine Agency, he wrote, "I have [Francois] Roi in custody & four other half breeds who are respected. If John Moore or any other person can serve as witnesses against the former they should be on hand when wanted. Jo Campbell should be here also."[49] He wrote an additional letter to J. C. Whitney, also at Yellow Medicine, reiterating that he wanted John Moore and Antoine Joseph Campbell, whom he referred to as "Joe," to get to Camp Release as soon as they could. He also reported that Joseph Laframboise Jr. had arrived the night before.[50] To General Pope, Sibley wrote that the full-ancestry Dakota forced their mixed-ancestry relatives to participate in the war, suggesting he trusted some mixed-ancestry Indians enough to rely on them for their testimony against the full-ancestry Dakota.[51] By October 20, however, Sibley's attitude toward some of the mixed-ancestry Dakota changed: "The developments show that the greater part of the Indian men now prisoners, & several half breeds among them richly deserve the halter which they will assuredly receive." He explained that one of the Dakota who had killed several white settlers was hiding in Saint Paul: "There is a half breed named Hypolite Auge said to be in St. Paul who is implicated. He is a half breed, please have him arrested if he be found. . . . He is doubtless known to many French people in St. Paul."[52] Auge was eventually found, tried, and hanged, but the fact that he could hide in the most populous city in the state, its capital, suggests that white Minnesotans did not feel the same enmity toward mixed-ancestry Dakota as they did against those of full-ancestry.

Now that he had a number of captives under his control, Sibley ordered that they be used for labor just days into the military tribunals. On October 4, he ordered Major Thomas Galbraith to "take charge of the Indians, and such of the half breeds & mixed bloods as may be designated" to go to the Indian agencies to collect the crops that had been growing unattended for the previous six weeks. Galbraith employed both men and women to collect the crops.[53] When Galbraith returned with the laborers, Sibley began to suspect that some of them had been involved in the war. He ordered that they be watched carefully and prevented from leaving.[54] The first weeks after the surrender were chaotic; the army had difficulty delineating between friend and foe, often changing their minds about individuals. Some were immediately considered friendly and used for labor and then returned to Camp Release under guard because the army now felt they should be tried for their involvement in the war.

However, the military officials at Camp Release were more lenient to the mixed-ancestry Dakota held there. When Joseph and Alexis Laframboise requested to go home with their families, Henry Sibley explained on November 28, "there is no objection to their being allowed to do so, as they are not prisoners." He also ordered that they receive several days' rations for their journey.[55] R. C. Olin had no problem employing Antoine Frenier as interpreter for the military tribunal despite the fact that four of his relatives, Louis, Thomas, John, and Joseph Frenier, were tried and convicted.[56] This leniency carried over into the trials. As missionary Stephen R. Riggs noted, if a full-ancestry Indian was present at a battle "with a gun and ammunition, and had fired off that gun, there was one law of condemnation for him. In addition to this, it was held that a half-breed might be forced to go to these battles, but not a pure Indian."[57] Quite often white contemporaries were willing to believe that when mixed-ancestry Indians fired their weapon in battle, they were not guilty and had been forced to by their full-ancestry relatives.

Mixed-ancestry interpreter Antoine Frenier, however, did not believe that the mixed-ancestry Dakota were in Táoyateduta's camp against their will. "It has been alleged that the half-breeds were held as prisoners by Little Crow at the time of the outbreak. I deny this. There was no guard placed around the Indian camp at any time during the continuance of the outbreak." Frenier continued, "It is a fact which the Indians and half-breeds admit, that on the morning of the outbreak, the Indians held a council at which it was unanimously agreed that none of the half breeds would be killed, and they should be allowed to go where they pleased." Not only did Frenier not believe in the innocence of the mixed-ancestry prisoners; he also downplayed the danger that they were in from their full-ancestry relatives. Despite Frenier's accusations, the fact that a council occurred on whether or not to kill the mixed-ancestry Dakota, even if they were unanimously against killing them, shows that there were significant rumblings, and the mixed-ancestry Dakota continued to live in fear.

Frenier accused the prisoners at Fort Snelling: "Two thirds of the half-breeds and Indians who are here were guilty of participation in the late outrages upon the whites." Considering there were over 1,600 Dakota held at Fort Snelling, and 112 were of mixed-ancestry, his accusations are significant. Certainly at least half of the prisoners at Fort Snelling were noncombatants, women and children, but if Frenier's claims are correct, a significant number of mixed- and full-ancestry Dakota men fought against the white settlers. He claimed to know only "two half breeds and one Indian who are entirely innocent"—Jack Frazier, Joseph Coursolle, and Aŋpétuthokeča (Other Day). Frenier told of Jack Frazier's refusal to fight against the white settlers:

> Jack Frazier was asked by his Indian relatives if he would join them, and he told them that he was a white man and would not do so, and requested them to bring him a horse to leave with. They complied with his request, and he then openly left the Indians and came down the river with his wife to Fort Ridgely, unmolested. Well now I ask why did not the half-breeds and other Indians leave as well as these? The reason was that they preferred to remain with those who were committing the murders and robbing the people of their property.[58]

Frenier's assertions are at odds with the accounts of the mixed-ancestry prisoners in Táoyateduta's camp who genuinely feared for their lives. His statements reveal that there was a deep factionalization of Dakota people during the war and that the mixed-ancestry Dakota were also factionalized and blamed each other for their actions. If his relation of Frazier's comment that "he told them he was a white man" is to be believed, this too reveals this factionalization. By refusing to fight with his relatives, his claim to whiteness separated him from them and established an attempt to erase the kinship connections he held with them.

A mixed-ancestry woman who was a captive of the Dakota responded in the *St. Paul Daily Press* to Frenier's letter in the *St. Paul Pioneer.* Signing as "M.A.H.," most likely Marion Robertson Hunter, she disputed his claims. "About a week before Gen. Sibley arrived at Camp Release," she wrote, "some of the half-breeds formed a plan to escape at midnight and come down to his camp, but so closely were they watched, their plan was discovered, notwithstanding all possible secrecy." After their escape attempt, she wrote, the full-ancestry Dakota placed guards around the camp and on the roads, making escape for the mixed-ancestry Dakota impossible. The full-ancestry Dakota did not permit the mixed-ancestry Dakota to leave, Hunter said in her response, even though many wanted to. She went on to express her gratitude to the full-ancestry Indians who protected their mixed-ancestry relatives. The full-ancestry Dakota "protected us from Little Crow and his murderous bands and restored us to our friends."[59]

Hunter took particular umbrage with Frenier's accusation that only two mixed-ancestry Dakota in the camp were innocent: "Surely Mr. Frenier does not mean to include . . . his own nephew Mr. Angus Brown. I never heard him charged with the least participation in the outbreak. I can assure Mr. Frenier, for his gratification, of my full belief that the reason Mr. Brown with his wife and father's family, remained among the Indians until the arrival of Gen. Sibley at Camp Release, was that they in common with the half-breeds were as really prisoners as the white captives."[60] More significant than Frenier's accusation of the mixed-ancestry Dakota and Hunter's full-throated defense of them is the fact that two Dakota Indians, just months after the war ended in Minnesota, were able to conduct their debate publicly in the Saint Paul newspapers. As mixed-ancestry Dakota, they had the privilege to have their voices heard, and the fact that they were able to publish their accounts suggests that the Saint Paul populace did not feel the enmity against them that they held for their full-ancestry relatives.

The mixed-ancestry Dakota soon found an avenue to punish the Dakota who had captured and threatened mixed-ancestry prisoners as witnesses in the military trials after the war. In less than six weeks, the military tribunal tried 391 full- and mixed-ancestry Dakota men (Charles Crawford was tried twice), resulting in 323 guilty verdicts. Of these, the tribunal sentenced twenty men to prison sentences of one to ten years; the tribunal sentenced 303 to death by hanging. Joseph Godfrey, or Ótakte (Many Kills), an African American man married into Wápahaša's band, is often noted for giving damning testimony against Dakota defendants.[61] He testified in nearly sixty trials, resulting in over fifty guilty verdicts and twelve executions. The mixed-ancestry Dakota, however, played a more crucial role in these trials as witnesses. In a total of 392 trials, mixed-ancestry Dakota served as witnesses in 288 cases. Of those, 240 were found guilty; a conviction rate of over 83 percent. Unfortunately, Isaac Heard, official recorder for the trials, failed to record the questions asked of the witnesses, failed to record much of the witness testimony, and occasionally failed to record the names of witnesses. At least thirty-three separate mixed-ancestry Indians participated as witnesses in the trials, but several were witnesses in dozens of trials. David Faribault Sr. and David Faribault Jr. served as witnesses in 151 cases. Unfortunately, as Heard infrequently recorded which David Faribault testified, it is unclear which of the two men was testifying in most of the cases. Between the two of them, of the 151 defendants, 136 were found guilty, and the army executed fifteen of them. Thomas Robertson, who had served as a go-between during the war, was a witness in ninety trials, with eighty-four guilty verdicts, resulting in nine executions. Alex Graham was a witness in sixty-three trials, resulting in fifty guilty verdicts and three executions. Participating in thirty trials, Michael Renville's witness testimony resulted in twenty-four guilty verdicts but no executions. Numerous other mixed-ancestry Dakota participated in multiple trials, and only thirteen of the thirty-eight were executed without mixed-ancestry witnesses. The witnesses did not provide damning evidence in all these cases, and many of these witnesses were involved in the same trials. Although the mixed-ancestry witnesses had no power themselves to order a guilty verdict, their testimony was the crucial component in the tribunal members' decision-making process in finding Dakota warriors guilty.[62]

Serving as witnesses did not save mixed-ancestry men from suspicion and trial. Thomas Robertson was himself accused of killing a man at the Battle of Fort Ridgely. Robertson admitted to being present at the battle and the Battle of New Ulm but claimed to have been there against his will. Joseph Godfrey testified that he was told by several Indians that Robertson killed a man, but he corroborated Robertson's story: "I don't think Tom is a bad man. I believe he was forced to fight."[63] The tribunal found Robertson not guilty. Likewise, the tribunal charged David Faribault Jr. despite he and his father testifying as witnesses in 151 cases. He admitted to firing shots at multiple battles but said he did not fire at anyone and testified he was told by full-ancestry Indians to engage in the fights.[64] The tribunal found him guilty and sentenced him to death.

In view of the testimony, it is clear that dozens of mixed-ancestry Dakota men were present at the major battles and fought on the side of their Dakota relatives. Of the nineteen mixed-ancestry men charged by the tribunal, most claimed that full-ancestry Dakota men intimidated or coerced them to participate in the war. Many, like Antoine Frenier, challenged this claim. Regardless, the tribunal often sentenced the mixed-ancestry men, like their full-ancestry relatives, on flimsy evidence. The only recorded evidence in the case of Wakháŋhdamani, or George Quinn, was his testimony, "I fired (at the Fort) two shots at the buildings," for which he was "to be hanged by the neck until he is dead."[65] Unlike other mixed-ancestry Dakota, Quinn was unapologetic about his support of the Dakota Nation: "I am half white man and half Indian. . . . But I never learned to speak English and I was raised among the Indians as one of them. So when the outbreak came I went with my people against the whites."[66]

The vast majority of defendants in the tribunals were Dakota men of full ancestry, yet many were the friends or loved ones of mixed-ancestry people. Henry Waŋbdíšuŋ, brother of Ičíyapiwiŋ, fought on the Dakota side of the war and was one of the 391 Dakota men tried by military tribunal afterward. Henry admitted he was at the Battle of Birch Coulee on September 2, a victory for the Dakota, and the Battle of Wood Lake on September 23, a major defeat. At his trial, the tribunal charged: "The said Wa-mde-shoon a Sioux Indian did between the 18th day of August 1862 and the 28th day of September 1862 join with and participate in the various Murders Robberies and outrages committed by the Sioux Tribe of Indians on the Minnesota Frontier and particularly in the battles at the Fort, New Ulm, Birch Coolie, and Wood Lake." Through an interpreter, and without council, Henry responded to the charges: "Was at [Little] Crow's village the time of the battle at the Fort. Have sore eyes and was not at any of the battles. Was at Birch Coulie. Was on the side of the prairie on top of the hill. Had a gun. Did not fire. Had sore eyes. Was at Wood Lake. Did not fire." Later in the trial, Waŋbdíšuŋ said, "I was running away at the time the Indians attacked Marsh's command" at Redwood Ferry. Wakháŋ Wašté testified that he "heard nothing about prisoner" while mixed-ancestry Dakota Thomas Robinson testified, "I know prisoner. Know nothing against him."[67] Henry was one of the lucky few found not guilty. Despite the divisions between those of mixed and full ancestry during the war, mixed- and full-ancestry families continued to intermarry. After the war, Frank Trudell married the daughter of Thatéibobdu and Henry Trudell married the daughter of Thatéiyayedaŋ, both of whom had been sentenced to death in the tribunals yet avoided execution. Their white father's service in the army did not impede their relationships with full-ancestry Dakota people.

The tribunal completed their work on November 5, and General Pope forwarded the trial transcript to President Abraham Lincoln on November 15.[68] This same month, the army marched a party of about 1,700 Dakota, mostly women and children, to Fort Snelling where they would spend the winter. The army moved the 303 men condemned to death to Mankato. On their way to their destinations, white settlers occasionally attacked the two parties, killing a handful of Dakota people. By December 6, Lincoln reduced the number of Dakota men to be executed to thirty-nine, later reduced to thirty-eight when new evidence cast doubt on the guilt of a prisoner. Mixed-ancestry Dakota had served as witnesses in twenty-five of their trials. At Mankato, the army separated the thirty-eight condemned from the others, where they awaited their execution on December 26.[69]

In the days leading up to the execution, missionaries, newspaper reporters, and others visited the condemned men. Reporters paid particular

Figure 19. Hypolite Auge, 1836–1862. He was a mixed-ancestry Waȟpéthuŋwaŋ Dakota. Robert O. Sweeny drew him on the day of his death in 1862. Like Baptiste Campbell, he was sentenced to death by the military tribunal and hanged by the army on December 26, 1862. Accession no. AV2017.203.9, Minnesota Historical Society, Saint Paul.

attention to the three mixed-ancestry Dakota men, Hypolite Auge, Baptiste Campbell, and Henry Milord, who had all been sentenced to death for participation in the same event. Correspondents for *Frank Leslie's Illustrated Newspaper* described meeting the condemned Indians in Mankato. One mentioned sitting down with the three mixed-ancestry men, and "they spoke to us both in French and English, both of which they spoke very well, particularly Hypolite Auge. He was a handsome young fellow. But both he and Baptiste Campbell, as well as Henry Milord, all three half-breeds, wore a very sorrowful and dejected mien. These three were dressed as citizens, with a blanket thrown around their shoulders."[70] Auge, Campbell, and Milord in fact were U.S. citizens, but this distinction was never noted during the trials. They also continued to wear "citizen's clothing," which set them apart from the other Dakota men.

The *Goodhue Volunteer* conducted interviews with all three men. Auge had worked as a clerk at one of the trading posts at the Redwood Agency for a year by the time the war started. "He was sent down the Minnesota river with Baptiste Campbell and others by Little Crow. He shot the white man, but not until after he had been killed by others." The newspaper noted that Baptiste Campbell felt that the Dakota should have new trials. He reiterated Auge's story that "they were sent over by Little Crow, and told to get all the cattle they could and kill every white man—if they did not the Soldier's Lodge would take care of them." Campbell admitted to firing his gun first but denied hitting the man. Milord told a similar story, that Little Crow forced him to go. He admitted to firing at a woman "but does not think that he killed her." When writing of Milord, the *Goodhue Volunteer* made an astute observation: "He is a smart, active, intelligent young man; and as such, would be likely to be drawn into the Dakota rebellion. Indeed it was next to impossible for young men, whether half-breeds or full bloods, to keep out of it. They are to be pitied as well as blamed."[71] As the newspaper noted, even mixed-ancestry Dakota could not avoid the war; in the case of Auge, Campbell, and Milord, they felt the pressure of their full-ancestry kin to fight on their side, while others had felt pressure from their white neighbors to join the army as scouts or soldiers. The mixed-ancestry Dakota, especially, faced difficult decisions: to fight against their Dakota relatives or to fight against their fathers' people.

Reporters also recorded their final moments. In the last hour before their execution, Father Augustin Ravoux addressed the prisoners in Dakota and read from a Dakota-language prayer book. Afterward, he "addressed them again, first in Dakota, then in French, which was interpreted by Baptiste Campbell, one of the condemned half-breeds."[72] The *Mankato Weekly Record* reported that little emotion was shown by the condemned but that "a half breed named Milord seemed much depressed in spirits." As they ascended the steps of the gallows, they began singing death songs, while "Baptiste Campbell remained perfectly quiet."[73] Another reporter recorded that in the final moments before the execution "the three half-breeds were the most of all affected, and their dejection of countenance was truly pitiful to behold."[74] While they died with their full-ancestry relatives, even in death they were set apart.

On December 26, 1862, Francis Trudell's Company K presided over the hanging of thirty-eight Dakota prisoners at Mankato, the largest mass execution in American history. The muster rolls for January and February 1863 place Trudell in the military hospital at Mankato; it is unknown whether he was present at the hanging or whether he was well enough to do his duties as a wagoner, which would have demanded that he haul away the bodies for burial. He was well enough to travel from Fort Snelling to Mankato in December and may have been well enough to participate in the executions. Whether he was present at the hanging or not, Trudell and his family were acquainted with at least some of the victims. In 1893, Antoine Joseph Campbell, a mixed-ancestry Dakota, testified that he had known Trudell since his marriage to Ičíyapiwiŋ around 1835 and had known Ičíyapiwiŋ since childhood.[75] Indeed, Henry Trudell swore to his acquaintance with the Campbells and recounted the Campbell family history years later in the probate of Antoine Campbell's mother, Margaret Campbell.[76] The Campbell family had been involved on both sides of the U.S.-Dakota War, and Antoine Campbell's younger brother, Baptiste Campbell, was one of the thirty-eight Dakota men executed on December 26. These Dakota kinship connections to both sides of the U.S.-Dakota War were common in extended Dakota families. Trudell did not enlist to simply fight the Dakota; he enlisted to fight against his wife's people and kin, including his brother-in-law Henry Waŋbdíšuŋ.

In the aftermath of the U.S.-Dakota War, the kinship relations between Dakota people of mixed and full ancestry were deeply strained but not broken. The war had lain bare the growing animosities that full-ancestry Indians had for their mixed relatives who were increasingly less likely to fulfill their kinship obligations, even when they had received windfalls of money through the 1837 Treaty of Washington or the sales of their scrip lands. The collapse of the fur trade also made it more difficult for Dakota people of mixed ancestry to make their livings as they had in previous decades, leaving them to increasingly gravitate toward white American society. Indians of mixed ancestry soon found that white Minnesotans no longer needed their votes, nor were whites interested in voting for Indians. Hundreds of mixed-ancestry Dakota people continued to try to eke out a living in their ancestral homelands, but most eventually moved to the various Dakota reservations in Dakota Territory and Nebraska or those that were founded later in Minnesota. Over time, the mixed- and full-ancestry Dakota mended their strained kinship connections on the reservations.

CHAPTER 8

The Rise of Blood Quantum as an Exclusionary Tool

After the U.S.-Dakota War, life for most Dakota people changed dramatically. Thousands of Dakota people fled north and west, fearing the genocidal tactics of the U.S. Army in American attempts at revenge. The army temporarily held over 1,600 Dakota people in a concentration camp at Fort Snelling over the winter and hundreds more in prison at Camp McClellan in Davenport, Iowa. In the spring of 1863, the army removed those held at Fort Snelling to a new Indian reservation far to the west, on the Missouri River, called Crow Creek, where hundreds more Dakota people, mostly women and children, died of disease, starvation, and exposure. Many mixed-ancestry Dakota people were part of these experiences, but the majority were able to avoid this treatment and continued to live off reservation in Minnesota and the surrounding states and territories. They usually lived as small minority communities within larger white settlements and villages, while their full-ancestry relatives often lived lives of fear, violence, imprisonment, or constant movement.

Dozens of other mixed-ancestry Dakota, along with approximately three hundred full-ancestry Dakota, lived at outposts in the region between Minnesota and Dakota Territory where they worked for the army as scouts until 1866. The army permitted families of scouts to remain in Minnesota while their scout relatives patrolled the border for the purpose of repelling any additional Dakota attacks. The scouts had numerous violent encounters with other Dakota people, sometimes against people they knew. Wičháȟpi Núŋpa (Two Stars), while leading a group of scouts in a skirmish in which the scouts killed fourteen Dakota warriors, felt compelled to kill his own nephew whom they had captured.[1] After the army dissolved the Dakota scout unit, most of the scouts moved to various Dakota reservations and lived among those they had fought.

In the decades following the war, most mixed-ancestry Dakota people gravitated toward their full-ancestry relatives and moved to various Dakota or Lakota Indian reservations. Before the war, Dakota people of mixed ancestry had been moving away from Dakota culture and kinship practices as they assimilated deeper into American society. Most never left their Dakota identities behind but found numerous irresistible economic opportunities among white Americans. Even before the war, however, the mixed-ancestry Dakota began to find these opportunities evaporating. The massive influx of white settlers led to the solidification of racial hierarchies in the region, and being of mixed Indian and white ancestry began to hold fewer benefits. There were no further treaty provisions of land or money for those of mixed ancestry, and after the war mixed-ancestry Indians, even those who were not Dakota, found it more difficult to exercise their citizenship rights or successfully run for political office.

The mixed-ancestry Dakota experience after the war was varied and diverse. Some had always maintained their connections with their full-ancestry relatives and shared their difficulties and privations with them. Some eventually fully acculturated into American society and passed as white by the twentieth century, fully leaving behind their Indigenous identities. Most others moved to reservations after experimenting with various tactics to make a future for themselves off reservation. Most of the Trudell family lived on both the Minnesota and Wisconsin sides of the Mississippi before finally moving to the Santee Indian Reservation in the late 1870s, where they reunited with their full-ancestry kin.

Despite these changes, there were more "mixed-blood" histories to come, as some Dakota people fought to maintain their Indian identities while others tried to leave them behind. The General Allotment Act of 1887 set in place a process by which the federal government would allot Indian reservations into individual parcels of land. Some scholars have erroneously credited the law with setting a blood quantum definition of Indian identity, but numerous amendments and related laws used blood quantum in decisions related to eligibility for inheritance of lands and "competency" to own land without a guardian.[2] This chapter examines how blood quantum came into play for two mixed-ancestry Dakota people in relation to land allotments at the end of the century. One of those, Jane Van Meter Waldron, successfully defended a challenge to her Indianness and therefore her eligibility to acquire an allotment under the General Allotment Act. Conversely, Barney Traversie tried to give up his Indian allotment and take a homestead under the Homestead Act of 1862 as a white person so that he could avoid the paternalism of life under the control of the Office of Indian Affairs. Traversie ultimately failed in his attempt, the court reaffirming his Indian status despite his attempt to relinquish it in exchange for whiteness.

The impacts of blood quantum in federal legislation and eligibility requirements for enrollment in tribes continues today. The animosities between Indians of mixed and full ancestry revealed in the U.S.-Dakota War also persist, although they have evolved over time. Additionally, confusion over definitions of Indianness based in race remains.[3] These "mixed-blood" histories are not exclusive to the nineteenth century, but it was in the nineteenth century when American and Indigenous ideas about race and mixedness came to prominence and came to dominate such discussions.

The war resulted in a vast Dakota diaspora across the northern Great Plains into Dakota Territory, Montana, Manitoba, and Saskatchewan. Dakota people used the international border to escape genocide and domination by the U.S. government, while others formed the basis for at least part of the populations at the Fort Peck Reservation in Montana, the Spirit Lake Reservation in North Dakota, and the Lake Traverse Reservation, which straddles the South Dakota–North Dakota border.[4] Those incarcerated or removed by the federal government primarily populated the Santee Indian Reservation in Nebraska and later the tiny Flandreau Reservation in eastern South Dakota. The punitive expeditions in 1863 and 1864 led by Generals Henry Sibley and Alfred Sully were a major catalyst for Dakota movement. Especially after Sully and his troops massacred between 150 and 300 Dakota and Lakota people at Whitestone Hill in North Dakota in 1863, most of whom were Iháŋkthuŋwaŋna Dakota and Lakota who had taken no part in the war.[5]

After the military tribunals at Mankato and the army's execution of thirty-eight Dakota men, the army marched those Dakota people who had surrendered at Camp Release over 130 miles to Fort Snelling, where they were held in an internment camp. They lived the winter of 1862–1863 in squalid conditions. A census taken December 2, 1862, at Fort Snelling recorded 1,601 prisoners, 112 of whom were Dakota people of mixed ancestry.[6] By all accounts, conditions in the camp were brutal, but there is evidence that mixed-ancestry prisoners received preferential treatment from the guards. A. D. Campbell was permitted "to proceed to St. Peter on private business, to be absent not more than ten days."[7] Lieutenant McKasick, the superintendent of the camp of Indian prisoners, complained of the whiskey trade in Mendota and how it was becoming a problem for the camp. He said the soldiers guarding the camp would often procure whiskey, "which is often given to Half Breeds and I fear in many cases the Half Breeds buy it themselves at the saloon."[8] This illustrates how mixed-ancestry Dakota could, in some circumstances, come and go as they wished while their full-ancestry relatives could not.

In light of the proposed removal of the Dakota from the state, local white settlers in eastern Minnesota clamored for the removal of Dakota people in the area to Fort Snelling and eventually to Crow Creek, Dakota Territory. Governor Alexander Ramsey complained to Sibley that a small band of Dakota had returned, hunting and fishing around Pig's Eye Lake, just across the Mississippi from Saint Paul. Ramsey requested that Sibley remove them to Fort Snelling.[9] White residents of Wabasha also wished to have the Dakota in their vicinity removed. Artemas Sharpe, the same man who tried to pay Frank and August Trudell to remove Mary Wacouta from her land several years earlier, wrote to Henry Sibley in the spring of 1863 in hopes of having the Dakota at Wabasha, mostly of mixed ancestry, removed. Sharpe wrote, "There are some remaining here yet which if not removed will be a nest egg for a further increase of them. Wabashaw has been long cursed by their presence, and as their now occurs an opportunity of being relieved of them altogether I trust that a clean sweep will be made so that neither root nor branch remains." Sharpe requested that Sibley order the county sheriff to round up the Dakota at Wabasha and take them to Fort Snelling.[10] The Trudell family continued to reside in the Wabasha area throughout the war, except Francis Trudell, who was serving in the army at the time. Sharpe's attempt to have the Indians in the area removed is probably the only time the Trudell family felt directly threatened by the U.S.-Dakota War and its consequences. However, the army never removed the Indians from Wabasha, and the Dakota community there continued to grow. In the immediate aftermath of the war in Minnesota, most Dakota either fled or suffered removal by the army. But pockets of Dakota people remained, the majority of whom were of mixed ancestry.

After the weather had warmed enough to travel by late April 1863, the army removed the unlucky prisoners at Fort Snelling by steamboat. Most were bound for the new reservation to be built at Crow Creek, while steamboats carried 272 Dakota passengers who had been found guilty and held prisoner in Mankato over the winter to imprisonment at Camp McClellan, later renamed Camp Kearny, in Davenport, Iowa. At least a dozen mixed-ancestry Dakota men found guilty in the military tribunals were also imprisoned at Davenport. Conditions in the prison were horrific. The prisoners were underfed and lacked proper clothing and blankets. Many died due to illness and cold winters. They also lived in constant fear. Most of the prisoners had been sentenced to death, sentences that, as far as they knew, might be carried out at any time.[11] Thomas and John Frenier, either brothers or cousins, only lasted about six months, dying on the same day, November 18, 1863, while imprisoned at Davenport. Joseph Frenier, who had also been found guilty, died on January 9, before they even left Mankato. Louis and Augustin Frenier survived their internment at Camp Kearny, both pardoned and released in 1866.[12]

It was not only these initial prisoners whom army officers found guilty in the military tribunals; the army continued to send prisoners to Davenport whom they had captured in Dakota Territory, including dozens of women who served as cooks and laundresses and their children. The population of the prison fluctuated as new prisoners were brought in, some were pardoned early, and others died. As many as 120 of the prisoners at Davenport died during their incarceration, due to the lack of health care and poor conditions. In addition, the prisoners were dehumanized and treated as a tourist attraction for local white settlers who paid to come into the prison to observe the Dakota inmates. Along with the Frenier family, members of the Provencalle, Faribault, LaBelle, Rouillard, and Quinn families endured incarceration.[13] About conditions in the camp, Augustin Frenier wrote simply, "Dehan terika nakax" ("It is terrible here").[14] Some Dakota inmates were able to obtain early releases, but most remained in prison until pardoned by President Andrew Johnson in 1866, when they reunited with their loved ones.

While the prisoners at Davenport suffered, their relatives on the Crow Creek Reservation fared little better. Because so many men had been killed in the war or were executed, imprisoned, or took flight to avoid capture, over 90 percent of the Dakota removed to Crow Creek were women and children. They suffered greatly and because of the gender imbalance: Women had to perform not only their own tasks but also men's tasks like hunting, when allowed, and they faced sexual abuse at the hands of soldiers and settlers. Even more so than at the prison at Davenport, the early years at Crow Creek are seared into Dakota memory as a period of privation and suffering.[15]

Henry Waŋbdíšuŋ, brother of Ičíyapiwiŋ and uncle to the Trudell children, was held with the condemned prisoners at Mankato over the winter, but he suffered three years at Crow Creek when the government forced him and hundreds of others onto the barren reservation. His wife Nancy Wakíŋyaŋtowiŋ and their young daughter Toíčiyewiŋ were held in the Fort Snelling concentration camp over the winter of 1862–1863.[16] They eventually reunited at Crow Creek, if not earlier on the steamboats. Those sent to the prison at Davenport included Henry's father-in-law, Tuŋkáŋhnamani, who had been sentenced to death, but his sentence had been commuted to imprisonment by President Abraham Lincoln. After dropping off the prisoners at Camp McClellan, the remaining Dakota continued on their journey up the Missouri River, where they landed on the Crow Creek Reservation in modern-day South Dakota. Henry Waŋbdíšuŋ and his family resided at Crow Creek, where they were listed as members of Wápahaša's band in 1864.[17] At Crow Creek, the family endured the brutal conditions, starvation, and inadequate clothing and blankets.[18] Henry and Nancy had nine children who died young; it is likely that several died at Crow Creek, their deaths exacerbated by the harsh conditions. They remained there until 1866, when the government removed the Dakota to the Santee Indian Reservation in northeastern Nebraska. The experience of Henry Waŋbdíšuŋ and his family in the immediate aftermath of the war was typical of the full-ancestry Dakota who had not fled Minnesota.

The Dakota worked to make peace, or wódakhota, with the United States. "Wódakhota," a concept that means "peace," "treaty," or "peace treaty," is essentially a kinship term. The prefix "wo-" is added to mean that through this act of peace they are making another people Dakota, making them relatives, and therefore in a state of peace.[19] By 1867, although few of them had been involved in the U.S.-Dakota War, the Sisíthuŋwaŋ and Waȟpéthuŋwaŋ achieved peace through an 1867 treaty, which founded the Lake Traverse and the Devil's Lake (since more accurately renamed

Figure 20. Thíwakhaŋ (Sacred Lodge), or Gabriel Renville, 1823–1892. A mixed-ancestry Bdewákhaŋthuŋwaŋ Dakota, but he lived his life among the Sisíthuŋwaŋ and Waȟpéthuŋwaŋ. He was head chief of the Lake Traverse Reservation from 1867 until his death and served as chief of Indian scouts during and after the U.S.-Dakota War. Edward E. Ayer Digital Collection, Newberry Library, Chicago.

Spirit Lake) Reservations. Mixed-ancestry Dakota Gabriel Renville signed the treaty as the head chief of both bands and for years was the head chief at Lake Traverse.[20] In the 1870s, another mixed-ancestry Dakota came to be head chief at Spirit Lake in North Dakota, a reservation for Sisíthuŋwaŋ, Waȟpéthuŋwaŋ, and Iháŋkthuŋwaŋna Dakota people. Hoǧáŋ Čík'ana (Little Fish), sometimes called Thiyówašte (Good House)—a mixed-ancestry Dakota, the son of a French fur trader named Carre or Le Carre and a Sisíthuŋwaŋ mother—became head chief of Spirit Lake.[21] Hoǧáŋ Čík'ana lived his life as a full-ancestry Dakota but acknowledged his mixed heritage. Similarly, by the late 1860s, mixed-ancestry leaders William Bean, Frank Jandron, and Francois Deloria were the heads of three of the eight bands on the Yankton Reservation.[22] The wódakhota that was achieved between the Dakota and the United States also saw peace between mixed- and full-ancestry Dakota people, with some mixed-ancestry Indians taking up important leadership roles in the nation.

The life of the Trudell family was much different from the experiences of Henry Waŋbdíšuŋ's family at Crow Creek. At the start of the war, Waŋbdíšuŋ and most other Dakota people lived on the Dakota reservation in western Minnesota on the south bank of the Minnesota River. The Trudell family lived on the eastern border of Minnesota in Wabasha, on the Mississippi River near the defunct Lake Pepin Reservation. Mixed-ancestry Dakota people lived in several communities in the eastern and southern reaches of Minnesota. These Dakota people lived far away from the war and remained integrated into these predominantly white towns years after the war. While the army forcibly removed most full-ancestry Dakota and some of mixed ancestry from Minnesota, many Dakota families of mixed ancestry remained in Minnesota after the war, especially in the eastern part of the state. A report of August 18, 1866, by Shubael Adams claimed there were 374 Dakota people living in Minnesota, including 12 at Wabasha, 35 at Faribault, 158 at the scout camp seventy miles south of Yellow Medicine, and 139 at the head of Big Stone Lake. "More than half of the two last mentioned numbers are half breeds," he wrote.[23] However, Adams's report undercounted the mixed-ancestry Dakota population that remained in Minnesota.

Considering that the 1865 Minnesota State Census listed at least ninety-five Indians at Wabasha, all of mixed ancestry, Adams's report was not accurate. Most of these residents of Wabasha had lived there for decades, and their existence was probably not known to federal officials.[24] Five years earlier, the 1860 U.S. Federal Census records over seven hundred mixed-ancestry Dakota people in 150 households spread over several states, but over four hundred of those in Minnesota. The census for Dakota Territory, Nebraska Territory, and Wisconsin enumerated approximately one hundred, seventy-four, and fifty-eight mixed-ancestry Dakota people, respectively. The largest communities were at Redwood Agency, Hastings, Mendota, Traverse des Sioux, Hawk River, and rural Wabasha County, all containing communities of at least twenty-five known mixed-ancestry Dakota people. Outside the state, there were large communities at Yankton Agency in Dakota Territory, Sioux City, Iowa, Rulo, Nebraska, and Prairie du Chien, Wisconsin, likewise with at least twenty-five known Dakota people of mixed ancestry.[25]

The 1870 U.S. Federal Census lists at least sixteen mixed-ancestry Dakota families living in Wabasha, made up of 89 people, the largest Dakota community. Eight families, made up of 35 people, resided in and around Faribault in southern Minnesota. Approximately 25 more mixed-ancestry Dakota lived in Saint Paul. A community of six mixed-ancestry families, comprising 21 people, resided in Granite Falls near the old Yellow Medicine Agency. Few Dakota of full ancestry appear in the 1870 census: a family of 5 in Wabasha and a small community of 14 in Bloomington, a suburb of the Twin Cities. Dozens of other mixed-ancestry Dakota families lived in other communities across the eastern and southern portions of the state, comprising at least 290 people in Minnesota. The census recorded over 200 mixed-ancestry Dakota people living in Dakota Territory and 44 in Wisconsin, half of them at Prairie du Chien. The Trudell family appeared in the 1870 census in Wabasha but erroneously under the names of Madeleine and Augustus Trudell.[26] Mixed-ancestry Dakota people were much more likely than their full-ancestry relatives to show up in federal, state, and territorial censuses, and the census records a significant population of mixed-ancestry Dakota people in Minnesota and surrounding states in the years following the war.

Unlike their full-ancestry relatives, the Trudell family and other mixed-ancestry families had the choice to remain in Minnesota or move to a reservation as they pleased. An 1867 issue of the *Wabasha Weekly Herald* listed several old fur traders and their families, including that "Francois Trudell, who was a long time 'baker' for the old company, is now living with his old Sioux squaw, about a mile below on an island."[27] Continued residence in Minnesota did come with dangers. The U.S. Army in Minnesota placed a bounty on Dakota scalps of $25, which was subsequently raised to $200, remaining in effect as late as 1868.[28] Mixed-ancestry Dakota people were probably in little danger, but the possibility of violence to them or their relatives certainly weighed upon them. Sometime in the late 1870s, the Trudell family decided to leave Wabasha and moved to the Santee Indian Reservation in Nebraska. Moses Trudell described how his father, Frank Trudell, moved from Minnesota to Nebraska in the 1870s: "He just packed up and left. He had an oxen team, you know. And it took him about ten days . . . two weeks to move out here. . . . He just come over because he wanted to move. They established a reservation and they gave each person a land deed for 160 . . . 160 acres of land. My dad got one and all my uncles got—got five uncles—all got land."[29] As Moses explains, his father and uncles had the choice and incentive to move to the reservation, a choice that Henry Waŋbdíšuŋ and the full-ancestry Dakota did not have.

One of the Trudell brothers stayed even longer in the east. Henry Trudell, by now in his thirties and married, is recorded in the 1880 Federal Census and the 1885 Wisconsin State Census as living in Maiden Rock, Wisconsin, next door to the Dakota family of Will Rock.[30] Soon after, Henry Trudell and his family moved to Wabasha, where they sold a parcel of land in 1887.[31] The family probably moved to Santee soon after, and they begin appearing on the Office of Indian Affairs census rolls in 1890.

Mixed-ancestry Dakota people maintained communities at Wabasha and other parts of Minnesota much later than historians realize. The *Iapi Oaye,* a Dakota-language newspaper published at Santee, occasionally published the goings-on among Dakota people living in the town of

Wabasha. For example, George Moose, a resident of Wabasha, sent in a brief letter that was published in the March 1890 issue.[32] In the 1880s, Congress appropriated funds to purchase small tracts of land in Minnesota for those Dakota people who had stayed or those from Santee who returned. In the 1880s and 1890s several purchases were made for lands in Dakota, Goodhue, Scott, and Wabasha Counties, totaling well over five hundred acres.[33] Dakota communities continued on these purchased lands for decades and, in the case of purchased land in Mendota in Dakota County, arguably continues today. The 1937 Bureau of Indian Affairs census of Pipestone Agency enumerates twenty-two federally enrolled tribal members living on purchased lands in Mendota, thirty in Hastings, and fifty-five in Wabasha.[34]

Unlike those Dakota that fought on the side of the Dakota in the U.S.-Dakota War, white and Dakota soldiers who served in the U.S. Army received pension benefits years later. Francis Trudell applied for an invalid pension in 1877 with the help of his mixed-ancestry attorney, Alexis P. Bailly but was denied because he could not prove his ailments were service related. After his death on the Santee Indian Reservation in 1881, Ičíyapiwiŋ applied for and received a widow's pension for her husband's military service, receiving eight dollars per month from 1890 to 1908 and then twelve dollars per month until her death in 1911.[35] Dozens of mixed-ancestry Dakota people received disability pensions or widows' pensions for service in the Civil War and U.S.-Dakota War. Dakota people who fought on the Dakota side in the war received no such pensions, despite the hardships they might have endured.

In the decades following the U.S.-Dakota War, the families of Mary Ičíyapiwiŋ and her brother Henry Waŋbdíšuŋ had very different experiences, based on the racial differences of the family. For Henry Waŋbdíšuŋ, he had no white or mixed-ancestry members in his immediate family and would not have felt split loyalties in the same way that mixed-ancestry Dakota people did. In addition, his full-ancestry Dakota friends and kin likely pressured him to participate in the war. For the Trudell family, any decision to go to war would mean fighting against one of the racial groups that made up their diverse family, with the potential to alienate family members. The army held Henry Waŋbdíšuŋ and his family as prisoners and forcibly removed them to Crow Creek in 1863 and forced them to move again in 1866 to Santee. Mary Ičíyapiwiŋ received a pension from the army for twenty-one years, and her family continued to live in the predominantly white community of Wabasha over a decade after the war and moved to Santee in the 1870s by choice. The root of their different experiences rested in the fact that Ičíyapiwiŋ's family contained a white man and mixed-ancestry children. Local white settlers tolerated her residence in the community because she had a white husband. As evidenced by the 1870 census, local white people were also willing to permit mixed-ancestry Dakota people to continue living in the state and the capital city of Saint Paul, despite meeting the full-ancestry Dakota with hate and violence just a few short years earlier. However, most mixed-ancestry Dakota lived on the periphery of these communities, and like the Trudell family, most mixed-ancestry Dakota eventually made their way to Indian reservations or banded together to make their own communities, such as those at Mendota and Prairie Island.

The U.S.-Dakota War remained in the minds of Dakota people as an important turning point in their history, and they often invoked the war when pressing their rights. In 1905, Henry Trudell wrote to the commissioner of Indian Affairs concerning a petition he signed in 1901, part of a group of petitioners at Santee who hoped to reaffirm or reacquire U.S. citizenship based on the fact that they did not fight in the U.S.-Dakota War. He asserted, "All the signers to said are loyals, and was not near or took part in the outbreak of the massacre in Minnesota in the year of 1862."[36] He also inquired about his treaty rights. Like many other Dakota families, relatives of the Trudell family fought on both sides of the war. Francis Trudell, the French Canadian father of the Trudell children, joined the army days after the start of the U.S.-Dakota War to fight against his wife's people. Their uncle, Henry Waŋbdíšuŋ, fought on the Dakota side at the Battles of Birch Coulee and Wood Lake. For Indians of mixed ancestry, having kinship connections to both sides of the war was common and must have been heart-wrenching. Henry Trudell received no answer to his letter and died in 1921, three years before the Indian Citizenship Act. He and the other petitioners used their neutrality or alliance with the United States during the war to make claims to rights of citizenship, suggesting that which side of the war one fought on had deep and lasting effects.

The divisions between full- and mixed-ancestry Dakota came to a head during and in the immediate aftermath of the U.S.-Dakota War. A wound was opened when the war faction captured their mixed-ancestry relatives and threatened them with death. The wound was opened further in the battles that pitted full- and mixed-ancestry kin against each other and in the military tribunals when mixed-ancestry Dakota were instrumental in finding Dakota warriors guilty. This wound is still open today. In 1894, Nancy McClure Faribault, by this time Nancy Huggan, wrote, "The Indians have always bitterly hated the half-breeds for their conduct in favor of the whites in that and other wars, and they hate them still. It seems they can forgive everybody but us."[37] In the years following the war, the federal government forcibly removed the full-ancestry Dakota and many mixed-ancestry Dakota from Minnesota. Some mixed-ancestry Dakota fled with their full-ancestry relatives. Although some mixed-ancestry Dakota blended into white communities in the decades following the war, most, like the Trudell family, eventually made their way to various Dakota reservations in Minnesota, Nebraska, and Dakota Territory. These wounds have healed to a degree, but ongoing political differences and the internalization of colonial-imposed blood-quantum rules have continued to divide Dakota communities today.

Two court cases involving mixed-ancestry Dakota people at the turn of the twentieth century reveal how American perceptions of race and mixedness had evolved in the three decades since the U.S.-Dakota War. In one case, *Waldron v. United States et al.*, a mixed-ancestry Dakota woman named Jane Waldron saw her status as an Indian challenged, while in another case, Barney Traversie saw his bid for "whiteness" challenged by the American legal system. Much had changed by this time, but much had stayed the same. I use the stories of Waldron and Traversie to illustrate the changes that occurred after the previous "mixed-blood" histories.

American officials were still mystified as to the legal rights and racial status of mixed-ancestry Indians. H. E. Dewey, an attorney for Čhaŋȟpí

Sápa (Black Tomahawk), a full-ancestry Lakota Indian on the Cheyenne River reservation, argued that mixed-ancestry Indians "are not Indians and are not whites." He argued that Indians of mixed ancestry had received separate treatment and "during the whole period of Government dealings with the Indians, whenever any half-breed or mixed-blood has received any advantage, benefit or privilege, under any law or treaty, that he has not received it under the name or word 'Indian,' but always under the name of half-breed or mixed-blood." "In determining the rights and privileges of mixed bloods," he argued, "we must give to the term 'Indian' a liberal and not a technical or restrictive construction."[38] The legal arguments used in the Waldron and Traversie cases were less about defining "mixedness" than they were about defining "Indian" and "white."

Jane Waldron, born Jane Van Meter in 1861, was the daughter of a white man named Arthur Van Meter and a mixed-ancestry Dakota mother. Her mother, Mary Aungie, was a mixed-ancestry Dakota of Bdewákhaŋthuŋwaŋ descent, but she was closely connected with the Iháŋkthuŋwaŋ band. According to Waldron, her mother held five-eighths Dakota blood quantum and was the granddaughter of white fur trader Robert Dickson and his wife Totówiŋ. Mary Aungie's father Henry was a descendant of Chief Wápahaša. Waldron's mother and both of her maternal grandparents had received land scrip at Lake Pepin as mixed-ancestry Dakota Indians. Born in contemporary southeastern South Dakota, Waldron grew up among mixed-ancestry Iháŋkthuŋwaŋ families. By the late 1870s, Waldron's family resided on and were enrolled on the Cheyenne River reservation. Under the General Allotment Act, Waldron filed for a 320-acre allotment in the southeast corner of the Cheyenne River reservation on September 10, 1890. Less than a month later, a Lakota named Čhaŋȟpí Sápa filed for the same allotment, setting off a long legal dispute.[39]

Čhaŋȟpí Sápa filed a complaint, to which the federal government made the initial decision that Waldron was not an Indian and not eligible to take an allotment. However, Waldron and Čhaŋȟpí Sápa continued to live on the same allotment for years. When Čhaŋȟpí Sápa received a trust patent in 1899, the Indian Agent at Cheyenne River, Ira Hatch, ordered Waldron to vacate the land. At that point, Waldron filed her lawsuit in federal court.[40]

Waldron's case rested on two questions: Was she an Indian? And if so, as a Dakota, was she eligible to receive an allotment on a Lakota reservation? I will focus on the former question. The attorney for Čhaŋȟpí Sápa, H. E. Dewey, based his rejection of Waldron's status as an Indian on her white father. Dewey argued that children inherit the status of their fathers; because Waldron's father was white, she too was white. Similarly, Dewey asserted that her marriage to a white man resulted in the loss of her status as an Indian. American marriage laws were at the heart of Dewey's assertions: "The offspring of all married people follow the status of the father," but "the offspring of unmarried Indian mothers are Indians."[41] Rather than basing his argument in race, Dewey understood Indianness as based in nationhood. When marrying a citizen of the United States, Dewey argued, an Indian woman gave up her tribal relationship and her children would also be American citizens, unaffiliated with a tribal nation. In essence, Dewey equated whiteness with citizenship and Indianness with noncitizenship. In his mind, the fact that Waldron had a white father and white husband meant she was now white, regardless of her race. Dewey further played up Waldron's non-Indianness by arguing that she had neither lived among Dakota people nor practiced Dakota culture.

Waldron vociferously refuted Dewey's claims. In her deposition, Waldron successfully painted a picture of her life as deeply moored in Dakota culture. Although she did not live on any reservation, she grew up in a community of Dakota people in southeastern South Dakota. In her childhood, the family was enrolled at the Yankton Reservation and her mother regularly traveled to the reservation to collect annuities and rations for herself and her children. Waldron spoke only Dakota until she was eight years old, when she started attending public school. She spoke about the importance of kinship in Dakota society and claimed to have kin on many different Dakota and Lakota reservations, including Fort Peck in Montana; Standing Rock, Cheyenne River, Rosebud, Yankton, and Lake Traverse in South Dakota; and the Santee Indian Reservation in Nebraska. She nicely summed up Dakota kinship: "Well the custom is to claim relationship to one another and when they don't know each other they find out who their relatives are or who their ancestors are, they talk a little while and pretty soon they find out they are some related; they all claim kinship."[42]

Waldron did not deny her mixed ancestry but gave a full-throated defense of her Dakotaness. When her attorney asked about her mother she stated, "She was born an Indian and I was born an Indian, we always have been Indians, mixed up with them and always known as Indians." On cross-examination, Assistant U.S. Attorney W. G. Porter scoffed at her claims to Indianness. He asked, "You say that you claim membership with the tribe of Sioux Indians because you are an Indian, that is your ground?" "I claim it because I am an Indian," she responded, "my mother and all her ancestors were Indians, we have always been Indians, we were born Indians, that is the reason I claim to be an Indian." Porter countered that mixed-ancestry Indians were not like other Indians and did not live in camps the way Indians did. In response, Waldron said, "No, the mixed bloods try to imitate and take on civilization, some of them live in houses, log houses, I presume if we had been aware that we were going to have everything taken away from us the minute we began to be white we would not have striven so hard to be anybody." Porter shot back, "You don't claim to have maintained tribal relations do you?" "Yes sir, I have always maintained tribal relations, we can't do away with them, those are born with us and they die with us," she responded.[43]

In her deposition, Waldron made it clear, from her perspective, that she was a Dakota person regardless of her mixed ancestry. In opposition to Dewey's assertion that a woman could give up her Indianness and "become white" through marriage to a white man, she argued that being Dakota was for life. For Waldron, Dakotaness was acquired at birth and based in culture and kinship connections. Indeed, to Waldron's point, one is born into kinship connections, and just as the children of American citizens are born into American citizenship, Waldron argued that she was Dakota at birth. But like Dewey, she equated whiteness with citizenship and non-Indianness. She claimed that mixed-ancestry Indians "began to be white," meaning they became acculturated into American culture. As we have seen, two generations earlier, mixed-ancestry Dakota people were more comfortable proclaiming their mixed status. Before the U.S.-Dakota War, mixed-ancestry Dakota people had little to lose and much to gain in emphasizing their mixedness. They could acquire land, money, or citizenship. Conversely, in Waldron's time, mixed-ancestry Indians did not hold separate rights and had to fight tooth and nail to retain their rights as Indians. Waldron finally won her case; nearly fifteen years after the initial decision that declared Waldron ineligible for allotment, Judge John Carland ruled on July 1, 1905, that she was indeed an Indian and was eligible to receive an allotment on the Cheyenne River reservation.

Some mixed-ancestry Indians, however, had a similar fight when they tried to give up their status as Indians and blend into white communities. At the same time as the Waldron case, another mixed-ancestry Dakota, Barney Traversie, tried to give up his Indian status and take up a homestead as a white citizen of the United States. Traversie was born in January 1860 to a French Canadian fur trader, Augustus Traversie, and a mixed-ancestry Isáŋathi Dakota woman, Felicia Dusant or Šináthowiŋ (Blue Blanket Woman). Traversie's mother and eight older siblings had received allotments on the Great Nemaha Reservation.

Like Waldron, Traversie was enrolled on the Cheyenne River reservation, and this story begins when he claimed an allotment April 23, 1891. By the end of the year, however, Traversie tried to relinquish his 320-acre allotment and take up a 160-acre homestead under the Homestead Act as a white American citizen. While Waldron based her Indianness in her immersion in Dakota culture, her kinship connections, and her birth as an Indian, Traversie minimized his connection to Dakota culture and Dakota people. In a letter dictated by his lawyer Owen Rowe on January 16, 1893, after hearing the decision of the commissioner of Indian Affairs and the secretary of the interior that he would not be permitted to relinquish his allotment, Traversie wrote,

> I made application about a year ago to relinquish, but the Secretary of the Interior denied my right to relinquish. He seems to think that I am an ignorant Indian who is not able to take care of himself. The facts are that I am not an Indian at all. I was born among and brought up with white people. My parents tell me that my mother had some Santee Indian blood in her veins, but my father is a white man. I have voted at all elections for about twenty-one years and my right to do so has never been questioned except at the last

> election, when I was denied the right to vote because my name was on the roll at the agency. When the allotting agent allotted me land I did not understand how it was or I would not have signed the papers. I do not want any land, rations, or annuities as an Indian. I want to take 160 acres—the land where I have lived for over nine years—as my homestead, as other people do.

Traversie used his voting history as a claim to whiteness and U.S. citizenship. Traversie explained his decision: "I would rather have 160 acres of land in my own name than many times that amount held in trust for me twenty-five years, as I understand the law to be. I want to live like other white people and I do not want to be under the control of the Indian agent."[44] Traversie wanted land but he objected to the paternalism in the General Allotment Act that forced Indians to hold their allotments under American trust for twenty-five years. Additionally, he opposed the paternalism of the Office of Indian Affairs itself. Traversie perceived whiteness and American citizenship as freedom and resented the way the federal government controlled Indians and restricted their rights.

Citizenship was the basis of Traversie's claim to whiteness, but his testimony about his whiteness and citizenship changed over time. In a deposition on January 12, 1892, he proclaimed that he "is not now, never has been, and never desired to be a Sioux Indian" but that he was "a white man, a citizen of the United States, had been since birth." Here Traversie was staking a claim similar, albeit opposite, to Waldron's: that he was a white American citizen at birth. In reality, Traversie and Waldron were both correct. As mixed-ancestry Indians, the children of white American fathers and Dakota mothers, they should have been affirmed both as U.S. citizens and as citizens of the Dakota Nation. In both cases they chose one of the two options, and both experienced extensive pushback from American officials on their respective choices.

Traversie said that his mother "is not a Sioux Indian—that she is in fact a white woman, and dresses and acts like other white people; that her habits are those of other white people." She was "only a half blood," he claimed, and he asserted that "he exercised the right of an American citizen, by voting at the elections held in his county" and that he was "living and associating with white people only."[45] When he was deposed again on September 3, 1892, his story changed. When asked, "Have you at any time or before any official ever stated or swore that you were not an Indian, but a citizen?" Traversie responded, "Not that I know of or that I so understood. I never was a citizen and I have never given up my tribal relations. I have voted and have said so, but not that I was a citizen." He claimed to have voted in Yankton County, Dakota Territory, in the 1870s but contended, "I did not know what I was voting for." Without identifying who "they" were, Traversie deposed that he "voted just because they wanted me to" and put the tickets he was given into the ballot box.[46]

The historical record does not show why his story changed in his second deposition or why he again forcefully asserted his whiteness and citizenship in the letter dictated by his lawyer, but Traversie had mixed feelings toward Indianness when it came to his family. When asked, "Do you understand that in becoming a citizen you sever your tribal relations and all rights as an Indian, or not?" Traversie replied, "Yes, I understand that I will not be an Indian, but can still draw my rations, and that the allotment to my wife and children and their Indian rights will not be affected by my becoming a citizen."[47] He wanted his wife and children to retain their Indian status and their allotments because he thought that that was best for them. Despite his claims to whiteness, Traversie continued to live on the Cheyenne River reservation until his death in the 1930s.

There is a glaring contrast between the views of Waldron and Traversie. Waldron believed her interests would best be served as an Indian while Traversie believed that the freedom of white American citizenship was preferable to being an Indian. In previous "mixed-blood" histories, mixed-ancestry Indians held their own racial status and legal rights that afforded them many benefits. But by the turn of the century that middle category no longer existed. The strict racial hierarchy of American society demanded that mixed-ancestry Indians fit into the category of "Indian" or "white." Holding mixed status was no longer beneficial and, as we have seen with the examples of Waldron and Traversie, could make life difficult. Waldron finally won her case fifteen years after applying for her allotment, but in both cases, the American colonial state defined their whiteness or Indianness for them. Given their mixedness, Traversie and

Waldron were in the position, as Karen Isaksen Leonard calls it, of "making an ethnic choice."[48] In practice, however, as we see from their cases, they had no choice at all. In the end, American officials decided for them that both were Indians.

The federal government did not challenge the Indianness or whiteness of the Trudell family as they did Waldron and Traversie, but by the turn of the twentieth century, government documents meticulously recorded the blood quanta of family members. The annual census rolls of the Office of Indian Affairs recorded the blood quantum of individual family members every available year between 1885 and 1937. Since the late nineteenth century, blood quantum follows all tribal members; enrolled members of federally recognized tribes, as proof of their Indianness, are issued a Certificate of Degree of Indian Blood by the federal government.

In the second half of the nineteenth century, questions still frequently arose concerning the rights of mixed-ancestry Indians. The Indian Agent at Cheyenne River, J. Lee Englebert, asked the commissioner of Indian Affairs in 1871, does a mixed-ancestry man "possess the rights & privileges of an Indian, of whites, or both, or otherwise?"[49] Similarly, the subagent at Flandreau, John P. Williamson, asked in 1876, "Have Half-Breeds who received 'Scrip' any further Tribal Rights?"[50] An Indian trader at Spotted Tail Agency in 1879 complained about Charles Tackett, a descendant of the Dorion family. He claimed that Tackett was trading without a license and argued that by the 1868 Fort Laramie Treaty, "half-breeds are concluded to be another class of persons, other than Indians."[51] Such concerns came up frequently, but most often Indians of mixed ancestry on reservations were treated the same as their full-ancestry relatives.

For their part, full-ancestry chiefs frequently attested to how they wanted their relatives to have the same rights as them and to be considered Indians by the government. During negotiations to break up the Great Sioux Reservation in 1888, several Lakota chiefs made this clear. Wizí (Old Tipi) was an Iháŋkthuŋwaŋna leader at Crow Creek; interpreted by mixed-ancestry Dakota Mark Wells, Wizí proclaimed that mixed-ancestry Indians "are just the same as we." Expressing similar sentiments, Mathȟó Héȟloǧeča (Hollow Horn Bear), a Sičháŋǧu chief at Rosebud Agency, through a mixed-ancestry Lakota interpreter, Thomas Flood, asserted that "we have made up our minds that we want to hold the mixed bloods and have them incorporated solidly into the tribe with us."[52] Legal and racial questions around the rights and status of mixed ancestry continued to be asked, but Očhéthi Šakówiŋ people made it clear that their mixed-ancestry relatives were Indians and had the same rights as them. Mixed-ancestry Dakota and Lakota people continued to reside at or near various Očhéthi Šakówiŋ reservations, and many of their descendants are still enrolled members of these tribes today.

From the perspective of mixed-ancestry Indians, some wanted more. A petition signed by mixed-ancestry Sičháŋǧu Lakota from the Whetstone Agency intended to "solicit the assistance of the Great Father to enable us to become something more than Indians." They wanted part of the reservation to be set aside for their use so that they would "not be interfered with by Indians."[53] While their full-ancestry relatives affirmed their kinship relations to the mixed-ancestry Dakota and Lakota in the face of ongoing questions of the legal and racial status of mixed-ancestry Indians by white Americans, mixed-ancestry Indians themselves questioned their own role. They wanted education and wanted the full rights of U.S. citizenship. As seen by the examples of Waldron and Traversie, mixed-ancestry Indians continued to look for various strategies to meet their wishes, whether it was as an Indian or as something else.

Most mixed-ancestry Dakota people, however, were content with being Indians. They continued to live on Indian reservations and enroll their children generation after generation. Many of the descendants of my Trudell, Dorion, and Langdeau ancestors are enrolled members of federally recognized tribes today. In fact, many descendants served as tribal leaders. Michael Jandreau, a descendant of the Langdeau family, served eighteen terms as tribal chairman of the Lower Brule Sioux Tribe from 1974 until his death in 2015. Roger Trudell served twenty years as the chairman of the Santee Sioux Tribe. A descendant of the Dorion family, Charles Colombe served as president of the Rosebud Sioux Tribe from 2003 to 2005. Despite Barney Traversie's attempt to leave his Indian identity behind, many of his descendants are enrolled members of the Cheyenne River Sioux Tribe today. Indeed, many of the surnames mentioned in this book can still be found among the enrolled members of many of the modern Očhéthi Šakówiŋ tribal nations. The "mixed-blood" histories of the nineteenth century gave way to the unambiguous incorporation of mixed-ancestry Dakota people into modern tribal nations of the twentieth century. Unfortunately, the ongoing usage of blood quantum as a membership requirement in many of the nations of the Očhéthi Šakówiŋ means that many Indigenous people of mixed ancestry are unable to enroll in their tribal nations despite their ongoing connections to culture and community.

Conclusion

Things have changed dramatically since the middle of the nineteenth century. The various "mixed-blood" histories in the Midwest have instilled ideas about Indianness, whiteness, and mixedness among white Americans and American Indians. The first mixed-blood history was inaugurated among the Dakota with the Treaty of Prairie du Chien in 1830, which created a new racial legal category. This new legal category nearly resulted in the recognition of the mixed-ancestry Dakota as a distinct nation in the 1840s, but instead they acquired citizenship in the American nation. American officials' confusion over the racial and legal standing of mixed-ancestry Indians, their attempts to define their legal rights, and the struggle to fit them into American binary conceptions of race led to a varying and contradictory mélange of legal rulings, racial misunderstandings, and unintended consequences.

As early as 1805, American officials began to develop a policy to put land in the hands of mixed-ancestry Indians not only as a way to assimilate them but so that mixed-ancestry Indians with land would act as an assimilative influence on their full-ancestry relatives. A byproduct of this policy was that treaty-makers established "half-breed" as a legal category. This had the consequence of creating two categories of Indigenous people in the United States with different sets of legal rights. Dakota people of mixed ancestry had additional entitlements to land and money in the treaties while they retained their rights as Indian people. The assimilation policy continued after the Indian Removal Act of 1830, which meant that instead of land, treaties offered cash payments to mixed-ancestry Indians. This had the effect of mixed- and full-ancestry Indians placing monetary value on the kinship obligations performed by mixed-ancestry Indians. The mixed-ancestry assimilation policy of the early nineteenth century contributed to divisions between mixed- and full-ancestry Indians.

When mixed-ancestry Dakota people and the U.S. government negotiated treaties in the 1840s, they almost created a nation. In fact, the mixed-ancestry Dakota were central to a proposed radical shift in Indian–white relations in the unratified treaties of 1841. While this radical shift never occurred and the creation of a mixed-ancestry nation was narrowly avoided, legislators in the Upper Midwest instead incorporated mixed-ancestry Indians into the American nation through citizenship. Initially meant to increase the voter base of the Democratic Party, mixed-ancestry Indians took advantage of this citizenship to exercise their own political power through elected offices. During these decades of confusion when it was uncertain if mixed-ancestry Indians would be part of their tribal nation, the American nation, or their own nation, they saw the erosion of their land bases at Lake Pepin and Great Nemaha. They were eventually dispossessed of their lands, and in the aftermath of the U.S.-Dakota War in 1862, the mixed-ancestry Dakota effectively lost their American citizenship.

Like other Indians, Indians of mixed ancestry were subject to the twists and turns of federal Indian policy. Mixedness became a focal point in American society and contributed to intratribal divisions. The "half-breed" became the subject of American literature and scientific racism.[1] Local lawmakers debated whether to enfranchise mixed-ancestry Indians and federal policymakers exploited Indians of mixed ancestry as a means to their own ends. Treaty negotiators created "half-breed" as a legal category in an attempt to use them for assimilative purposes. After the establishment of the Indian Removal Act in the early 1830s, they half-heartedly continued the mixed-ancestry assimilation policy through cash payments, contributing to the monetization of mixed-ancestry kinship obligations. In the 1840s, policymakers nearly recognized the nationhood status of mixed-ancestry Dakota people in the process of trying to acquire their land. American policymakers continued their obsession with Indians and mixedness until the present, but after these mixed-blood histories the focus was on the sophisticated colonial concept of blood quantum, which the federal government used to exclude Indians of mixed ancestry.

During these mixed-blood histories, being a mixed-ancestry Indian in the Midwest could be beneficial. Mixed-ancestry Indians gained land, money, legal rights, and American citizenship without losing their status as Indian people. During these moments, the American obsession with blood quantum did not hurt mixed-ancestry Indians; indeed, there was much to gain and little to lose in proclaiming one's status as a mixed-ancestry Indian. But through the process of these mixed-blood histories and the legal and racial confusion that accompanied them, American officials learned to use blood quantum against Indians. After the U.S.-Dakota War, it was no longer beneficial to be an Indian of mixed ancestry. Now there was much to lose and little to gain. Jane Waldron saw intense resistance to her claims to Indianness, while Barney Traversie saw his bid for whiteness rejected.

It was mixed-blood histories like these among the Dakota and other Indigenous nations that led directly to the colonial imposition of blood quantum as a tool of exclusion. The policies of the late nineteenth and twentieth centuries were aimed at excluding Indians of mixed ancestry. The American race-based understandings of Indians that grew out of these moments resulted in a conception of Indians today as racial minorities rather than as members of sovereign Indigenous nations. Americans today continue their obsession with "blood," calling people "part Indian" as a way to minimize Indian identity and ongoing Native presence in the United States. Indians of mixed ancestry are perceived by Americans and sometimes other Indigenous people as not Indigenous enough or are mislabeled as Métis. To a large extent, Indians have internalized this colonial racism and the misguided assumptions of racial purity that come with it, which contributes to ongoing divides between mixed- and full-ancestry Indians today.

Thinking back to the Trudell family reunion on the Santee Reservation in 2007, I realized that it is not some racial determinant that made us Dakota or not Dakota; it is our kinship connections that continue to bind us together and inform who we are. Mixed ancestry does not make one less Indian, nor does the presence of some Indian "blood" automatically make one Indigenous. Indigeneity comes through culture, through connection to community, through our relationships to our Native relatives. It is not the two hundred years of the American settler colonial obsession with blood quantum that makes us who we are as Indigenous people. For me, it was a family reunion over a long weekend that reinforced the importance of kinship and acceptance by a Native community that makes us who we are.

Acknowledgments

This book could not have been written without the assistance and encouragement of many people. Jean O'Brien and David Chang provided invaluable support and guidance. Jeani in particular was the best mentor anyone could ever hope for. I would also like to thank Katherine Hayes, Brenda Child, and Barbara Welke at the University of Minnesota. I am especially appreciative of my Dakota language instructors, Šišóka Dúta Joe Bendickson and Čhaŋté Máza Neil McKay, as well as the Dakota Language Program at the University of Minnesota for funding a year of my graduate work. Sam Majhor, John Reynolds, Ethan Neerdaels, Darlene St. Clair, Dawí Westerman, Lorna Her Many Horses, Kirk Perez, and Steve Trettel were the best classmates one could ask for.

I received inestimable help, encouragement, and inspiration from the members of the American Indian and Indigenous Studies Workshop at the University of Minnesota, who pored over iterations of each chapter and provided invaluable feedback. My thanks to Katie Phillips, Kasey Keeler, Sam Majhor, Jess Arnett, John Little, Rose Miron, Sasha Suarez, Amber Annis, Marie Balsley Taylor, Bernadette Perez, Boyd Cothran, Joanne Jahnke Wegner, Akikwe Cornell, Evan Taparata, Juliana Hu Pegues, Kai Pyle, Jason Herbert, Chris Pexa, Agléška Cohen-Rencountre, Adrian Chavana, Robert Gilmer, Mike Wise, and Jesus Estrada-Perez.

I am indebted to many scholars who provided feedback, advice, encouragement, and help in innumerable ways. I would like to thank Chris

Andersen, Nicole St-Onge, Bruce White, Mattie Harper, Robert Morrissey, Linda Waggoner, Robert Warrior, Margaret Huettl, Tanis Thorne, Lucy Murphy, Kate Beane, John Reynolds, Fred Hoxie, Anne Hyde, Tiya Miles, Kyle Mays, K. Tsianina Lomawaima, cousin John Lavelle, John Legg, Elizabeth Ellis, Joshua Lynn, Ned Blackhawk, Kelly Fayard, Michael Witgen, Larry Nesper, Mary Murphy, Billy Smith, and Robert Campbell. Thank you also to John Craig Hammond for sharing documents and Robert Englebert and Olivier Genger for help translating documents from French. Thank you also to my colleagues at Rutgers for their support: Louis Masur, Maria Kennedy, Carla Cevasco, Allan Isaac, Ben Sifuentes-Jáuregui, Andrew Urban, Sylvia Chan-Malik, Jefferson Decker, Angus Gillespie, Maya Mikdashi, and Camilla Townsend.

Numerous institutions supported my research. Thank you to the Ford Foundation, William Nelson Cromwell Foundation, the Newberry Library, the Buffalo Bill Historical Center, the American Historical Association, the American Philosophical Society, and the State Historical Society of Iowa. A special thank you to Yale University and the Henry Roe Cloud Postdoctoral Fellowship. This book could not have been possible without the help of archivists and numerous other workers at numerous archives, many of whose names I never learned. Thank you to those who helped me at the Minnesota Historical Society, the Newberry Library, the State Historical Society of Iowa, the Wisconsin Historical Society, the National Archives, the Nebraska State Historical Society, the Archives of Manitoba, and the North Dakota State Historical Society.

Over the years, several researchers in the Dakota community helped me along the way; a special thank you to Vicky Valenta, Franky Jackson, Tamara St. John, Sarah James-Childers, and cousin Sallie Greystone. A special thank you for my aunt and uncle, Barbara and Francis Bettelyoun. Finally, thank you to my wife Elizabeth, son James, and daughter Josephine —I could not have done this without you.

Notes

Introduction

1. Wolfchild v. United States, No. 12-5035 (Fed. Cir. 2013).

2. Affidavit #125, Francis Trudell, entry 529, Miscellaneous Reserve Papers, 1825–1907, box 359, RG 75, National Archives, Washington, D.C.

3. Quoted in Linda M. Waggoner, ed., *"Neither White Men nor Indians": Affidavits from the Winnebago Mixed-Blood Claim Commissions, Prairie du Chien, Wisconsin, 1838–1839* (Park Genealogical Books, 2002), 2.

4. Patrick Wolfe, "Settler Colonialism and the Elimination of the Native," *Journal of Genocide Research* 8, no. 4 (December 2006): 388–89.

5. Wolfe, "Settler Colonialism and the Elimination of the Native," 387–88.

6. Jennifer S. H. Brown, *Strangers in Blood: Fur Trade Company Families in Indian Country* (University of British Columbia Press, 1980); Sylvia Van Kirk, *Many Tender Ties: Women in Fur-Trade Society, 1670–1870* (University of Oklahoma Press, 1980); Jacqueline Peterson, "The People in Between: Indian-White Marriage and the Genesis of Métis Society and Culture in the Great Lakes Region, 1680–1830" (PhD diss., University of Illinois at Chicago, 1981); Jacqueline Peterson, "Prelude to Red River: A Social Portrait of the Great Lakes Métis," *Ethnohistory* 25, no. 1 (Winter 1978): 41–67; Jacqueline Peterson, "Ethnogenesis: The Settlement and Growth of a 'New People' in the Great Lakes Region, 1702–1815," *American Indian Culture and Research Journal* 6, no. 2 (1982): 23–64; Jacqueline Peterson and Jennifer S. H. Brown, eds., *The New Peoples: Being and Becoming Métis in North America* (University of Manitoba Press, 1985).

7. Jace Weaver, *The Red Atlantic: American Indigenes and the Making of the Modern World, 1000–1927* (University of North Carolina Press, 2014), xi.

8. Chris Andersen, "Moya 'Tipimsook ('The People Who Aren't Their Own Bosses'): Racialization and the Misrecognition of 'Métis' in Upper Great Lakes Ethnohistory," *Ethnohistory* 58, no. 1 (Winter 2011): 37–63; Chris Andersen, *"Métis": Race, Recognition, and the Struggle for Indigenous Peoplehood* (University of British Columbia Press, 2014); Adam Gaudry and Darryl Leroux, "White Settler Revisionism and Making Métis Everywhere: The Evocation of Métissage in Quebec and Nova Scotia," *Critical Ethnic Studies* 3, no. 1 (Spring 2017): 116–42; Darryl Leroux, *Distorted Descent: White Claims to Indigenous Identity* (University of Manitoba Press, 2019); Adam Gaudry, "Communing with the Dead: The 'New Métis,' Métis Identity Appropriation, and the Displacement of Living Métis Culture," *American Indian Quarterly* 42, no. 2 (Spring 2018): 162–90; Chris Andersen, "'I'm Métis, What's Your Excuse?' On the Optics and the Ethics of the Misrecognition of Métis in Canada," *Aboriginal Policy Studies* 1, no. 2 (2011): 161–65.

9. James Garvie, "The Race Problem," *Word Carrier* (Santee Agency, Nebraska), November–December 1896.

10. Marie L. McLaughlin, *Myths and Legends of the Sioux* (Bismarck Tribune Company, 1916).

11. Raymond J. DeMallie, "Kinship: The Foundation for Native American Society," in *Studying Native America: Problems and Prospects,* ed. Russell Thornton (University of Wisconsin Press, 1998).

12. Eastman left two autobiographical writings, Charles Alexander Eastman, *Indian Boyhood* (McClure, Phillips & Co., 1902); *From the Deep Woods to Civilization: Chapters in the Autobiography of an Indian* (Little and Brown, 1916).

13. Susan Bordeaux Bettelyoun and Josephine Waggoner, *With My Own Eyes: A Lakota Woman Tells Her People's History,* ed. Emily Levine (University of Nebraska Press, 1999).

14. Josephine Waggoner, *Witness: A Húŋkpapȟa Historian's Strong-Heart Song of the Lakotas,* ed. Emily Levine (University of Nebraska Press, 2013).

15. Zitkala-Ša wrote numerous short pieces, which she later published as *American Indian Stories* (Hayworth Publishing House, 1921), and *Old Indian Legends* (Ginn & Company, 1904). Deloria wrote numerous works of fiction and nonfiction, most notably *Speaking of Indians* (Friendship Press, 1944); *Dakota Texts* (University of Nebraska Press, 2006); *Waterlily* (University of Nebraska Press, 2009).

16. William J. Bordeaux, *Conquering the Mighty Sioux* (William J. Bordeaux, 1929). See also the historical account of William Red Cloud Jordan (1884–1975), William Red Cloud Jordan, "Eighty Years on the Rosebud," ed. Henry W. Hamilton, *South Dakota Report and Historical Collections* 35 (1970): 323–83.

17. Julian Rice, "'It Was Their Own Fault for Being Intractable': Internalized Racism and Wounded Knee," *American Indian Quarterly* 22, nos. 1 and 2

(Winter–Spring 1998): 63–82. Also see Penelope Myrtle Kelsey, *Tribal Theory in Native American Literature: Dakota and Haudenosaunee Writing and Indigenous Worldviews* (University of Nebraska Press, 2008).

18. Gary B. Nash, "The Hidden History of Mestizo America," *Journal of American History* 82 (December 1995): 941–62; Anne F. Hyde, "Hard Choices: Mixed-Race Families and Strategies of Acculturation in the U.S. West after 1848," in *On the Borders of Love and Power: Families and Kinship in the Intercultural American Southwest,* ed. David Wallace Adams and Crista DeLuzio (University of California Press, 2013).

19. William J. Sheick, *The Half-Blood: A Cultural Symbol in Nineteenth-Century American Fiction* (University of Kentucky Press, 2015), ix. See also Harry J. Brown, *Injun Joe's Ghost: The Indian Mixed-Blood in American Writing* (University of Missouri Press, 2004); Peter G. Beidler, "The Indian Half-Breed in Turn-of-the-Century Short Fiction," *American Indian Culture and Research Journal* 9, no. 1 (1985): 1–12.

20. Lauren L. Basson, *White Enough to Be American? Race Mixing, Indigenous People, and the Boundaries of State and Nation* (University of North Carolina Press, 2008), 1.

21. Lucy Eldersveld Murphy, *Great Lakes Creoles: A French-Indian Community on the Northern Borderlands, Prairie du Chien, 1750–1860* (Cambridge University Press, 2014); Susan Sleeper-Smith, *Indian Women and French Men: Rethinking Cultural Encounter in the Western Great Lakes* (University of Massachusetts Press, 2001); Robert Englebert and Guillaume Teasdale, *French and Indians in the Heart of North America, 1630–1815* (Michigan State University Press, 2013); Kathleen DuVal, *The Native Ground: Indians and Colonists in the Heart of the Continent* (University of Pennsylvania Press, 2006); Tanis C. Thorne, *The Many Hands of My Relations: French and Indians on the Lower Missouri* (University of Missouri Press, 1996); Jay Gitlin, *The Bourgeois Frontier: French Towns, French Traders, and American Expansion* (Yale University Press, 2010); Sophie White, *Wild Frenchmen and Frenchified Indians: Material Culture and Race in Colonial Louisiana* (University of Pennsylvania Press, 2012); Thomas N. Ingersoll, *To Intermix with Our White Brothers: Indian Mixed Bloods in the United States from Earliest Times to the Indian Removals* (University of New Mexico Press, 2005).

22. Alaina E. Roberts, *I've Been Here All the While: Black Freedom on Native Land* (University of Pennsylvania Press, 2021); James F. Brooks, ed., *Confounding the Color Line: The Indian-Black Experience in North America* (University of Nebraska Press, 2002); Tiya Miles, *Ties That Bind: The Story of an Afro-Cherokee Family in Slavery and Freedom,* 2nd ed. (University of California Press, 2015); A. B. Wilkinson, *Blurring the Lines of Race and Freedom: Mulattoes and Mixed Bloods in English Colonial America* (University of North Carolina Press, 2020).

23. Sleeper-Smith, *Indian Women and French Men,* 4. For more on kinship and especially on mixed-ancestry families, see William E. Foly and C. David Rice, *The First Chouteaus: River Barons of Early St. Louis* (University of Illinois Press, 2000); Stan Hoig, *The Chouteaus: First Family of the Fur Trade* (University of New Mexico Press, 2008); Robert Silbernagel, *The Cadottes: A Fur Trade Family on Lake Superior* (Wisconsin Historical Society Press, 2002); Hugh M. Lewis, *Robidoux Chronicles: French-Indian Ethnoculture of the Trans-Mississippi West* (Trafford, 2004); Robert J. Willoughby, *The Brothers Robidoux and the Opening of the American West* (University of Missouri Press, 2012); David C. Beyreis, *Blood in the Borderlands: Conflict, Kinship, and the Bent Family, 1821–1920* (University of Nebraska Press, 2020); Andrew R. Graybill, *The Red and the White: A Family Saga of the American West* (Liveright Publishing, 2013); Heather Devine, *The People Who Own Themselves: Aboriginal Ethnogenesis in a Canadian Family, 1660–1900* (University of Calgary Press, 2004).

24. J. Kēhaulani Kauanui, *Hawaiian Blood: Colonialism and the Politics of Sovereignty and Indigeneity* (Duke University Press, 2008), 2. For more on this issue of "blood," see Katherine Ellinghaus, *Blood Will Tell: Native Americans and Assimilation Policy* (University of Nebraska Press, 2017); Jill Doerfler, *Those Who Belong: Identity, Family, Blood, and Citizenship Among the White Earth Anishinaabeg* (Michigan State University Press, 2007).

25. Theda Perdue, *"Mixed Blood" Indians: Racial Construction in the Early South* (University of Georgia Press, 2003), 102.

26. Vine Deloria Jr. and David E. Wilkins, *Tribes, Treaties, and Constitutional Tribulations* (University of Texas Press, 1999), 26.

27. David E. Wilkins, *American Indian Sovereignty and the U.S. Supreme Court: The Masking of Justice* (University of Texas Press, 1997), 3–4.

28. David E. Wilkins and Heidi Kiiwetinepenisiik Stark, *American Indian Politics and the American Political System,* 3rd ed. (Rowman & Littlefield, 2011), 33–50. For work on Native American sovereignty, see Deloria and Wilkins, *Tribes, Treaties, and Constitutional Tribulations*; David E. Wilkins and K. Tsianina Lomawaima, *Uneven Ground: American Indian Sovereignty and Federal Law* (University of Oklahoma Press, 2001); Sidney L. Harring, *Crow Dog's Case: American Indian Sovereignty, Tribal Law, and United States Law in the Nineteenth Century* (Cambridge University Press, 1994).

29. Deborah A. Rosen, *American Indians and State Law: Sovereignty, Race, and Citizenship, 1790–1880* (University of Nebraska Press, 2007). For more on Indian law, especially how it relates to race, see Charles E. Cleland, *Faith in Paper: The Ethnohistory and Litigation of Upper Great Lakes Indian Treaties* (University of Michigan Press, 2011); Martin Case, *The Relentless Business of Treaties: How Indigenous Land Became U.S. Property* (Minnesota Historical Society Press, 2018);

Robert A. Williams Jr., *Like a Loaded Weapon: The Rehnquist Court, Indian Rights, and the Legal History of Racism in America* (University of Minnesota Press, 2005); Paul Spruhan, "A Legal History of Blood Quantum in Federal Indian Law to 1935," *South Dakota Law Review* 51 (2006): 1–50; Ariela J. Gross, *What Blood Won't Tell: A History of Race on Trial in America* (Harvard University Press, 2008); Kathleen Ratteree and Norbert Hill, eds., *The Great Vanishing Act: Blood Quantum and the Future of Native Nations* (Fulcrum, 2017); Circe Sturm, *Blood Politics: Race, Culture, and Identity in the Cherokee Nation of Oklahoma* (University of California Press, 2002).

30. Andersen, "*Métis*."

31. James A. Clifton, "Personal and Ethnic Identity on the Great Lakes Frontier: The Case of Billy Caldwell, Anglo-Canadian," *Ethnohistory* 25 (Winter 1978): 82; Jennifer S. H. Brown, "Métis, Halfbreeds, and Other Real People: Challenging Cultures and Categories," *History Teacher* 27, no. 1 (November 1993): 20; Jack D. Forbes, "Mustees, Halfbreeds and Zambos in Anglo North America: Aspects of Black-Indian Relations," *American Indian Quarterly* 7, no. 1 (1983): 72–73.

32. David Treuer, "How Do You Prove You're an Indian?," *New York Times*, December 20, 2011.

33. Viola A. Burnette, *Confessions of an Iyeska* (University of Utah Press, 2018), 51–56.

34. Scott Richard Lyons, *X-Marks: Native Signatures of Assent* (University of Minnesota Press, 2010), 54–55.

35. I implore all scholars to incorporate knowledge of Indigenous languages in their work. Douglas R. Parks, "The Importance of Language Study for the Writing of Plains Indian History," in *New Directions in American Indian History*, ed. Colin G. Calloway (University of Oklahoma Press, 1988); Gwen N. Westerman, "Treaties Are More than a Piece of Paper: Why Words Matter," *Albany Government Law Review* 10 (2017): 293–317.

36. Anne F. Hyde, *Empires, Nations, and Families: A History of the North American West, 1800–1860* (University of Nebraska Press, 2011).

37. See Diane Wilson, *Spirit Car: Journey to a Dakota Past* (Borealis Press, 2006), 181. See also Clara Sue Kidwell, "It's All Relatives: Family History as a Strategy for Writing American Indian History," *Journal of the West* 49, no. 4 (Fall 2010): 20–29; Joseph A. Amato, *Jacob's Well: A Case for Rethinking Family History* (Minnesota Historical Society Press, 2008).

38. DeMallie, "Kinship," 341.

1. The Emergence of the Mixed-Ancestry Dakota Community

1. For more on Iháŋkthuŋwaŋ ethnohistory, see Alan R. Woolworth, *Ethnohistorical Report on the Yankton Sioux* (Garland Publishing, 1974); James H.

Howard, "Notes on the Ethnogeography of the Yankton Dakota," *Plains Anthropologist* 17, no. 58, pt. 1 (November 1972): 281–307.

2. Abraham P. Nasatir, "Anglo-Spanish Rivalry in the Iowa Country, 1797–1798," *Iowa Journal of History and Politics* 28, no. 3 (July 1930): 337–89; A. P. Nasatir, "Anglo-Spanish Rivalry on the Upper Missouri," *Mississippi Valley Historical Review* 16, no. 4 (March 1930): 507–28.

3. W. J. Eccles, "The Fur Trade and Eighteenth-Century Imperialism," in *Rethinking the Fur Trade: Cultures of Exchange in an Atlantic World,* ed. Susan Sleeper-Smith (University of Nebraska Press, 2009), 236–37; Barton H. Barbour, *Fort Union and the Upper Missouri Fur Trade* (University of Oklahoma Press, 2001), 6.

4. Robert S. Allen, *His Majesty's Indian Allies: British Indian Policy in the Defence of Canada, 1774–1815* (Dundurn Press, 1992); Barton H. Barbour, *Fort Union and the Upper Missouri Fur Trade* (University of Oklahoma Press, 2001), 8.

5. Henry S. Baird, "Recollections of the Early History of Northern Wisconsin," *Collections of the State Historical Society of Wisconsin* 4 (1906): 204.

6. Carolyn Podruchny, *Making the Voyageur World: Travelers and Traders in the North American Fur Trade* (University of Nebraska Press, 2006), 13.

7. David Andrew Nichols, *Engines of Diplomacy: Indian Trading Factories and the Negotiation of American Empire* (University of North Carolina Press, 2016); John S. Milloy, *The Plains Cree: Trade, Diplomacy and War, 1790 to 1870* (University of Manitoba Press, 1988).

8. Raymond J. DeMallie, "Kinship: The Foundation for Native American Society," in *Studying Native America: Problems and Prospects,* ed. Russell Thornton (University of Wisconsin Press, 1998), 307.

9. Richard White, *The Middle Ground: Indians, Empires, and Republics in the Great Lakes Region, 1650–1815* (Cambridge University Press, 1991); Kathleen DuVal, *The Native Ground: Indians and Colonists in the Heart of the Continent* (University of Pennsylvania Press, 2006); Juliana Barr, *Peace Came in the Form of a Woman: Indians and Spaniards in the Texas Borderlands* (University of North Carolina Press, 2007); Matthew Kruer, *Time of Anarchy: Indigenous Power and the Crisis of Colonialism in Early America* (Harvard University Press, 2021); Daniel P. Barr, ed., *The Boundaries Between Us: Natives and Newcomers Along the Frontiers of the Old Northwest Territory, 1750–1850* (Kent State University Press, 2006); Robert Englebert and Guillaume Teasdale, eds., *French and Indians in the Heart of North America, 1630–1815* (Michigan State University Press, 2013); Robert Michael Morrissey, *Empire by Collaboration: Indians, Colonists, and Governments in Colonial Illinois Country* (University of Pennsylvania Press, 2015).

10. See, for example, Gilles Havard, *The Great Peace of Montreal of 1701: French-Native Diplomacy in the Seventeenth Century,* trans. Phyllis Aronoff and Howard Scott (McGill-Queens University Press, 2001).

11. Sylvia Van Kirk, *Many Tender Ties: Women in Fur-Trade Society, 1670–1870* (University of Oklahoma Press, 1980); Jennifer S. H. Brown, *Strangers in Blood: Fur Trade Company Families in Indian Country* (University of British Columbia Press, 1980); Gary Clayton Anderson, *Kinsmen of Another Kind: Dakota-White Relations in the Upper Mississippi Valley, 1650–1862* (University of Nebraska Press, 1984); Susan Sleeper-Smith, *Indian Women and French Men: Rethinking Cultural Encounter in the Western Great Lakes* (University of Massachusetts Press, 2001).

12. Lesley Wischmann, *Frontier Diplomats: The Life and Times of Alexander Culbertson and Natoyist-Siksina'* (Arthur H. Clark, 2000), 21.

13. John T. Juricek, *Colonial Georgia and the Creeks: Anglo-Indian Diplomacy on the Southern Frontier, 1733–1763* (University Press of Florida, 2010).

14. Lakota Language Consortium, *New Lakota Dictionary: Lakȟótiyapi-English/English-Lakȟótiyapi & Incorporating the Dakota Dialects of Yankton-Yanktonai & Santee-Sisseton*, 2nd ed. (Lakota Language Consortium, 2001), 551–52.

15. Gideon D. Scull, ed., *Voyages of Peter Esprit Radisson, Being an Account of His Travels and Experiences Among the North American Indians, from 1652 to 1684* (Peter Smith, 1943), 213–14.

16. Carla Kelly, ed., *On the Upper Missouri: The Journal of Rudolph Friedrich Kurz, 1851–1852* (University of Oklahoma Press, 2005), 88–89; Mary K. Whelan, "Dakota Indian Economics and the Nineteenth-Century Fur Trade," *Ethnohistory* 40, no. 2 (Spring 1993): 253–57.

17. Podruchny, *Making the Voyageur World*, 227–28.

18. Dedication in Luther Standing Bear, *Land of the Spotted Eagle* (University of Nebraska Press, 1978).

19. Robert Englebert, "Between Obligation and Opportunity: St. Louis, Women, and Transcolonial Networks, 1764–1800," in *French St. Louis: Landscape, Contexts, and Legacy*, ed. Jay Gitlin, Robert Michael Morrissey, and Peter J. Kastor (University of Nebraska Press, 2021); Michael Lansing, "Plains Indian Women and Interracial Marriage in the Upper Missouri Trade, 1804–1868," *Western Historical Quarterly* 31, no. 4 (Winter 2000): 413–33.

20. Lansing, "Plains Indian Women."

21. For the sake of continuity, I'm writing in the past tense, but many of the aspects of kinship described here are still practiced by Lakota and Dakota people today.

22. Ella Deloria, *Speaking of Indians* (State Publishing, 1983), 17–18.

23. For more on the cultural differences in marriage practices, see Ann Marie Plane, *Colonial Intimacies: Indian Marriage in Early New England* (Cornell University Press, 2000); John Mack Faragher, "The Custom of the Country: Cross-Cultural Marriage in the Far Western Fur Trade," in *Western Women: Their Land, Their Lives*, ed. Lillian Schlissel, Vicki L. Ruiz, and Janice Monk (University of New Mexico Press, 1988).

24. Sophie White, *Wild Frenchmen and Frenchified Indians: Material Culture and Race in Colonial Louisiana* (University of Pennsylvania Press, 2012), 107.

25. Collette's Index of Marriages, Holy Family Parish, Cahokia, Illinois, Church Records, 1740–1950, microfilm, Family History Library, Salt Lake City, Utah.

26. Scull, *Voyages of Peter Esprit Radisson,* 208–9.

27. Scull, 216.

28. John Gilmary Shea, *Discovery and Exploration of the Mississippi Valley: With the Original Narratives of Marquette, Allouez, Membré, Hennepin, and Anastase Douay* (Redfield, 1852), 117–18.

29. Shea, *Discovery and Exploration of the Mississippi Valley,* 129–30.

30. Louis Hennepin, *A Description of Louisiana,* trans. John Gilmary Shea (John G. Shea, 1880), 293.

31. Joseph Buisson papers, Wisconsin Historical Society, Madison, Wisc.

32. Doane Robinson, *A History of the Dakota or Sioux Indians* (New Printing, 1904), 49.

33. Reuben Gold Thwaites, ed., "Mackinac Register of Baptisms and Internments, 1695–1821," *Collections of the State Historical Society of Wisconsin* 19 (1910): 23.

34. Luce Eldersveld Murphy, *A Gathering of Rivers: Indians, Métis, and Mining in the Western Great Lakes, 1737–1832* (University of Nebraska Press, 2000), 58.

35. Brett Rushforth, *Bonds of Alliance: Indigenous and Atlantic Slaveries in New France* (University of North Carolina Press, 2012).

36. Gwen Westerman and Bruce White, *Mni Sota Makoce: The Land of the Dakota* (Minnesota Historical Society Press, 2012), 38.

37. John S. Wozniak, *Contact, Negotiation, and Change: An Ethnohistory of the Eastern Dakota, 1819–1839* (University Press of America, 1978), 7.

38. Roy W. Meyer, *History of the Santee Sioux: United States Indian Policy on Trial* (University of Nebraska Press, 1980), 10.

39. Westerman and White, *Mni Sota Makoce,* 62–63.

40. Peter Lawrence Scanlan, *Prairie du Chien: French, British, American* (Collegiate Press, 1937), 26–27.

41. Westerman and White, *Mni Sota Makoce,* 65; Anderson, *Kinsmen of Another Kind,* 19–20; Scanlan, *Prairie du Chien,* 26–28.

42. Scanlan, *Prairie du Chien,* 29–46.

43. Louis Houck, *The Spanish Regime in Missouri,* vol. 1 (R. R. Donnelley & Sons, 1909), 145.

44. Sharon K. Person, "St. Louis Trade & Traders in Indian Country, 1766–1774: Valentin Devin & Jean-Baptiste Papillon," *Nebraska History* 99, no. 4 (Winter 2018): 252–65.

45. Lucy Eldersveld Murphy, *Great Lakes Creoles: A French-Indian Community on the Northern Borderlands, Prairie du Chien, 1750–1860* (Cambridge University

Press, 2014); Karen L. Marrero, *Detroit's Hidden Channels: The Power of French-Indigenous Families in the Eighteenth Century* (Michigan State University Press, 2020); Patricia Cleary, *The World, the Flesh, and the Devil: A History of Colonial St. Louis* (University of Missouri Press, 2011); Charles E. Hoffhaus, *Chez Les Canses: Three Centuries at Kawsmouth; The French Foundations of Metropolitan Kansas City* (Lowell Press, 1984); Kerry A. Trask, "Settlement in a Half-Savage Land: Life and Loss in the Metis Community of La Baye," *Michigan Historical Review* 15, no. 1 (Spring 1989): 1–27; Colin G. Calloway, *"The Chiefs Now in This City": Indians and the Urban Frontier in Early America* (Oxford University Press, 2021).

46. Murphy, *Great Lakes Creoles,* 6.

47. Barry Gough, "Michilimackinac and Prairie du Chien: Northern Anchors of British Authority in the War of 1812," *Michigan Historical Review* 38, no. 1 (Spring 2012): 83–84.

48. J. Frederick Fausz, "The Capital of St. Louis: From Indian Trade to American Territory, 1764–1825," in *French St. Louis: Landscape, Contests, and Legacy,* ed. Jay Gitlin, Robert Michael Morrissey, and Peter J. Kastor (University of Nebraska Press, 2021).

49. Mark Diedrich, *The Chiefs Wapahasha: Three Generations of Dakota Leadership, 1740–1876* (Coyote Books, 2004), 21–25, 36; John Francis McDermott, ed., *Old Cahokia: A Narrative and Documents Illustrating the First Century of Its History* (St. Louis Historical Documents Foundation, 1949), 213n36; Cleary, *World, the Flesh, and the Devil,* 222–48.

50. These were the families of Jacques l'Arrivée, Jean Tomaso Uvaldy, and Joseph Pineau. Cleary, *World, the Flesh, and the Devil,* 157; Carl J. Ekberg, *Stealing Indian Women: Native Slavery in the Illinois Country* (University of Illinois Press, 2007), 78–79; J. Frederick Fausz, *Founding St. Louis: First City of the New West* (History Press, 2011), 131–32.

51. Pierre Dorion to George Rogers Clark, May 31, 1780, in *Collections of the Illinois State Historical Library,* vol. 8, *George Rogers Clark Papers, 1771–1781,* ed. Clarence Walworth Alvord (Illinois State Historical Library, 1912), 420–21.

52. Cleary, *World, the Flesh, and the Devil,* 222–48; Carolyn Gilman, "L'Anneé du Coup: The Battle of St. Louis, 1780, Part 1," *Missouri Historical Review* 103, no. 3 (April 2009): 133–47; Carolyn Gilman, "L'Anneé du Coup: The Battle of St. Louis, 1780, Part 2," *Missouri Historical Review* 103, no. 4 (July 2009): 195–211.

53. Charles Gratiot to Pierre Dorion, August 18, 1779, in McDermott, *Old Cahokia,* 218–19.

54. A. P. Nasatir, "The Anglo-Spanish Frontier in the Illinois Country During the American Revolution, 1779–1783," *Journal of the Illinois State Historical Society* 21, no. 3 (October 1928): 352–54.

55. Henry H. Sibley, "Memoir of Jean Baptiste Faribault," *Collections of the Minnesota Historical Society* 3 (1880): 170–72; Cynthia L. Peterson, "Historical Tribes and Early Forts," in *Frontier Forts of Iowa: Indians, Traders, and Soldiers, 1682–1862,* ed. William E. Whittaker (University of Iowa Press, 2009), 20–21; Jacob Van der Zee, "Fur Trade Operations in the Eastern Iowa Country from 1800 to 1833," *Iowa Journal of History and Politics* 12, no. 4 (October 1914): 481–83.

56. Cailhol quoted in Nasatir, "Anglo-Spanish Rivalry in the Iowa Country," 384–85.

57. Pierre Dorion to Charles de Hault Delassus, August 4, 1799, Papers of the St. Louis Fur Trade, part 1, microfilm reel 1, Wisconsin Historical Society, Madison (hereafter PSLFT).

58. Jacob Van der Zee, "Fur Trade Operations in the Eastern Iowa Country Under the Spanish Régime," *Iowa Journal of History and Politics* 12 (1914): 369–70; Gordon Speck, *Breeds and Half-Breeds* (Clarkson N. Potter, 1969), 151.

59. L. Honore Taisont (Tesson) to Charles de Hault Delassus, August 18, 1799, PSLFT, part 1, reel 1.

60. L. Honore Taisont (Tesson) to Charles de Hault Delassus, October 10, 1799, PSLFT, part 1, reel 1; Speck, *Breeds and Half-Breeds,* 151.

61. Jean Baptiste Baupelar to Carlos de Hault Delassus, March 29, 1800, PSLFT, part 1, reel 1.

62. L. Honore Taisont (Tesson) to Charles de Hault Delassus, April 29, 1800, PSLFT, part 1, reel 1. For another view of Dorion's activities at this time, see Martha Royce Blaine, *The Ioway Indians* (University of Oklahoma Press, 1995), 78–79.

63. For more on winter counts, see James H. Howard, "Yanktonai Ethnohistory and the John K. Bear Winter Count," *Plains Anthropologist* 21, no. 73, pt. 2 (August 1976): 1–78; Barbara Risch, "Wife, Mother, Provider, Defender, God: Women in Lakota Winter Counts," *American Indian Culture and Research Journal* 27, no. 3 (2003): 1–30; Candace S. Greene and Russell Thornton, eds., *The Year the Stars Fell: Lakota Winter Counts at the Smithsonian* (Smithsonian Institution, 2007); Ron McCoy, "'A People Without History Is like Wind on the Buffalo Grass': Lakota Winter Counts," *South Dakota History* 32, no. 1 (Spring 2002): 65–86.

64. Howard, "Yanktonai Ethnohistory," 21.

65. Howard, 21–25.

66. Howard, 38.

67. Risch, "Wife, Mother, Provider, Defender, God," 13.

68. Roger T. Grange Jr., "The Garnier Oglala Winter Count," *Plains Anthropologist* 8, no. 20 (May 1963): 75; Eli Waktegli, "Waniyetu Yawapi Watapeta Kağa Kin," *Iapi Oaye* 21, no. 5 (May 1892): 18.

69. Lucy Kramer Cohen, "Big Missouri's Winter Count: A Sioux Calendar, 1796–1926," *Indians at Work* 6, no. 6 (February 1939): 17.

70. Edward S. Curtis, *The North American Indian,* vol. 3 (Edward S. Curtis, 1908), 170.

71. Kingsley M. Bray, "Making the Sichangu Hoop: Brule Tribal Organization, 1750–1804," in *Generous Man = Ahxsi-tapina: Essays in Memory of Colin Taylor, Plains Indian Ethnologist,* ed. Arni Brownstone and Hugh Dempsey (Tatanka Press, 2008), 153.

72. Annie Heloise Abel, ed., *Tabeau's Narrative of Loisel's Expedition to the Upper Missouri* (University of Oklahoma Press, 1939), 119–20.

73. Reuben Gold Thwaites, ed., *Original Journals of the Lewis and Clark Expedition, 1804–1806,* vol. 1 (Dodd, Mead, 1904), 46–47.

74. Milo M. Quaife, ed., *The Journals of Captain Meriwether Lewis and Sergeant John Ordway: Kept on the Expedition of Western Exploration, 1803–1806* (Wisconsin Historical Society, 1916), 85.

75. Brad Tennant, "Reading Between the Lines," *We Proceeded On* 35, no. 1 (January 2007): 7–8; Harry H. Anderson, "The Diplomacy of Lewis and Clark Among the Teton Sioux, 1804–1807," *South Dakota History* 35, no. 1 (Spring 2005): 40–70.

76. Quaife, *Journals of Captain Meriwether Lewis,* 119–23; Thwaites, *Original Journals of the Lewis and Clark Expedition,* 1:129–33; Doane Robinson, "Our First Family," *South Dakota Historical Collections* 13 (1926): 47–50.

77. Quaife, 121.

78. Quoted in Robinson, "Our First Family," 53.

79. Quaife, *Journals of Captain Meriwether Lewis,* 398–99; Reuben Gold Thwaites, ed., *Original Journals of the Lewis and Clark Expedition, 1804–1806,* vol. 5 (Dodd, Mead, 1905), 370–72, 383. See also Kingsley M. Bray, "'Singing the Big Belly Song': The Making of the Robe Trade Alliance with the Lakota," *Museum of the Fur Trade Quarterly* 43, nos. 3–4 (Fall–Winter 2007): 90–91.

80. Harry H. Anderson, ed., "Transcript of William Clark's Council with the Sioux, 22 May, 1807, Saint Louis, Missouri," *South Dakota History* 35, no. 1 (Spring 2005): 71–87; Bray, "'Singing the Big Belly Song,'" 90–91.

81. Gary Clayton Anderson, "American Agents vs. British Traders: Prelude to the War of 1812 in the Far West," in *The American West: Essays in Honor of W. Eugene Hollon,* ed. Ronald Lora (University of Toledo, 1980).

82. Frederick Bates to William Clark, December 1807, in *The Life and Papers of Frederick Bates,* vol. 1, ed. Thomas Maitland Marshall (Missouri Historical Society, 1926), 247–50.

83. William Clark to Henry Dearborn, June 1, 1807, in *The Territorial Papers of the United States,* vol. 14, *The Territory of Louisiana-Missouri, 1806–1814,* ed. Clarence Edwin Carter (Government Printing Office, 1949), 126–27; "The Story of Big White and His Trip to Washington," *South Dakotan* 6, no. 9 (January 1904):

9–14; Doane Robinson, "Lewis and Clark in South Dakota," *South Dakota Historical Collections* 9 (1918): 594–96; Hiram Martin Chittenden, *The American Fur Trade of the Far West,* vol. 1 (Francis P. Harper, 1902), 119–24.

84. Tracy Potter, *Sheheke, Mandan Indian Diplomat: The Story of White Coyote, Thomas Jefferson, and Lewis and Clark* (Farcountry Press, 2003), 139–44; Robinson, "Lewis and Clark in South Dakota," 594–96; Chittenden, *American Fur Trade,* 1:119–24.

85. Meriweather Lewis to Henry Dearborn, July 1, 1808, and William Eustis to William Clark, August 7, 1809, in Carter, *Territorial Papers of the United States,* 14:196–204, 289–90; William E. Foley and C. David Rice, *The First Chouteaus: River Barons of Early St. Louis* (University of Illinois Press, 2000), 125.

86. William Clark to Henry Dearborn, May 18, 1807, in Carter, *Territorial Papers of the United States,* 14:122–25.

87. Probate and Inventory of Pierre Dorion, 1810, Probate Case Files, St. Louis County, Missouri, roll 2, Missouri State Archives, Jefferson City, Mo.

88. Washington Irving, *Astoria, or Anecdotes of an Enterprise Beyond the Rocky Mountains,* vol. 1 (Carey, Lea, & Blanchard, 1836), 149–53; Chauncey Pratt Williams, "The Dorions" [Part 1], *Overland Monthly and Out West Magazine* 88, no. 4 (April 1930): 107–108; Chittenden, *American Fur Trade,* 1:182–99; Jean Barman, *French Canadians, Furs, and Indigenous Women in the Making of the Pacific Northwest* (UBC Press, 2014), 47–49.

89. Irving, *Astoria,* 1:149–53.

90. Irving, 1:149–53; Williams, "Dorions" [Part 1], 107–8; Robinson, "Our First Family," 56–57; Chittenden, *American Fur Trade,* 1:182–99.

91. Irving, *Astoria,* 1:149–53; John Bradbury, *Travels in the Interior of America, in the Years 1809, 1810, and 1811* (Sherwood, Neely, and Jones, 1817), 11–14; Chittenden, *American Fur Trade,* 1:182–99.

92. Irving, *Astoria,* 1:149–53; Bradbury, *Travels in the Interior of America,* 11–14; Williams, "Dorions" [Part 1], 107–8; Chittenden, *American Fur Trade,* 1:182–99; Barman, *French Canadians, Furs, and Indigenous Women,* 47–49.

93. Irving, *Astoria,* 1:149–53; Bradbury, *Travels in the Interior of America,* 11–14; Chittenden, *American Fur Trade,* 1:182–99.

94. Irving, *Astoria,* 1:160–61; Bradbury, *Travels in the Interior of America,* 43; Williams, "Dorions" [Part 1], 107–8; J. Neilson Barry, "Madame Dorion of the Astorians," *South Dakota Historical Collections* 17 (1934): 7–13; Chittenden, *American Fur Trade,* 1:182–99.

95. Henry M. Brackenridge, "Journal of a Voyage up the River Missouri," in *Early Western Travels, 1748–1846,* vol. 6, ed. Reuben Gold Thwaites (Arthur H. Clark, 1904).

96. Bradbury, *Travels in the Interior of America,* 102–3; Richard Edward Oglesby, *Manuel Lisa and the Opening of the Missouri Fur Trade* (University of Oklahoma Press, 1963), 107–13.

97. Irving, *Astoria,* 1:204–6; Bradbury, *Travels in the Interior of America,* 102–3; Brackenridge, "Journal of a Voyage up the River Missouri," 106–7; Williams, "Dorions" [Part 1], 127–28; Oglesby, *Manuel Lisa,* 107–13.

98. J. M. Bumsted, *Fur Trade Wars: The Founding of Western Canada* (Great Plains Publications, 1999).

99. Irving, *Astoria,* 1:234–35; Chauncey Pratt Williams, "The Dorions" [Part 2], *Overland Monthly and Out West Magazine* 88, no. 5 (May 1930): 137.

100. Podruchny, *Making the Voyageur World,* 25–26.

101. Washington Irving, *Astoria, or Anecdotes of an Enterprise Beyond the Rocky Mountains,* vol. 2 (Carey, Lea, & Blanchard, 1836), 38–39.

102. Katherine M. Weist, "Beasts of Burden and Menial Slaves: Nineteenth Century Observations of Northern Plains Indian Women," in *The Hidden Half: Studies of Plains Indian Women,* ed. Patricia Albers and Beatrice Medicine (University Press of America, 1983).

103. Hoyt C. Franchère, ed. and trans., *The Overland Diary of Wilson Price Hunt* (Oregon Book Society, 1973), 43.

104. Irving, *Astoria,* 2:47–49; Franchère, *Overland Diary of Wilson Price Hunt,* 48.

105. Irving, *Astoria,* 2:47–51.

106. Franchère, *Overland Diary of Wilson Price Hunt,* 52–53.

107. Irving, *Astoria,* 2:58–62.

108. Irving, 2:73; Franchère, *Overland Diary of Wilson Price Hunt,* 59.

109. Robert F. Jones, ed., *Annals of Astoria: The Headquarters Log of the Pacific Fur Company on the Columbia River, 1811–1813* (Fordham University Press, 1999), 92–93.

110. Jones, *Annals of Astoria,* 102.

111. Jones; Melinda Marie Jetté, *At the Heart of the Crossed Races: A French-Indian Community in Nineteenth-Century Oregon, 1812–1859* (Oregon State University Press, 2015), 12–41.

112. Alexander Ross, *Adventures of the First Settlers on the Oregon or Columbia River: Being a Narrative of the Expedition Fitted Out by John Jacob Astor, to Establish the "Pacific Fur Company"* (Smith, Elder, 1849), 276–82; Gabriel Franchère, "Franchère's Narrative of a Voyage to the Northwest Coast, 1811–1814," in *Early Western Travels, 1748–1846,* vol. 6, ed. Reuben Gold Thwaites (Arthur H. Clark, 1904); Irving, *Astoria,* 2:253–57.

113. Ross, *Adventures of the First Settlers,* 276–82; Franchère, "Franchère's Narrative," 342–44; Irving, *Astoria,* 2:253–57; Williams, "Dorions" [Part 2], 144.

114. Ross, *Adventures of the First Settlers,* 276–82; Franchère, "Franchère's Narrative," 342–44; Irving, *Astoria,* 253–57.

115. Franchère, "Franchère's Narrative," 342–44; Robinson, "Our First Family," 63–67; Barman, *French Canadians, Furs, and Indigenous Women,* 123–25.

116. For more on Marie's later life, see J. Neilson Barry, "Astorians Who Became Permanent Settlers," *Washington Historical Quarterly* 24, no. 3 (July 1933): 229; Jerome Peltier, *Madame Dorion* (Ye Galleon Press, 1980); Barry, "Madame Dorion of the Astorians," 7–13.

117. Elliott Coues, ed., *The Manuscript Journals of Alexander Henry, Fur Trader of the Northwest Company, and of David Thompson, Official Geographer and Explorer of the Same Company, 1799–1814,* vol. 1, *The Red River of the North* (Francis P. Harper, 1897), 245.

118. "Talk of Big Elk to Governor Clark," *Missouri Gazette and Public Advertiser* (St. Louis, Mo.), August 5, 1815.

2. The Creation of "Half-Breed" as a Legal Concept

1. Treaty with the Sauk and Foxes, 1824, in *Indian Affairs: Laws and Treaties,* vol. 2, *Treaties,* ed. Charles J. Kappler (Government Printing Office, 1904), 207–8.

2. B. L. Wick, "Struggle for the Half-Breed Tract," *Annals of Iowa* 7 (April 1905): 16–29; Jacob Van der Zee, "The Half-Breed Tract," *Iowa Journal of History and Politics* 13 (April 1915): 151–64; Isaac Galland, "Dr. Galland's Account of the Half-Breed Tract," *Annals of Iowa* 10 (July 1912): 450–66.

3. Isaac Galland, "Claimants of the Sac and Fox Half Breed Reservation," undated, Robert Lucas papers, State Historical Society of Iowa, Iowa City.

4. E. D. Neill, "A Sketch of Joseph Renville, a 'Bois Brule,' and Early Trader of Minnesota," *Collections of the Minnesota Historical Society* 1 ([1853] repr. 1902): 158.

5. A. B. Wilkinson, *Blurring the Lines of Race and Freedom: Mulattoes and Mixed Bloods in English Colonial America* (University of North Carolina Press, 2020); Paul Spruhan, "A Legal History of Blood Quantum in Federal Indian Law to 1935," *South Dakota Law Review* 51 (2006): 1–50.

6. Ariela J. Gross, *What Blood Won't Tell: A History of Race on Trial in America* (Harvard University Press, 2008); Deborah A. Rosen, *American Indians and State Law: Sovereignty, Race, and Citizenship, 1790–1880* (University of Nebraska Press, 2007); Stephen Middleton, *The Black Laws: Race and the Legal Process in Early Ohio* (Ohio University Press, 2005); Ann McGrath, *Illicit Love: Interracial Sex and Marriage in the United States and Australia* (University of Nebraska Press, 2015); Werner Sollors, ed., *Interracialism: Black-White Intermarriage in American History, Literature, and Law* (Oxford University Press, 2000).

7. "To Captain Hendrick, the Delawares, Mohicans, and Munries, December 21, 1808," in *Letters and Addresses of Thomas Jefferson,* ed. William B. Parker and Jonas Viles (Unit Book Publishing, 1905), 190.

8. Charles J. Kappler, ed., *Indian Affairs: Laws and Treaties,* vol. 2, *Treaties* (Government Printing Office, 1904), 148.

9. Kappler, *Indian Affairs,* 2:173.

10. Kappler, 2:218–19.

11. Kappler, 2:269.

12. Kappler, 2:147.

13. Kappler, 2:347.

14. Quoted in Tanis C. Thorne, *The Many Hands of My Relations: French and Indians on the Lower Missouri* (University of Missouri Press, 1996), 135. For more on mixed-ancestry Indians as an assimilative influence, see Kristen Tegtmeier Oertel, *Bleeding Borders: Race, Gender and Violence in Pre-Civil War Kansas* (Louisiana State University Press, 2009), 27–28.

15. Ratified Treaty No. 126, Documents Relating to the Negotiation of the Treaty of June 2, 1825, with the Osage Indians, Documents Relating to the Negotiation of Ratified and Unratified Treaties with Various Indian Tribes, 1801-1869, T494, Records of the Bureau of Indian Affairs, RG 75, National Archives, Washington, D.C.

16. John W. Johnson to Commissioner of Indian Affairs, March 21, 1826, Letters Received by the Office of Indian Affairs, 1824–1881, M234, Sac and Fox Agency, microfilm reel 728, National Archives, Washington, D.C. (hereafter LROIA).

17. James D. Doty to John Bell, August 4, 1841, LROIA, St. Peter's Agency, reel 759.

18. D. D. Mitchell to Luke Lea, *Annual Report of the Commissioner of Indian Affairs* (Office of the Commissioner of Indian Affairs, 1852), 325–26; John J. Killoren, *"Come, Blackrobe": De Smet and the Indian Tragedy* (University of Oklahoma Press, 1994), 168–70.

19. D. D. Mitchell to Luke Lea, *Annual Report of the Commissioner of Indian Affairs,* 325–26.

20. D. D. Mitchell to Luke Lea, October 25, 1851, *Annual Report of the Commissioner of Indian Affairs* (Gideon & Co., 1851), 64.

21. Quoted in R. W. Haskins, *History and Progress of Phrenology* (Steele & Peck, 1839), 110–11. See also Josiah C. Nott, *Two Lectures, on the Natural History of the Caucasian and Negro Races* (Dade and Thompson, 1844), 38.

22. Alexander Berghold, *The Indians' Revenge, or Days of Horror: Some Appalling Events in the History of the Sioux* (P. J. Thomas, 1891), 69. See also Abigail Gardiner, *History of the Spirit Lake Massacre! And of Miss Abigail Gardiner's Three*

Months' Captivity Among the Indians According to Her Own Account (L. P. Lee, 1857), 13.

23. Alfred Brunson to Arnold Plumer, June 14, 1838, in *The Territorial Papers of the United States,* vol. 27, *The Territory of Wisconsin, Executive Journal, 1836–1848, Papers, 1836–1839,* ed. John Porter Bloom (Government Printing Office, 1969), 1033–34.

24. William Davenport to T. Cross, August 31, 1838, in Bloom, *Territorial Papers of the United States,* 27:1061–62.

25. Frederick Marryat, "Captain Marryat in Minnesota, 1838," *Minnesota History* 6, no. 2 (June 1925): 175.

26. Elizabeth Thérèse Baird, "Reminiscences of Life in Territorial Wisconsin," *Collections of the State Historical Society of Wisconsin* 15 (1900): 213.

27. Elisha Dorian, "Early Indian History," in *History of Richardson County Nebraska: Its People, Industries and Institutions,* vol. 1, ed. Lewis C. Edwards (B. F. Bowen, 1917), 731.

28. Keith R. Widder, *Battle for the Soul: Métis Children Encounter Evangelical Protestants at Mackinaw Mission, 1823–1837* (Michigan State University Press, 1999), 107. For more on early schools and education of Indian children in the region, see Thomas S. Williamson, "Earliest Schools in Minnesota Valley," *Collections of the Minnesota Historical Society* 6 (1894): 410–12.

29. Caleb Atwater, *Remarks on a Tour to Prairie du Chien; Thence to Washington City, in 1829* (Isaac N. Whiting, 1831), 114–15.

30. Census of Mixed-Ancestry Dakota Indians, 1838, Special Files of the Office of Indian Affairs, 1807–1904, microfilm, M574, reel 59, file 200, Claims Filed Under the Treaty of September 29, 1837, with the Sioux of the Mississippi, 1838, National Archives, Washington, D.C.

31. 1850 U.S. Federal Census, District No. 1, Dubuque County, Iowa.

32. Nancy Huggan, "The Story of Nancy McClure: Captivity Among the Sioux," *Collections of the Minnesota Historical Society* 6 (1894): 443.

33. Huggan, "Story of Nancy McClure," 445.

34. Waldron v. United States et al., 143 F. 413 (Circuit Court, D. South Dakota, July 1, 1905).

35. William D. Green, "Race and Segregation in St. Paul's Public Schools, 1846–69," *Minnesota History* 55, no. 4 (Winter 1996–1997): 138–49.

36. File 851, Ellen Brown, box 1724, and file 213, Antoine Frenier, box 1713, entry 525, Indian Accounts, Records of the Accounting Officers of the Department of the Treasury, RG 217, National Archives, Washington, D.C.

37. Petition of Mixed-Ancestry Dakota to Governor Willis Gorman, Redwood Agency, November 4, 1853, entry 529, Miscellaneous Reserve Papers, 1825–1907,

box 360, Records of the Bureau of Indian Affairs, RG 75, National Archives, Washington, D.C.

38. Quoted in Robert Joseph Keckeisen, "The Kansas 'Half-Breed' Lands: Contravention and Transformation of United States Indian Policy in Kansas" (master's thesis, Wichita State University, 1977), 8.

39. Royal B. Hassrick, *The Sioux: Life and Customs of a Warrior Society* (University of Oklahoma Press, 1964), 36–38, 296–302.

40. Quoted in Charles E. Hoffhaus, *Chez Les Canses: Three Centuries at Kawsmouth; The French Foundations of Metropolitan Kansas City* (Lowell Press, 1984), 149.

41. Deed, Augustin Rock to Francois LaBathe, June 7, 1837, book D, Register of Deeds Records, Crawford County, Wisconsin, microfilm reel 1, Wisconsin Historical Society, Madison.

42. Deed, William Laidlaw and Mary Ann Laidlaw to William Dawson, October 10, 1838, Clay County, Missouri Deeds, book F, microfilm reel 4, Family History Library, Salt Lake City, Utah.

43. Deed, William Laidlaw and Mary Ann Laidlaw to Moore K. Lurtey, October 28, 1844, Clay County, Missouri Deeds, book I, microfilm reel 5, Family History Library, Salt Lake City, Utah.

44. 1840 U.S. Federal Census for Clay County, Missouri, and 1850 U.S. Federal Census Slave Schedule for Washington Township, Clay County, Missouri.

45. 1850 U.S. Federal Census Slave Schedule for Washington Township, Clay County, Missouri.

46. Deeds, William Laidlaw to Mary Laidlaw, and William Laidlaw to Elizabeth Laidlaw Wallis, September 4, 1848, Clay County, Missouri Deeds, book M, microfilm reel 6, Family History Library, Salt Lake City, Utah.

47. Deeds, William Laidlaw to Jane Laidlaw, and William Laidlaw to Julia Laidlaw, September 4, 1848, Clay County, Missouri Deeds, book N, microfilm reel 6, Family History Library, Salt Lake City, Utah.

48. Rather than as a result of a decline in fur-bearing animals, Rhoda R. Gilman argues that the fur trade collapsed as a result of a decline of Indian laborers in the trade, who were increasingly confined to reservations and ceded their hunting lands. See Rhoda R. Gilman, "Last Days of the Upper Mississippi Fur Trade," *Minnesota History* 42, no. 4 (Winter 1970): 122–40.

49. Lesley Wischmann and Andrew Erskine Dawson, *This Far-Off Wild Land: The Upper Missouri Letters of Andrew Dawson* (Arthur H. Clark, 2013), 65–69.

50. Mortgage, William Laidlaw to Elizabeth Wallis, June 22, 1850, Clay County, Missouri Deeds, book L, microfilm reel 5, Family History Library, Salt Lake City, Utah.

51. Mortgage, William Laidlaw to Michael Arthur, Madison Miller, Greenup Bird, and Darius Gittings, August 22, 1850, and Mortgage, William Laidlaw to Calvin B. Hodges, August 21, 1850, Clay County, Missouri Deeds, book L, microfilm reel 5, Family History Library, Salt Lake City, Utah.

52. Power of Attorney, Moore K. Lurtey and Mary Lurtey to Henry E. Vanosdell, April 10, 1850, Clay County, Missouri Deeds, book M, microfilm reel 6, Family History Library, Salt Lake City, Utah.

53. Power of Attorney, Moore K. Lurtey and Mary Lurtey to Henry E. Vanosdell, April 10, 1850, Clay County, Missouri Deeds, book M, microfilm reel 6, Family History Library, Salt Lake City, Utah.

54. Quit Claim Deeds, Mary Ann Laidlaw to L. W. Leavell and Mary Ann Laidlaw to Nairy Cave, October 3, 1853, Clay County, Missouri Deeds, book N, microfilm reel 6, Family History Library, Salt Lake City, Utah.

55. Deed, Mary Ann Laidlaw to Joseph A. Sire, November 3, 1853, Clay County, Missouri Deeds, book O, microfilm reel 7, Family History Library, Salt Lake City, Utah.

56. Deed, Robert G. Gilmer, Hugh J. Robertson, and Elizabeth C. Robertson to Mary Ann Laidlaw, February 10, 1854, Clay County, Missouri Deeds, book N, microfilm reel 6, Family History Library, Salt Lake City, Utah.

57. Deed, Mary Ann Laidlaw to Robert G. Gilmer, April 27, 1868, Clay County, Missouri Deeds, book 29, microfilm reel 14, Family History Library, Salt Lake City, Utah.

58. Probate of William Laidlaw Sr., 1851, Clay County, Missouri Probate Case Files, microfilm reel 19, Family History Library, Salt Lake City, Utah.

59. Probate of William Laidlaw Jr., 1859, Clay County, Missouri Probate Case Files, microfilm reel 19, Family History Library, Salt Lake City, Utah.

60. For more on the legal realm of marriage in the United States, see Hendrik Hartog, *Man and Wife in America: A History* (Harvard University Press, 2000).

61. Elizabeth Wallis vs. William Wallis and Mary Lurty vs. Moore K. Lurty, Clay County, Missouri Circuit Court Records, microfilm reel 46, Family History Library, Salt Lake City, Utah.

62. Toby L. Ditz argues that the importance of kinship in white American society has been overlooked because of the influence of the myth of American exceptionalism through "rugged individualism." Toby L. Ditz, *Property and Kinship: Inheritance in Early Connecticut, 1750–1820* (Princeton University Press, 1986).

63. B. B. Paddock, *History and Biographical Record of North and West Texas*, vol. 2 (Lewis Publishing, 1906), 165–66.

64. Power of Attorney, Pierre, Louis, and Martin Dorion to Pierre Chouteau, December 9, 1808; Power of Attorney, John Baptiste Dorion to Pierre Chouteau, July 14, 1808, St. Louis, Missouri Deeds, book B, microfilm reel 179, Family History

Library, Salt Lake City, Utah; Power of Attorney, Louis Dorion to Peter Chouteau, May 12, 1809, St. Louis Deeds, book B, microfilm reel 179, Family History Library, Salt Lake City, Utah; Power of Attorney, Jean Baptiste Dorion to Pierre Chouteau, May 12, 1809, St. Louis Deeds, book B, microfilm reel 179, Family History Library, Salt Lake City, Utah.

65. John Dougherty to William Clark, July 4, 1836, LROIA, Council Bluffs Agency, reel 215.

66. John Dougherty to William Clark, July 4, 1836, LROIA, Council Bluffs Agency, reel 215.

67. William Clark to Elbert Herring, July 18, 1836, and John Dougherty to William Clark, July 4, 1836, LROIA, Council Bluffs Agency, reel 215.

68. "Names of a Deputation of Indians of the Council Bluffs Agency on a Visit to Washington," 1837, LROIA, Council Bluffs Agency, reel 215.

69. Alan R. Woolworth, *Ethnohistorical Report on the Yankton Sioux* (Garland, 1974), 57.

70. Dorian, "Early Indian History," 731–33.

71. Joshua Pilcher to Elbert Herring, July 1, 1835, and William Clark to Elbert Herring, August 1, 1835, LROIA, Upper Missouri Agency, reel 883.

72. Joshua Pilcher to William Clark, July 1, 1835, LROIA, Upper Missouri Agency, reel 883.

73. John E. Sunder, *Joshua Pilcher: Fur Trader and Indian Agent* (University of Oklahoma Press, 1968), 113–16.

74. See Treaty with the Teton, 1815, Treaty with the Sioux of the Lakes, 1815, Treaty with the Sioux of St. Peter's River, 1815, Treaty with the Yankton Sioux, 1815, Treaty with the Iowa, 1815, and Treaty with the Mahah, 1815, in Kappler, *Indian Affairs,* 2:112–56

75. Treaty with the Teton, Etc., Sioux, 1825, and Treaty with the Oto, Etc., 1836, in Kappler, *Indian Affairs,* 2:227–30, 479–81.

76. Vine Deloria Jr., *Custer Died for Your Sins: An Indian Manifesto* (University of Oklahoma Press, 1988), 46.

77. Berlin Basil Chapman, *The Otoes and Missourias: A Study of Indian Removal and the Legal Aftermath* (Times Journal, 1965), 21.

78. Gwen Westerman and Bruce White, *Mni Sota Makoce: The Land of the Dakota* (Minnesota Historical Society Press, 2012), 149.

79. Westerman and White, *Mni Sota Makoce,* 152.

80. Kappler, *Indian Affairs,* 2:305–10.

81. Roy W. Meyer, *History of the Santee Sioux: United States Indian Policy on Trial* (University of Nebraska Press, 1980), 51.

82. John Connolly to Lewis Cass, November 1, 1831, U.S. Congress, *Correspondence on the Subject of the Emigration of Indians, Between the 30th November,*

1831, and 27th December, 1833, with Abstracts of Expenditures by Disbursing Agents, in the Removal and Subsistence of Indians, 23rd Cong., 1st Sess., S.Doc.512, pt. 2, 639.

83. Kappler, *Indian Affairs,* 2:307.

84. Kappler, 2:307.

85. Entry 402, List of Allotted and Unallotted Mixed-Bloods, RG 75, National Archives; entry 378, Sioux Half Breed Census, 1856, RG 75, National Archives, Washington, D.C.

86. Westerman and White, *Mni Sota Makoce,* 154–55.

87. Kappler, *Indian Affairs,* 2:305–10.

88. Margaret Hess to Lawrence Taliaferro, September 28, 1836, Lawrence Taliaferro papers, microfilm reel 1, Minnesota Historical Society, Saint Paul (hereafter MHS).

89. List of claimants, 1838, Special Files of the Office of Indian Affairs, 1807–1904, RG 75, M574, reel 59, file 200, National Archives, Washington, D.C.

90. Entry for September 19, 1823, Taliaferro journals vol. 7, Lawrence Taliaferro papers, MHS.

91. Lizzie Ehrenhalt, "'The Most Satisfactory Proof': Revising an Anglo-Dakota Family History," *Minnesota History* 63, no. 4 (Winter 2012–2013): 146.

92. Margaret Hess to Lawrence Taliaferro, September 28, 1836, Lawrence Taliaferro papers, reel 1, MHS.

93. Ehrenhalt, "'Most Satisfactory Proof,'" 148.

94. Kappler, *Indian Affairs,* 2:411.

3. The Economics of Racial Mixedness and Kinship

1. The treaty had broader significance as a point of contention between the Dakota people and Christian missionaries. See Linda M. Clemmons, *Conflicted Mission: Faith, Disputes, and Deception on the Dakota Frontier* (Minnesota Historical Society Press, 2014).

2. Some scholars do argue for the existence of commodification of Indianness by Euro-Americans, such as George Pierre Castile, "The Commodification of Indian Identity," *American Anthropologist* 98, no. 4 (December 1996): 743–49.

3. Nancy Leong, "Racial Capitalism," *Harvard Law Review* 126, no. 8 (June 2013): 2151–226; Cedric J. Robinson, *Black Marxism: The Making of the Black Radical Tradition,* 3rd ed. (University of North Carolina Press, 2020); Destin Jenkins and Justin Leroy, eds., *Histories of Racial Capitalism* (Columbia University Press, 2021); Susan Koshy, Lisa Marie Cacho, Jodi A. Byrd, and Brian Jordan Jefferson, eds., *Colonial Racial Capitalism* (Duke University Press, 2022).

4. Lance Greene and Mark R. Plane, eds., *American Indians and the Market Economy, 1775–1850* (University of Alabama Press, 2010); Brian C. Hosmer,

American Indians in the Marketplace: Persistence and Innovation Among the Menominees and Metlakatlans, 1870–1920 (University of Kansas Press, 1999).

5. Brian Gettler, *Colonialism's Currency: Money, State, and First Nations in Canada, 1820–1950* (McGill-Queen's University Press, 2020).

6. Ned Blackhawk, *The Rediscovery of America: Native Peoples and the Unmaking of U.S. History* (Yale University Press, 2023), 182–98.

7. Entry of October 9, 1819, Journal of Transactions in the Sioux District by John Bourke, 1819–1820, vol. 1, Hudson's Bay Company Archives, Winnipeg, Manitoba (hereafter HBC).

8. Thomas G. Anderson, "Personal Narrative of Capt. Thomas G. Anderson," *Report and Collections of the State Historical Society of Wisconsin* 9 (1882): 160–65, 179, 192.

9. Entries of October 27, 1820, and March 20, 1821, Upper Red River Journal Commencing September 23rd 1820 & Ending 31 May 1821, J. P. Bourke, vol. 2, HBC.

10. Entry of October 31, 1820, Upper Red River Journal Commencing September 23rd 1820 & Ending 31 May 1821, J. P. Bourke, vol. 2, HBC.

11. Entry of March 20, 1821, Upper Red River Journal Commencing September 23rd 1820 & Ending 31 May 1821, J. P. Bourke, vol. 2, HBC.

12. Entry of April 23, 1821, Upper Red River Journal Commencing September 23rd 1820 & Ending 31 May 1821, J. P. Bourke, vol. 2, HBC.

13. Entry of November 2, 1820, Upper Red River Journal Commencing September 23rd 1820 & Ending 31 May 1821, J. P. Bourke, vol. 2, HBC.

14. Entry of November 13, 1820, Upper Red River Journal Commencing September 23rd 1820 & Ending 31 May 1821, J. P. Bourke, vol. 2, HBC.

15. Entry of February 4, 1820, Journal of Transactions in the Sioux District by John Bourke, 1819–1820, vol. 1, HBC.

16. Mary K. Whelan, "Dakota Indian Economics and the Nineteenth-Century Fur Trade," *Ethnohistory* 40, no. 2 (Spring 1993): 252–57.

17. Grace Lee Knute, "Hudson's Bay Company Posts in the Minnesota Country," *Minnesota History* (September 1941): 282–83.

18. Deposition of Henry H. Sibley, December 11, 1841, Miscellaneous Records, Depositions Taken in Disputed Election, 1841, in *Minnesota Beginnings: Records of St. Croix County Wisconsin Territory, 1840–1849*, by History Network of Washington County (Washington County Historical Society, 1999).

19. Sioux Outfit Account, August 10, 1835, Henry H. Sibley papers, microfilm reel 1, Minnesota Historical Society, Saint Paul (hereafter MHS); Balance Sheet, Sioux Outfit, 1852, Henry H. Sibley papers, reel 9, MHS; Henry H. Sibley, Agt. Sioux Outfit v. Francois Trudell, 1841, in History Network of Washington County, *Minnesota Beginnings*.

20. See the voyageur database entry for Francois Prince Dt Trudelle at the Centre du patrimoine, https://archivesshsb.mb.ca/link/voyageurs25356. The coincidence of the similarity in names and time of contract makes it highly likely that this is indeed the same person.

21. "Old Fur Traders," *Wabasha Weekly Herald* (Wabasha, Minn.), August 22, 1867.

22. Rhoda R. Gilman, "Last Days of the Upper Mississippi Fur Trade," *Minnesota History* 42, no. 4 (Winter 1970): 123–24, 138–39; Whelan, "Dakota Indian Economics," 269–71.

23. Gilman, "Last Days of the Upper Mississippi Fur Trade," 123–24.

24. Richmond Clow, "Bison Ecology: Brulé and Yankton Winter Hunting, and the Starving Winter of 1832–33," *Great Plains Quarterly* 15, no. 4 (Fall 1995): 259–70; Alan R. Woolworth and Nancy L. Woolworth, "Eastern Dakota Settlement and Subsistence Patterns Prior to 1851," *Minnesota Archaeologist* 39 (1980): 70–89; Jeffrey Ostler, "'They Regard Their Passing as Wakan': Interpreting Western Sioux Explanations for the Bison's Decline," *Western Historical Quarterly* 30, no. 4 (Winter 1999): 475–97.

25. Kathleen Pickering, "Articulation of the Lakota Mode of Production and the Euro-American Fur Trade," in *The Fur Trade Revisited: Selected Papers of the Sixth North American Fur Trade Conference, Mackinac Island, Michigan, 1991,* ed. Jennifer S. H. Brown, W. J. Eccles, and Donald P. Heldman (Michigan State University Press, 1994).

26. Henry H. Sibley papers, microfilm reel 19, vol. 25, September 15, 1838, MHS.

27. Ledger, vol. 52, 1834, Alexis Bailly papers, box 2, MHS.

28. Henry H. Sibley papers, microfilm reel 19, vol. 27, October 15, 1838, MHS.

29. Account Book, 1843–1844, vol. 61, Alexis Bailly papers, box 2, MHS.

30. Account Book, 1843–1844, vol. 61, Alexis Bailly papers, box 2, MHS.

31. Henry H. Sibley papers, microfilm reel 18, vol. 22, 1852, MHS.

32. Indian Credit Book, 1844–1845, vol. 39, Alexis Bailly papers, box 3, MHS.

33. Account Book, 1843–1844, vol. 61, Alexis Bailly papers, box 2, MHS.

34. Pay Voucher to Francis Trudelle, May 20, 1857, Charles Eugene Flandrau and family papers, box 1, MHS.

35. 1857 Minnesota Territorial Census, Red Wing, Goodhue County, October 26, 1857, microfilm reel 2, T1175, National Archives, Washington, D.C.

36. 1860 U.S. Federal Census, Hastings, Dakota County, Minnesota, July 16, 1860.

37. Civil War Service Record of Francis Trudell, Co. K, 9th Minnesota Infantry, RG 94, National Archives, Washington, D.C.

38. Affidavit of Charles Mitchell, April 27, 1892, Civil War Pension Record of Francis Trudell, Co. K, 9th Minnesota Infantry, RG 15, National Archives, Washington, D.C.

39. Dorothy Eaton Ahlgren and Mary Cotter Beeler, *A History of Prescott, Wisconsin: A River City and Farming Community on the St. Croix and Mississippi* (Prescott Area Historical Society, 1996), 21.

40. Chantal Norrgard, *Seasons of Change: Labor, Treaty Rights, and Ojibwe Nationhood* (University of North Carolina Press, 2014), 2.

41. 1854 Mdewakanton Dakota Annuity Roll, Sioux #1 Various Bands, entry 906, Annuity Payment Rolls, 1841–1949, RG 75, National Archives, Washington, D.C.

42. Charles J. Kappler, *Indian Affairs: Laws and Treaties,* vol. 2, *Treaties* (Government Printing Office, 1904), 493–94.

43. William Davenport to T. Cross, August 31, 1838, in *The Territorial Papers of the United States,* vol. 27, *The Territory of Wisconsin, Executive Journal, 1836–1848, Papers, 1836–1839,* ed. John Porter Bloom (Government Printing Office, 1969), 1061–62.

44. Alfred Brunson to Arnold Plumer, June 14, 1838, in Bloom, *Territorial Papers of the United States,* 27:1033–34; Alfred Brunson to James Duane Doty, January 6, 1843, Letterbook, 1835–1842, Alfred Brunson papers, box 1, Wisconsin Historical Society, Madison (hereafter WHS).

45. Affidavit of Frank Trudell, July 28, 1897, Civil War Pension Record of Joseph Young, RG 15, National Archives, Washington, D.C.

46. Lawrence Taliaferro to Henry Dodge, August 21, 1837, Letters Received by the Office of Indian Affairs, 1824–1881, St. Peter's Agency, M234, reel 758, RG 75, National Archives, Washington, D.C. (hereafter LROIA).

47. Alfred Brunson to James Duane Doty, January 6, 1843, Letterbook, 1835–1842, Alfred Brunson papers, box 1, WHS.

48. Robert Stuart to Alfred Brunson, March 10, 1843, Letterbook, 1835–1842, Alfred Brunson papers, box 1, WHS.

49. Robert Stuart to T. Hartley Crawford, March 15, 1843, Letterbook, 1842–1844, Alfred Brunson papers, box 2, WHS.

50. Statement of Chief Buffalo, January 5, 1843, enclosure in Alfred Brunson to James Duane Doty, January 6, 1843, Letterbook, 1835–1842, Alfred Brunson papers, box 1, WHS.

51. Statement of Chief Martin, December 18, 1842, enclosure in Alfred Brunson to James Duane Doty, January 6, 1843, Letterbook, 1835–1842, Alfred Brunson papers, box 1, WHS.

52. Kappler, *Indian Affairs,* 2:452.

53. Kappler, 2:452.

54. Kappler, 2:464–65.

55. Roy Meyer, *History of the Santee Sioux: United States Indian Policy on Trial* (University of Nebraska Press, 1993), 56–60.

56. There is no indication in the historical record why the church was chosen for the negotiation site. For more on the negotiations, see Chad Delano Ronnander, "Many Paths to the Pine: Mdewakanton Dakotas, Fur Traders, Ojibwes, and the United States in Wisconsin's Chippewa Valley, 1815–1837" (PhD diss., University of Minnesota, 2003), 284–349.

57. Ratified Treaty No. 224, Documents Relating to the Negotiation of the Treaty of September 29, 1837, with the Sioux of the Mississippi Indians, Documents Relating to the Negotiation of Ratified and Unratified Treaties with Various Indian Tribes, 1801–1869, T494, Records of the Bureau of Indian Affairs, RG 75, National Archives, Washington, D.C. (hereafter Treaty Files).

58. Lawrence Taliaferro to Henry Dodge, August 21, 1837, LROIA, St. Peter's Agency, reel 758.

59. Dakota Chiefs to Joel R. Poinsett, September 1837, LROIA, St. Peter's Agency, reel 758.

60. "Indian Council," *Daily National Intelligencer* (Washington, D.C.), September 26, 1837.

61. Ratified Treaty No. 224.

62. "Indian Council," *Daily National Intelligencer* (Washington, D.C.), September 29, 1837.

63. See Special Files of the Office of Indian Affairs, 1807–1904, M574, reel 59, file 200, Claims Filed Under the Treaty of September 29, 1837, with the Sioux of the Mississippi, 1838, National Archives, Washington, D.C. (hereafter SFOIA).

64. Ratified Treaty No. 224.

65. Ratified Treaty No. 224.

66. Lawrence Taliaferro, "Auto-Biography of Maj. Lawrence Taliaferro," *Collections of the Minnesota Historical Society* 6 (1894): 223–24.

67. Statement of Dakota Chiefs, January 10, 1837, LROIA, St. Peter's Agency, reel 758.

68. Kappler, *Indian Affairs,* 2:493–94.

69. "Indian Council," *Daily National Intelligencer* (Washington, D.C.), September 30, 1837.

70. Lucius Lyon to T. Hartley Crawford, December 16, 1839, in *The Territorial Papers of the United States,* vol. 28, *The Territory of Wisconsin, 1839–1848,* ed. John Porter Bloom (Government Printing Office, 1975), 94.

71. Pease and Ewing to Carey Harris, November 5, 1838, SFOIA.

72. Ida M. Street, "The Simon Cameron Indian Commission of 1838," *Annals of Iowa* 7, no. 2 (July 1905): 115–39; Taliaferro, "Auto-Biography of Maj. Lawrence Taliaferro," 231–32.

73. Lawrence Taliaferro journals, vol. 15, MHS.

74. Lorraine T. Pease and William L. D. Ewing, Register of Claims, September 19, 1838, SFOIA. For more on similar payments to other tribes, see Theresa M. Schenck, *All Our Relations: Chippewa Mixed-Bloods and the Treaty of 1837* (Centre for Rupert's Land Studies, 2010); Linda M. Waggoner, ed., *"Neither White Men nor Indians": Affidavits from the Winnebago Mixed-Blood Claim Commissions, Prairie du Chien, Wisconsin, 1838–1839* (Park Genealogical Books, 2002).

75. Lorraine T. Pease and William L. D. Ewing, Register of Claims, September 19, 1838, SFOIA.

76. Pease and Ewing.

77. Pease and Ewing.

78. Pease and Ewing.

79. Pease and Ewing.

80. Pease and Ewing.

81. Linda M. Waggoner, "Sibley's Winnebago Prisoners: Deconstructing Race and Recovering Kinship in the Dakota War of 1862," *Great Plains Quarterly* 33, no. 1 (Winter 2013): 27.

82. Pelagie LaChapelle affidavit, August 28, 1837, September 19, 1838, SFOIA.

83. Pelagie LaChapelle affidavit and Francois Labathe affidavit, August 17, 1838, SFOIA.

84. Affidavit of Pelagie Farrebault, September 1, 1838, SFOIA.

85. Alexis Bailly affidavit, September 3, 1838, SFOIA.

86. Madeline Campbell affidavit, SFOIA.

87. Mr. Quin affidavit, SFOIA.

88. Lawrence Taliaferro affidavit, SFOIA.

89. Pease and Ewing.

90. Mary Woodbury and Elizabeth Odell (to Accompany Bill H.R. No. 451), 31st Cong., 2nd Sess., 1851, H.R. Rep. No. 19, serial 606; Elizabeth Odell, Mary Woodbury, and Others (to Accompany Bill H.R. No. 276), 37th Cong., 2nd Sess., 1862, H.R. Rep. 27, serial 1144.

91. Catherine Denial, "Pelagie Faribault's Island: Property, Kinship, and the Meaning of Marriage in Dakota Country," *Minnesota History* 62 (Summer 2010): 48–59.

92. See Jeanne Boydston, *Home and Work: Housework, Wages, and the Ideology of Labor in the Early Republic* (Oxford University Press, 1994).

93. Pease and Ewing.

94. Lorraine T. Pease and William L. D. Ewing, Roll of Claimants Under the Third Clause of the Second Article of the Treaty of the 29th Sept 1837 with the Sioux Indians, SFOIA.

95. Kappler, *Indian Affairs,* 2:778–79.

96. Alexander Redfield to Alfred Greenwood, February 20, 1860, LROIA, Yankton Agency, reel 959.

97. Minutes of a Council Held at Yancton Agency, February 4, 1860, LROIA, Yankton Agency, reel 959.

4. An Unintended Nation

1. Treaty with the Half Breeds of the Dakota or Sioux Nation, July 31, 1841, Letters Received by the Office of Indian Affairs 1824–1881, M234, St. Peters Agency, reel 759, National Archives, Washington, D.C. (hereafter LROIA); Vine Deloria Jr. and Raymond J. DeMallie, eds., *Documents of American Indian Diplomacy: Treaties, Agreements, and Conventions, 1775–1979,* vol. 2 (University of Oklahoma Press, 1999), 787–90.

2. See Vine Deloria Jr. and Clifford M. Lytle, *The Nations Within: The Past and Future of American Indian Sovereignty* (Pantheon Books, 1984).

3. See William E. Unrau, *The Rise and Fall of Indian Country, 1825–1855* (University Press of Kansas, 2007).

4. David E. Wilkins, *American Indian Politics and the American Political System* (Rowman & Littlefield, 2002), 338.

5. Edward H. Spicer, "The Nations of a State," in *American Indian Persistence and Resurgence,* ed. Karl Kroeber (Duke University Press, 1994), 32.

6. Chris Andersen, *"Métis": Race, Recognition, and the Struggle for Indigenous Peoplehood* (UBC Press, 2014), 15–19.

7. Sami Lakomäki, *Gathering Together: The Shawnee People Through Diaspora and Nationhood, 1600–1870* (Yale University Press, 2014), 8.

8. Ella Cara Deloria, *The Dakota Way of Life,* ed. Raymond J. DeMallie and Theirry Veyrié (University of Nebraska Press, 2022), 1.

9. For small-scale Dakota political units exercising political autonomy or a kind of nationhood, see "Convention with the Sioux of Wa-ba-shaw's Tribe," in *Indian Affairs: Laws and Treaties,* vol. 2, *Treaties,* ed. Charles J. Kappler (Government Printing Office, 1904), 466–67; also see the various treaties of 1865 with various bands of the Thíthuŋwaŋ or Lakota and Iháŋkthuŋwaŋna in the same volume, 896–908.

10. The political organization of the Dakota tribes has received significantly less scholarly attention than that of the Lakota. For a deeper dive into Lakota political structures, see Kingsley M. Bray, "Making the Sichangu Hoop: Brule Tribal Organization, 1750–1804," in *Generous Man = Ahxsi-tapina: Essays in Memory of Colin Taylor, Plains Indian Ethnologist,* ed. Arni Brownstone and Hugh Dempsey (Tatanka Press, 2008); Kingsley M. Bray, "Before Sitting Bull: Interpreting Hunkpapa Political History, 1750–1867," *South Dakota History* 40, no. 2 (Summer 2010): 97–135; Catherine Price, *The Oglala People, 1841–1879: A*

Political History (Bison Books, 1998). For Indigenous understandings of nationhood, see Christina Gish Hill, *Webs of Kinship: Family in Northern Cheyenne Nationhood* (University of Oklahoma Press, 2017); Chantal Norrgard, *Seasons of Change: Labor, Treaty Rights, and Ojibwe Nationhood* (University of North Carolina Press, 2014); Nancy Shoemaker, *A Strange Likeness: Becoming Red and White in Eighteenth-Century North America* (Oxford University Press, 2004); Brad D. E. Jarvis, *The Brothertown Nation of Indians: Land Ownership and Nationalism in Early America, 1740–1840* (University of Nebraska Press, 2010). For Euro-American perceptions of nationhood in the nineteenth century and their views of Indigenous nationhood, see Peter S. Onuf, *Jefferson's Empire: The Language of American Nationhood* (University Press of Virginia, 2000); Deborah A. Rosen, *American Indians and State Law: Sovereignty, Race, and Citizenship, 1790–1880* (University of Nebraska Press, 2007); Lauren L. Basson, *White Enough to Be American? Race Mixing, Indigenous People, and the Boundaries of State and Nation* (University of North Carolina Press, 2008); Rochelle Raineri Zuck, *Divided Sovereignties: Race, Nationhood, and Citizenship in Nineteenth-Century America* (University of Georgia Press, 2016).

11. Allan Greer, "Commons and Enclosures in the Colonization of North America," *American Historical Review* 117, no. 2 (April 2012): 365–86.

12. Philander Prescott in Henry R. Schoolcraft, *Information Respecting the History, Condition, and Prospects of the Indian Tribes of the United States,* vol. 2 (Lippincott, Grambo, 1853), 194.

13. Resolution in the Executive Session of the U.S. Senate, Asbury Dickins, Secretary, March 1, 1839, LROIA, Council Bluffs Agency, reel 215.

14. For a discussion of the treaty, see Berlin Basil Chapman, *The Otoes and Missourias: A Study of Indian Removal and the Legal Aftermath* (Times Journal, 1965), 54–57.

15. For more on the Great Nemaha Reservation, see Robert L. Bohlken and C. James Keck, "An Experience in Territorial Social Compensation: Half Breed Tract, Nebraska Territory," *Northwest Missouri State University Studies* (February 1973): 3–12; Berlin B. Chapman, "The Nemaha Half-Breed Reservation," *Nebraska History* 38 (1957): 1–23; Gregory J. Johansen, "'To Make Some Provision for Their Half-Breeds': The Nemaha Half-Breed Reserve, 1830–1866," *Nebraska History* 67, no. 1 (March 1986): 8–29; William T. Moran, "A Fortune Is Near at Hand: White Land Buyers on the Nemaha Half-Breed Tract, 1857–1860" (master's thesis, University of Nebraska at Omaha, 1992).

16. Treaty with the Omaha, Iowa, Otoe, and the Yancton and Santie Band of Sioux, May 5, 1838, Unratified, LROIA, Council Bluffs Agency, reel 215.

17. Treaty with the Omaha, Iowa, Otoe, and the Yancton and Santie Band of Sioux.

18. Iaton, Hahchegebuga, Big Elk, and Little Dish to William Clark, October 15, 1836, Ratified Treaty no. 217, Documents Relating to the Negotiation of the Treaty of October 15, 1836, with the Oto, Missouri, and Omaha Indians, and Yankton and Santee Sioux Indians, M668, Ratified Indian Treaties 1722–1869, roll 8, RG 75, National Archives, Washington, D.C.

19. Quoted in Chapman, *Otoes and Missourias,* 56–57.

20. Martin Van Buren to the Senate of the United States, January 24, 1839, in *Journal of the Executive Proceedings of the Senate of the United States of America, 1837–1841,* vol. 5 (Government Printing Office, 1887), 185.

21. Cynthia Cumfer, "Local Origins of National Indian Policy: Cherokee and Tennessean Ideas About Sovereignty and Nationhood, 1790–1811," *Journal of the Early American Republic* 23, no. 1 (Spring 2003): 21–46.

22. See Patrick J. Jung, "Judge James Duane Doty and Wisconsin's First Court: The Additional Court of Michigan Territory, 1823–1836," *Wisconsin Magazine of History* 36, no. 2 (Winter 2002–2003): 32–41; Alice Elizabeth Smith, *James Duane Doty: Frontier Promoter* (State Historical Society of Wisconsin, 1954).

23. Proposals for an Indian Territory north of the Indian Territory that became the state of Oklahoma were not new, nor were considerations over the creation of an Indian state. See John P. Bowes, *Land Too Good for Indians: Northern Indian Removal* (University of Oklahoma Press, 2016); Annie H. Abel, "Proposals for an Indian State, 1778–1878," *Annual Report of the American Historical Association* 1 (1907): 87–104; Rhoda R. Gilman, "A Northwestern Indian Territory—The Last Voice," *Journal of the West* 39, no. 1 (January 2000): 16–22.

24. James D. Doty to John Bell, August 4, 1841, in *The Territorial Papers of the United States,* vol. 27, *The Territory of Wisconsin, 1839–1848,* ed. John Porter Bloom (Government Printing Office, 1975).

25. *Journal of the House of Representatives, Second Session of the Third Legislative Assembly of Wisconsin* (C. Latham Sholes, 1842), 62–63.

26. Deloria and DeMallie, *Documents of American Indian Diplomacy,* 2:783–87; *Journal of the House of Representatives,* 546–53.

27. Deloria and DeMallie, *Documents of American Indian Diplomacy,* 2:783–87; *Journal of the House of Representatives,* 546–53.

28. Deloria and DeMallie, *Documents of American Indian Diplomacy,* 2:783–87; *Journal of the House of Representatives,* 546–53; Gilman, "Northwestern Indian Territory," 16–22.

29. Deloria and DeMallie, *Documents of American Indian Diplomacy,* 2:783–87; *Journal of the House of Representatives,* 546–53; Gilman, "Northwestern Indian Territory," 16–22.

30. Deloria and DeMallie, *Documents of American Indian Diplomacy,* 2:783–87; *Journal of the House of Representatives,* 546–53; Gilman, "Northwestern Indian Territory," 16–22.

31. Deloria and DeMallie, *Documents of American Indian Diplomacy,* 2:787–90.

32. Deloria and DeMallie, *Documents of American Indian Diplomacy,* 2:787–90.

33. "New Indian Territory—No. V," *Daily National Intelligencer* (Washington, D.C.), October 23, 1841.

34. James D. Doty to John Bell, August 4, 1841, LROIA, St. Peters Agency, reel 759.

35. James D. Doty to John Bell, August 9, 1841, LROIA, St. Peters Agency, reel 759.

36. Lawrence Taliaferro to William Clark, July 25, 1836, LROIA, St. Peters Agency, reel 757.

37. Mixed-Ancestry Petition to Henry Dodge, August 15, 1837, LROIA, St. Peters Agency, reel 758.

38. Mixed-Ancestry Petition to Henry Dodge.

39. Mixed-Ancestry Petition to Henry Dodge.

40. Memorial by Sioux Halfbreeds to the Secretary of War, 1839, in Bloom, *Territorial Papers of the United States,* 27:103–4.

41. Although there is no evidence to suggest it was a fake, Colonel Samuel C. Stambaugh accused the American Fur Company of forging, or at least heavily influencing, the mixed-ancestry petition of August 15, 1837. See S. C. Stambaugh to C. Harris, September 23, 1837, LROIA, St. Peters Agency, reel 758.

42. Resolution of the Wisconsin Territorial Legislature to the Commissioner of Indian Affairs, December 16, 1839, LROIA, St. Peters Agency, reel 758.

43. Lawrence Taliaferro to John C. Spencer, November 27, 1841, LROIA, St. Peters Agency, reel 759.

44. James D. Doty to John C. Spencer, November 9, 1841, LROIA, St. Peters Agency, reel 759.

45. Darren O'Toole, "From Entity to Identity to Nation: The Ethnogenesis of the Wiisakodewininiwag (Boise-Brûlé) Reconsidered," in *Métis in Canada: History, Identity, Law and Politics,* ed. Christopher Adams, Gregg Dahl, and Ian Peach (University of Alberta Press, 2013), 150–51.

46. O'Toole, "From Entity to Identity to Nation," 150.

47. Objection to the Sioux Treaty, Senator Thomas Hart Benton, September 22, 1841, LROIA, St. Peters Agency, reel 759.

48. Smith, *James Duane Doty,* 257–62.

49. Journal of Proceedings, September 29–October 5, 1849, Documents Relating to the Negotiation of an Unratified Treaty of October 9, 1849, with the Sioux Indians (hereafter Unratified Treaty of 1849), Documents Relating to the Negotiation of Ratified and Unratified Treaties with Various Indian Tribes, 1801–1869, microfilm reel 4, T494, RG 75, National Archives, Washington, D.C.

50. Report of Orlando Brown, Commissioner of Indian Affairs, August 25, 1849, U.S. Congress, House of Representatives, in *Message from the President of*

the United States to the Two Houses of Congress, at the Commencement of the First Session of the Thirty-First Congress, 31st Cong., 1st Sess., 1850, H.Exec.Doc. 5 pt. 2, serial 570, 943.

51. Proceedings of a Council Held at Mendota, October 8, 1849, Unratified Treaty of 1849, microfilm reel 4, T494, RG 75, National Archives, Washington, D.C.

52. Proceedings of a Council Held at Mendota.

53. Proceedings of a Council Held at Mendota.

54. Deloria and DeMallie, *Documents of American Indian Diplomacy,* 2:791–98.

55. Report of Alexander Ramsey and John Chambers, October 15, 1849, Unratified Treaty of 1849, microfilm reel 4, T494, RG 75, National Archives, Washington, D.C.

56. Report of Alexander Ramsey and John Chambers.

57. Report of Alexander Ramsey and John Chambers.

58. Report of Alexander Ramsey and John Chambers.

59. *Journal of the Senate of the United States of America, Being the First Session of the Thirty-First Congress,* Serial Set vol. 548, 31st Cong., 1st Sess., 1850, 944–46.

60. *Acts, Joint Resolutions and Memorials Passed by the First Legislative Assembly of the Territory of Minnesota* (James M. Goodhue and Nathaniel M'Lean, 1850), 6.

61. William Watts Folwell, *A History of Minnesota* (Minnesota Historical Society Press, 1921), 324.

62. J. Owen Dorsey, "The Social Organization of the Siouan Tribes," *Journal of American Folklore* 4, no. 14 (July–September 1891): 260–63; Vine Deloria Jr., *Singing for a Spirit: A Portrait of the Dakota Sioux* (Clear Light Publishers, 2000), 30.

63. Joseph Plympton to General Atkinson, August 13, 1838, in Bloom, *Territorial Papers of the United States,* 27:1053–55.

64. Nicole St-Onge, "Familial Foes? French-Sioux Families and Plains Métis Brigades in the Nineteenth Century," *American Indian Quarterly* 39, no. 3 (Summer 2015): 302–37.

65. Matthew L. M. Fletcher, "Treaties As Recognition of a Nation-to-Nation Relationship," in *Nation to Nation: Treaties Between the United States and American Indian Nations,* ed. Suzan Shown Harjo (Smithsonian Institution, 2014), 34–35.

66. Duane Champagne, "Federal Recognition and Unratified Treaties," *Indian Country Today,* September 20, 2014, https://indiancountrymedianetwork.com/history/events/federal-recognition-and-unratified-treaties/.

67. Miscellaneous Records, Depositions Taken in Disputed Election, 1841, in *Minnesota Beginnings: Records of St. Croix County Wisconsin Territory, 1840–1849,*

by History Network of Washington County (Washington County Historical Society, 1999), 266.

68. For more about interracial marriages and specifics about Brown's marriages, see Catherine J. Denial, *Making Marriage: Husbands, Wives, and the American State in Dakota and Ojibwe Country* (Minnesota Historical Society Press, 2013); "An Act for the Relief of Joseph R. Brown," in *Laws of the Territory of Wisconsin, Passed at Madison, By the Legislative Assembly, at Its Annual Session of 1838–40* (Harrison Reed, 1840).

69. *Milwaukie Sentinel* (Milwaukee, Wis. Ter.), January 26, 1842.

70. Miscellaneous Records, Depositions Taken in Disputed Election, 1841, in History Network of Washington County, *Minnesota Beginnings,* 266.

71. Letter of Theophile LaChapelle dated August 4, 1845, *Wisconsin Herald* (Lancaster, Wisc.), August 9, 1845.

72. *Milwaukie Sentinel* (Milwaukee, Wis. Ter.), March 16, 1844.

73. Lucy Eldersveld Murphy, *Great Lakes Creoles: A French-Indian Community on the Northern Borderlands, Prairie du Chien, 1750–1860* (Cambridge University Press, 2014), 16–17.

74. William P. Murray, "Recollections of Early Territorial Days and Legislation," *Collections of the Minnesota Historical Society* 12 (December 1908): 103–4; Bruce M. White, "The Power of Whiteness: Or, the Life and Times of Joseph Rolette Jr.," *Minnesota History* 56, no. 4 (Winter 1998–1999): 178–97.

75. Denial, *Making Marriage,* 4.

76. Hill, *Webs of Kinship*; Christina Gish Hill, "Kinship as an Assertion of Sovereign Native Nationhood," in *Tribal Worlds: Critical Studies in American Indian Nation Building,* ed. Brian Hosmer and Larry Nesper (State University of New York Press, 2013).

77. Champagne, "Federal Recognition and Unratified Treaties."

5. Native Suffrage

1. List of Voters, Mendota Precinct, Dakota County, Minnesota Territory, October 12, 1852, Henry H. Sibley papers, microfilm reel 9, Minnesota Historical Society, St. Paul (hereafter MHS).

2. List of Voters, Mendota Precinct, Dakota County, Minnesota Territory, February 14, 1851, Henry H. Sibley papers, reel 8, MHS.

3. Executive Proceedings of Michigan Territory July 1, 1823–December 31, 1823, in *Territorial Papers of the United States,* vol. 11, *The Territory of Michigan 1820–1829,* ed. Clarence Edwin Carter (Government Printing Office, 1948), 481–82.

4. Lucy Eldersveld Murphy, *Great Lakes Creoles: A French-Indian Community on the Northern Borderlands, Prairie du Chien, 1750–1860* (Cambridge University Press, 2014), 65–107.

5. Numerous Indians of mixed ancestry voted in the contested 1824 election for Michigan Territory's delegate to Congress. "A Report of the Proceedings in Relation to the Contested Election for Delegate to the Nineteenth Congress, from the Territory of Michigan," 1825, in Carter, *Territorial Papers of the United States,* 11:711–69. See *Constitution of the State of Wisconsin, Adopted in Convention, at Madison, on the First Day of February, in the Year of Our Lord One Thousand Eight Hundred and Forty-Eight; The Revised Constitution of the State of Michigan, Adopted in Convention, August 15, 1850* (R. W. Ingals, 1850).

6. George D. Pappas, *The Literary and Legal Genealogy of Native American Dispossession: The Marshall Trilogy Cases* (Routledge, 2017); Eric Eisner, "The Law-of-Nations Origins of the Marshall Trilogy," *Yale Law Journal* 133, no. 3 (January 2024): 998–1038; Blake A Watson, *Buying America from the Indians: "Johnson v. McIntosh" and the History of Native Land Rights* (University of Oklahoma Press, 2012).

7. See Earl M. Maltz, "The Fourteenth Amendment and Native American Citizenship," *Constitutional Commentary* 17, no. 3 (Winter 2000): 555–73; Stephen D. Bodayla, "'Can an Indian Vote?' Elk v. Wilkins, A Setback for Indian Citizenship," *Nebraska History* 67 (1986): 372–80.

8. Daniel McCool, Susan M. Olson, and Jennifer L. Robinson, *Native Vote: American Indians, the Voting Rights Act, and the Right to Vote* (Cambridge University Press, 2007), ix. For a brief but good overview of the history of American Indian citizenship, see Laughlin McDonald, *American Indians and the Fight for Equal Voting Rights* (University of Oklahoma Press, 2010), 3–29. For an overview of mixed-ancestry suffrage see Jeremy Mumford, "Métis and the Vote in 19th-Century America," *Journal of the West* 39, no. 3 (Summer 2000): 38–45.

9. Deborah A. Rosen, *American Indians and State Law: Sovereignty, Race, and Citizenship, 1790–1880* (University of Nebraska Press, 2007), 155–201. See also Stephen Kantrowitz, "Jurisdiction, Civilization, and the Ends of Native American Citizenship: The View from 1866," *Western Historical Quarterly* 52 (Summer 2021): 189–208; Stephen Kantrowitz, "White Supremacy, Settler Colonialism, and the Two Citizenships of the Fourteenth Amendment," *Journal of the Civil War Era* 10, no. 1 (March 2020): 29–53; Stephen Kantrowitz, *Citizens of a Stolen Land: A Ho-Chunk History of the Nineteenth-Century United States* (University of North Carolina Press, 2023); Jameson Sweet, "Native Suffrage: Race, Citizenship, and Dakota Indians in the Upper Midwest," *Journal of the Early Republic* 39, no. 1 (Spring 2019): 99–109.

10. William E. Unrau, *Mixed-Bloods and Tribal Dissolution: Charles Curtis and the Quest for Indian Identity* (University Press of Kansas, 1989).

11. S. G. Heiskell, *Andrew Jackson and Early Tennessee History,* vol. 1 (Ambrose Printing, 1920), 210; Charles J. Kappler, ed., *Indian Affairs: Laws and Treaties,* vol. 2,

Treaties (Government Printing Office, 1904), 310–19, 439–49; Willard Hughes Rollings, "Citizenship and Suffrage: The Native American Struggle for Civil Rights in the American West, 1830–1965," *Nevada Law Journal* 5, no. 126 (Fall 2004): 129–31; Mary Lethert Wingerd, *North Country: The Making of Minnesota* (University of Minnesota Press, 2010), 232.

12. Murphy, *Great Lakes Creoles,* 6–12. See also Bethel Saler, *The Settlers' Empire: Colonialism and State Formation in America's Old Northwest* (University of Pennsylvania Press, 2015).

13. *Acts, Joint Resolutions and Memorials Passed by the First Legislative Assembly of the Territory of Minnesota* (James M. Goodhue and Nathaniel M'Lean, 1850), 6.

14. Henry Trudell to Commissioner of Indian Affairs Francis E. Leupp, August 12, 1905, letter #63942, 1905, box 2868, entry 91, Letters Received, 1881–1907, Records of the Bureau of Indian Affairs, RG 75, National Archives, Washington, D.C.

15. Trudell to Leupp.

16. Eugene Buechel, *A Dictionary: Oie Wowapi Wan of Teton Sioux,* ed. Paul Manhart (Red Cloud Indian School, 1983), 51–52.

17. Stephen R. Riggs, ed., *Grammar and Dictionary of the Dakota Language* (Smithsonian Institution, 1852), 254, 289; *An English and Dakota Vocabulary, by a Member of the Dakota Mission* (R. Craighead, 1852), 23.

18. For more on women and American citizenship, see Nancy F. Cott, "Marriage and Women's Citizenship in the United States, 1830–1934," *American Historical Review* 103, no. 5 (December 1998): 1440–74.

19. Stephen R. Riggs, *A Dakota-English Dictionary,* ed. James Owen Dorsey (Government Printing Office, 1890), 18, 356. Eugene Buechel's Lakota dictionary, completed in manuscript form in 1917 but not published until 1970, uses "aígluha," the Lakota dialect version of "aíhduha," to mean "citizen." Buechel, *Dictionary.*

20. John P. Williamson, *An English-Dakota School Dictionary* (Iapi Oaye Press, 1886), 34. Fred Hans uses the same term for "citizenship" in his 1907 dictionary. Fred M. Hans, *The Great Sioux Nation* (M. A. Donohue, 1907), 318.

21. John P. Williamson, *An English-Dakota Dictionary* (American Tract Society, 1902), 32.

22. Williamson, *English-Dakota School Dictionary,* 34.

23. Williamson, *English-Dakota Dictionary,* 33.

24. Williamson, *English-Dakota School Dictionary,* 34; Williamson, *English-Dakota Dictionary,* 33.

25. Hans, *Great Sioux Nation,* 318.

26. Williamson, *English-Dakota School Dictionary,* 34.

27. Williamson, 34.

28. *St. Cloud Democrat* (St. Cloud, Minn.), September 9, 1858.

29. *Stillwater Messenger* (Stillwater, Minn.), November 30, 1858.

30. *Rochester City Post* (Rochester, Minn.), December 22, 1860.

31. "Douglas for Dunn," *Grant County Herald* (Lancaster, Wisc.), November 20, 1858.

32. "Will Do," *Council Bluffs Nonpareil* (Council Bluffs, Iowa), November 19, 1859.

33. "The Topeka Constitution," *White Cloud Kansas Chief* (White Cloud, Kans.), December 10, 1857.

34. Dakota County, Minnesota Territory, District Court Naturalization Records, 1854–1943, reel 3, MHS.

35. Charles E. Flandrau, "Lawyers and Courts of Minnesota Prior to and During Its Territorial Period," *Collections of the Minnesota Historical Society* 8 (1898): 89–91. For examples of mixed-ancestry Indians serving in public office, as jurors, and as voters going back to the 1820s in Wisconsin, see Murphy, *Great Lakes Creoles,* 65–107.

36. "By Authority," *Minnesota Democrat* (St. Paul, Min. Ter.), September 8, 1852.

37. *Minnesota Democrat* (St. Paul, Min. Ter.), October 5, 1853.

38. "The Returns—Mendota," *St. Paul Daily Times* (St. Paul, Min. Ter.), October 13, 1854.

39. "Public Meeting at Wabashaw," *St. Paul Daily Pioneer* (St. Paul, Min. Ter.), July 16, 1855.

40. "Public Meeting at Wabashaw."

41. Renée Sansom-Flood, *Lessons from Chouteau Creek: Yankton Memories of Dakota Territorial Intrigue* (Center for Western Studies, 1986), 39–40.

42. This was not the only time a group of Dakota chose to create a separate Christian community. See Elwin E. Rogers, *For God & Land: Brown Earth, a Dakota Indian Community, 1876–1892* (Pine Hill Press, 2002).

43. Joseph R. Brown to W. J. Cullen, Superintendent of Indian Affairs, September 10, 1859, Annual Report of the Secretary of Interior, 1860, in *Message from the President of the United States to the Two Houses of Congress at the Commencement of the First Session of the Thirty-Sixth Congress,* vol. 1 (George W. Bowman, 1860), 453.

44. For more on clothing in Dakota–American relations, see David John Trayte, "The Roll of Dress in Eastern Dakota and White Interaction, 1834–1862: A Symbol in Contending Cultures" (PhD diss., University of Minnesota, 1993).

45. Constitution of the Hazelwood Republic, M842, Records of the Minnesota Superintendency of Indian Affairs, 1849–1856, roll 8, RG 75, National Archives, Washington, D.C.; Stephen R. Riggs to S. B. Treat, July 31, 1856, Transcripts of

Letters from Missionaries Among the Indians of Minnesota, Dakota, and Oregon, 1830–1878, Ayer MS 16, Newberry Library, Chicago.

46. Memorial from the Hazelwood Republic, *The Debates and Proceedings of the Minnesota Constitutional Convention Including the Organic Act of the Territory* [Democratic] (Earle S. Goodrich, 1857), 430–31.

47. Stephen R. Riggs, trans., *The Constitution of Minnesota in the Dakota Language* (Press of T. R. Marvin & Son, 1858).

48. William D. Green, *A Peculiar Imbalance: The Fall and Rise of Racial Equality in Early Minnesota* (Minnesota Historical Society Press, 2007), 114–16.

49. "An Act Granting the Privileges of Citizenship Under Certain Restrictions to the Civilized Indians of This State," in *General and Special Laws of the State of Minnesota, Together with the Joint Resolutions and Memorials, Passed During the Third Session of the State Legislature* (Wm. R. Marshall, 1861), 171–72.

50. F. Curtiss-Wedge, Susan Bahr's Personal Reminiscences of Early Minnesota, October 12, 1936, Works Progress Administration, copy in the Alan R. Woolworth papers, box 145.I.16.4F, MHS.

51. Charles S. Bryant and Abel B. Murch, *A History of the Great Massacre by the Sioux Indians, in Minnesota, Including the Personal Narratives of Many Who Escaped,* 2nd ed. (Rickey & Carroll, 1864), 267.

52. S. C. Armstrong, "Present Condition and Prospects of the Indians," *Misk-Wi-Nen-Ne* 1, no. 2 (February 1889): 3.

53. Horst Dippel, ed., *Constitutional Documents of the United States of America 1776–1860* (K. G. Saur, 2009), 214–15.

54. Letter of Theophile LaChapelle dated August 4, 1845, *Wisconsin Herald* (Lancaster, Wisc.), August 9, 1845.

55. "From the Hazelwood Republic," *St. Paul Daily Times* (St. Paul, Min. Ter.), March 24, 1857.

56. "Indians Adopting Civilization," *Public Ledger* (Philadelphia, Penn.), September 15, 1858.

57. *Journal of the Constitutional Convention of State of Michigan, 1850* (R. W. Ingals, 1850), 539.

58. An Act to Establish the Territorial Government of Minnesota, March 3, 1849, 9 Stat. 403 (chap. 21).

59. *Acts, Joint Resolutions and Memorials,* 6.

60. Charles E. Flandrau, "Reminiscences of Minnesota During the Territorial Period," *Collections of the Minnesota Historical Society* 9 (1901): 199. For more on race and the Bonga family, see Mattie Marie Harper, "French Africans in Ojibwe Country: Negotiating Marriage, Identity and Race, 1780–1890" (PhD diss., University of California, Berkeley, 2012).

61. Green, *Peculiar Imbalance.*

62. For more on debates over citizenship in state constitutional conventions, see Silvana R. Siddali, *Frontier Democracy: Constitutional Conventions in the Old Northwest* (Cambridge University Press, 2016).

63. *Debates and Proceedings of the Constitutional Convention for the Territory of Minnesota, to Form a State Constitution Preparatory to Its Admission into the Union as a State* [Republican] (George W. Moore, 1858), 359–60.

64. *Debates and Proceedings of the Constitutional Convention* [Republican], 345, 394.

65. *Debates and Proceedings of the Constitutional Convention* [Republican], 399.

66. Stephen R. Riggs to S. B. Treat, August 13, 1857, Transcripts of Letters from Missionaries Among the Indians of Minnesota, Dakota, and Oregon, 1830–1878, Ayer MS 16, Newberry Library, Chicago.

67. Murphy, *Great Lakes Creoles*, 15–17.

68. *The Debates and Proceedings of the Minnesota Constitutional Convention Including the Organic Act of the Territory* [Democratic] (Earle S. Goodrich, 1857), 154.

69. Bruce M. White, "The Power of Whiteness: Or, the Life and Times of Joseph Rolette Jr.," *Minnesota History* 56, no. 4 (Winter 1998–1999): 186.

70. "Daily's Vote in Nemaha," *Nebraska Advertiser* (Brownville, Neb. Ter.), October 11, 1860.

71. U.S. Congress, House of Representatives, *Contested Election—Samuel G. Daily vs. J. Sterling Morton*, 37th Cong., 1st Sess., 1861, H. Mis. Doc. 4, serial 1115, 1–3.

72. U.S. Congress, *Contested Election*, 11–31.

73. U.S. Congress, 32–48.

74. Fillisita Beddow to Alfred Greenwood, May 11, 1860, Letters Received by the Office of Indian Affairs, 1824–1881, M234, Great Nemaha Agency, reel 310, RG 75, National Archives, Washington, D.C. (hereafter LROIA).

75. Moses K. Armstrong, *The Early Empire Builders of the Great West* (E. W. Porter, 1901), 73–74; Howard Roberts Lamar, *Dakota Territory 1861–1889: A Study of Frontier Politics* (Yale University Press, 1956), 87–88.

76. Lamar, *Dakota Territory*, 87–88.

77. Armstrong, *Early Empire Builders*, 73–74.

78. *General Laws, and Memorials and Resolutions of the Territory of Dakota, Passed at the First Session of the Legislative Assembly* (Josiah C. Trask, 1862), 1–2; *General Laws, and Memorials and Resolutions of the Territory of Dakota, Passed at the Second Session of the Legislative Assembly* (Kingsbury & Ziebach, 1863), 285; *General and Private Laws, Memorials and Resolutions, of the Territory of Dakota, Passed at the Third Session of the Legislative Assembly* (G. W. Kingsbury, 1864),

129; *General and Private Laws, and Memorials and Resolutions, of the Territory of Dakota, of the Fourth Session of the Legislative Assembly* (G. W. Kingsbury, 1865), 276; *Laws, Memorials and Resolutions of the Territory of Dakota, Passed at the Fifth Session of the Legislative Assembly* (G. W. Kingsbury, 1866), 577; *Public and Private Laws, Memorials and Resolutions, of the Territory of Dakota, Passed by the Legislative Assembly at the Seventh Session Thereof* (Geo. W. Kingsbury, 1868), 266–67.

79. "Charles Mix County," *Yankton Press and Dakotan* (Yankton, Dak. Ter.), July 9, 1864.

80. "Officers of Bon Homme County," *Yankton Press and Dakotan* (Yankton, Dak. Ter.), November 3, 1866.

81. *Turner County Herald* (Hurley, S.D.), December 15, 1892.

82. Adeline S. Gnirk, *The Saga of Sully Flats* (Gregory Times-Advocate, 1977), 133–34.

83. Affidavit of Sefroy Iott, June 25, 1864, LROIA, Upper Platte Agency, M234, reel 891.

84. John B. Colomb Testimony, in U.S. Congress, House of Representatives, *Papers and Testimony in the Case of W. A. Burleigh vs. M. K Armstrong, as Delegate from Dakota Territory*, 42nd Cong., 2nd Sess., 1872, H.Misc.Doc 47, serial 1525, 137. For more on the case, see Harry H. Anderson, "Fur Traders as Fathers: The Origins of the Mixed-Blooded Community Among the Rosebud Sioux," *South Dakota History* 3, no. 3 (Summer 1973): 233–70.

85. John B. Colomb Testimony, *Papers and Testimony in the Case of W. A. Burleigh vs. M. K Armstrong, as delegate from Dakota Territory*, 138–39.

86. Zack T. Sutley, *The Last Frontier* (Macmillan, 1930), 177–78.

87. Sansom-Flood, *Lessons from Chouteau Creek*, 47–52.

88. R. W. Andrews Testimony, in U.S. Congress, House of Representatives, *Papers and Testimony in the Case of W. A. Burleigh vs. M. K Armstrong, as Delegate from Dakota Territory*, 42nd Cong., 2nd Sess., 1872, H.Misc.Doc 47, serial 1525, 26–27.

89. John L. Turner Testimony, in U.S. Congress, House of Representatives, *Papers and Testimony in the Case of W. A. Burleigh vs. M. K Armstrong, as Delegate from Dakota Territory*, 42nd Cong., 2nd Sess., 1872, H.Misc.Doc 47, serial 1525, 31.

90. Lester E. Wood Testimony, in U.S. Congress, House of Representatives, *Papers and Testimony in the Case of W. A. Burleigh vs. M. K Armstrong, as Delegate from Dakota Territory*, 42nd Cong., 2nd Sess., 1872, H.Misc.Doc 47, serial 1525, 24–25.

91. Ray D. Andrews Testimony and Alexander Keeler Testimony, in U.S. Congress, House of Representatives, *Papers and Testimony in the Case of W. A. Burleigh*

vs. M. K Armstrong, as Delegate from Dakota Territory, 42nd Cong., 2nd Sess., 1872, H.Misc.Doc 47, serial 1525, 121.

92. Lester E. Wood Testimony, Nathan McDaniels Testimony, in U.S. Congress, House of Representatives, *Papers and Testimony in the Case of W. A. Burleigh vs. M. K Armstrong, as Delegate from Dakota Territory,* 42nd Cong., 2nd Sess., 1872, H.Misc.Doc 47, serial 1525, 25, 37–40.

93. *General Laws, Memorials and Resolutions of the Territory of Dakota, Passed at the Ninth Session of the Legislative Assembly* (Stone & Kingsbury, 1871), 10.

94. *General and Private Laws, Memorials and Resolutions, of the Territory of Dakota,* 1864, 56–57.

95. "A Bill to Outlaw Indians," *Wabashaw County Herald* (Wabasha, Min. Ter.), January 1863.

96. Levi Trudell to W. A. Jones, Commissioner of Indian Affairs, January 22, 1899, letter #4574, 1899, box 1621, entry 91, Letters Received, 1881–1907, RG 75, National Archives, Washington, D.C.

97. "A Democratic Indian Delegate," *Omaha World-Herald* (Omaha, Neb.), October 13, 1887.

98. *The Word Carrier* (Santee, Neb.), November 1887, originally published in the *Knox County Democrat* (Niobrara, Neb.).

6. Land Scrip and Allotment

1. Wabasha County, Minnesota District Court, Civil Case Files, box 2, case #247, *Mary Wacoutah v. A. T. Sharpe et al.,* 1866, Minnesota Historical Society, St. Paul (hereafter MHS).

2. See Petition of the Mixed-Ancestry Dakota to President Franklin Pierce, June 30, 1853, Letters Received by the Office of Indian Affairs, 1824–1881, Minnesota Superintendency, 1849–1856, roll 428, RG 75, National Archives, Washington, D.C. (hereafter LROIA); Petition of the Mixed-Ancestry Dakota to Minnesota Territorial Governor Willis Gorman, November 5, 1853, entry 529, Miscellaneous Reserve Papers, 1825–1907, box 360, RG 75, National Archives, Washington, D.C. (hereafter MRP); Petition of the Mixed-Ancestry Dakota to President Franklin Pierce, January 11, 1854, MRP, box 360.

3. 1830 Treaty of Prairie du Chien, in *Indian Affairs: Laws and Treaties,* vol. 2, *Treaties,* ed. Charles J. Kappler (Government Printing Office, 1904), 305–10.

4. Lucy Eldersveld Murphy, *Great Lakes Creoles: A French-Indian Community on the Northern Borderlands, Prairie du Chien, 1750–1860* (Cambridge University Press, 2014), 12.

5. Cheryl I. Harris, "Whiteness as Property," *Harvard Law Review* 106, no. 8 (June 1993): 1714.

6. Harris, "Whiteness as Property," 1724.

7. Harris, 1724.

8. See Stuart Banner, *How the Indian Lost Their Land: Law and Power on the Frontier* (Belknap Press of Harvard University Press, 2005); Paula Mitchell Marks, *In a Barren Land: American Indian Dispossession and Survival* (William Morrow, 1998); David J. Wishart, *An Unspeakable Sadness: The Dispossession of the Nebraska Indians* (University of Nebraska Press, 1994). For Indian dispossession through allotment, see Joseph Genetin-Pilawa, *Crooked Paths to Allotment: The Fight over Federal Indian Policy After the Civil War* (University of North Carolina Press, 2012); Emily Greenwald, *Reconfiguring the Reservation: The Nez Perces, Jicarilla Apaches, and the Dawes Act* (University of New Mexico Press, 2002).

9. Brad D. E. Jarvis, *The Brothertown Nation of Indians: Land Ownership and Nationalism in Early America, 1740–1840* (University of Nebraska Press, 2010).

10. Jean M. O'Brien, *Dispossession by Degrees: Indian Land and Identity in Natick, Massachusetts, 1650–1790* (Cambridge University Press, 1997), 8–9.

11. Melissa L. Meyer, *The White Earth Tragedy: Ethnicity and Dispossession at a Minnesota Anishinaabe Reservation, 1889–1920* (University of Nebraska Press, 1994).

12. David A. Chang, *The Color of the Land: Race, Nation, and the Politics of Landownership in Oklahoma, 1832–1929* (University of North Carolina Press, 2010).

13. Petition of Mixed-Ancestry Dakota of the Bdewákhaŋthuŋwaŋ Band to Governor Willis A. Gorman, October 14, 1853, MRP, box 360.

14. Petition of Mixed-Ancestry Dakota of the Bdewákhaŋtuŋwaŋ Band to Governor Willis A. Gorman.

15. For more on Indian women and American coverture laws, see Robert Gilmer, "Chickasaws, Tribal Laws, and the Mississippi Married Women's Property Act of 1839," *Journal of Mississippi History* 68, no. 2 (June 2006): 131–48.

16. Petition of Mixed-Ancestry Dakota to Governor Willis A. Gorman.

17. D. H. Dustin, U.S. District Attorney, to Governor Willis A. Gorman, December 8, 1853, MRP, box 360.

18. Nathaniel McLean to Alexander Ramsey, September 24, 1850, and Philander Prescott to Nathaniel McLean, September 24, 1850, LROIA, St. Peter's Agency, reel 761.

19. An Act to Authorize the President of the United States to Cause to Be Surveyed the Tract of Land in the Territory of Minnesota, Belonging to the Half-Breeds or Mixed-Bloods of the Dacotah or Sioux Nation of Indians, and for Other Purposes, July 17, 1854, in *The Statutes at Large and Treaties of the United States of America from December 1, 1851, to March 3, 1855*, vol. 10, ed. George Minot (Little, Brown, 1855), 304.

20. "Sioux Lands or Reservation in Minnesota Territory," Serial Set Vol. 743, Session Vol. No. 2, 33rd Cong., 1st Sess., 1854, 1–2.

21. "Sioux Lands or Reservation in Minnesota Territory," 1–2.

22. "Sioux Lands or Reservation in Minnesota Territory," 1–2.

23. George Manypenny, Commissioner of Indian Affairs, to Robert McClelland, Secretary of Interior, March 14, 1855, RG 75, entry 529, MRP, box 360.

24. Robert McClelland, Secretary of Interior to George Manypenny, Commissioner of Indian Affairs, June 30, 1856, RG 75, entry 529, MRP, box 360.

25. Henry Sibley, Alexis Bailly, and Alexander Faribault to George H. Manypenny, Commissioner of Indian Affairs, July 25, 1855, RG 75, entry 529, MRP, box 360.

26. C. Billinghurst to Robert McClelland, Secretary of Interior, March 1, 1856, RG 75, entry 529, MRP, box 360.

27. Petition of Citizens of Wabasha and South Wabasha to President James Buchanan, undated, entry 529, MRP, box 358.

28. Petition of Mixed-Ancestry Dakota to President Franklin Pierce, undated (received May 6, 1856), entry 529, MRP, box 360.

29. For an example of a notice, see "Notice to the Sioux Half-Breeds & Mixed Bloods, Having an Interest in the Reservation on Lake Pepin, Minnesota Ter'ry," *Minnesota Democrat* (St. Paul, Min. Ter.), July 18, 1855.

30. "Notice to the Sioux Half-Breeds & Mixed Bloods."

31. Affidavit #51, Charlotte Mercier, entry 529, MRP, box 359.

32. Affidavit #139, Theophile Bruguier, entry 529, MRP, box 359.

33. Affidavit #125, Francis Trudell, entry 529, MRP, box 359.

34. Affidavit #126, George H. Farribault, entry 529, MRP, box 359.

35. Affidavit #124, Francis Trudell, entry 529, MRP, box 359.

36. Affidavit #123, George H. Farribault, entry 529, MRP, box 359.

37. Entry 378, Sioux Half Breed Census, 1856, RG 75, National Archives, Washington, D.C.

38. George W. Manypenny to R. McClelland, June 22, 1856, entry 529, MRP, box 360.

39. George W. Manypenny to R. McClelland, November 21, 1856, entry 529, MRP, box 360.

40. Affidavit of Baptiste DeLoney, May 19, 1857, entry 529, MRP, box 358.

41. Affidavit of Amable Morrin, July 30, 1857, entry 529, MRP, box 358.

42. Schedule Containing the Names, Age, Sex, and Tribe of Certain Mixed Blood Sioux Indians Who Are Believed to Be Entitled, September 11, 1860, entry 529, MRP, box 362.

43. Petition of Mixed-Ancestry Dakota to George Manypenny, Commissioner of Indian Affairs, November 15, 1856, entry 529, MRP, box 360.

44. Petition of Mixed-Ancestry Dakota to George Manypenny.

45. Petition of Mixed-Ancestry Dakota to George Manypenny.

46. "Constitution and By-Laws of the Settlers' Protection," undated and unidentified newspaper clipping, entry 529, MRP, box 360.

47. Alexis Bailly to Henry M. Rice, August 2, 1856, entry 529, MRP, box 360.

48. Carey A. Harris, Commissioner of Indian Affairs, to Alexis Bailly, August 4, 1837, Letters Sent by the Office of Indian Affairs, 1824–1882, M21, roll 22, June 21–November 27, 1837, RG 75, National Archives, Washington, D.C.

49. Alexis Bailly to George Manypenny, Commissioner of Indian Affairs, June 21, 1856, entry 529, MRP, box 360.

50. George Manypenny, Commissioner of Indian Affairs, to Robert McClelland, Secretary of Interior, June 22, 1856, entry 529, MRP, box 360.

51. Thomas Hendricks, Commissioner of General Land Office to Charles Mix, Acting Commissioner of Indian Affairs, June 12, 1857, entry 529, MRP, box 361.

52. Alexis Bailly to George Manypenny, Commissioner of Indian Affairs, June 25, 1856, entry 529, MRP, box 360.

53. Israel Garrard to George Manypenny, Commissioner of Indian Affairs, August 11, 1856, entry 529, MRP, box 360.

54. Notice of Delivery of Scrip, George Manypenny, Commissioner of Indian Affairs, February 5, 1857, entry 529, MRP, box 361.

55. Receipt of James Shields, Washington, D.C., March 7, 1857, entry 529, MRP, box 361.

56. James Shields to James W. Denver, Commissioner of Indian Affairs, June 8, 1857, entry 529, MRP, box 361.

57. Relinquishments of Sioux Half Breeds, Lake Pepin, entry 381, RG 75, National Archives, Washington, D.C.

58. Entry 380, Receipts for Land Certificates for Lake Pepin Half-Breed Scrip, 1857, and entry 379, Stubs of Land Certificates for Lake Pepin Half-Breed Sioux, 1856–1915, box 2, RG 75, National Archives, Washington, D.C.

59. James Shields to Commissioner of Indian Affairs, December 1, 1857, entry 529, MRP, box 361.

60. Entry 381, Relinquishments of Sioux Half Breeds, Lake Pepin, RG 75, National Archives, Washington, D.C.

61. Entry 379, Stubs of Land Certificates for Lake Pepin Half-Breed Sioux, 1856–1915, box 2, RG 75, National Archives, Washington, D.C.; entry 380, Receipts for Land Certificates for Lake Pepin Half-Breed Sioux, 1857, RG 75, National Archives, Washington, D.C.

62. Goodhue County Probate Court, 1854–1862, vol. 1, MHS; "Guardian's Sale," *Red Wing Sentinel* (Red Wing, Minn.), August 29, 1857.

63. 1860 U.S. Federal Census, Hastings, Dakota County, Minn., July 16, 1860.

64. Augustus Trudell to S. J. Willard, August 28, 1886, enclosure in S. M. Hockslager to Lucius Q. C. Lamar, October 25, 1886, letter #28701, 1886, box 349, entry 91, Letters Received, 1881–1907, Records of the Bureau of Indian Affairs, RG 75, National Archives, Washington, D.C. (hereafter LR). For more on the National Indian Defense Association, see Jo Lea Wetherilt Behrens, "In Defense of 'Poor Lo': National Indian Defense Association and *Council Fire's* Advocacy for Sioux Land Rights," *South Dakota History* 24 (Fall/Winter 1994): 153–73.

65. Statement of Leon [Levi] Trudell, enclosure in S. M. Hockslager to Lucius Q. C. Lamar, October 25, 1886, letter #28701, 1886, box 349, LR.

66. D. H. Talbot to William Arthur Jones, Commissioner of Indian Affairs, November 18, 1897, letter #49155, 1897, box 1479, LR.

67. D. H. Talbot to William Arthur Jones, Commissioner of Indian Affairs, January 25, 1898, letter #4726, 1898, box 1501, LR.

68. Clinton Gurnee Jr., attorney of Francis Trudell, located scrips A, B, and D of Elizabeth Trudell, deceased, January 23, 1860. Scrip D was located on land abandoned by James W. Edward, and scrips A and B were located on land abandoned by C. Williams. See Abstracts of Sioux Half-Breed Scrip, UD 2258, RG 49, National Archives, Washington, D.C.

69. For more on what was going on in the region with Dakota and Ojibwe "half-breed" scrip, see Larry Nesper, *"Our Relations . . . the Mixed Bloods": Indigenous Transformation and Dispossession in the Western Great Lakes* (State University of New York Press, 2021).

70. Red Wing Land District, Register of Sioux Half Breed Scrip Entries, 1857–1861, U.S. General Land Office Records, MHS.

71. See McLeod County Tax Lists for 1861 and 1863, MHS.

72. Deed, Francis and Mary Trudell, heir at law of Joseph Trudell to William H. Grant, July 22, 1867, Goodhue County, Minnesota Deeds, vol. B-2, roll 7, MHS.

73. Deed, Augustus Trudell to Daniel G. Shillock, July 19, 1871, Goodhue County, Minnesota Deeds, vol. S-2, roll 9, MHS.

74. Court order, Augustine, Henry, and Peter Trudell, defendants, George Wilkinson, plaintiff, December 3, 1867, Goodhue County, Minnesota Deeds, vol. C-2, roll 7, MHS.

75. Deed, Francis Trudell [Jr.] to Joshua Egbert, December 28, 1867, Sibley County, Minnesota Deeds, vol. J, roll 1, MHS.

76. Deed, Francis Trudell [Jr.] to Daniel G. Shillock, July 19, 1871, Sibley County, Minnesota Deeds, vol. J, roll 1, MHS.

77. Deed, Frank and Maggie Trudell to J. B. Lucas, August 14, 1897, Sibley County, Minnesota Deeds, vol. 12, roll 15, MHS.

78. See James Olson and Abraham Mendoza, *American Economic History: A Dictionary and Chronology* (ABC-CLIO, 2015), 366.

79. Dakota County, Minnesota Deeds, Book A, page 46, June, 1855, and Book B, page 60, January 29, 1856, Dakota County, Minnesota Register of Deeds, Hastings.

80. See digital copy of Francis Trudell's land patent, accession no. MN0010.317, General Land Office Records, U.S. Department of the Interior, Bureau of Land Management, accessed November 13, 2024, https://glorecords.blm.gov/results/default.aspx?searchCriteria=type=patent|st=MN|cty=|ln=trudelle|fn=francois|sp=true|sw=true|sadv=false.

81. Deed, Francis Trudell [Jr.] to William and Esther Curtis and David Hughes, November 4, 1857, Goodhue County, Minnesota Deeds, book F, reel 3, MHS; Deed, Francis Trudell Jr. to Arne Henrickson, December 1, 1857, Goodhue County, Minnesota Deeds, book F, reel 3, MHS.

82. Deed, George and Hannah Wilkinson to Francis Trudell, October 14, 1858, Goodhue County, Minnesota Deeds, book I, reel 4, MHS; Deed, Francis and Mary Trudell to Edward Kiernan, October 15, 1858, book I, reel 4, MHS.

83. Deed, Francis and Mary Trudell to Edward Kiernan, October 15, 1858, book I, reel 4, MHS.

84. Dakota County, Minnesota District Court, Civil and Criminal Case Files, 1853–1937, box 3, John Kennedy v. Augustus Trudell, Peter Trudell, Leon Trudell, and Francois Trudell, 1861, MHS.

85. See Charter of the Dakota County Association, March 9, 1855, and List of Members of the Dakota County Association, March 10, 1855, Henry H. Sibley papers, reel 10, MHS.

86. Thomas B. Walker, "Memories of the Early Life and Development of Minnesota," *Collections of the Minnesota Historical Society* 15 (1915): 462–68.

87. William Millikan, "The Great Treasure of the Fort Snelling Prison Camp," *Minnesota History* 62, no. 1 (Spring 2010): 4–17.

88. Franklin Steele papers, MHS.

89. Walker, "Memories," 462–65.

90. C. S. Rice to Samuel Brown, December 7, 1863, Joseph and Samuel Brown papers, MHS.

91. Petition of Great Nemaha Mixed-Bloods to George W. Manypenny, March 1, 1854, LROIA, Great Nemaha Agency, reel 308.

92. Gregory J. Johansen, "'To Make Some Provision for Their Half-Breeds': The Nemaha Half-Breed Reserve, 1830–1866," *Nebraska History* 67, no. 1 (March 1986): 13; "Half Breed Lands," *Nebraska Advertiser* (Brownville, Neb. Ter.), December 20, 1856.

93. List of civilian employees at Fort Pierre, November 1855, Returns from U.S. Military Posts, 1800–1916, reel 920, M617, RG 94, Records of the Adjutant General's Office, National Archives, Washington, D.C. For more on the First Sioux War, see Paul N. Beck, *The First Sioux War: The Grattan Fight and Blue Water*

Creek, 1854–1856 (University Press of America, 2004); R. Eli Paul, *Blue Water Creek and the First Sioux War, 1854–1856* (University of Oklahoma Press, 2004).

94. Affidavit of William Kinsler, June 2, 1860, LROIA, Great Nemaha Agency, M234, reel 310.

95. Affidavit of William Kinsler.

96. Affidavit of Struck by the Ree, Crazy Bull, and Long Foot, June 19, 1858, LROIA, Great Nemaha Agency, reel 309.

97. Thomas Sloan to James Denver, July 19, 1857, LROIA, Great Nemaha Agency, reel 309.

98. J. Sharp to James Denver, April 24, 1857, LROIA, Great Nemaha Agency, reel 309; List of the Names of Those Rejected by This Office on Account of African Blood or by Reason of Their Being on the Lake Pepin List, LROIA, Great Nemaha Agency, reel 309.

99. Petition of Margaret Sloan, Pelagie Ritter, and Mary Rodgers to George W. Manypenny, May 21, 1856, LROIA, Great Nemaha Agency, reel 308.

100. Petition of Great Nemaha Mixed-Bloods to James W. Denver, July 17, 1858, LROIA, Great Nemaha Agency, reel 309.

101. Petition to Congress and Nathaniel G. Taylor, November 16, 1867, LROIA, Upper Platte Agency, reel 892.

102. J. B. S. Todd to Charles Mix, April 12, 1858, LROIA, Great Nemaha Agency, reel 309.

103. Paul Daurion to Mr. Hicks, July 1, 1858, LROIA, Great Nemaha Agency, reel 309.

104. Kappler, *Indian Affairs,* 2:779.

105. Richardson County, Nebraska Territory Tax Lists, vols. 1–5, 1861–1866, microfilm, RG245, roll 1, Nebraska State Historical Society, Lincoln (hereafter NSHS).

106. Charles Rouleau to William P. Dole, April 2, 1864, LROIA, Great Nemaha Agency, reel 311.

107. Numerical Index of Lands, Richardson County, Range 17–18, NSHS.

108. See William T. Moran, "A Fortune Is Near at Hand: White Land Buyers on the Nemaha Half-Breed Tract" (master's thesis, University of Nebraska at Omaha, 1992), 94–124.

109. Numerical Index of Lands, Richardson County, Range 17–18, NSHS.

110. Land Deed, Morris and Margaret Langdeau to Thomas Harrison, October 19, 1860, Fremont County, Iowa Deeds, book D, microform, Family History Library, Salt Lake City, Utah.

111. Affidavit of Mary Woodbury, May 6, 1872, MRP, box 357.

112. Robert H. Bradford and James L. Bradford to Edward Smith, Commissioner of Indian Affairs, July 8, 1873, MRP, box 364.

113. Willis Drummond, Commissioner of the General Land Office, to Secretary of Interior Columbus Delano, August 6, 1873, MRP, box 364.

114. Affidavit of Angelique Boyer, May 6, 1872, MRP, box 357.

115. Willis Drummond, Commissioner of the General Land Office, to Secretary of Interior Columbus Delano, August 6, 1873, MRP, box 364.

116. Walter Bourke to Ely S. Parker, Commissioner of Indian Affairs, November 29, 1870, MRP, box 363.

117. Affidavit of Henry Welles, Stearns County, Minnesota, October 26, 1870, MRP, box 363.

118. Joseph Wilson, Commissioner of the General Land Office, to Ely S. Parker, Commissioner of Indian Affairs, November 23, 1870, MRP, box 363.

119. Nancy Campbell Bourke's scrip affidavit, June 25, 1875, Library and Archives Canada.

120. Nicole C. O'Byrne, "'A Rather Vexed Question . . .': The Federal-Provincial Debate over the Constitutional Responsibility for Métis Scrip," *Review of Constitutional Studies* 12, no. 2 (2007): 221–22. For more on Métis scrip, see Melanie Niemi-Bohun, "Colonial Categories and Familial Responses to Treaty and Metis Scrip Policy: The 'Edmonton and District Stragglers,' 1870–88," *Canadian Historical Review* 90, no. 1 (March 2009): 71–98; Gerhard J. Ens, "Taking Treaty 8 Scrip, 1899–1900: A Quantitative Portrait of Northern Alberta Metis Communities," *Lobstick: An Interdisciplinary Journal* 1, no. 1 (2000): 229–58; Brad Milne, "The Historiography of Métis Land Dispersal, 1870–1890," *Manitoba History* 30 (Autumn 1995): 30–41.

7. The U.S.-Dakota War of 1862

1. For more on Little Crow, see Gary Clayton Anderson, *Little Crow: Spokesman for the Sioux* (Minnesota Historical Society Press, 1986).

2. Gary Clayton Anderson, *Massacre in Minnesota: The Dakota War of 1862, the Most Violent Ethnic Conflict in American History* (University of Oklahoma Press, 2019), ix.

3. See Anderson, *Massacre in Minnesota.* For a Dakota perspective on the war, see Gary Clayton Anderson and Alan R. Woolworth, eds., *Through Dakota Eyes: Narrative Accounts of the Minnesota Indian War of 1862* (Minnesota Historical Society Press, 1988). William E. Lass provides a good historiographical treatment of the literature in "Histories of the U.S.-Dakota War of 1862," *Minnesota History* 63, no. 2 (Summer 2012): 44–57.

4. Most accounts of the war end with the mass execution of thirty-eight Dakota men on December 26, 1862, but the army continued to attack Dakota bands and villages in the years following as they fled westward, including many who had not been involved in the war. For a good account of the so-called punitive

expeditions, see Paul N. Beck, *Columns of Vengeance: Soldiers, Sioux, and the Punitive Expeditions, 1863–1864* (University of Oklahoma Press, 2013). For a broader scope on the aftermath of the war, see Linda M. Clemmons, *Dakota in Exile: The Untold Stories of Captives in the Aftermath of the U.S.-Dakota War* (University of Iowa Press, 2019).

5. Robert Hakewaste's Testimony, in Anderson and Woolworth, *Through Dakota Eyes,* 32. Táoyateduta also claimed starvation as the cause of the war, as told to Henry Sibley. See Kenneth Carley, ed., "The Sioux Campaign of 1862: Sibley's Letters to His Wife," *Minnesota History* 38 (September 1962): 106.

6. Account of Jerome Big Eagle, in Kenneth Carley, ed., "As Red Men Viewed It: Three Indian Accounts of the Uprising," *Minnesota History* 38 (September 1962): 131.

7. Wabasha's Statement, in Anderson and Woolworth, *Through Dakota Eyes,* 30.

8. Cecilia Campbell Stay's Account, in Anderson and Woolworth, *Through Dakota Eyes,* 46–48.

9. Joseph Coursolle's Story, in Anderson and Woolworth, *Through Dakota Eyes,* 58.

10. Nancy McClure Faribault Huggan's Account, in Anderson and Woolworth, *Through Dakota Eyes,* 82–84.

11. Trial of David Faribault Jr., case #134, in *The Dakota Trials: Including the Complete Transcripts and Explanatory Notes on the Military Commission Trials in Minnesota, 1862–1864,* ed. John Isch (Brown County Historical Society, 2013), 166–68.

12. Account of George Quinn, in Carley, "As Red Men Viewed It," 147–48.

13. Account of Jerome Big Eagle, in Carley, "As Red Men Viewed It," 136.

14. Baptiste Campbell Trial Transcript, in Isch, *Dakota Trials,* 173–75.

15. Gabriel Renville, "A Sioux Narrative of the Outbreak in 1862, and of Sibley's Expedition in 1863," *Collections of the Minnesota Historical Society* 10, pt. 2 (1905): 602.

16. Affidavit of F. H. Milligan, June 14, 1877, Francis Trudell Military Pension Record, RG 15, National Archives, Washington, D.C.

17. Military Service Record of Francis Trudell, Co. K, 9th Minnesota Infantry, RG 94, National Archives, Washington, D.C.

18. Military Service Record of Francis Trudell.

19. Certificate of Disability for Discharge, Military Service Record of Francis Trudell.

20. Joseph Allord to General Dodge, January 6, 1865, Service Record of Joseph Allord, Co. A, 6th Minnesota Infantry, RG 94, National Archives, Washington, D.C. The quoted material is from the contemporary loose English translation;

see the Dakota version in the same record. See also A. P. Connolly, *A Thrilling Narrative of the Minnesota Massacre and the Sioux War of 1862–63* (A. P. Connolly, 1896), 202–04.

21. Trial of Jo Allord, case #334, in Isch, *Dakota Trials*, 332.

22. Oscar Garrett Wall, *Recollections of the Sioux Massacre* (M. C. Russell, 1909), 95.

23. Renville, "Sioux Narrative of the Outbreak," 597.

24. Victor Renville, "A Sketch of the Minnesota Massacre," *Collections of the State Historical Society of North Dakota* 5 (1923): 257–58.

25. Joseph La Framboise Jr.'s Testimony, in Anderson and Woolworth, *Through Dakota Eyes*, 111.

26. Nancy McClure Faribault Huggan Account, in Anderson and Woolworth, *Through Dakota Eyes*, 138–39.

27. John Pope to Henry Sibley, September 28, 1862, Records of United States Army Continental Commands, 1821–1920, pt. 1, entry 3436, Letters Sent, September 1862–July 1865, Correspondence, Department of the Northwest, 1862–1865, vol. 3, RG 393, National Archives, Washington, D.C.

28. John Pope to Henry Sibley, October 10, 1862, entry 3436, vol. 3, RG 393, National Archives, Washington, D.C.

29. *Minnesota in the Civil and Indian Wars, 1861–1865*, vol. 1 (Pioneer Press Company, 1890), 309; Joseph Coursolle Account, in Anderson and Woolworth, *Through Dakota Eyes*, 164. For more on the battle, see John Christgau, *Birch Coulie: The Epic Battle of the Dakota War* (University of Nebraska Press, 2012).

30. John Pope to Norman Kittson, September 23, 1862, entry 3436, vol. 3, RG 393, National Archives, Washington, D.C.

31. John Pope to Edward Salomon, November 6, 1862, entry 3436, vol. 3, RG 393, National Archives, Washington, D.C.

32. Account of George Quinn, in Carley, "As Red Men Viewed It," 148.

33. Account of Jerome Big Eagle, in Carley, 139.

34. Alexis Demars Military Pension Record, RG 15, National Archives; Francis Demars Military Pension Record, RG 15, National Archives, Washington, D.C.

35. Charles S. Bryant and Abel B. Murch, *A History of the Great Massacre of the Sioux Indians, in Minnesota, Including the Personal Narratives of Many Who Escaped* (Rickey & Carroll, 1864), 200.

36. Joseph Coursolle Account, in Anderson and Woolworth, *Through Dakota Eyes*, 163–64.

37. Thomas A. Robertson, "Reminiscence of Thomas A. Robertson," *South Dakota Historical Collections* 20 (1940): 559–601; Isaac V. D. Heard, *History of the Sioux War and Massacres of 1862 and 1863* (Harper & Brothers, 1865), 147–50.

38. Henry Sibley to the Half Breeds and Sioux Indians, September 13, 1862, Records of United States Army Continental Commands, 1821–1920, pt. 1, entry

3480, Letters Sent, Sept.–Oct. 1862, Field Records, Sibley's Indian Expedition, 1862, Department of the Northwest, 1862–1865, RG 393, National Archives, Washington, D.C.

39. Renville, "Sioux Narrative of the Outbreak," 605.

40. Renville, 601.

41. Renville, 603.

42. Joseph La Framboise Jr.'s Account, in Anderson and Woolworth, *Through Dakota Eyes,* 198–99.

43. Nancy McClure Faribault Huggan Account, in Anderson and Woolworth, 244–45.

44. Good Star Woman's Recollections, in Anderson and Woolworth, 263.

45. Nancy McClure Faribault Huggan Account, in Anderson and Woolworth, 245.

46. Nancy McClure Faribault Huggan Account, 244–45.

47. Henry Sibley to John Pope, October 3, 1862, entry 3480, RG 393, National Archives, Washington, D.C.; Alan R. Woolworth, "The Significance and Challenge of Camp Release 1862–2012," *Minnesota's Heritage* 5 (January 2012): 5–10.

48. This racial terminology was boilerplate language in all of the trials. See Isch, *Dakota Trials.*

49. Henry Sibley to Thomas Galbraith, October 17, 1862, entry 3480, RG 393, National Archives, Washington, D.C.

50. Henry Sibley to J. C. Whitney, October 17, 1862, entry 3480, RG 393, National Archives, Washington, D.C.

51. Henry Sibley to John Pope, October 17, 1862, entry 3480, RG 393, National Archives, Washington, D.C.

52. Henry Sibley to John Pope, October 20, 1862, entry 3480, RG 393, National Archives, Washington, D.C.

53. Henry Sibley to Thomas Galbraith, October 4, 1862, entry 3480, RG 393, National Archives, Washington, D.C.

54. Henry Sibley to J. C. Whitney, October 16, 1862, entry 3480, RG 393, National Archives, Washington, D.C.

55. Henry Sibley to William Crooks, November 28, 1862, Records of United States Army Continental Commands, 1821–1920, pt. 3, entry 343, Letters and Telegrams Sent, Nov. 1862–Oct. 1873, District of Minnesota, RG 393, National Archives, Washington, D.C.

56. R. C. Olin to Thomas Galbraith, December 20, 1862, entry 343, RG 393, National Archives, Washington, D.C.

57. Stephen R. Riggs, *Tah-koo Wah-kan; or The Gospel Among the Dakotas* (Cong. Sabbath-School and Publishing Society, 1869), 334.

58. "Another Communication from Antoine Frenier, the Indian Interpreter," *St. Paul Pioneer* (St. Paul, Minn.), February 23, 1863.

59. "Did the Indians Hold the Half Breeds as Prisoners? A Female Captive Versus Mr. Frenier," *St. Paul Daily Press,* March 3, 1863.

60. "Did the Indians Hold the Half Breeds as Prisoners?"

61. Carol Chomsky, "The United States-Dakota War Trials: A Study in Military Injustice," *Stanford Law Review* 43, no. 1 (November 1990): 50–51.

62. For more on the trials, see Maeve Herbert, "Explaining the Sioux Military Commission of 1862," *Columbia Human Rights Law Review* 40 (2009): 743–98.

63. Trial of Thomas Robertson, case #135, in Isch, *Dakota Trials,* 168–70.

64. Trial of David Faribault Jr., case #134, in Isch, *Dakota Trials,* 166–68.

65. Trial of Wa-kan-hda-ma-ne, case #200, in Isch, *Dakota Trials,* 228.

66. Account of George Quinn, in Carley, "As Red Men Viewed It," 147–48.

67. Trial of Wa-mde-shoon, case #371, in Isch, *Dakota Trials,* 360.

68. See John Pope to Abraham Lincoln, November 7, 1862, Abraham Lincoln papers, series 1, General Correspondence, 1833–1916, Library of Congress. This was the list of the names of condemned prisoners sent to Lincoln. He asked for the documents relating to the trial, which Pope sent on November 15 but that have since been lost.

69. For a list of the thirty-eight, see Stephen Miller to R. C. Olin, December 26, 1862, Records of United States Army Continental Commands, 1821–1920, pt. 3, entry 346, Letters Received, 1862–1869, District of Minnesota, RG 393, National Archives, Washington, D.C.

70. "Prison of the Sioux Indian Murderers at Mankato, Minn.," *Frank Leslie's Illustrated Newspaper* (New York, N.Y.), January 31, 1863.

71. "The Indian Execution," *Goodhue Volunteer* (Red Wing, Minn.), January 7, 1863.

72. "Indian Execution."

73. "Execution of 38 Sioux," *Mankato Weekly Record* (Mankato, Minn.), December 26, 1862.

74. "The Indian Executions," *Chicago Daily Tribune* (Chicago), January 1, 1863.

75. Affidavit of Charles Mitchell and A. J. Campbell, February 9, 1893, Francis Trudell Military Pension Record, RG 15, National Archives, Washington, D.C.

76. Testimony of Henry Trudell, February 17, 1913, Probate of Margaret Campbell, RG 75, National Archives, Washington, D.C.

8. The Rise of Blood Quantum as an Exclusionary Tool

1. Curtis A. Dahlin, *The Fort Sisseton Dakota Scouts and Their Camps in Eastern Dakota Territory, 1863–1866* (Curtis A. Dahlin, 2017), 122. See also Alan R. Woolworth, "Dakota Indian Scouts on the Minnesota/Dakota Territory Frontier, 1863–1866," *Minnesota's Heritage* 6 (2012): 60–77; Linda M. Clemmons, *Dakota in*

Exile: The Untold Stories of Captives in the Aftermath of the U.S.-Dakota War (University of Iowa Press, 2019), 131–53.

2. John P. LaVelle, "The General Allotment Act 'Eligibility' Hoax: Distortions of Law, Policy, and History in Derogation of Indian Tribes," *Wicazo Sa Review* 14, no. 1 (Spring 1999): 251–302. LaVelle is a descendant of the Trudell family.

3. Paul Robertson, *The Power of the Land: Identity, Ethnicity, and Class Among the Oglala Lakota* (Routledge, 2002).

4. See John R. Legg, "'In Our Own Rightful Territory': Dakota Mobility, Diplomacy, and Belonging in Mni Sota Makoce after the US-Dakota War" (PhD diss., George Mason University, 2024); Robert J. Werner, "Dakota Diaspora After 1862," *Minnesota's Heritage* 6 (2012): 28–59; Alexander Dietz, "Wapahaska: The Early History of the Whitecap Band," *Saskatoon History Review* 6 (1991): 36–45; Roy W. Meyer, "The Canadian Sioux: Refugees from Minnesota," *Minnesota History* 41, no. 1 (Spring 1968): 13–28.

5. Paul N. Beck, *Columns of Vengeance: Soldiers, Sioux, and the Punitive Expeditions, 1863–1864* (University of Oklahoma Press, 2013), 153–76; Aaron L. Barth, "Imagining a Battlefield at a Civil War Mistake: The Public History of Whitestone Hill, 1863 to 2013," *Public Historian* 35, no. 3 (August 2013): 72–97; Clair Jacobson, "The Battle of Whitestone Hill," *North Dakota History* 44, no. 3 (Summer 1972): 4–14.

6. Census of Indian Camp at Ft. Snelling, December 2, 1862, Records of United States Army Continental Commands, 1821–1920, pt. 1, entry 3457, "Two or More Name File," 1862–1865, Correspondence, Department of the Northwest, 1862–1865, RG 393, National Archives, Washington, D.C.

7. R. C. Olin to William Crooks, February 10, 1863, Records of United States Army Continental Commands, 1821–1920, pt. 3, entry 343, Letters and Telegrams Sent, Nov. 1862–Oct. 1873, District of Minnesota, RG 393, National Archives, Washington, D.C.

8. Lt. McKasick to William Crooks, December 8, 1862, Records of United States Army Continental Commands, 1821–1920, pt. 3, entry 346, Letters Received, 1862–1869, District of Minnesota, RG 393, National Archives, Washington, D.C.

9. Alexander Ramsey to Henry Sibley, February 24, 1863, entry 346, RG 393, National Archives, Washington, D.C.

10. Artemas Sharpe to Henry Sibley, April 5, 1863, entry 3457, RG 393, National Archives, Washington, D.C.

11. Linda M. Clemmons, *Dakota in Exile: The Untold Stories of Captives in the Aftermath of the U.S.-Dakota War* (University of Iowa Press, 2019), 63–90; Linda M. Clemmons, "'The Young Folks [Want] to Go in and See the Indians': Davenport Citizens, Protestant Missionaries, and Dakota Prisoners of War, 1863–1866," *Annals of Iowa* 77, no. 2 (Spring 2018): 121–50; Sarah-Eva Ellen Carlson, "They Tell Their

Story: The Dakota Internment at Camp McClellan in Davenport, 1862–1866," *Annals of Iowa* 63, no. 3 (Summer 2004): 251–78.

12. John Isch, ed., *The Dakota Trials: The 1862–1864 Military Commission Trials* (Brown County Historical Society, 2013), 162–63, 179–80, 182–86.

13. Clemmons, *Dakota in Exile,* 63–90; Clemmons, "'Young Folks [Want] to Go In and See the Indians.'" See also Clifford Canku and Michael Simon, eds., *The Dakota Prisoner of War Letters: Dakota Kaškapi Okicize Wowapi* (Minnesota Historical Society Press, 2013).

14. Canku and Simon, *Dakota Prisoner of War Letters,* 31.

15. Clemmons, *Dakota in Exile,* 41–61; Edmund J. Danziger Jr., "The Crow Creek Experiment: An Aftermath of the Sioux War of 1862," *North Dakota History* 37, no. 2 (1970): 104–23; Colette A. Hyman, "Survival at Crow Creek, 1863–1866," *Minnesota History* 61, no. 4 (Winter 2008–2009): 148–61.

16. List of Indians in Prison at Mankato [January 1863], Records of the Adjutant General's Office, entry 173, Indian Prisoners, RG 94, National Archives, Washington, D.C.; F. Curtiss-Wedge, Susan Bahr's Personal Reminiscences of Early Minnesota, October 12, 1936, Works Progress Administration, copy in the Alan R. Woolworth papers, box 145.I.16.4F, Minnesota Historical Society, Saint Paul (hereafter MHS).

17. Census of Mdewakanton at Ft. Thompson, May 1864, Joseph and Samuel Brown papers, reel 3, MHS.

18. See Hyman, "Survival at Crow Creek," 148–61.

19. Ella C. Deloria, *Speaking of Indians* (State Publishing, 1983), 21–22.

20. Treaty with the Sioux—Sisseton and Wahpeton Bands, 1867, in *Indian Affairs: Laws and Treaties,* vol. 2, *Treaties,* ed. Charles J. Kappler (Government Printing Office, 1904), 956–59; Gary Clayton Anderson, *Gabriel Renville: From the Dakota War to the Creation of the Sisseton-Wahpeton Reservation, 1825–1892* (South Dakota Historical Society Press, 2018).

21. Mark Diedrich and Louis Garcia, *Little Fish: Head Chief of the Dakota on the Fort Totten Reservation* (Coyote Books, 2009), 9.

22. Thomas Constantine Maroukis, *Peyote and the Yankton Sioux: The Life and Times of Sam Necklace* (University of Oklahoma Press, 2004), 36–37.

23. Shubael Adams to D. N. Cooley, August 10, 1866, Letters Received by the Office of Indian Affairs, 1824–1881, M234, St. Peter's Agency, reel 765, RG 75, National Archives, Washington, D.C. (hereafter LROIA).

24. 1865 Minnesota State Census, Minnesota State Population Census Schedule, microfilm, MHS.

25. 1860 U.S. Federal Census.

26. 1870 U.S. Federal Census, July 28, 1870, Wabasha, Wabasha County, Minn.

27. "Old Fur Traders," *Wabasha Weekly Herald* (Wabasha, Minn.), August 22, 1867.

28. Colette Routel, "Minnesota Bounties on Dakota Men During the U.S.-Dakota War," *William Mitchell Law Review* 40, no. 1 (2013–2014): 1–77.

29. Herbert Hoover, Interview of Moses Trudell and Minnie Goodteacher Trudell, August 11, 1970, American Indian Research Project, South Dakota Oral History Center, University of South Dakota, Vermillion.

30. 1880 U.S. Federal Census; 1885 Wisconsin State Census.

31. Land Deed, Henry and Louisa Trudell to Louis Sharo, July 7, 1887, Wabasha County, Minnesota Deeds, reel 33.

32. George Moose, "Wowapi Maqupi," *Iapi Oaye* (Santee Agency, Neb.), March 1890.

33. Roy W. Meyer, "The Prairie Island Community: A Remnant of Minnesota Sioux," *Minnesota History* 37, no. 7 (September 1961): 275. See also Jeff Williamson, "The Dakota Indian Settlement at the Gideon Pond Farm, 1863 to 1891," *Minnesota's Heritage* 2 (2010): 114–20; Howard J. Vogel, "Rethinking the Effect of the Abrogation of the Dakota Treaties and the Authority for the Removal of the Dakota People from Their Homeland," *William Mitchell Law Review* 39, no. 2 (2013): 550.

34. 1937 Pipestone Census, reel 385, M595 Indian Census Rolls, 1885–1940, RG 75, National Archives, Washington, D.C.

35. Francis Trudell Military Pension Record, RG 15, National Archives, Washington, D.C.

36. Henry Trudell to Commissioner of Indian Affairs Francis E. Leupp, August 12, 1905, Letter #63942, 1905, box 2868, entry 91, Letters Received, 1881–1907, Records of the Bureau of Indian Affairs, RG 75, National Archives, Washington, D.C.

37. Nancy McClure Faribault Huggan Account, in *Through Dakota Eyes: Narrative Accounts of the Minnesota Indian War of 1862*, ed. Gary Clayton Anderson and Alan R. Woolworth (Minnesota Historical Society Press, 1988), 244–45.

38. U.S. Congress, Senate, *Letter from the Secretary of the Interior*, Ex. Doc. 59, 53rd Cong., 2nd Sess., March 12, 1894, serial 3160, 23.

39. For more on the case, see Harry H. Anderson, "The Waldron-Black Tomahawk Controversy and the Status of Mixed Bloods Among the Teton Sioux," *South Dakota History* 21, no. 1 (Spring 1991): 69–83; Lauren L. Basson, *White Enough to Be American? Race Mixing, Indigenous People, and the Boundaries of State and Nation* (University of North Carolina Press, 2008), 29–56.

40. Anderson, "Waldron-Black Tomahawk Controversy," 71–72.

41. U.S. Congress, *Letter from the Secretary of the Interior*, 10–11.

42. Waldron v. United States et al., 143 F. 413 (Circuit Court, D. South Dakota, July 1, 1905).

43. Waldron v. United States et al.

44. U.S. Congress, *Letter from the Secretary of the Interior,* 128–30.

45. U.S. Congress, 149.

46. U.S. Congress, 136–37.

47. U.S. Congress, 137.

48. See Karen Isaksen Leonard, *Making Ethnic Choices: California's Punjabi Mexican Americans* (Temple University Press, 1992).

49. J. Lee Englebert to Ely S. Parker, February 4, 1871, LROIA, Cheyenne River Agency, reel 127.

50. John P. Williamson to John Q. Smith, October 7, 1876, LROIA, Nebraska Agencies, reel 519.

51. Oscar M. Carter to H. C. Bulis, May 2, 1879, LROIA, reel 843.

52. U.S. Congress, Senate, *Report Relative to Opening a Part of the Sioux Reservation,* 50th Cong., 2nd Sess., 1888, Ex.Doc. 17, 223–25.

53. Petition of Half-Breeds, July 8, 1871, LROIA, Whetstone Agency, reel 925.

Conclusion

1. See William J. Scheick, *The Half-Blood: A Cultural Symbol in Nineteenth-Century American Fiction* (University Press of Kentucky, 1979); David Hurst Thomas, *Skull Wars: Kennewick Man, Archaeology, and the Battle for Native American Identity* (Basic Books, 2000); Reginald Horsman, "Scientific Racism and the American Indian in the Mid-Nineteenth Century," *American Quarterly* 27, no. 2 (May 1975): 152–68.

Index

JAMESON R. SWEET (Lakota and Dakota, unenrolled) is associate professor of American studies at Rutgers University.